CARNIVAL

Traditional carnival theory, based mainly on the work of Mikhail Bakhtin and Victor Turner, has long defined carnival as inversive or subversive. The essays in this groundbreaking anthology collectively reverse that trend, offering a redefinition of "carnival" that is focused not on the social hierarchies it challenges, but on the values and sense of community that it affirms. This book details its new theory with reference to a carnival that is at once representative and distinctive: the Carnival of Trinidad – the most copied yet least studied major carnival in the world.

Milla Cozart Riggio has compiled a body of work that takes the reader on a fascinating journey exploring the various aspects of carnival – its traditions, its history, its music, its politics – and prefaces each section with an illuminating introductory essay. This beautifully illustrated volume features an introduction by world-renowned performance theorist Richard Schechner and varied essays by leading writers and experts on Trinidad Carnival. It provides an introduction to a festival that has been copied in more than five dozen North American, European, Middle Eastern, Asian, and Australian cities, but that has traditionally been described solely within the frame of West Indian culture. *Carnival* represents the first theoretical redefinition of its subject and will be essential reading for the study of Trinidad Carnival in particular and for the general study of the carnivalesque in performance.

Milla Cozart Riggio is the James J. Goodwin Professor of English at Trinity College, Connecticut. She is the writer and editor of a number of books, and her essays and reviews have appeared in a variety of journals, including *The Shakespeare Quarterly* and *TDR: The Drama Review*. She has also worked as a consultant to the National Carnival Commission of Trinidad and Tobago and in 1999 held a government-appointed post on the World Conference on Carnival organizing committee in Trinidad.

WORLDS OF PERFORMANCE

What is a "performance"? Where does it takes place? Who are the participants? What is being enacted? Does it make a difference if the performance is embodied by live performers or represented on film, video, or digital media? How does the performance interact with individuals, societies, and cultures? Not so long ago, many of these questions were settled. But today, orthodox answers are misleading, limiting, and unsatisfactory.

"Performance" as a practice and as a theoretical category has expanded exponentially. It now comprises a panoply of genres, styles, events, and actions ranging from play, sports, and popular entertainments, to theatre, dance and music, secular and religious rituals, the performances of everyday life, intercultural experiments, and more. And beyond performance proper is the even more dynamically unsettled category of the performative.

For nearly fifty years, *The Drama Review* (*TDR*), the journal of performance studies, has been at the cutting edge of exploring performance. In *TDR*, artists and scholars introduce and debate new ideas; historical documents are published; new performance theories expounded. The Worlds of Performance Series is designed to mine the extraordinary resources and diversity of *TDR*'s decades of excellence.

Each Worlds of Performance book is a complete anthology, arranged around a specific theme or topic. Each volume contains hard-to-get seminal essays, artists' notes, interviews, creative texts, and photographs. New materials and careful introductions insure that each book is up to date. Every Worlds of Performance editor is a leader in the field of performance studies. Each Worlds of Performance book is an excellent basic resource for scholars, a textbook for students, and an exciting eye-opener for the general reader.

Richard Schechner
Editor, *TDR*
Series Editor

OTHER TITLES IN THE SERIES

Acting (Re)Considered 2nd Edition edited by Phillip B. Zarrilli

Happenings and Other Acts edited by Mariellen R. Sandford

A Sourcebook of Feminist Theatre and Performance: On and Beyond the Stage edited by Carol Martin

The Grotowski Sourcebook edited by Richard Schechner and Lisa Wolford

A Sourcebook of African-American Performance: Plays, People, Movements edited by Annemarie Bean

Brecht Sourcebook edited by Carol Martin and Henry Bial

Re:Direction. A Theoretical and Practical Guide by Rebecca Schneider and Gabrielle Cody

Popular Theatre: A Sourcebook edited by Joel Schechter

CARNIVAL

CULTURE IN ACTION – THE TRINIDAD EXPERIENCE

Edited by Milla Cozart Riggio

NEW YORK AND LONDON

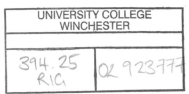

First published 2004
by Routledge
270 Madison Ave, New York, NY 10016

Simultaneously published in the UK
by Routledge
2 Park Square, Milton Park, Abingdon, Oxon, OX14 4RN

Routledge is an imprint of the Taylor & Francis Group

Typeset in Times New Roman by RefineCatch Limited, Bungay, Suffolk
Printed and bound in Great Britain by TJ International Ltd, Padstow, Cornwall

Library of Congress Cataloging in Publication Data
Carnival: culture in action: the Trinidad experience / [edited by] Milla Cozart Riggio.
     p. cm. – (Worlds of performance)
   Includes bibliographical references and index.
   1. Carnival – Trinidad.   2. Trinidad – Social life and customs.   I. Riggio, Milla Cozart.   II.
Series.
GT4229.T7C37 2004
394.26972983 – dc22   2004001267

British Library Cataloguing in Publication Data
A catalogue record for this book is available from the British Library

ISBN 0–415–27128–2 (hbk)
ISBN 0–415–27129–0 (pbk)

For Carlisle Chang and Theresa Morilla Montano

The passing of Carlisle Chang in May, 2001, was more than the death of one man. It was the stilling of a hand and the silencing of a voice that for more than half a century exacted a standard of precision, accuracy, and honesty for himself and for other Trinidadian artists, designers, and masmen. Carlisle's voice was soft, gentle, at times almost inaudible. But the absence of that voice is deafening. Though his paintings were exhibited in Europe, London, and the US, leaving the island of his birth never occurred to Carlisle. It is thus fitting that his memory should be silently honored everywhere the Trinidad flag, which he designed, is flown or the Trinidad coat of arms, also designed by him, is shown.

Theresa Morilla Montano, who styled herself as "born a long time but not old," lived with her husband Joseph on Morne Cocoa Road in Maraval, at the foot of Paramin Mountain. There she sewed the village shrouds, taught French patois, maintained a patois choir for the churches of Paramin and Maraval, cooked, and cared for children. For more than sixty years she played mas, winning the Jouvay Queen title sixteen times and leading her Minstrel Boys through grueling ten-hour carnival days until in the fall of 2001 at age 84 she died with the same dignity with which she lived. The hills around her home will for ever be filled with a voice that death cannot silence.

CONTENTS

ILLUSTRATIONS

CONTRIBUTORS

Dawn K. Batson is currently the Chairman of the Board of the Trinidad and Tobago National Steel Orchestra. She holds a PhD and is Assistant Professor of Music at Florida Memorial College and the Musical Director of the Florida Memorial Steelband, joint winners of the 2000 World Steelband Festival Ensemble Class. She has long been involved with the steelband movement as teacher, arranger, conductor, administrator, and composer.

Hélène Bellour is coauthor of *Censure et bibliothèques au XXe siècle* (Editions du Cercle de la Librairie, 1989). Cofounder and contributor to *Histoires d'Elles*, a French feminist periodical, she works as a translator, editor, and French instructor. Since 1996 she has pursued further research on Indian mas In Trinidad and supervised editorship of *Renegades: The History of the Renegades Steel Orchestra of Trinidad and Tobago* (Macmillan Caribbean, 2002).

Bridget Brereton is Professor of History at the University of the West Indies, St Augustine Campus, Trinidad and Tobago. She is the author or editor of many books and articles, mainly on the social history of Trinidad and of the anglophone Caribbean in the nineteenth and twentieth centuries. A past President of the Association of Caribbean Historians, she is editor of Volume V of the UNESCO General History of the Caribbean.

Carlisle Chang (d. 2001) was a native of Trinidad. Although he was better known in his country as a mural and easel painter, he also designed for theatre and ballet. He was involved in the promotion of art throughout his sixty-year-long career, holding the Hummingbird Medal for Community Service, the bronze medal of the VII São Paulo Bienal for painting (1963), and a citation from the Press Club of Lausanne (1972) for Best Foreign Pavilion at the Comptoire Suisse. His paintings have been exhibited in group shows in Europe, including London, and the United States. Carlisle Chang was also responsible for designing his country's flag and coat of arms.

Jeffrey Chock is a freelance photographer in Port of Spain, Trinidad, who for the past three decades has photographed many aspects of his culture, particularly carnival and other arts. He was the photographic editor of *Renegades: The History of the Renegades Steel Orchestra of Trinidad and Tobago* (Macmillan Caribbean, 2002). He is affiliated with the Trinity College in Trinidad Global Learning Site. His photographs have appeared in a wide range of journals and books; they have been exhibited in Trinidad and the United States.

Geraldine Connor is a freelance theatre director. An ethnomusicologist, she was Senior Lecturer at the University of Leeds (1992–2004), and holds an MMus. (London), LRSM,

Dip. Ed. She held a two-year appointment as Associate Director of Music at the West Yorkshire Playhouse (2001–2003). A composer, performer, musical director, and vocal animator specializing in mainstream rock and pop, Caribbean carnival, Caribbean folk and African-American gospel, she conceived, composed, and directed *Carnival Messiah*, a radical theatrical reinvention inspired by George Frederick Handel's *Messiah* (1999 and 2002, West Yorkshire Playhouse; 2003 and 2004, Port of Spain), and also directed the acclaimed premiere coproduction between the West Yorkshire Playhouse and Adzido Pan African Dance, *Yaa Asantewaa, Warrior Queen*, which successfully toured Britain and Ghana, Africa, in 2001/2. Most recently she has directed *Blues in the Night* (West Yorkshire Playhouse, 2003), and *Vodou Nation* (UK Arts and West Yorkshire Playhouse, 2004).

Pablo Delano was born in San Juan, Puerto Rico. He holds a BFA in painting from Temple University and an MFA in painting from Yale University School of Art. He has completed numerous community-based public art projects, including commissions from the New York City Department of Cultural Affairs and the US Department of the Interior. His photographs of Caribbean communities have been exhibited at galleries and museums in the US, Puerto Rico, and Latin America. He is the author of *Faces of America*, a book of photographs published by Smithsonian Institution Press (1992). He teaches photography at Trinity College in Hartford, CT, and is working on several books of photographs portraying the rich cultural diversity of life in Trinidad.

J.D. Elder (d. 2003) received his PhD in anthropology from the University of Pennsylvania in 1965. He did extensive field research in the history of kalinda, pan, calypso, and other aspects of carnival. His publications included *From Congo Drum to Steelband* (University of the West Indies, 1969) and, most recently, *Brown Girl in the Ring* (Pantheon, 1998), which was coedited with Alan and Bess Lomax. At the time of his death he was building a Heritage Village in Tobago.

Max Farrar currently teaches sociology in the School of Cultural Studies at Leeds Metropolitan University, Leeds, UK. He lived for nearly thirty years in the Chapeltown area of Leeds. His PhD research on social movements in that area was published in 2002 by the Edwin Mellen Press, titled *The Struggle for Community in a British Multi-ethnic Inner City Area*. Prior to joining the university he worked in community education, legal advice, publishing, and journalism. He has participated in and photographed the Leeds Carnival since the early 1970s. Visit his website at www.maxfarrar.org.uk

Pamela R. Franco is an assistant professor in the Newcomb Art Department at Tulane University. She teaches courses in the arts, both plastic and performance, of Africa and the African diaspora, with special emphasis on the anglophone Caribbean. She is the author of several articles on women maskers. She is currently working on a book on women and the performance of gender in nineteenth-century Trinidad carnival.

Jocelyne Guilbault is Professor of Ethnomusicology in the Music Department of the University of California, Berkeley. She is the author of *Zouk: World Music in the West Indies* (1993) and coeditor of *Border Crossings: New Directions in Music Studies* (1999–2000). Her current research focuses on the politics and aesthetics of the calypso music scene in the Caribbean and its diaspora.

Tony Hall is a playwright and moviemaker. In the theatre, he worked extensively in western Canada and in the Caribbean with Derek Walcott's Trinidad Theatre Workshop. With Banyan he codirected and appeared in *And the Dish Ran Away with the Spoon* (1992), an award-winning Banyan Film for a BBC/TVE series. His plays include: *Jean & Dinah . . .* (1994); *Red House [Fire! Fire!]* (1999), *Twilight Café* (2002), and the book for *The Brand New Lucky Diamond Horseshoe Club*, a Blues Kaiso written in collaboration with composer David Rudder, premiered in Indiana, July 2004. He is the Academic Onsite Director of the Trinity College in Trinidad Global Learning Site each spring term and, in most fall terms, is Visiting Artist in Residence at Trinity College. He lives in Tobago.

Kim Johnson is a journalist and cultural researcher who holds a PhD from the University of the West Indies. He has authored several books, most recently *Renegades: The History of the Renegades Steel Orchestra of Trinidad and Tobago* (Macmillan Caribbean, 2002). His book-length study of the oral history of the steel band is forthcoming from Macmillan Caribbean.

Philip Kasinitz is currently the Executive Officer of the CUNY PhD Program in Sociology and associate director of the CUNY Center for Urban Research. He received his PhD from New York University in 1987. His book *Caribbean New York: Black Immigrants and the Politics of Race* (Cornell University Press, 1992) won the Thomas and Znaniecki Award from the International Migration Section of the American Sociological Association. In addition to numerous academic journals, his work has appeared in *Dissent, The Nation, The City Journal, The Wall Street Journal, Lingua Franca*, and *Common Quest: The Magazine of Black Jewish Relations*.

Samuel Kinser is Presidential Research Professor in History at Northern Illinois University. His books include *Rabelais's Carnival: Text, Context, Metatext* (University of California Press, 1990) and *Carnival American Style, Mardi Gras at New Orleans and Mobile* (University of Chicago Press, 1990). His present project is a comparative history of festive representations of Amerindians in Europe and the Americas from 1500 to the present.

Earl Lovelace is a prize-winning novelist who was born in Toco, Trinidad, and grew up in Tobago. He has taught at the University of the West Indies and Wellesley College; he currently teaches at Pacific Lutheran University in Tacoma, Washington. He has written six volumes of fiction including the novels *The Dragon Can't Dance* (Longman, 1979), *The Wine of Astonishment* (André Deutsch, 1982), and *Salt* (Faber & Faber, 1996). He received the British Commonwealth Prize for Literature in 1997 and was named the *Trinidad Express* Man of the Year for 1997. He received an honorary doctorate from the University of the West Indies in 2002. He is currently working on a collection of essays and a new novel.

Carol Martin, PhD – books include: *Brecht Sourcebook*; *A Sourcebook of Feminist Theatre: On and Beyond the Stage*; and *Dance Marathons: Performing American Culture of the 1920s and 1930s*. Martin's essays on performance and interviews with artists have appeared in journals and anthologies, including the *New York Times*, and have been translated into French, Polish, Chinese, and Italian. She has lectured and given papers on theatre and performance in Singapore, Shanghai, Tokyo, and Paris. Martin is an Associate Professor of Drama at Tisch School of the Arts, New York University.

Keith Nurse is a Senior Lecturer at the Institute of International Relations, University of the West Indies, Trinidad and Tobago, and President of the Association of Caribbean Economists (2004). He is the academic coordinator of the Arts and Cultural Enterprise Management programme at the Festival Centre of the Creative Arts. Recent publications include *Festival Tourism in the Caribbean* (2004). He is also the coeditor of *Globalization and Caribbean Popular Culture* (2004).

Milla Cozart Riggio, James J. Goodwin Professor of English at Trinity College (Hartford, CT) and coordinator of the Trinity-in-Trinidad Global Learning Site, received her PhD from Harvard University. Her books include *The Wisdom Symposium, Ta'ziyeh: Ritual and Drama in Iran* (a monograph), *The Play of Wisdom: Its Texts and Contexts*, and *Teaching Shakespeare through Performance*. She coedited *Renegades: The History of the Renegades Steel Orchestra of Trinidad and Tobago*, as well as a special edition of *Mediaevalia* on medieval drama; she edited a special issue of *TDR: The Drama Review* on Trinidad and Tobago Carnival. Her essays and reviews have appeared in a wide range of scholarly journals, including *The Shakespeare Quarterly, Speculum*, and *TDR*.

Gordon Rohlehr is Professor of West Indian Literature at the University of the West Indies, Trinidad. Born in Guyana, he is author of *Pathfinder: Black Awakening in the Arrivants of Edward Kamau Brathwaite* (Gordon Rohlehr, 1981); *Calypso and Society in Pre-Independence Trinidad* (Gordon Rohlehr, 1990); *My Strangled City and Other Essays* (Longman Trinidad, 1992); and *The Shape of That Hurt and Other Essays* (Longman Trinidad, 1992). He is also coeditor of *Voiceprint: An Anthology of Oral and Related Poetry from the Caribbean* (Longman, 1989). His latest book is *A Scuffling of Islands: Essays on the Calypso* (Lexican Trinidad Ltd, 2004).

Burton Sankeralli is a theologian whose area of research is religion, culture, and society in Trinidad. He is a freelance writer for the *Sunday Express* newspaper in Port of Spain, Trinidad, and the editor of *At the Crossroads: African Caribbean Religion and Christianity*, a collection of conference papers for the Caribbean Conference of Churches.

Richard Schechner is University Professor and Professor of Performance Studies at the Tisch School of the Arts, New York University. He is artistic director of East Coast Artists and editor of *TDR: A Journal of Performance Studies*. He is general editor of the Worlds of Performance book series. Schechner's own books include *Environmental Theater, Between Theater and Anthropology, The End of Humanism, Performance Theory, The Future of Ritual*, and *Performance Studies – An Introduction*. His books have been translated into many languages, including Chinese, German, Japanese, Spanish, Italian, and Serbo-Croat. He founded and directed The Performance Group, with which he directed *Dionysus in 69, Tooth of Crime, Mother Courage and Her Children*, and many other works. His most recent works for the stage are productions of Anton Chekhov's *Three Sisters*, Shakespeare's *Hamlet*, and Samuel Beckett's *Waiting for Godot*. Schechner has directed plays, conducted performance workshops, and lectured in Asia, Africa, Europe, Australia, and the Americas. He is the recipient of numerous fellowships and awards including a Lifetime Achievement Award from Performance Studies International. He is an honorary professor at the Shanghai Theatre Academy and the Institute of Fine Arts, Havana.

Martin W. Walsh is head of the Drama Concentration in the Residential College and Professor of Theatre History in the Department of Theatre and Drama at the University of Michigan. He holds a PhD from Cambridge University and is widely published in early drama and popular culture, having recently coedited and translated the Dutch morality play *Mariken van Nieumeghen*. Actor, director, and dramaturg for Ann Arbor's Brecht Company for many years, he is also the Artistic Director of the Harlotry Players, a university-based early drama group.

ACKNOWLEDGMENTS

My greatest debt for the production of this book is to my Editorial Associate Tracy Knight, without whom the project could not have been completed. Also important was the clerical assistance given by Dorothy Francoeur, Julie Decatur, and Erica Mace. Jeffrey Chock offered irreplaceable help with graphic editing, choosing and assembling photographs. Pablo Delano was, likewise, an invaluable graphic editor and adviser. Richard Schechner provided the impetus for the creation of the book; his support saw me through a difficult and sensitive process. Rosie Waters, Diane Parker, Talia Rodgers, and Ruth Whittington of Routledge made the difficult task of assembling this text much easier with their enthusiastic support. John Banks provided excellent copy-editing. At Trinity College, I owe thanks to our affiliated faculty Janet Bauer, Raymond Baker, Brigitte Schulz, Dario Euraque, Luis Figueroa, Leslie Desmangles, Ellison Findly, Joan Morrison, Joe Palladino, and to Lise Waxer, who lived more actively in her 37 short years than most manage in four score and whose love of life and dancing energy continue to inspire me each day. In Trinidad, I owe many debts of gratitude. John Cupid has since 1995 been my mentor; the National Carnival Commission has consistently supported this work, through Carol Wolfe and a series of NCC Chairmen beginning with Alfred Aguiton, including Roy Augustus, and the current Chairman Kenny de Silva. Dr Hollis "Chalkdust" Liverpool has been a valuable friend and adviser. At the University of the West Indies, Professor Bridget Brereton supported the Trinity College in Trinidad Global Learning Site, which has helped to spawn this book. Thanks are due also to my colleague Tony Hall, our administrative coordinator Naima Mohammad, and our partners Lloyd Best of the Trinidad and Tobago Institute of the West Indies, Bhai Ravi Ji for his continuing support and advice, Peter Minshall, Nestor Sullivan of Pamberi and the National Steel Orchestra, Professor Gordon Rohlehr, Noble Douglas, the late André Tanker, Wendell Manwarren, Earl Lovelace, the late Merwyn Williams, Dr Joan Kazim of the Islamic Institute, Dr Rhoda Reddock, Halima-Sa'adia Kassim, Rawle Gibbons of the Creative Arts Centre, Norvan Fullerton and Gemma Jordan of the Malick Folk Performance Group, Eintou Springer, Christopher Laird of Banyan, Narrie Approo, Felix Edinburgh, Brian Honoré, Michael Cooper, Jill and Sue Singh and the Carapichaima Carnival Committee, along with others too numerous to name. My personal thanks go to Ron and Jackie Rose, Gina Humphrey, and Ivan LaRose, and of course to my own family, Thomas I, II, and III, Anna, Daniel, Rob, and Laura, all of whom have had an opportunity to share with me the magic island nation with its richly sophisticated culture, where I have found aspects of myself I might never have realized elsewhere.

The following chapters were previously published in *TDR: The Drama Review*, special issue ed. Milla Cozart Riggio, *Trinidad and Tobago Carnival*, 42 (3) (Fall 1998) and are republished by permission: J.D. Elder, "Cannes brûlées"; Carlisle Chang, "Chinese in

Trinidad Carnival"; and Burton Sankeralli, "Indian presence in carnival." Earlier versions of the following essays, likewise published in *TDR: The Drama Review*, 42(3) (Fall 1998), have been edited or updated for this volume and are republished by permission: Hélène Bellour and Samuel Kinser, "Amerindian masking in Trinidad Carnival: the House of Black Elk in San Fernando"; Kim Johnson, "Notes on pan"; Earl Lovelace, "The emancipation jouvay tradition and the almost loss of pan"; Carol Martin, "Trinidad Carnival glossary"; and Richard Schechner and Milla Riggio, "Peter Minshall: a voice to add to the song of the universe." Portions of Milla Riggio, "The carnival story – then and now: introduction to Part I," were adapted from "Resistance and Identity: Carnival in Trinidad and Tobago," published in *TDR: The Drama Review* (T159); portions of Milla Riggio, "Time out or time in," were published as the "Carnival" entry in the *Oxford Encyclopedia of Theatre and Performance* (ed. Dennis Kennedy, 2003). Both are reprinted by permission of Oxford University Press. Portions of Philip Kasinitz, " 'New York equalize you?' Change and continuity in Brooklyn's Labor Day Carnival," were published in Philip Kasinitz, *Caribbean New York: Black Immigrants and the Politics of Race* (Ithaca: Cornell University Press, 1992) and are reprinted by permission.

INTRODUCTION:
THEORIZING CARNIVAL

CARNIVAL (THEORY) AFTER BAKHTIN

Richard Schechner

Bakhtin's notions of carnival are founded on a settled, stratified society – a non-democratic society. In such a setting, authority can be suspended or set aside temporarily, and "the people" given a chance to act out their desires freely if temporarily. But today's world is not that kind of world. In the places where carnival as a formal institution is performed (Trinidad and Tobago, New Orleans Mardi Gras, and Rio de Janeiro, for example), the social "baseline" is democracy or the illusion of democracy. It is not that "the people" really have power on a daily basis or ultimately. But from time to time there are elections in which "the people" are appealed to, their votes sought, bought, and manipulated. This kind of democracy is both dysfunctional (in the US, nearly half the eligible voters do not vote) and illusory. The image-makers provide a daily diet of patriotism linked to democracy. But even if untrue, the "make believe" of democracy depends on the psychosocial phenomenon that "the people" are sovereign. If people believe that they are collectively sovereign, then against whom is carnival staged? From what overall authority is carnival a relief?

There are at least two ways to solve this problem. One is to wonder what the *actual* power arrangements are in so-called democratic societies; and another is to analyze carnival as an enactment that at one and the same time plays out democratic illusions, giving temporary relief from the authority (if not oppression and downright tyranny) imposed in the name of "democracy."

Prior to making such an analysis with regard to Trinidad Carnival, I need to say a little about "the people" in Third World societies – cultures that have suffered colonialism and whose current experience is that of postcolonialism and globalization. Such societies are not the same as First World societies – or even Russia (and other nations of the former USSR) – under whose auspices Bakhtin lived, thought, and wrote.

Bakhtin's model of carnival was developed in terms of the medieval European practices as Bakhtin reconfigured them while living in the dangerous, totalitarian world of Stalinism. Bakhtin stressed carnival's rebelliousness as he explained how carni-revellers act out their hatred for official culture. Trinidad Carnival developed under very different historical circumstances. Trinidad Carnival emerged in the nineteenth century from the celebrations of liberated African slaves embodying African ways and values and the carnival traditions of Catholic Europe as carried to the Caribbean perhaps by Spanish and certainly by French planters–slave owners. Ironically, Trinidad Carnival is a celebration of former slaves and former masters enjoying – and to some degree satirizing – each other's cultural heritages. As Trinidad Carnival continues to develop in the twenty-first century, its cultural complexity multiplies to include, and rebroadcast to the world at large, musical and visual performance languages that are intriguingly Afro-Euro-Caribbean-South-Asian-global. Thus Trinidad Carnival has become both a centripetal hub and a centrifugal force for carnival, musical, and masking styles that flow inward to the islands of Trinidad and Tobago and radiate outward from them to the world at large. This kind of complexity confounds Bakhtinian theory.

Trinidad Carnival actually both critiques official culture and supports it. It is an event both "of the people" and "of the nation." As Allesandro Falassi (1987: 3) wrote:

> If we consider that the primary and most general function of the festival is to renounce and then to announce culture, to renew periodically the life stream of a community by creating new energy, and to give sanctions to its institutions, the symbolic means to achieve it is to represent the primordial chaos before creation, or a historical disorder before the establishment of the culture, society, or regime where the festival happens to take place. Such representation cannot be properly accomplished by reversal behavior or by rites of intensification alone, but only by the simultaneous presence in the same festival of all the basic behavioral modalities of daily social life, all modified – by distortion, inversion, stylization, or disguise – in such a way that they take on an especially meaningful symbolic character. [. . .] In sum, festival presents a complete range of behavioral modalities, each one related to the modalities of normal daily life. At festival times, people do something they normally do not; they abstain from something they normally do; they carry to the extreme behaviors that are usually regulated by measure; they invert patterns of daily social life. Reversal, intensification, trespassing, and abstinence are the four cardinal points of festive behavior.

But how is this accomplished in Trinidad? Carnival is financially, artistically, and conceptually supported from the bottom up and from the top down. These two systems – "top-down" and "bottom-up" – must be studied independently and in relation to each other. Being a Third World country populated mostly by peoples of color – African, South Asian, remnants of the Caribs – in relation both to Europe and the US (the inheritor of the European desire for global hegemony), Trinidad is "other." This is borne out in Carnival, which – despite much boundary-crossing interculturality – is partially a festival of "differences" demarking the urban from the rural, the African from the European, the Asian from the African, and so on. From this perspective, Trinidad Carnival is in its largest frame a Festival of the Other, no matter how "official" it is within its own national-cultural boundaries. In the Trinidad diaspora even more so, the spin-off carnivals are each regarded as "exotic" within the cultures of the US, Canada, and the UK.

But what about the thousands of Trinidadians and other West Indians who come back to this island for carnival? They are in a uniquely postmodern circumstance. In the US, they are a minority within a minority within a minority within a minority: "Trinidadians" amidst "islanders" amidst "African-Americans" amidst "people of color." South Asian-American-Trinidadians are not regarded as "Indians" because in the popular imagination they have been absorbed into the African group. Nor do these designations take into account the equally complex presence in carnival of people and practices that are Christian, Orixan (Yoruban African), Hindu, and Muslim. For "West Indian Carnival" day in Brooklyn, celebrated in early September, all these differences and more are temporarily set aside: warm weather trumps the church's Lenten ritual calendar, Trinidad is absorbed into "West India", itself a bizarre designation founded on a geo-culture error.

In Trinidad and Tobago itself, even though carnival originated as a liberationist exuberance celebrating emancipation from enslavement, it never was "freely free." From its very inception, the carnival was policed and controlled. Increasingly, the culture of surveillance is penetrating to the heart of carnival – sometimes simply to steal "good ideas" from rival bands or mas camps; sometimes as a means of social control. Even the presence of interested scholars, of books like the one you are reading, hedge in carnival's spontaneity. Sometimes this kind of limitation can take the form of "saving" carnival – as with the interventionist activities of those who want to preserve and reinstate the "traditional" carnival figures regarded collectively as an endangered species: Midnight Robber, Dame Lorraine, White Faced Minstrels, and so on. But, as in zoos and game parks, or with animals reintroduced into the wild, there is a difference both on the theoretical and on the practical level between the wild and the protected.

In terms of Carnival, what appears to be free, licentious, and spontaneous – the enactment of the most-of-the-time forbidden – upon examination proves to occur between the three poles of the permitted, the perpetrated, and the reinstated. Without "excess" what would the Tourism and Industrial Development Company of Trinidad and Tobago Ltd (TIDCO) sell? Without the traditional characters what would Trinidad Carnival be? If the oil business is what underlies Trinidad's wealth, setting it apart from the other Caribbean islands, carnival runs an important second as a "cultural product" of great market value. Too valuable to let run freely free.

This is not to deny the reality of the element of resistance in the evolution of Trinidad Carnival, as freed slaves, later joined by enfranchised former indentured laborers, combined African, European, and Asian celebratory techniques and practices to embody in the streets of Port of Spain and elsewhere on the island a range of community values: individual and corporate (band) expression and artistic creativity; release from the daily grind in an ecstasy of dancing, music-making, sexplay, drinking, and other similar entertainments. Taken together these constituted both a nonconscious and a highly self-conscious celebration of Trinidad and Tobago (TT)[1] as a "culturally diverse nation" emerging from colonialism. Official promotion of its unique qualities helped sell Trinidad on the global tourist market. These values cannot be reduced to a single overall item.

Some scholars argue that a "real" carnival is no longer possible because there are no coherent communities to stage the carnivals or to rebel against. This may be true on the grand scale. But one of the functions of Trinidad Carnival is to sustain smaller, local communities. At least in Port of Spain what happens in the mas camps, steel band yards, and the calypso tents is the formation and maintenance of tight-knit communities. Unlike European carnivals or American Mardi Gras (but like carnival in Rio de Janeiro), Trinidad Carnival dominates the national consciousness and occupies the time, work, and imagination of many people for much of the year. Next year's carnival begins the day after this year's ends. Not only are local communities formed and sustained by carnival, carnival brings together performance events that do not necessarily belong together. Masking, calypso, and steel band are "natural" to carnival simply because they occur within the carnival frame. Actually, carnival taken as a whole is a hybrid. Within the overall event many different kinds of performances rub up against each other, sometimes uncomfortably, such as when the Blue Devils of Paramin Village perform right after the French patois Mass in the village. Or how the orderly processions of King and Queen contestants and mas bands across formal stages compare to the bursting chaos of the street celebrations and local parties. There are historical-traditional rather than performance-logical reasons why mas, new characters and traditional characters, various official competitions, calypso, pan, and kalinda are all performed at carnival. In fact, multiplicity and contradictory intentions are the hallmark of Trinidad Carnival. For the time being (carnival time), contradictions are supported and not challenged. A "forgiveness of illogic" allows contradictory values to be simultaneously expressed.

There are historical reasons, not inherent reasons of cultural affinity, that bring together African, European, and South Asian practices in Trinidad. What's even more amazing is that, once thrown together by historical circumstances, the hybrid arts that emerge make perfect sense and are coherent. Soca makes sense, even if its *causes* could not be predicted. The convergence of Shango, Christian, Hindu, and Islamic practices gives rise to both a unity and a tension that are extremely creative. The tensions separating various cultural practices also require hard work to maintain at least a working cooperation among African, European, South Asian, and Chinese individuals and groups who all exist cheek-by-jowl in a small territory. Daily life in Trinidad requires a keen sense of both unique and shared social, political, geographical, religious, and artistic histories and proclivities. No matter how celebratory, Trinidad Carnival lives within the shadows of slavery, indentured labor, colonialism, imperialism, and, now, globalization. Carnival is not sunshine dispelling these shadows but a means of overcoming them, assimilating them, and playing them out. Carnival is a celebration of freedom – yes, but not only or even mostly, individual freedom, but social, collective, national freedom – a liberty that is tenuous, hard-won, and still felt as threatened.

The contradictions, shadows, and threats mean that that Trinidad Carnival is not now, nor was it ever, nor can it ever be, static. Today carnival is not what it was in the nineteenth or the mid-twentieth century. I have no doubt that in 2050 it will be much different than it is now. At first emancipation, then independence, and then the emergence of TT on the world stage, have all affected carnival. TT is an independent nation and a robust culture, but it also is a Third World developing nation living in postcolonial circumstances in a period of rampant globalization. Trinidad Carnival exists as a centerpiece in a vast diasporic network which circulates mas, concepts, persons, and all kinds of specific carnival practices. The celebratory imperative – and carnival can really happen only in outdoor spaces, in the streets – overpowers the religious calendar. Also certain masks travel and therefore carnival in different regions of the Trinidad and Tobago diaspora needs to be scheduled at different times. In other words, the diasporic carnivals are not simply exports but also redistributions and reinterpretations of the "original." But what is the original? Masks, music, dances, and styles happening in TT may, in fact, be very influenced by what happens in the diaspora. People, masks, music, and ideas circulate. And behind the diaspora are Africa and the Indian subcontinent. African and Indian cultures are a driving force in a process of retro-colonization whereby practices, styles, and beliefs from the former colonies are affecting the cultures of the former colonial homelands.

Its hybridity gives Trinidad Carnival both its particular qualities and its edginess. It is not only or even mostly the release of some kind of popular Bakhtinian voice of the people. Instead, what is played out is a dangerous, almost about to come apart, coalition of traditions and socio-political arrangements. This threat and danger inherent in carnival explains why the TT government has tried to control what calypsonians sing about – trying to make sure especially that they don't exacerbate tensions between Indians and Africans. It is why scholars argue so heatedly about the various sources of Trinidad Carnival: is it "really" African, how important is the European influence, what about the South Asians, the East Asians? Are there any echoes of Carib culture in it? As in TT politics, each group wants to claim its primacy without upsetting the balance. None of these arguments can be settled. Trinidad culture, and carnival as the prime vehicle of that culture, expresses dynamic relationship among contending components. A very tense, energetic, and creative interculturality.

Unlike the popular democracy of Bakhtin's model, Trinidad Carnival is fiercely competitive and hierarchical. The official carnival, which climaxes with competitors performing on the Queen's Park Savannah stage to determine the kings and queens, the top steel bands and calypsonians, involves fierce struggles decided by judges. But whatever the judges decide, people supporting the losers aver that the competition was fixed, that unfair influence swayed the judges, or something else undercut their objectivity. At the same time, once the prizes have been awarded, the winners take great pride in them. There is an almost obsessional quality about hierarchy: "Am I eighth, am I ninth, am I tenth, am I first?" From the competitor's point of view – not necessarily from the point of view of individual players – Trinidad Carnival is anything but fun as popularly defined.

There are, in fact, several great divisions separating out different kinds of participation, different classes of people, different versions of "fun." The Savannah stage is itself a sharply binary space. The great runway where the competitors show their stuff lies between the North Stand and the Grandstand. The more commodious Grandstand is full of people who have paid fancy prices, official guests, and other VIPs (including visiting scholars). At the base of the Grandstand are the judges. The North Stand has as its mythos that it belongs to "the people," though in reality it has become itself the more chic place for upscale middle-class celebration. The seats are cheaper and less comfortable, and the comportment of the crowd is noisier, more boisterous. The style of dressing is different, also, south to north – with fancier outfits more likely to be found in the Grandstand. The performers, however, play both to the upper crust and to "the people." The enormous king full-body masks rotate and spin round; the calypso balladeers strut to the north and to the south. Pan, of course, can be heard and seen from either perspective, though the primary "show" faces the judges. It is as if the competitors have two audiences to satisfy: that of official culture and that of "the people."

The street celebrations and the myriad of individual parties are a different matter altogether. Once jouvay literally opens the official carnival in the wee hours of Monday, the streets are crammed with dancers, drunks, and assorted masqueraders. But even here there is a big difference between the massed followers of sound-blasting eighteen-wheelers, hard core "wining" through the night and into the morning, crossing the downtown judging venue that is located on the street itself, and the relatively more sedate bands who chip and wine through either Adam Smith Square or onto the Queen's Park Savannah stage (this venue tends to differ from year to year).

If we consider only the period from Sunday to Tuesday night before Lent, what we have, in practice (and therefore what needs to be better theorized), are at least two masquerade carnivals running simultaneously and often intermixing with each other: Carnival 1 focuses on the official stages and competitions and Carnival 2 erupting in the streets and permeating the many private parties and more hidden venues that have been filled with carnival revelry for many weeks, dissolving the boundaries between inside and outside, private and public, the church calendar and the "real" calendar of celebration.

Carnival 1 is a climax of intense months of preparation, training, and highly disciplined behavior leading to hysterical last-minute plans – very much like the opening of a play where everything depends on the public's and the critics' reactions on opening night. Carnival 1 is extremely hierarchical. Internationally known calypsonians, band and pan leaders call the shots. Everyone appears according to a pre-arranged sequence and schedule (often enough, dramatically late as the tradition has it). Those in the stands know who the time-tested great ones are, who this year's favorites are, and who are ambitious upstarts. Carnival 2 is a letting go of all that in a deliriously wild, paint- and mud-spattered, actually more dangerously chaotic playfulness inaugurated in the dark of jouvay and, building on the momentum gained throughout the carnival season, weaving through to las' lap.

Before the masquerade carnival begins officially, most of the major competitions have already been concluded – Panorama champions chosen, stickfighting champion, calypso and soca monarchs, and masquerade King and Queen of Carnival crowned, multiple children's carnivals concluded. Surrounding and in between all these competing activities are the remnants of "traditional carnival," the time-honored figures who show themselves in Woodford Square during the day on Friday before the official carnival starts, as well as at Victoria Square and other "traditional character festival" venues. Some of these figures appear awkwardly on the Queen's Park Savannah stage. At the same time, these restorations have started to take root. Children mask as Bats or Burroquites; a few Midnight Robbers can be heard expostulating. The input of "lovers of the tradition," such as John Cupid, abetted by scholars both Trinidadian and foreign, plays no small part in integrating the old with the new. There is, in fact, a flux of activities and priorities. Supporters of the "tradition" are valued as much by the promoters of Trinidad tourism as by those who value the beauty, wit, and historical fetch of figures such as the White Faced Minstrels or Baby Doll.

One must never forget that Trinidad Carnival is played out on the world stage as well as on the island. Far from being an eruption of "the people," it is the signature happening of an entire nation, the most prominent mark of its culture. And by means of its carnival, Trinidad continues to make an impression on the world stage far beyond its size geographically or its numbers in terms of population. Whether Trinidad Carnival is a great art-form in itself, as mas master Peter Minshall avers, or whether it is an eruption of popular culture, or whether it is a marketable performance commodity does not constitute a set of choices but a complex of probabilities. Trinidad Carnival is all of the above.

The aspect of official carnival – like its counterparts in New Orleans Mardi Gras or Rio de Janeiro Carnival – includes the active involvement of government, businesses, and educational institutions who want to understand, broadcast, exploit, and sell Trinidad Carnival on the world markets – including the scholarship market. That is, many persons both inside of and beyond Trinidad want carnival to be "attractive," both as entertainment and as a focus for serious scholarly work. Oil and natural gas are depletable resources, but carnival is forever. This global approach to carnival – its treatment as a cultural resource to be exploited as you would any other marketable resource – is part of the postmodern phenomenon of intellectual property, which assigns an economic value to the creation, ownership, and buying and selling of information.

It is from this perspective that we must understand the desire to restore the traditional characters. I am among those who strongly support such restoration. But I am also keenly aware of the tensions marking such a preservation and restoration. The past is restored in order to assure a future of carnival diversity. What carnival was is posited as being performed within what it is and what it ought to become. Carnival needs to be contemporary but it also needs to be old-fashioned. It needs to include the formal competitions, the displays of the big bands and masks, even as it needs also the wild street excesses and the much more delicate exposition of the traditional characters. It needs to satisfy up-to-date desires as reflected in the most advanced technologies, but it also needs to "remember" and replay its past, its honored originary traditions. It is precisely at this juncture that the desires of scholars and promoters of tourism coincide. Only if Trinidad Carnival includes all of the above can its supporters truly claim it is "authentic." And, of course, by including all of its components Trinidad Carnival will appeal simultaneously to many different kinds of publics, both domestic and foreign. It will be, in short, a better product.

Can the five key aspects (or themes) of Trinidad Carnival be explained by a single theory? The five aspects are:

- hybridity
- competition
- hierarchy
- inversion
- playing on the world stage.

Don Handelman and David Shulman suggested that play or playing could be theorized from two perspectives: top-down and bottom-up. Top-down playing is based on the Sanskrit-Hindu notion of *maya-lila*, a concept meaning that the whole world exists as the playing of the gods.

> In such a cosmology, the presence of the ludic is what may be called a top-down idea. Here, qualities of play are integral to the operation of the hierarchical cosmos, from its very apex, throughout its levels and domains. In this regard, to be involved in conditions of play, to partake of the qualities of play, is to be in tune with cosmic processes and their self-transformations. To be in play is to reproduce, time and again,

the very premises that inform the existence of this kind of cosmos. [. . .] It is worth noting that in cosmologies where premises of the ludic are not embedded at a high level of cosmos, and are not integral to the workings of cosmos, the phenomenon of play seems to erupt more from the bottom. Bottom-up play means that the ludic is often formulated in opposition to, or as a negation of, the order of things. This is the perception of play as unserious, illusory, and ephemeral, but it is also the perception of play as subversive and as resisting the order of things. [. . .] Bottom-up play has deep roots in monotheistic cosmologies. In related societies, the bottom-up entry of the ludic into routine living is often a battle for presence, a struggle over space and time devoted to their practices, and a confrontation over legitimacy, apart from those special occasions and places that indeed are set apart. So, play is often perceived to lurk within the interstices and spill over from the margins. Although the effortless, quicksilver qualities of play are always the same, the ontic and epistemic statuses of these qualities differ radically between cosmologies that embed such qualities at the top of the cosmic hierarchy and cosmologies that locate such qualities nearer the bottom.

(Handelman and Shulman 1997: 44–5)

Playing, pretending, masking, or taking on different forms or appearances is what the gods do all the time. The ever-changing forms of things and experiences are all "plays" in both the theatrical and the playful senses. The whole cosmos is a playground. From the top-down perspective, carnival is celebratory but not rebellious. The "gods" are the various authorities and their official instruments. They more than permit carnival; they encourage and indeed depend on it. Carnival 1 is a top-down set of events.

To some degree an African–South-Asian cosmology prevails over the European –Judaeo-Christian. Or, perhaps, in a paradoxical conundrum each contains the other, the Afro-Asian including and being included by the Euro-Christian. During Trinidad Carnival what the gods do all the time ordinary people are allowed to do, or cannot be stopped from doing, or are urged to do – for a brief time. Yet, even as the people play, they are controlled by the authorities; their playing is channeled according to what the authorities wish carnival to express and represent. Of course, such control – especially when drunkenness and giddiness are let loose – is potentially dangerous. The top can lose control; the bottom – Carnival 2 – can suddenly surge outwards and upwards.

This outward/upward surge is bottom-up playing. Bottom-up playing is more the Bakhtinian mode of rebellion, the mockery of authority, a freedom from constraints. Trinidad Carnival is both top-down and bottom-up playing. Carnival's deepest springs are the tensions between top-down and bottom-up playing. The top-down predictable structured set of events is always on the verge of collapsing into bottom-up chaotic unending creativity. Or is it the other way round? Is it that the predictably bottom-up Euro-Christian pre-Lenten "permitted" carnival may suddenly be transformed into an Afro-South-Asian never-ending cosmos-at-play? Which will it be, Trinidad Carnival asks, top-down or bottom-up? Each kind of playing wants to prevail over the other; but each needs the other. When successful, the result is an ongoing creative tension between the top-down and the bottom-up.

Let me further complicate matters theoretically speaking. Trinidad Carnival presents a peculiar situation, and perhaps not one that would be anticipated – given that the Europeans were the enslavers and colonizers. But I see in the intense competitions, the stickfighting, the trance-inducing rhythms of pan, the public displays of power-as-play Afro-South-Asian kinds of public social behavior. Contrastingly, the drunkenness, the rejection of work, the rebelliousness, and the inversion of social roles I see as European. I am not referring to who the performers are, but to the structure of the performing itself. Of course, it is not so simple. To put it more bluntly: the official competitions, the formal parades across the Queen's Park Savannah stage, the emphasis on a clearly demarcated hierarchy, the way the carnival dominates the press during carnival season, the participation of the Prime Minister and other top government officials, these are top-down activities and their structures and origins ought to be sought in African practices firstly and Asian practices secondly. The street playing, even jouvay itself, are bottom-up playing whose structures and origins ought to be sought in European practices.

It gets complicated because, for example, while on the street, band members may be acting bottom-up, once the band displays itself on the stage, where it will be judged, the participants shift performance mode and play top-down. If you have ever played, you know when you get close to the stage, the section leader says, "Okay now jump this way, make sure you know where you are going, that everyone is going to be watching you! When you are off the stage, hey, then you can let go." People are very flexible, they can play more than one kind of role in a very short stretch of time.

Finally, let me note that Trinidad Carnival is more intercultural than multi-cultural. Multicultural is where every culture performs in its assigned place. In New York, for example, there is St Patrick's Day, a Korean Day, a Caribbean Festival, various feast days for specific Roman Catholic saints, Purim in Crown Heights, etc. Trinidad Carnival as it has developed from Harlem earlier to Brooklyn these days has become part of New York's multicultural agenda. Intercultural is different. It is where cultural practices are obliged to share the same time-space. In this situation, things do not fit together neatly. There are tensions and ongoing (if sometimes non-conscious) negotiations, like sharing space and air in a crowded elevator. By deeming TT Carnival intercultural I mean it does not elide or alleviate differences but boldly displays and highlights them. These differences occur on all levels – individual, neighborhood, top-down/bottom-up, competitive, collaborative, and generic (steel band is different than calypso is different than mas is different than stickfighting is different than traditional characters . . .). What makes Trinidad Carnival such a stupendously energetic and "global" event – culturally and person-ally comprehensive – is its ability not only to tolerate but actually to raise to high consciousness and put into play, in the actual practices of Trinidad Carnival, the performances of these differences.

1   [Editor's note]. The Republic of Trinidad and Tobago, established at Independence in 1962 from the former British colony of Trinidad and Tobago, will be collectively referred to in this chapter as TT. Trinidad Carnival, which evolved throughout the nineteenth century, was not exported to Tobago until the twentieth century; in form and substance it remains Trinidad Carnival.

TIME OUT OR TIME IN?
THE URBAN DIALECTIC OF CARNIVAL

Milla Cozart Riggio

> Despising . . . the City, thus I turn my back. There is a world elsewhere.
>
> Shakespeare, *Coriolanus*, 3.3.134–5

In his chapter in this volume ("Carnival (theory) after Bakhtin"), Richard Schechner identified "hybridity, competition, hierarchy, inversion, and playing on the world stage" as central aspects of Trinidad and Tobago Carnival. In so doing, he differentiated between so-called democratic and non-democratic societies, past and present concepts of play, and cultures with a cosmic sense of the ludic and those without. Such distinctions are basic to understanding the function of festivity in general and carnival in particular in any given society. By examining what carnival affirms rather than what it negates and focusing on its essentially urban nature, both as a European pre-Lenten festival and as an African-influenced celebratory ritual throughout the Americas and especially in Trinidad, this essay augments Schechner's argument.

More than a festival, carnival (from Italian *carnevalare*, literally "removal of meat") was in its European origins a period of ritualized conflict and celebration identified with the pre-Lenten period between Christmas and Ash Wednesday.[1] Thus celebrated at the crossroads between winter and spring, indulgence and abstinence, death and rebirth, work and leisure, so-called civilization and what is perceived as savage or "wild," carnival has always licensed the crossing of many kinds of boundaries – between classes or estates, genders, races, ethnicities, carefully guarded geographical territories or neighborhoods.

From its first recorded instances in the twelfth century to the present, carnival history has been inseparable from the processes of urban expansion and capital development that led to the Industrial Revolution, the colonial and postcolonial plantation histories of the Americas, and to the nascent post-national globalism of the early twenty-first century. During the European Renaissance when establishing continuities with pre-Christian Greece and Rome was an important priority, carnival was erroneously traced to Greek and Roman celebrations, such as the Dionysia, Lupercalia, and Saturnalia, festivals to which carnival may in certain respects be

but with which it has no verifiable historical links and from which it
sential respects.

val celebrations have always been distinguished by time and location.
Historically, European carnival traditions have been strong in France, Spain,
Italy, southern Germany and the southern areas of the Netherlands, primarily
though not exclusively in Catholic countries. Venetian masks embody the Italian
commedia dell'arte spirit. In Spain, carnival was and still is primarily a village event.
In France, elite aristocratic masquerade parties, especially at the Paris Opera,
and large public balls often outside the city had by the eighteenth century set the
tone for aristocratic and popular carnival, which maintained a strong tradition
of street masking (see Kinser 1990). Hans Sachs's sixteenth-century *Fastnachtspiele*, or comic carnival plays, reflect the Burgher character of Protestant
Nuremberg.

Though literally hundreds of "carnivals" are chronicled in contemporary
England, almost all of them out of the official carnival season, ranging from
autumnal Guy Fawkes carnivals in Somerset to the August West Indian festivals
across the island (see Connor and Farrar in this volume), carnival as such never
fully reached early England, which has only scattered records of Shrove Tuesday
masquerading (alluded to in Norwich, 1443). However, carnival can be linked to
the season of masquerade balls and plays that began at Christmas and carried
through Shrovetide leading up to Ash Wednesday (see Introduction to Part II in
this volume). In its broader sense, carnival can also be linked to the Feast of Fools
or the Boy Bishop and to warm-weather festivities such as May Day or midsummer
games and St John's celebrations as times of license, revelry, masquerading, often
associated with the social inversion that is but part of the carnival story.

In the nineteenth and twentieth centuries, carnival emerged in the Americas.
Though individual carnivals differ as much in the so-called "New World" as they
do in Europe, carnivals throughout the Americas have encoded the processes
of cultural resistance and assimilation (at times annihilation) that constitute the
complex colonial and postcolonial history in areas ranging from Cuba to Brazil,
Uruguay, and Louisiana (especially the cities of Mobile and New Orleans). As
in earlier Europe (e.g. fifteenth-century Ferrara), masking was often allowed in
American plantation cultures only in the days leading up to Ash Wednesday. Thus,
Emancipation festivals of the street – as for example the *cannes brûlées* (canboulay
or cane burning; see Elder in this volume) harvest ritual in Trinidad – were
celebrated as carnival rites, often alongside the Governor's ball, house-to-house
visits, or other European-style celebrations. Contemporary carnivals of the
Americas often reflect African influences, as in the Samba schools of Rio, the
calinda and calypso of Trinidad, or the St James the Apostle vegigante processions
in July in Loiza, Puerto Rico. At times, they subtly encode interactive relationships
between indigenous peoples and colonial/postcolonial cultures, as for example in
the Murgas of Uruguay (see Remedi 1996, 2004).

As in the development of carnival in Europe, the carnivals of the Americas –
positioned in the margins between the past and the future – both resist and assimilate a broad range of folk traditions and disparate cultural influences reflected in
the ethnic intermixtures of its celebrants (Amerindian and Asian as well as African
and European; see chapters in Part I of this volume). By creating a diaspora of
its own, in cities ranging from Toronto, London (Notting Hill), Tokyo, Brooklyn,

Boston, Miami and fifty-odd other US, English, and European cities, with influences in Asia and Australia, West Indian Carnival has added a new chapter to the carnival story (see Part IV of this volume).

Despite their independent history, carnival masquerades in the Americas involve many of the same traditions and emblems as those of earlier Europe: phallic symbols such as the Roman *nasos longos et grossos in formam priaporum sive membrorum virilium in magna quantitate* (noses long and great like priapuses or male members of an enormous size; Burchard 1502, see Twycross and Carpenter 2001; similar noses are attested in *Fastnachtspiele* in Germany), mud masking, satirical songs that mock authorities (Venetian or Florentine *canti carnascialeschi*, Spanish *picardia*, Trinidad calypso), wild man masking, and animal masks as well as fancy masquerades. Cross-gender dressing and transvestism characterize both, as does the presence of the grotesque (Bakhtin's "laugher of the marketplace"). In Caribbean-based carnivals, playing royal has a more serious, powerful, and often beautiful significance – reflecting African notions of masking and festive play – than the parodic concept of the Carnival King might imply in European festivals (see figures Intro.1–3). But the essence of carnival remains its inherent capacity to appropriate spaces and transgress boundaries in order to manifest and celebrate aspects of human community.

TIME OUT OR TIME IN?

From the perspective of Mikhail Bakhtin, Victor Turner, and other twentieth-century theorists, carnival is a liminal festival that reverses social hierarchies during a circumscribed period of release, enthroning and then scapegoating temporary carnival monarchs (see Bakhtin [1968] 1984, Turner 1988, Burke [1978] 1994; see also Schechner in this volume). By taking "time out of time," i.e. suspending what is regarded as "normal" time, carnival is thought to temporarily release its revelers from all that *really* matters in the world. As stereotypically portrayed, the Carnival King is the figure imagined in 1559 by Pieter Bruegel in *The Fight Between Carnival and Lent*: lecherous, gluttonous, parodic, and obese – fattened for the kill after a short reign (see figures Intro.1 and Intro.2). This carnival subverts through parody or as epitomized by wildness of many kinds – devils, demons, furred or feathered Amerinidan or African warriors – threatens dangerously.

Indeed, this description is not essentially wrong. In burlesques, parodies, and satirical songs or skits, carnival provides a stabilizing vehicle for critiquing social authority and civic pretension. Moreover, carnival does partially ally itself with that which is dirty, bestial, or mythically primal: feces, mud, menstrual blood are parodically worn or demonstrated in many carnivals. Carnival "dirt" has both a sociology and a mythos. Carnival devils, for instance, are simultaneously characters of resistance to authority and emblems of primal essence: Trinidadian "molasses devils" recall the cane burning on the plantations of the nineteenth century, evoke the earth itself as that substance from which humanity emerged and to which it will return, and embody the mutinous energy of forces mythically arrayed against so-called civilization.

Nevertheless, despite its subversive elements, to describe carnival as liminal ("time out of time") is to see it as a photographic negative defined by the dark shadow of what it displaces rather than by the positive images of what it affirms.

Intro. 1 Pieter Bruegel, detail of Carnival King from *The Fight Between Carnival and Lent*.
Photograph courtesy of the Kunsthistorisches Museum, Vienna; published by permission.

Intro. 2 In its display of pleasures, Trinidad Carnival provides a parallel to the obese Carnival King image. The parallel here recorded is accidental; the man in the photograph is waving a flag for a small band on a truck, not a carnival king competitor. Carnival Tuesday, 1997. Photograph by Pablo Delano.

Intro. 3 "Playing royal" – Carnival Queen costume emphasizes grandeur and beauty. Carnival, Port of Spain, 1996. Photograph by Pablo Delano.

Carnival's primary source of energy – and this has a lot to do with its flexibility – is located neither fully in inversion nor in affirmation but in the tension between subverting and affirming, or, put another way, in its dialectic between civilized respectability and vagabondage. By expressing the tension between that which is regarded as respectable, often embodied in civic and urban infrastructures (town hall, corporate centers, policing authorities, the church as an institution, the workaday world), and community (the family with its many rites of passage, neighborhoods, carnival-producing societies, Krewes, or camps; see Table 1 below), carnival may be said to affirm the village within the city. By privileging leisure over work, it recalls pre-industrial social rhythms. By affirming the power of imagination and fantasy against the logic of reason and by resisting the tyranny of clock time in favor of an organic and seasonal temporal flow, carnival offers what Goethe called "der Menschen wunderliches Weben" (the wonderful texture of humanity; quoted in Catannés) – the "confusion, chaos . . . pushing, pressing, and rubbing" not only of the neighborhood marketplace but even more potently of the extended family, street festival, or artist colony as an alternative to the efficiency of the producing, industrializing world.

Carnival is, thus, characterized by paradox and contradiction. Its lifeblood flows from competition; it revels in the potential danger and threatened violence of massing in public places or at sensitive social margins. And yet, it manifests community. Its masks reveal identity as much as they conceal it. Indeed, in the Americas the festival itself was often a disguise for emancipation celebrations masked as carnival (see Introductions to Parts I, II, and III, Brereton, Elder, and Lovelace in this volume). By calling basic bodily functions to parodic attention, carnival reaches the human spirit through the flesh, fueled by too much food, too much drink, and too much sex. Its feasts include rich and fatty foods such as pancakes and sausages (in Koenigsberg in 1583 butchers carried a 440-pound sausage in procession; see Twycross and Carpenter 2001). It releases the spirit of intoxication inherent in aesthetic creativity and communion with fellow revelers as much as in its free-flowing alcoholic libations. Though contemporary carnivals are sometimes celebrated in seasons other than spring (particularly in northern climates in mid or late summer), the festival retains its link with fertility, licensing otherwise forbidden sexual freedom, even as its feasts affirm and reinforce communal sharing.

Part of the carnival paradox – and one of its main boundary crossings – is its positioning between pre-industrial, traditional cultural norms and highly industrialized contemporary settings. Modern carnivals, despite their many particular distinctions, collectively evoke the world of so-called "traditional" communities which, in the words of French sociologist Roger Caillois, live "in remembrance of one festival and in expectation of the next" (quoted in Burke [1978] 1994: 179). Despite nineteenth-century attempts to link carnival to agrarian origins (epitomized by the Grimm brothers and Frazer[2]), carnival – though seasonal – is neither agrarian nor essentially rural, even though many of its rituals commemorate harvest practices, such as slaughtering of fatted cows or pigs or Caribbean cane-burning ceremonies. Centered in villages (Eastern Europe, Spain), towns or settled regions (Bavaria, southern Netherlands, Bahia in Brazil, the island of Trinidad), and cities (Venice, Rome, Paris, Cologne, Nice, Nuremberg, New Orleans, Rio de Janeiro, Port of Spain), it is at base an urban festival, its history associated with the history of the cities with which it is largely identified.

Carnival is not only often in cities, it is in some respects also "of" the city. Grounded in antithesis and opposition, its driving engine is competition, often with territorial implications. The festival ritualizes, sublimates, and sometimes overtly threatens violence, often in defense of territory. Early carnival "bands" in Trinidad were, essentially, paramilitary groups, "bands" in the sense of territorial street gangs, rather than performing groups, defending individual turf, primarily as determined by city streets: Henry Street, French Street.[3] Fighting to protect urban spaces bounded by city streets, or taking over city or town squares, "clashing" or competing for artistic primacy are – like striking and massing in protest – urban activities, functions of cohabiting with others in a densely populated area.

Other aspects of urbanity in carnival include: its size and noise, its multiplex character (pan, steel drums, calypso, folk dance, carnival plays, street festivals, elite masquerade balls), its density and its intensity. In Trinidad, carnival has also appropriated discarded objects of urban industrialization: wheel hubs, used as percussive instruments in the "engine room" of steel orchestras; the discarded American oil drums used to create the one new acoustic instrument of the twentieth century, the steel drum. And, most recently, the highly controversial use of the big truck, the eighteen-wheel semi-trailer flatbeds on which are mounted the electronic bands (David Rudder and Charlie's Roots; Byron Lee and the Dragonaires) or dee jays who blare soca into the streets, in a thundering, driving rhythm that shakes houses. Such is not a country sound (though it has been imported to small village squares all over Trinidad).

In other ways, however, carnival does not initially seem to belong to the "city" as we usually think of it. By affirming the values of neighborhood and community, carnival may be said in a sense to bring the village, in the form of the neighborhood, the ghetto, the family, the community, into the city.[4] Carnival, thus, affirms not only the restorative value of festivity but also a concept of cultural and individual history, seen not as the story of public institutions, centralized governments, systems of law and order, governing economies, or even the conquering or the subjugating of peoples, but as the encoding and imprinting of genetic, cultural, and artistic legacies, of cultural memory embodied in dance, music, and fantasy. Carnival in Trinidad offers any individual on the island an opportunity, in the local parlance, to "play yuhself," to find the authentic link between the person and the disguise, which as often as not leaves the face painted but unmasked.

To put it simply, carnival does more than invert hierarchy or provide a socially stabilizing, temporary outlet or relief. The festival manifests what Shakespeare called "a world elsewhere," a festive world of community, when community is allied with artistic expression manifest in public celebration. As one of the basic antinomies of culture, community/neighborhood always fights city hall, the local against the central, private versus public, family versus government. Every time a local organization tries to get money for neighborhood community centers, or fights to restore art and music to public education, it is affirming an important aspect of the carnivalesque.

To be sure, carnival allies itself with festive consumption, rather than with thrift: Eat, drink, be merry and spend in a day what you may have worked a year to save, says the carnival reveler. And the prudent among us often cluck our tongues and say, reproachfully, "But what about shoes for the children and bread for the table?" No one condones poverty or neglect of the family. To the extent that the hedonism of carnival may lead to such, its excesses are dangerous as well as attractive. But the antithesis between consumerism and festivity, capital accumulation and festive generosity, which is at the base of carnival, underlies many other social oppositions. Those who have forgone large salaries, possible wealth, prestige, and visible social position in order to produce theater, build masks, make films, or in some other way to dwell in the world of the arts espouse values that carnival takes over the road "make to walk on carnival day" to affirm in a festival mode (quotation from Kitchener calypso).

Carnival is not always benign in claiming its space and affirming its values. Indeed, without at least the threat of danger and a whiff of potential violence, carnival loses its potency. Contemporary carnival violence is ordinarily ritualized and sublimated in informal or organized competitions. However, the festival has periodically provided the occasion for actual violence, sometimes as clashes between organized groups of carnival celebrants, sometimes as social protest arising from class or race conflicts (Romans in 1580, Trinidad 1881, Notting Hill, London, 1976). Santiago de Cuba, celebrated each July, was used as a cover for an unsuccessful Castro rebellion in 1953, and, when Castro came to power in 1959 under the cover of a raucous New Year's Day celebration, carnival was officially canceled (though subversively celebrated) for nearly forty years.

Though it revels in excess and may be subversive, carnival is not Saturnalian. Its celebration is typically governed by a process of restraint – order within license – amidst the excesses of consumption and revelry. It has its own sense of limits that stops far short of the true Dionysian. In celebrating sexuality and fertility, carnival affirms both the power of the libido and its inevitable result – the birth of children (often, it is said, by producing them; the birth rate is presumed to go up in carnival cultures nine months after carnival). Nevertheless, carnival has its own rules, expressed through a sense of internal decorum that limits excess and creates courtesy, even in the midst of what is called the bacchanal of its celebration.

"WOULD HE WERE FATTER" – THE FESTIVAL WORLD VS. THE WORKADAY WORLD

> Yond Cassius has a lean and hungry look . . . Would he were fatter . . . He loves no plays . . . hears no music; seldom he smiles . . . Such men are dangerous.
>
> Shakespeare, *The Tragedy of Julius Caesar*, 1.2.194–205

Like linguistic dialects that were once thought to be debased versions of a master tongue but are now recognized as having their own internal structure, the carnival ethos may best be understood in holistic terms, as part of what we may call the "festival world." Its epistemology and concepts of space, time, and value resemble those often associated with festivity in writers such as Shakespeare. They systematically contrast to values of earnestness and sobriety commonly identified with what we may call "the workaday world," especially in post-industrial capitalist economies. The virtues of carnival, which reside partly in the healing power of laughter, play, and fantasy, are, thus, embedded in an internally consistent structure, which may be diagrammed as in Table 1.

Table 1 The festival world vs. the workaday world

The festival world	The workaday world
Concepts of time: seasonal	*Concepts of time: clock time*
Movements of the ocean	Regularity
Diurnal – light	Punctuality
Agrarian (mango, puoi)	Steady measurement
Sense of the eternal	Temporal materiality
Social structuring	*Social structuring*
Family	Urban infrastructures
Neighborhood	Government
Community	Policing agencies
Church as folk worship	Church as institution
Significant social spaces	*Significant social spaces*
Yards	Factories
Streets as festive arenas	Streets as thoroughfares
Domestic spaces	Corporate/government offices
Public space, freely accessed	Regulated public spaces
Epistemology	*Epistemology*
Imagination, intuition	Rationality, logic, logical cause and effect
Activities (vocations) of value	*Activities of value*
Rites of passage	Money making
Art in all its forms	Commerce, trade, manufacturing
Music, painting, costume-making	Consumerism
Poetry, drama	Law and legal processes
Imaginative creativity	Progressive development
Resistive/constructive play	Obedient behavior
Transgressive behavior	
Essences	*Essences*
Spiritual, metaphysical	Material
Fantasy, magic	Science
The primacy of the unseen	Phenomenology

Trinidad Carnival, the self-styled Mecca of Caribbean celebrations, exemplifies the notions of time, concepts of space, sense of community, and epistemology associated with the carnival world.

"Trini Time"

Time is basic to carnival theory. The concept of "liminality" (the word meaning threshold) is usually glossed as time taken out of "real" time, a period of suspension when the time clock stops. Conversely, what is called "Trini Time" – which grants a license to disregard punctuality – is the defining feature of ordinary "time," not only in Trinidad but under other names throughout much of the Caribbean. The term is often used deprecatingly, in a tone of apology, without recognition of the extent to which this simple phrase denotes a concept of time more fluid and organic but no less "real" than that measured by the regularity of a clock.

The concept of a "time clock" is derived from modern industrial development, particularly of nineteenth-century factories that required workers to be simultaneously present on the job. Modern weekends are a way of regulating labor by keeping it at work during the week. The weekend, as an extension of nineteenth-century Sabbatarianism, replaces festival and holy days as times of work stoppage.[5] In this sense, the clock is and has always been the enemy of the festival world. Trini Time, which disregards this clock, is antithetical to "production" in the modern industrial sense of the term.

Trini Time – carnival time – is in itself a concept of time, with its own value, not the absence of time or the suspension of time, but another way of measuring time – the time scheme if you will, of carnival's world elsewhere. As such, it is "measured," if at all, not by the clock but by the sun and the moon, the tides, the seasons in a culture that still marks the seasons in festival terms, moving from one festival to another, often cross-celebrated by peoples of diverse religions and races.[6]

How, one may ask, can the time scheme of an urban festival in Trinidad, a gas, oil, and ammonia producing nation that is among the most industrialized of the Caribbean, recall the pre-industrial, seasonal rhythm of the sun and the moon? What have harvest festivals to do with the city? In this very contradiction lies the essence of this paradoxical celebration as well as one key to the character of Trinidad as a carnival culture. Just as Charles Dickens, the most urban of English nineteenth-century novelists, used parables of "sowing," "reaping," and "garnering" to affirm the value of imagination and fantasy as educators of city children in *Hard Times*, so too carnival recalls the cyclical rhythms of the seasons not as an echo of a lost way of life but as a reminder amidst the bustle of modernity that there is a present cosmic temporality that supersedes the manufactured time scheme of the factory world. It is again a way of affirming within the urban context an alternative rhythm of life.

This festive sense of time resists the rational assumption that time marches along a never-varying path. In contrast, from this point of view time varies with human perception, rather than being controlled by the merciless regularity of the clock. Ask any school child waiting for recess, and you will hear that not all minutes are the same length, no matter what the clock says. Time, which "drags" and "flies," is a flexible commodity, to be valued, used, and spent in individual ways. Pace is important, and it varies. For many Trinidadians, for instance, the pace of life is speeded up, rather than slowed down, by carnival. For those working in mas camps where costumes are made – all but the "factory" camps where costumes are completed and neatly hanging in rows weeks before carnival – the pressure to produce carnival forces both paid workers and volunteers to work long nights, often "around the clock." As any performer knows, intensely focused, sleep-deprived concentration releases a level of energy and, epistemologically, a different kind of perception than one finds within the regularity of a controlled and methodical routine: dangerous on the production line or in the hospital emergency room, but effective for the artist.

What is important about Trinidad as a carnival culture is or has until very recently been the fact that such a notion of time is not limited to the period of the festival itself. One of Trinidad's most influential and longest-lasting journals, the *Trinidad and Tobago Review*, published continuously since the mid-1960s by distinguished economist and cultural activist Lloyd Best under the auspices of Tapia House, has for years appeared in editions named for the fruit or flowers of the season: the Mango edition, Puoi, etc. Best has long understood that social and economic value for a culture such as that of Trinidad ought to adhere in the potential distinction of a way of life that can incorporate the local into the national, that uses steel pan as a teaching tool as well as a musical instrument, and that moves to the rhythm of its own notion of the seasons more than its ability to rival Venezuelan production of oil or to mimic the industrial output of larger nations. An understanding of time is crucial to such knowledge. Carnival does not stop the clock so much as it affirms this fluid and organic, seasonal, festive notion of time.

Appropriating space

However central time is to understanding the ethos of carnival, space is equally important – though less readily apparent. Whereas time might because of its seasonal nature appear to link the festival world somewhat misleadingly with agrarian rhythms, carnival's relationship to space can best be understood as a way of claiming, appropriating, and dominating urban spaces. Notions of time were long ago associated with festivity. However, the debate about space still belongs mainly to philosophers, city planners, and urban theorists, who though they recognize the "physical form of the urban environment," including its aesthetic dimensions, as a "central aspect of the social world itself, contributing to the constitution of the world through every dimension from the economic, to the biotic, to the aesthetic," have not dealt directly with the festive appropriations of space (quotation from Martinez 2001).[7]

This makes our work a little harder and requires a bit of theoretical background not necessary to the arguments about time. As the aesthetic equivalent of social protest, carnival claims city streets and other urban spaces or village squares not only for the momentary pleasures of play but also implicitly (and for many of the participants probably unconsciously) to affirm its right to those streets. The transforming energies of mas link the festival world to social practice, crossing boundaries, defining territory, marking places as their own in a variety of ways. Claiming the streets and replacing the corporate and governmental infrastructure with festive exuberance for a day or two may seem like nothing more than a temporary inversion of the classic kind. However, by bridging the gap between the material and the aesthetic and by transforming the space itself, such an appropriation creates a more lasting effect throughout the culture.

This is to say that just as time can be either linear or variably transformative, so too space has a cosmic as well as a material dimension, an idea that Cecilia Martinez de la Macorra, an architect and professor of urban planning, traces primarily to Henri Lefebvre:

> There has been a growing interest in theorizing space over the last two decades, and the spatial lexicon (border, territory, place, mobility) is now part and parcel of debates within social theory. Henri Lefebvre's work *The Production of Urban Space* marks the first attempt to bridge the gap between the theoretical (epistemological) realm and

the practical one; between mental space and social structure; between the space of philosophers and the space of people who deal with material things. Before him, this connection presumed to be self-evident from the point of view of the scientific discourse was never conceptualized. With this new "knowledge of space" Lefebvre moved from descriptions and cross sections to a "science of space . . . to discover or construct a theoretical unity between . . . physical-nature, the Cosmos, mental [concepts of space] . . . and the social. Lefebvre thus gave structure to the epistemological space, as well as the space of social practice and to the space occupied by sensory phenomena, including products of the imagination.

(Martinez 2001)

In a world so dominated by the notions of private property and ownership that we lay legal claim not only to all our own ideas and words but often even to the air around us, space itself has become one of the contested arenas of modern life: gaining access to, then appropriating, dominating and finally creating (or "producing") space is – according to urban theorist David Harvey – a vital, ongoing process. The very transgressive nature of the appropriation may add to its power. To give a non-festive example, urban squatters, for instance, change the landscape of the city in just this way, by creating the space they appropriate. Stumbling over mattresses as one walks through the city changes the nature of the sidewalk and impacts the surrounding architecture. Similarly though more positively, carnival transforms the streets it claims as its own.

In Trinidad, where the festival has been appropriated as the signifier of the nation and is thought to be national, democratic, free, and open, there is no barrier between the masqueraders on the street on carnival Tuesday and the onlookers on the sidewalk. Despite sometimes heavy-handed "security guards" hired by profit-minded mas band leaders to prevent intruders from crashing their bands, the line between those participating and those watching the festival is consistently blurred. Indeed, while this massive street festival is boring to watch, it is a mesmerizingly heady experience to play. The streets belong to the festival – to those playing mas, who often rove between their own band and those of their friends, and the thundering semi-trailers and smaller vehicles that carry their music. Such a massive takeover marks the space permanently.

In contrast, in diasporic carnivals, such as those in Toronto, Notting Hill, or Brooklyn, there is a much sharper line of division between the maskers who more normally "parade" through the streets and the watching public (in Toronto an actual fence separates the two). This line of division reduces or alters the ultimate impact of the event. The "parade" may own the streets for a time, but always with the awareness that this is either by permission or, conversely, in a hostile environment. The audacity of the transgressive appropriation is to some extent limited by the powerfully countering corporate or ethnic force squeezing the masqueraders – who are themselves sometimes seen as cultural intruders in territory not their own. In Trinidad, where carnival is more naturally at home, the appropriation of space has a somewhat different set of epistemological, spatial, and social dimensions. Carnival leaves its indelible mark on the spaces it occupies, its aggressive freedom and domination remembered throughout the year, whereas in cities where it is more contained and restricted its effect seems more limited, or at least more contested and controversial.[8]

Carnival and community

Carnival involves more than the festive takeover of public spaces. At the heart of the opposition between the festival and the workaday worlds is the battle between neighborhood and city hall – the community with its many needs for services opposing what is normally thought of as the urban infrastructure, embedded in corporate wealth, government, and institutional religion. Carnival manifests the power of community within the urban sphere, in festive rather than ideological terms. Time combines with space in helping to establish the sense of community within the festive realm.

One of the important aspects of carnival's allocation of space and time is the nature of the communities created by or for the festival – and, conversely, the way in which the presence of carnival impacts the idea of community itself. Pan yards, for example, where steel bands rehearse, are often community centers, where food and drink are sold, visitors come to listen to rehearsals, and pannists can hang out as well as play. In the late 1940s and 1950s and into the 1960s, pan yards were territorial strongholds, replacements in their way for the bands of stickfighters of an earlier period, defended when necessary by violence. But even then, the yards provided a haven for young men who sought their identity on the streets (see Bellour et al. 2002). The yard itself provided a sense of place, an alternative family that understood the needs of young men at risk better perhaps than their own families.[9] For many poor boys, pan provided the only meaningful "time in" in their lives.

The early steel bands not only provided a home and a haven for boys of the street, but they also brought middle-class boys into forbidden pleasures, often across class lines. In the inevitable period of rebellion against parental authority that accompanies the rites of passage to adulthood, sneaking out to play pan provided a creative world elsewhere for middle-class boys. Taking time out from the disciplined training of a middle-class home provided constructive, rather than destructive, time in the pan yard, a training ground for maturation (see Johnson in this volume). Such training expands horizons, allows independence, and creates social awarenesses that cross class lines at the crucial stages of adolescence when youth develops autonomy, separating itself from parents to establish its own identity.

Calypso and mas, the other two forms of carnival, also create communities. The pan yard, calypso tents, and mas camps are strongest during the high carnival season, from January 6 to Ash Wednesday, though they often function all year round. But the effect of carnival on community in Trinidad is not limited to the communities that carnival actually creates. It also impacts existing neighborhoods, communities, and families in significant ways. The United States national, state, and local governments spend millions of dollars, often unsuccessfully, attempting to generate a link between art and community. In Trinidad and Tobago, such arts spring as if from the soil itself: the narrow lanes of Belmont may now house folks who live more apart from their neighbors than they were once wont to do. Yet, these small houses still contain home-run businesses, such as tailoring or automobile repair shops. The neighborhood is internally secured by those who live there more than by the police. And at the corner of Clifford Street and Belmont Circular Road, a small steel band thrives each year in hope and expectation, until it falls silent after the preliminary pan competitions.

Similar small pan yards can be found in Port of Spain, Woodbrook, Diego Martin and throughout the island; children's mas camps are set up in front rooms of tiny houses or elaborate homes. Competitions in both impoverished and affluent schools train students to write songs, draw carnival pictures, play pan, and develop a sense of national pride through the festival. Indeed, the Michael K. Hall Community School in Tobago, which in 1998 won the Better Business Award as the best small business in the Republic of Trinidad and Tobago, uses carnival arts as a thematic center for teaching elementary-aged children the basic lessons they need to learn: mathematics, reading, social studies.

Epistemology and social value

> There are more things in heaven and earth, Horatio, than are dreamt of in your philosophy.
>
> Shakespeare, Hamlet, 1.5.166–7

Walking with a friend down Frederick Street in Port of Spain one day, I suddenly slipped and fell for no apparent reason, badly injuring my foot. A well-known Trinidadian singer, who came quickly to my rescue, later explained my fall by saying that he had seen my friend and me generating a force field of energy through our conversation. We then entered the energy field emanating from the singer and his companions; while my spirit could handle the intense concentration of energies, my body could not. And I fell. What was striking to me about this story was the assurance with which the narrator described what he had seen. As surely as I myself had seen him as he bent over to help me, he had seen emanations invisible to me.

Such a story epitomizes the epistemology of the carnival world, which, because it is centered in imagination and intuition rather than in logic or reason, privileges things of the spirit over the material or phenomenological. Such an ethos is consistent with attitudes toward time, space, and the creation of community within carnival. Moreover, the emphasis on imaginative fantasy and intuitive knowing reinforces carnival's historical identification with the organic, seasonal rhythms of the pre-industrial world, even in a modern urban setting. Sociologists have since Max Weber assumed the link between capitalism and the Protestant work ethic, with its attendant sense of duty (see Weber 1930, Tawney 1926). Similarly, the development of modern industrial, corporate infrastructures emphasizes the material and presumes a rational world ordered by logical cause and effect.

Such is not the carnival world. Indeed, one of the reasons that carnival provided an important festive vehicle in the Americas for emancipated Africans in the nineteenth century was the link between the sense of fantasy in the festival and a powerful, ancestor-based belief in the primacy of the unseen among the Afro-Trinidadians. Homage to the ancestors cohabits easily with a sense that life is governed by energies and forces beyond the material. It is no surprise that the Afro-Creole population in late nineteenth-century Trinidad – that group to which the origins of carnival as we now know it are attributed – looked more to education than to capital accumulation, shopkeeping, or property ownership as an avenue of advancement for their children. Moreover, in a situation such as that of slavery or its post-emancipation aftermath where the material world is arrayed against one's culture, limiting advancement in many different ways, achieving through festive media – through the arts (or sometimes sports) – provides an alternative path not only to personal satisfaction but also to social recognition.

As in every other area of carnival celebration, production and performance are not entirely dissociated from each other. Material success lures across the carnival divide, echoing and continuing the dialectic between the festival and the workaday worlds that is in itself basic to the very existence of carnival. This is true in Trinidad, where large mas camps sometimes resemble factories more than families, steel orchestras are partially seduced by corporate sponsorship, and calypsonians and soca artists are eager to get their share of the pie of plenty. Nevertheless, there remains throughout the culture of Trinidad – in keeping with the carnival ethos – a sense that value finally adheres more in family (especially extended families) and community than in vocation, in festive celebration at least as much as or more than in work. Indeed, there is among many Trinidadians an almost fatalistic belief in cosmic inevitability: "nothing happens before its time"; "when you reach you reach."

In such a society, power lies not in multinational corporate wealth but in the extraordinary range and reach of the culture with its many arts and festivals. These are hardly limited to carnival; they range across ethnic, religious, and racial boundaries throughout Trinidad. Many in the culture, particularly the cohesive Hindu and Islamic Indo-Trinidadian communities, might be offended by the idea that carnival, which they may see as vulgar and secular, represents an ethos with which they can identify. However, understood not as a debasement of the human spirit but as an expression of imagination and fantasy that captures the essential spirituality of the island, carnival epitomizes the link between festive epistemology and social value.

CONCLUSION: CARNIVAL AND MARKET FORCES

Of course, the opposition between the festival and the workaday worlds is both idealized and partial. Carnival is not free from market forces, especially in a nation such as Trinidad that attempts to market the festival itself as a national product. The impulse to make money, to mass-manufacture costumes, to develop the sort of consumerism that would regulate behavior in the name of "decency" partly to promote profit has from the beginning cohabited with the impulse to transgressive behavior in carnival. It is this very opposition between respectability and vaga-bondage that creates the central paradox of the festival and that to some extent accounts for both its flexibility and its essential urbanity. For all its link to tradition, its organic and seasonal sense of time, its ability to appropriate and transform space, its grounding in community, and its preference for imagination over reason, carnival is not at its base nostalgic. Governed, finally, by the laws of hospitality, which are always more courteous than the laws of production, carnival welcomes its revelers to its feast. But the feast itself embodies all the contradictions and paradoxes of modernity.

NOTES

1 Portions of the opening section of this chapter were previously published in Milla Cozart Riggio, "Carnival," an entry in Dennis Kennedy (ed.) *Oxford Encyclopedia of Theatre and Performance*, and are used with permission of Oxford University Press.

2 Sir James Frazer in particular was eager to see in carnival the universal agrarian myth of the burial and resurrection of a god that for him underlay all religions: "We have seen that many peoples have been used to observe an annual period of license, when the customary restraints of law and morality are thrown aside, when the whole population give themselves up to extravagant mirth and jollity, and when the darker passions find a vent which would never be allowed them in the more staid and sober course of ordinary life. Such outbursts of the pent-up forces of human nature, too often degenerating into wild orgies of lust and crime, occur most commonly at the end of the year, and are frequently associated, as I have had occasion to point out, with one or other of the agricultural seasons, especially with the time of sowing or of harvest. Now, of all these periods of license the one which is best known and which in modern language has given its name to the rest, is the Saturnalia . . . The resemblance between the Saturnalia of ancient and the Carnival of modern Italy has often been remarked; but in the light of all the facts that have come before us, we may well ask whether the resemblance does not amount to identity" (Frazer 1922, chapter 58).

3 This same kind of rivalry extended to the early steel band movement, when, following World War II, steel bands were "Bad John" enclaves fighting for their space, a struggle that climaxed in the 1970 Black Power movement, when all but one steel band in Port of Spain boycotted carnival in a collective moment of protest.

4 The distinction, basically, is that defined by Victor Turner as "communitas" vs. "societas," with communitas that place of communal "flow" that breaks the boundaries of society and is set against the corporative and centrally governing urban infrastructures, or societas.

5 Sabbatarianism was the practice of isolating the Sabbath (usually Sunday rather than Saturday) as a day away from work, as a replacement for midweek festivals and holidays. The practice gained widespread currency during the period of highest industrial development in the nineteenth century, though in England it is foreshadowed as early as the sixteenth century. Because the Sabbath itself was often appropriated by evangelical ministers and others as a day of worship and spiritual reflection rather than play, the effect of Sabbatarianism among the working poor was effectively to remove (or attempt to remove) almost all vestiges of play from their lives. Dickens deals with this issue, and also with the contrasting concepts of time, in *Hard Times*, when he portrays the churches of his industrial town as "pious warehouses" of red brick.

6 For a study that focuses on the Trinidadian concept of time, placing it in relationship to contemporary theoretical debates about the nature of time and its possible variants see Birth (1999).

7 Theorizing space has been a crucial preoccupation of urban specialists and philosophers of the last two decades of the twentieth century, just as theorizing about time was in the beginning of the century (see Martinez 2001). But those dealing with space have not developed theories linking space to festivity as Turner and others did for time.

8 The history of diasporic carnivals may challenge this rather simplistic opposition (see Part IV of this volume). Conflicts between various ethnic groups, as for example the Hasidic community and the West Indians in Brooklyn, are played out partly in the festive arenas of the city. And, in contrast, there are those in Trinidad who resist the ethos of carnival, from either religious persuasion or the opposite extreme, a commitment to the ethos of the workaday world.

9   The concept of family in this festive setting is extended to include an informal, non-biological family. Such a concept carries to an extent throughout Trinidad culture, in which nurturing adult women, such as teachers, are consistently called "Tanti" or "Aunty." The notion of a "family" composed of cultural relatives – brothers, sisters, aunties and so forth – is characteristic of many societies, and especially of Afro-Creole peoples in the Americas.

TRINIDAD CARNIVAL TIMELINE

Dawn K. Batson and Milla Cozart Riggio

Encounter and early settlement 1498–1782

1498 – Columbus encounters Trinidad and its Amerindian population.

1530 – Spanish establish limited settlements in Trinidad.

Pre-emancipation era 1783–1837

1783 – *Cédula de población* allows Catholic colonists and free people of color to settle in Trinidad. French planters migrate with their slaves to Trinidad, mainly from other West Indian islands. French planters probably initiate Mardi Gras Carnival, partially excluding slaves.

1797 – British capture Trinidad.

1802 – Treaty of Amiens formally cedes Trinidad to British.

1806 – First immigration of Chinese indentured workers.

1807 – Abolition of the slave trade in the British Empire.

1811 – Trinidad has largest free non-white population in the British Caribbean.

1834 – Emancipation Act passed in Britain, with stipulation of a five-year "period of apprenticeship" to last until 1840, when full emancipation was expected to take place.

Emancipation 1838

1838 – August 1, abolition of slavery. Unrest cut apprenticeship short, with full emancipation gained August 1, 1838. *Cannes brûlées* (burning of the cane) celebrations may have been initiated, later evolving into canboulay, though verified

Intro. 4 Map of Trinidad. Photograph provided by Jeffrey Chock.

records are not available this early. The drum trinity – bull, foulé, and the cutter – provide the rhythm for the songs and dances.

Domination of the skin drum; growth of jamette carnival 1838–81

1840–8 – Canboulay celebrations moved to carnival Sunday night. Immigration from neighboring islands, Europe, and America. French Creoles appear to be withdrawing from carnival.

1843 – Carnival limited to two days.

1845 – East Indian and later new wave of Chinese indentured laborers arrive.

1857 – First working oil well in the world outside the Caspian Sea region dug at La Brea in Trinidad by The American Merrimac Oil Company. Closed in 1859.

1866 – Chinese immigration ends.

1867 – Paria Oil Company formed; oil well dug; produces 60 gallons a week. Quickly closed down.

1881 – Canboulay riots.

Carnival 1881–1934: tamboo bamboo, emergence of English as language of calypsos; middle-class influence in carnival; competitions developed

1881–3 – Conflict between the authorities and the canboulay celebrants. Canboulay riots in 1881.

1883 – Music Ordinance effectively banning the drum, the calindas, and the canboulay processions.

1884 – Peace Ordinance establishes j'ouvert from dawn of carnival Monday. Indian Muharram Hosay riots. More rioting at Carnival.

1885 – Tamboo-bamboo bands replace the drums' boom, foule, and cutter with the bottle and spoon.

1898 – Process of replacing French Creole with English as language of choice in lavways well under way.

1901 – "Calypso" accepted as name of music.

1902 – The Oil Exploration Syndicate of Canada strikes oil. Beginning of industrial production in Trinidad.

1915 – Newly appointed Governor Sir John Chancellor declares intention to prohibit carnival because of war but does not do so.

1917 – Masking at carnival time prohibited. East Indian indentureship ends.

1919 – "Victory Carnival," masking permitted; carnival prizes established by the *Trinidad Guardian* and *Argos* newspapers.

1923 – "Sly Mongoose," a song brought to Trinidad from Jamaica in 1911, described by the *Trinidad Guardian* in terms that suggest the beginning of the Road March style of spontaneously using common melodies for bands on the street, rather than relying on compositions by the chantwell of each band (Rohlehr 1990: 117).

1934 – Theatres and Dance Halls Ordinance regulates safety features and prohibits "profane, indecent, or obscene songs or ballads" in theatres and dancehalls licensed for public entertainment, including calypso venues.

Biscuit tin bands; attempts to "improve" carnival 1935–39

1937 – Labor riots. Tamboo-bamboo bands start incorporating metal cans.

1939 – Trinidad Calypso and Musicians Advertising Association founded by calypsonians, including Hubert Raphael Charles (Lion), Raymond Ignatius Quevado (Atilla), Charles Grant (Gorilla), and W. Wilkinson; Trinidad Calypsonians Union founded; Carnival Improvement Committee attempted reorganization of festival; Alexander's Ragtime Band comes on the road with dust bins, cement pans, paint cans, biscuit tins and brake drums. Two to four notes heard.

War years and aftermath 1940–50

1941–5 – World War II. Carnival suspended, though calypsonians continued to perform. Experimentation with steel drums goes on in the "yards." More notes added to pans and more instruments created. Cuff boom or slap bass; du-dup or bass kettle, kettle, and later the ping-pong were the main instruments. Pans convex in shape until 1941 when Ellie Mannette sinks pan to create concave instrument. Burning of pans to remove chemicals improves sound. VE Day (May) and VJ Day (August) 1945 bands attract the attention of the public at victory celebrations.

1945–50 – Steelband development: 55-gallon drum now used for instruments. Larger surface, more notes. Pans still held in one hand and played with a stick held in the other. Run-ins with the law continue. Red Army band tours British Guiana.

1946 – Carnival resumed after war. Carnival Bands Union led by Patrick Jones rivals Savannah Carnival Committee, under James H. Smith. Rivalry between downtown and Queen's Park Savannah venues continues throughout decade. First Carnival Queen contest sponsored by the *Trinidad Guardian*.

1950 – Steelbands clash; Invaders and Tokyo, Casablanca and Invaders. Steelband Association formed.

Developments in period leading up to independence 1951–61

1951 – Trinidad All Steel Percussion Orchestra formed to go to Festival of Britain. Eleven of the top ping-pong players from Trinidad. Members: Sterling Betancourt – Crossfire, Belgrave Bonaparte – Southern Symphony, Philmore "Boots" Davidson – Syncopators, Andrew de la Bastide – Hill 60, Orman "Patsy" Barnes – Casablanca, Winston "Spree" Simon – Tokyo, Dudley Smith – Rising Sun, Ellie Mannette – Invaders, Granville Sealey – Tripoli, Theo Stephens – Free French, Anthony Williams – North Stars. Lieutenant Griffith of St Lucia Police Band – Musical Director. Toured Britain and France. Chromatic range established.

1952 – Steelband classes (soloist and orchestra) included in the Trinidad and Tobago Music Festival.

1953 – First national Calypso King competition, replacing competing king contests.

1956 – Anthony Williams introduces pan on wheels.

1957 – Government establishes Carnival Development Committee. The Mighty Sparrow boycotts the Calypso Monarch competition in protest against disparity in prizes given calypsonians and the Carnival Queen.

1958 – Steelband Association officially registered. George Goddard, President. *Trinidad Guardian* cancels Carnival Queen show, ending its sponsorship.

1959 – Carnival Queen show sponsored by the Jaycees. Eric Williams snubs Queen, in favor of newly established Queen of the Carnival Bands.

Musical war and peace 1962–70

1962 – Independence within the British Commonwealth. First Prime Minister of Trinidad and Tobago – Eric Williams of the People's National Movement (PNM) party. Steelband Association now National Association of Trinidad and Tobago Steelbandsmen. Anthony Williams introduces the Spider Web pan, forerunner of fourths and fifths pan.

1963 – Launch of the Panorama Competition. Establishment of National Steelband with government aid. Errol Hill Dimanche Gras plays to Celebrate Independence (1963–1964).

1965 – Bertie Marshall introduces amplified pans.

1969 – North Stars perform with acclaimed pianist Winifred Atwell "Ivory and Steel" recording.

1970 – Prime Minister Eric Williams meets with steelband leaders. Greater corporate sponsorship of bands. Black Power demonstrations.

A decade of innovation and invention 1971–79

1971 – National Association of Steelbandsmen becomes PanTrinbago. Bertie Marshall invents the Bertphone – combined tone control and amplification (lost in fire in 1980). The Carnival Queen contest ended because of Black Power demonstrations of previous year.

1975 – Rudolph Charles of Desperadoes introduces the quadrophonic pan. Also introduced chromed pans, nine bass, triple tenor, rocket bass, and aluminum canopies. DJs begin to supplant steelbands on roads and in parties. Steelband Music Festival in decline. Ras Shorty I records *Soul Calypso Music*.

1977 – Ras Shorty I names "the soul of calypso" music SOKAH.

1979 – Panorama boycott.

Consolidation and expansion 1980–2002

1980 – Denzil "Dimes" Fernandez creates bore pan. Grooves of pan bored by small holes giving a brighter sound. Steelband Music Festival reintroduced – as "Pan Is Beautiful Too," staged at Jean Pierre Complex. School Steelband Festival introduced. Number of innovations in pan world.

1986–8 – Jimi Phillip introduces collapsible pan stand, porta bass.

1991 – National Carnival Commission Act no. 9 created the National Carnival Commission, replacing the Carnival Development Committee.

1993 – First Soca Monarch competition established with Superblue as winner.

1995 – Election of United National Congress (UNC) candidate Basdeo Panday as first Indo-Trinidadian Prime Minister; A.N.R. Robinson swings three Tobago-based National Alliance for the Republic (NAR) seats to the UNC after a tied election to create majority. UNC comes in with a theme of "national unity."

1996 – First Chutney Soca Monarch competition established. Primary oversight of carnival placed in the hands of the three interest groups: PanTrinbago; Trinbago Unified Calypsonians' Organization (TUCO); and National Carnival Bands Association (NCBA), rather than the National Carnival Commission.

1998 – Trinidad and Tobago National Steel Orchestra formed.

2000 – World Steelband Festival held in Trinidad with bands from Europe, North America, the Caribbean, and Trinidad and Tobago.

2001 – Election tied between PNM and UNC. President Robinson appoints Patrick Manning of the PNM as Prime Minister for an interim period.

2002 – Election gives clear majority to PNM, with Patrick Manning as Prime Minister. In November, challenge to the National Carnival Bands Association (NCBA) under the leadership of Richard Afong (of Barbarossa) created by new "Carnival Improvement Committee" formed by leaders of large mas bands. The National Carnival Commission asserts its control of the "parade of the bands" on carnival Tuesday. Panorama prelims for the first time held in the panyards rather than the Queen's Park Savannah.

Part I

EMANCIPATION, ETHNICITY, AND IDENTITY IN TRINIDAD AND TOBAGO CARNIVAL – FROM THE NINETEENTH CENTURY TO THE PRESENT

1

THE CARNIVAL STORY – THEN AND NOW
Introduction to Part I[1]

Milla Cozart Riggio

Fact evaporates into myth. This is not the jaded cynicism which sees nothing new under the sun, it is an elation which sees everything as renewed.

Derek Walcott, "The Muse of History"

The history of Trinidad Carnival is essentially the history of the peoples of Trinidad – embedded in the stories of conquest, enslavement, resistance, and indentureship, and in commercial, cultural, and ethnic exchange among the many who were forcibly brought to the place or settled there after Columbus first named the island Trinidad in 1498: Spanish, French, English, Africans, (East) Indians, Irish, Germans, Corsicans, Chinese, Syrians, Portuguese, Canadians, Lebanese, and probably more. Also present are the vestigial influences of the estimated forty thousand indigenous people who lived in the island as of 1500, from five known groups (Nepuyo, Aruaca, Shebaio, Yaio, and Garini), with some evidence of the Warao from the Orinoco region and "increasing incursions of Island Carib, the Kalipurna or Califournians" (Elie 1997: 3). It is not clear exactly when enslaved Africans were first brought to Trinidad, but trading in human lives remained legal from the mid sixteenth century to the British Abolition Act of 1807, and was carried on illegally for several decades after that. Public records indicate that most of the enslaved were Igbos, Mandingoes, Yorubas, Asantes, Hausas, and Alladas from West Africa and Kongos from the Congo Basin (Public Record Office, Slave Registration Returns T1, 501–3, cited by Liverpool 1993: 11; see also Elder 1969: 5–6).

The Spanish controlled Trinidad from 1498 until 1797, when Governor Don José Maria Chacon surrendered to the British General Sir Ralph Abercromby, with Spain formally ceding the island to the British in the Peace of Amiens in 1802. The Spanish never fully inhabited the island. After almost three hundred years of neglect, in which Trinidad – valuable mainly for its location some six miles off the coast of Venezuela – served primarily as a jumping off place in the persistent search for El Dorado, the fabulous city of gold (not only for the Spanish but for others such as Sir Walter Raleigh (see Naipaul 1969)), the 1873 Cedula of Population invited Roman Catholic settlers who were willing to swear an oath of allegiance to the Spanish to settle in Trinidad. Catholic planters were given land according to the numbers of persons in their households, including the enslaved: white planters received approximately 30 acres each, with half as many for each laborer; African and free coloured planters were given roughly 15 acres each, again with half as many for each laborer. In this way, large numbers of French Creole planters and African workers came to Trinidad from neighboring Caribbean islands in the late eighteenth century, along with free coloured planters and some African estate owners, many of whom were rewarded for fighting with the British in the war of 1812.

Faced with the problem of administering a largely Roman Catholic French-speaking population that, if given home rule, could easily vote their conquerors out of power, the British fashioned for Trinidad (later including Tobago) a Crown Colony system of government, by which these islands – the only Crown Colony in the Caribbean – were ruled from Britain. This political, social, and religious climate was already complicated by the presence of many peoples. Into the rainbow of merging cultures others quickly migrated.

Spanish Capuchin monks from Aragon had established the Mission of Santa Rosa de Arima by the mid eighteenth century (Elie 1990: 2). The Germans, who had attempted to bargain Trinidad away from the Spanish in 1680, came in force with Abercromby in 1797, leading the attack on the Laventille hills (De Verteuil 1994: 1–2). In 1802, twenty-three Chinese laborers arrived, with approximately 190 following in 1806 in anticipation of the 1807 abolition of slave trade (Millett 1993: 17). Many of these early immigrants returned to their homelands, but they were the vanguard for later arrivals; most of all, they helped to set the character for an island that at no point in its history has been dominated by one clear hegemonic authority.

Against this background is set the story of the emerging African presence in carnival. The British Act of Emancipation was enacted in Trinidad on August 1, 1834, with an "apprenticeship" period that was to last until 1840. Unrest shortened the period, and full emancipation came throughout the British West Indies on August 1, 1838. With Africans fleeing the sugar plantations for the city, new labor had to be found. After an attempt to import free Africans from other islands as well as from Africa had failed to meet the labor need, (East) Indian indentured laborers – mainly Hindus and Muslims from Uttar Pradash, Bihar, and south India – were brought in to work the estates. Between 1845 and 1917, approximately 117,000 Indians came to Trinidad.

As a result of the interlaced patterns of migration and mission activity, and the persistence of African, Hindu, and Islamic cultural rituals, twenty-first-century Trinidad has a constellation of religions as well as a kaleidoscope of cultures: Roman Catholicism (French, some Spanish, along with others, such as Irish priests and nuns), Anglicanism, Hinduism, Islam (primarily Sunni), the Church of Scotland, the East Indian Presbyterians, African religions (initially called Shango, later Orisha), Spiritual Baptists and the emergent Pentecostals and fundamentalist Christians – all with their own religious rites and festivals, celebrated by Trinidadians who in festivity cross both religious and ethnic boundaries, playing and praying together: Siparia Mai – thousands of Hindus pay homage annually to a Black Madonna in a Catholic church on Good Friday in the borough of Siparia in the south central part of the island; Divali – the YMCA, a Christian organization, burns its name in lights on the Brian Lara promenade in Port of Spain as one of the sponsors of Divali, the Hindu fall festival of lights; Hosay – a Shi'ite funereal event in St James mainly by devout Muslims – is performed in the fishing village of Cedros primarily by Hindus and Christians. Despite such openness and cross-cultural sharing of festivals and holidays, Trinidadians do struggle to maintain a sense of ethnic as well as cultural identity, in a society in which politics themselves are to a large extent based on race and religion.

Crucial to the evolution of carnival has been the conflict among the elites of Trinidad, particularly between the Anglican bureaucracy that ruled the country and the Roman Catholic planters who owned many of the estates. The Cedula of Population of the 1780s had been designed largely to maintain the primacy of the Roman Catholic faith. Initially, the British reinforced the Catholic dominance, particularly during the period of Sir Ralph Woodford's governorship (1813–28). Determined to protect Spanish laws and customs, Woodford selected the site for the Catholic, as well as for the Anglican, cathedral. The British governor assumed a role as an officer of the Roman Catholic Church in Trinidad. However, this situation changed. In 1844, an Ecclesiastical Ordinance replaced the Roman Catholic Church by the Anglican Church, thus making the Anglican – often called the English Catholic (or EC) – Church the official religion of Trinidad until this ordinance was rescinded in 1870. During much of this period, Anglican priests were the only legal religious officers of the island; Catholic sacraments (such as marriage) were periodically unrecognized by British authorities.

Under British domination, there were effectively two – or if one counts the British as a Creole population, three – Creole traditions in Trinidad: the French Creole, of planters who had mostly been born in the Caribbean (Martinique, etc.), and the African Creole, created by enslavement. As carnival became associated with African-based street celebrations, a common Catholic sympathy as well as antagonism toward British rule evoked a partial tolerance among the French Creole elites for the canboulay revelry of the African Creole population, who after all largely spoke Afro-French patois and were Catholic-influenced if not converted. Such tolerance was on the whole not shared by the British, and often not by the industrious Bajans (Barbadians) whom the British – partly in need of an Anglican, English-speaking underclass to serve its clerical, educational, and policing needs – encouraged to enter the underpopulated island in the second half of the nineteenth century as policemen, teachers, and clerks.

CARNIVAL – THEN

Reminding us that "history" is the inevitably biased construction of those who configure our reading of the past, usually in their own image, Trinidad Carnival emerges as much from the mythology as from the history of the island. Documentary records, enmeshed in varieties of cultural mythos, weave an evolutionary narrative that merges two parallel festivals: first, that imported from Europe, primarily by French Creole planters, and including the fancy English governor's carnival balls, together with some street masking of elite and possibly plebian participation; second, that which emerged from the African Creole emancipation ritual that came to be known as *cannes brûlées* (canboulay).

Even this simple opposition must to some extent be qualified. Canboulay, the ceremony celebrating the burning of the cane (*cannes brûlées*), may help to explain the difficulty. On the one hand, this ceremony is thought to re-enact the extinguishing of illegal cane fires by "bands" of slaves with torches and drums in the night, as a form of emancipation celebration transferred at some point from August 1 to the two days before Ash Wednesday (when masking was allowed). From this perspective, canboulay is purely a festival of resistance, celebrating freedom and independence and linked to the notion of the reveler as vagabond. On the other hand, the cane was also burnt – as it still is today – as part of the harvest ritual. From this perspective, canboulay may be thought of as a harvest festival that in the pre-emancipation period may well have allied the planters with their field hands. Resistance existed, of course, and was feared even in its absence, but there was also at times a sense of collective destiny by a set of peoples who assimilated patterns of behavior and even moral codes that they simultaneously abhorred.

The narrative of nineteenth-century carnival has to a large extent been put together by connecting the historical dots established by relatively few eyewitness accounts (e.g. Bayley 1833; Borde 1876; Day 1852; Carmichael [1833] 1961), newspaper editorials that frequently complain about the vulgarity of street performances, and colonial records. Those who have attempted to find the figures buried in this sometimes scattered data are in themselves key shapers of the carnival story: Andrew Pearse, Andrew Carr, Daniel Crowley, Barbara Powrie, Errol Hill. In this volume, anthropologist J.D. Elder and historian Bridget Brereton, who helped to establish this historical reading, describe the structure of African canboulay celebrations and narrate a history in which carnival shifts from the elite celebrations of the first half of the century (from which the Africans and sometimes the free coloureds are to a large extent supposed to have been excluded) to the "jamette carnival" of the streets that emerged during the second part of the century, leading to what one commentator called the "legalized saturnalia of revenge" on the part of the police and especially the Barbadian Police Chief Captain Baker in the canboulay riots of 1881 (*New Era*, November 28, 1881), the interlocking histories of carnival and the (East) Indian Muharram celebration of Hosay, especially in the 1880s, and the middle-class takeover of carnival during the remainder of the century and into World War I. More and more complex competitions developed between the wars.

With reference to nineteenth-century carnival, this narrative has been both reinforced and complicated by the research of scholars such as John Cowley and the Afro-centric perspectives of historians such as Hollis "Chalkdust" Liverpool and Ian Smart. For instance, one must take into account the Afro-Creole fiddle-playing, drumming, probably territorial dancing societies of the early nineteenth century, with internal hierarchies ultimately reflected in the notions of what it means to be a "Carnival King" or "Queen" (see, for instance, Cowley 1996: 8, 17–18, 60; Liverpool 1993: 199–209; 1998: 30–1; 2001; Rohlehr in this volume).

The linear evolution is further troubled by the criss-crossing currents of history, the push and pull from one governor's reign to another, the infusion of Barbadians as teachers and policemen, and perhaps most of all by the awareness of what it means for an oral culture to have its history recorded by the literate: the deep divide between those describing the events and those whose experience is being described. In this regard, Pamela Franco's essay on the spectacular decorative quality of clothing styles and headdresses identified as "Martinican" – worn not in emulation of the ladies of the plantation culture, as has so often been assumed, but out of a daily sense of personal pride – qualifies our assumptions about the presumed inversive nature of "dressing up" as a carnival style among the so-called "jamette" women.

The unfolding picture is not yet clear. No one has fully evaluated, reconciled, and moved beyond the existing historical narratives – or considered those narratives within the perspective of specific ethnic populations. In particular, the story of the (East) Indian presence in Trinidad Carnival is yet to be explored from within the diverse Indo-Trinidadian community, though the essay by Burton Sankeralli, reprinted in this volume from *The Drama Review (TDR)* of 1998, does outline some of the major issues presented within the context of a particular sensibility and ritual structure. The late Carlisle Chang, in another essay reprinted from *TDR*, outlines but does not assess the significant Chinese presence in carnival since the 1920s. The roles of the Syrians, the Portuguese and the many ethnic "others" in the history of carnival have not been documented.

Much remains to be done. Among the many issues we are as yet unable to factor into the history of carnival is a clear understanding of the role of education in the nineteenth century, particularly among the African Creole population. What are the implications, for instance, of John Jacob Thomas – the son of freed slaves who was fluent in French patois (which he calls Creole), English, French, Latin, and Greek – at age 29 in 1869 writing *The Theory and Practice of Creole Grammar*, a language that he characterizes as "framed by Africans from a European tongue," the grammar of which he formulates from "*bellairs, calendas, joubas*, idioms, [and] odd sayings" (see Thomas [1869] 1969, Buscher: Introduction, iii, "Preface," v)? Or of the existence of *The Trinidad Sentinal*, an African-owned newspaper in the late nineteenth century (see Cowley 1996: 54)?

CARNIVAL – NOW

Since it was initially marketed as a tourist attraction by the newly established Carnival Improvement Committee, headed by the Mayor of Port of Spain and chaired by Captain A.A. Cipriani in the late 1930s (see Rohlehr 1990: 295, 328), carnival has been increasingly claimed as the signature event of the emerging nation. Sustaining this claim required cleaning up the festival, eradicating its vulgarity, violence, and danger in the name of "decency" and respectability. In the words of Eric Williams in 1962: "Play mask, stay sober, and do not misbehave" (*Trinidad Guardian*, February 3, 1962). In this vein, Panorama, first established to celebrate Independence in 1962, began the process of marketing steel drums as the national instrument of the newly independent Trinidad and Tobago, but at the cost (it is claimed) of taming the fiery "warriorhood" of the street-fighting gangs that formed many of the first steelbands. Errol Hill, who dramatized the link between nationhood and carnival in scripted Dimanche Gras plays in 1963 and 1964,[2] likewise struggled to bring a sense of decency and decorum into the carnival arena.

Not that this impulse was new. It was, in fact, a characteristic remnant of Victorianism, epitomized by L.A.A. De Verteuil, who in 1884 blasted female members of "*bands* notoriously formed for immoral purposes" for "singing . . . as if in defiance of . . . all decency" (De Verteuil [1858] 1884; quoted in Cowley 1996: 75). Indeed, the dialectical opposition between respectability and vagabondage lies at the heart of an event that is as competitive as it is celebratory. The vitalizing tension of Trinidad

Carnival results partly from the vulgarity that opposes even as it aspires to join so-called "civilized society." The struggle has a complex dialectical duality. Partly, it expresses the human need to resist authority, to "get on bad," to idealize the outlaw who has the nerve to break the rules. Such need is compounded in situations of racial or class oppression, in which those who make the laws impose them on groups or cultures other than themselves. In such situations, the outlaw becomes more than mythic lawbreaker. Almost inevitably masculine, he is also an avenger of wrongs. This energy, which operates throughout carnival, along with the more general impulse to "free" oneself from disciplined and legal constraints, associates the local history with the broader human impulse. It is no surprise that even in the United States during the masquerading season of 2002, among the most popular adult Halloween masks was that of Osama bin Laden.

On the other hand, the motivating impulse is also to obtain respectability: very few vagabonds treasure their poverty or their pariah status; mostly, they want to be respectable, to be enfranchised, to have a stake in the system they take so much pleasure in metaphorically (and sometimes literally) mooning. Once they have achieved such status (as for instance when steel drums ceased to be the forbidden pleasure of youth or the enclaves of the bad johns and became the highly marketed national instrument), then some other form of vulgarity inevitably arises to replace that which has been subsumed. The history of the festival – from the mid nineteenth century, when street vendors with the glint of profit in their eyes first began to defend carnival, to the present – is the continuous story of commercialization, assimilation, and nostalgia for a purer, if sometimes rougher past.

Part of this story that remains is the resistance to, as well as embracing of, the festival. There are those who still see it today as many saw it in the nineteenth century as degenerate, racist, and wasteful. These include many fundamental Christians, those who signed a petition in 1995 to try to force Peter Minshall to change the name of his mas band *Hallelujah* on the grounds of sacrilege; many devout Muslims and Hindus resist what they see as the debauchery of the event and the waste of money and national resources. Often those who feel this way take their children camping on the beach or in town centers for the two days of carnival to get them away from the festival, even on the television sets. This side of carnival is almost as complex as the event itself, since it involves resisters from many different walks of life, religions, and social positions. Even for the detractors, however, the period of carnival is a time away from the regular daily routine. For some, the event has a kind of historical and cultural significance that the – to them – "profane" and debauched street festival lacks: teach it in the schools; boycott it on the streets is one answer. For others, the event itself represents the failure of the island to achieve its potential either morally or socially. This critique, too, is part of the ongoing story of carnival.

What may be new – and dangerous in a different way – is that contemporary vulgarity in a carnival marketed as the culture-bearer of the nation does not in the main originate among the huddled masses. It is a function instead of the global commercial success of a festival now heard round the world. The new "vagabonds" – if you wish – are those who defy respectability not with mud, rags, or whips but with glitter, glamour, partial nudity, bikini costumes (as, for instance, the five to eight thousand masqueraders that each year swell the ranks of middle-class mas bands such as Poison) or, alternately, with loud, loud "party" music that for the most part eschews social commentary in favor of celebrating sexuality and youth, intruding "foreign" rhythms into the local soca. How carnival will vitally assimilate and move beyond this Philistinism – which may, of course, be one source of future energy (see, for instance, Guilbault in this volume) – is the story unfolding at the beginning of this new century. Some parts of it will be told in the later chapters of this book.

THE CARNIVAL SEASON

Despite its economy driven by oil and natural gas and its position at the economic center of the West Indies, Trinidad still marks its seasons with festivity, moving from festival to festival. And among its many celebrations – Eid, Divali, Ramleela, the Muharram Hosay, Phagwa, Easter, Christmas with its two months of Spanish parang music – carnival is the biggest and most engulfing. Violence – once a serious threat – is largely sublimated in a myriad complex of competitions, divided among the sometimes overlapping three main divisions, each with its own organizing union: Masquerade (under the auspices of the National Carnival Bands Association, which in 2002 came under serious attack), Calypso (Trinbago Unified Calypsonian Organization), and Pan (PanTrinbago). For the past few years, these interest groups replaced the National Carnival Commission as the primary organizers of carnival events, thus to a large extent increasing the sense of chaos that has always attended the structuring of a festival that will not allow itself to be contained.

It is impossible to pin Trinidad Carnival down. Always on the edge, always threatened by commercialization, the festival spins on, twisting and shifting in ways that are neither predictable nor essentially comforting. Nothing characterizes carnival more than its perpetual sense of change. Mostly, whatever one says today will not be true tomorrow. The essence of the event is ephemerality and endless renewal – death and rebirth of many kinds. Though in the past some old-time traditional characters took pride in storing and reusing their costumes, currently competitions require annual reconstruction: the costume must have been built, the calypso or soca composed the year it is performed.

Nevertheless, there is an *almost* predictable carnival season that stretches from Christmas to Ash Wednesday, a time determined though not limited by the Christian calendar. Pre-Lenten carnival is traditionally a Catholic, not Protestant festival, French or Spanish, not English. The British have few, if any, specific carnival traditions. However, English gentry of earlier centuries customarily filled the Christmas to Lenten period with gay indoor revels, including masqued balls, plays, dances, and so forth. This not only made it easy for English governors such as Sir Ralph Woodford annually to host a carnival masquerade ball but may well have helped to establish the extended carnival season that exists even now in Trinidad.[3]

In the broadest sense, this is the festival that never sleeps: it officially ends sharply at the stroke of twelve midnight that signals the beginning of Ash Wednesday and, for the planners and masmen and women, starts again the following morning. However, though costume designs are drawn, mas bands launched, calypsos and socas written and recorded throughout the year, the "carnival season" begins on or around Three Kings Day, just as the Christmas season fades out.

During the "hotting up" weeks of January, footfalls across the island quicken with expectation. Mas bands that have not already launched do so; pan yards come alive; calypso tents are opened; radio stations play soca more steadily; carnival fetes are held. The season is on. The latent energy explodes during the Panorama prelims that ordinarily take place some two weeks before carnival itself. For this event the red metallic north stands, which are constructed annually, stand ready to rock with the energy of their prelim magic[4]. From that day through the next two weeks, competitions are held at a dizzying rate – stickfighting, soca, calypso, pan in all its forms, traditional character festivals, King and Queen competitions, massive children's carnivals – and the frenzy of preparation continues in mas camps hastening to prepare for the street theater of carnival Monday and Tuesday.

Carnival itself – the event for which the nation stops for two full days despite the fact that it is not even yet an official holiday – is inaugurated by a proclamation from the Mayor of Port of Spain in the pre-dawn witching darkness of Monday morning: jouvay with its elemental mud masking ushers in the dawn and then gives way to the street festivals of Monday and Tuesday. The season itself has a maddening kind of elasticity, somewhere between four and eight weeks long. This paradoxical festival begins its high season on a somewhat fixed calendrical date (roughly January 6) and ends as a movable feast, keyed to the paschal full moon, expanding and contracting with the rhythms of this natural cycle.

Finally, it is impossible to track the contours of such an event that simultaneously enacts the mythos of unity – "All ah we is one" – and affirms the reality of separation and otherness. Trinidad Carnival reflects the energies of a nation that is entrepreneurial, individual and contrary and, at the same time, assimilative, intercultural, and buoyant. The massive carnival of today continues in some ways to radiate the energy of its myriad mythical and real origins as an intrusive annual festival invasion taking over the "streets make to walk on carnival day."

NOTES

1   Portions of this introduction, particularly the opening pages, were adapted from Riggio, "Resistance and Identity," first published in Riggio (1998a), now out of print.

2   The history of the Dimanche Gras show is in itself an important chapter in the unfolding of carnival. It was begun in 1946 as a showcase for the then new Carnival Queen contest, which was held until it was canceled in 1971, following the Black Power movement of 1970, before being renewed briefly in the later 1970s and again in the late 1990s. The issues of class and race in this event, and the relationship between this beauty queen contest and the Queen of the Bands costume competition (established 1958), help to chart the rise of carnival as the signifying cultural event of the new republic (see Riggio 1999, n.p.). Dimanche Gras has been the host venue for a variety of competitions, as well as varied carnival revues. The first effort to create a sustained theatrical event as a cultural tribute to carnival came with *Callaloo 1952*, directed by Jeffrey Holder. Hill's Independence Carnival productions followed in this vein but with more formal drama (see Hill 1972: 105–13). Currently, the Dimanche Gras show, during which the Calypso Monarch and the King and Queen of the carnival bands are customarily crowned, sells out each year; it attracts a posh, mature audience, but it lacks the dynamic youthful intensity of such events as, for example, the Soca Monarch competition.

3   Though French Mardi Gras is a two- or three-day festival (as it appears also to have been in some French colonial areas as, for instance, in Martinique), in other French-influenced areas,

such as Louisiana, the carnival season stretched from Twelfth Night (January 6) to Ash Wednesday, as it does in Trinidad. As early as 1833, according to one commentator, "bacchanal diversions" were extended "for the space of a month or two" (*Port of Spain Gazette*, January 22; quoted in Cowley 1996: 25). The festival would recurrently be limited to two days throughout the nineteenth century. But the natural season – apparently accepted by the British as well as the French – runs from Christmas to Ash Wednesday.

4   From 2002 the preliminary competition has, through at least 2004, been held in pan yard, rather than the Queen's Park Savannah.

2

CANNES BRÛLÉES

J.D. Elder

INTRODUCTION

Cannes brûlées (canboulay) as a Black artistic institution in Trinidad and Tobago should be defined as a multimedia symbolic ceremony in which its psychological messages take various forms and are manifested in a variety of artistic behaviors – music-making, poetics, vernacular languages, dramatics, dance, and other acrobatic gestures. Each of these media is anchored in the matrix of the African cultural traditions brought into the Caribbean by migrants mostly from West Africa and can be traced back to specific tribal origins whose cultural traces are still evident in contemporary Black Caribbean society, as in zoomorphic masks like the Cow/Bull dancers, Dragons, Serpents, butterflies, giant spiders, Burrokeet.

Music, theatre, handicraft, poetry, mythology, superstitions, religion, dance: each and every one of these features carries a dramatic "message" about the performers themselves, their worldview, belief system, philosophy of life. But above all, what the Africans are projecting is their aspiration for true liberty, freedom to pursue their own goals as human beings and not to be hampered in this effort by the White planter class or the European colonial rulership which regarded them as inferior or even savage and without civilization. This is the burden of the message of *cannes brûlées*. Whether we examine the songs or the dance, the theatre or the costumes worn by the actors, this eloquent declaration is symbolized – in satire, burlesque, in pornographic expletives and double entendre, in half-hidden verbal dualisms – and only the Africans are enabled to understand the "message" because the very medium *is* the message.

The Europeans who definitely did not know the medium missed the message over and over. They traditionally felt that something was wrong. The communication lines seemed fouled but, as in Greek tragedy, though they felt something awful was about to overcome them, they could do nothing to escape. Riots and rebellions followed and, finally, the abolition of colonial rule in 1962, more than a hundred years after the abolition of slavery in 1838 – one century of Black strategy and struggle.

Canboulay is basically a ceremony symbolizing cane burning that Africans of Trinidad devised to celebrate their "freedom from slavery" in 1838. The exact date of its original enactment and the prime movers are completely forgotten. We can, however, historically pinpoint this Black artistic pageant only from 1881, when the British administration in Trinidad decided to stamp it out, to suppress its annual celebration in the streets of Port of Spain using the police force to restrict its performance. Canboulay can be examined as: first, a Black resistance ceremony; second, a recreational pageantry of Africans; third, an anti-Catholic celebration of freedom from slavery and the origin of the present carnival; and fourth, a popular street theatre exhibiting African-style dance, theatre, and music. It can also be regarded as a boast – nonmoralistic exhibitionism – a duel between the European moral codes and the African canons of freedom, which in essence it was.

ELEMENTAL FEATURES OF *CANNES BRÛLÉES*

The elemental features of *cannes brûlées* are highly expressive of the symbolical functions of this ceremonial protest and resistance of European domination. These features include:

- enacting the African pageant inside the White-dominated carnival (trespassing)
- processing through the streets at dead of night
- satirizing the ruling class in popular song
- beating African drums – a symbol of savagery
- performing African-type dancing condemned by the White moralists as profane
- carrying lighted torches in a wooden city
- blowing cow horns and conch shells at dead of night
- burlesquing the Europeans' lifestyle, as in Dame Lorraine
- arming with bois for dueling (stickfighting) on the streets.

The White upper class, according to L.O. Inniss, condemned the Africans (as pagans) for entering carnival, a Christian religious ceremony. On this basis, *cannes brûlées* was deemed a savage pagan ceremony – in a Christian Catholic society. This to them was heresy for which Africans were persecuted cruelly for years.

In an effort to extinguish this African saturnalia (as the Whites deemed canboulay), it was decided to outlaw carnival. In 1884, a royal commission, under Sir Robert Hamilton, outlawed *cannes brûlées* in Trinidad. But kalinda (bois) continued, and the Africans promptly took over carnival. Caliso singing and kalinda dueling continued. Finally, African-type carnival, highly organized in "tents" – crude theatres erected in several points of the city of Port of Spain – sprang up, and carnival became African in terms of art, craft, music, and theatre. The White upper-class capitalists such as Sa Gomes invested heavily in carnival, but the prime movers in carnival had become all Africans – singers, dancers, shantwells (chantuelles), and organizers. By 1940 Trinidad calypsonians (such as Raphael DeLeon (Roaring Lion), Neville Marcano (Growling Tiger), Phillip Garcia (Lord Executor), and Raymond Quevado (Atilla the Hun)) were in the US recording their music and making history, and *cannes brûlées* had become just one type of mask in the Trinidad black carnival.

STRUCTURE OF CANBOULAY

The structure of canboulay reflects its psycho-sociological function, i.e., resistance and protest against White racism and social alienation in Trinidad. The major features include:

- iconoclastic objects, e.g. the lighted torch, the bois, the African drums (ka), the bull-mask
- the mass processional – the show of strength
- the simulation of Africans royally – kings, queens, princes
- the musical march – the blowing of cow horns and conch shells
- the satirical songs – the vitriolic Black poetics shouted in French Creole
- the performing of erotic pornographic dances and postures
- the physical defiance within the "encounter of resistance."

CANBOULAY: BASIS OF CONTEMPORARY CARNIVAL

Canboulay included:

- shantwells – song leaders, composers, etc.
- organizers of "tents" – crude theatres
- mask-makers and craftsmen/women
- music makers and organizers of song groups
- entrepreneurs in the entertainment industry.

Out of this body of organizers and recruitment of talent grew the contemporary carnival movement with "factories" that annually organized "bands" – people who "play mask [mas]" each year. These are "mask [mas] camps," which operate all through the year, holding shows at which calypso singers appear in regular concerts to exhibit new songs – originally composed and entered at carnival time in competitions for valuable prizes. Thus, out of the despised canboulay has risen the national carnival of Trinidad and Tobago. The traditional features still exist:

- massive music bands
- street processing, i.e. jumping-up
- stage competitions in singing
- stickfighting (kalinda/bois)
- costume competitions and Queen shows
- masquerades (Devils, Dragons).

Canboulay has become socially approved by the European element and, though once suppressed and despised, is now recognized as art by all classes. Trinidad Carnival is celebrated each year in foreign countries wherever there are Trinidadian Africans – Brooklyn, Toronto, London, Germany.

WOMEN'S ROLE IN CANBOULAY

In music and music-making, females formed a major part of the chorus led by the shantwells, who were always male. Several instances exist where the drum team included females. For example, Congo women played the *marli doundoun* (Tobagonian drums made of olive oil containers) for their *quelbe* dance in Tobago.

Lennox Pierre: Canboulay Riots

an interview by Tony Hall

The structure of the canboulay bands has long been a matter of conjecture and uncertainty. The following description and illustration were provided by musician and cultural researcher Lennox Pierre (1990) in an interview by Tony Hall, partly from an eyewitness account and from Edric Connor's descriptions. The interview was produced by Christopher Laird for "Late Night Lime" on Trinidad and Tobago Television.

Hall: Can you give us a quick view of the actual Canboulay Riots?

Pierre: J.D. Elder and I were fortunate to meet an old lady [Frances Edwards] in 1954 at 87 years of age, and she gave us this eyewitness account of the Canboulay Riots. What had, in fact, happened was that Captain Baker, who was the Superintendent of Police at the time, had attacked the canboulay revelers in 1880 and taken away their torches. And in 1881 the canboulay revelers prepared for Baker. According to the eyewitness account Edwards gave, the canboulay revelers from districts outside Port of Spain came into Port of Spain. And you had a Neg Jardin stickband that took the length from Medical Corner at the corner of Park Street and Tragarete Road, [i.e.,] Park Streets and St Vincent Streets, right down St Vincent Street into Park Street. When twelve midnight struck that year, 1881, the canboulay revelers moved out from the Medical Corner, and the band moved in darkness and without drums. And the old lady told us how there was an old patois woman at the front of the band. And she called out "Mssrs, Captain Baker et tout l'homme" (and all his men), "au cour de la rue" (at the corner of the street), just about where All Stars [steel orchestra] have their headquarters now. And at that signal the fellows light their torches and start up the drums and went for Baker. The story that she gave me and that Brierly said in *Then and Now* [1912] was that the canboulay revelers swept the ground with the police.

Hall: But this wasn't all men, was it? Wasn't there a role for women as well?

Pierre: A canboulay band, canboulay revelers moved with their women and children, too, but as I understand from [Edric] Connor's account, the Neg Jardin band was surrounded by stickfighters [see figure 2.1]. Each stickman had a flambeau in his left hand, and that left hand was interlaced with the right hand of the man next to him. The women and children were at the back with [some spare sticks and] some other kinds of weapons, stones and all.

During breaks in kalinda tournaments the females, according to Frances Edwards (1954), sang early original caiso (cariso, kaliso) in the ring. These songs were based on kalinda in structure, rhythm, language (French Creole). The original calypsos were sung in the minor mode, i.e. pentatonic.

As regards organization, females were members of the *cannes brûlées*. Several of them were stickfighting in their own right or wives of batonniers. Notorious stickfighting kalinda women existed. In Trinidadians' popular canboulay history, noted in the early nineteenth century, Sarah Jamaica, Boobull Tiger, Techselia, and B-Bar the Devil are called matador women.

On parade the canboulay band comprised several categories or ranks of roles – musicians (drummers), warriors, shantwells, and ammunition-bearers. These were mostly females bearing spare weapons (sticks), food (rum, pelau, etc.), and, according to L.M. Fraser (1881), Chief of Police, stones and bottles for war with

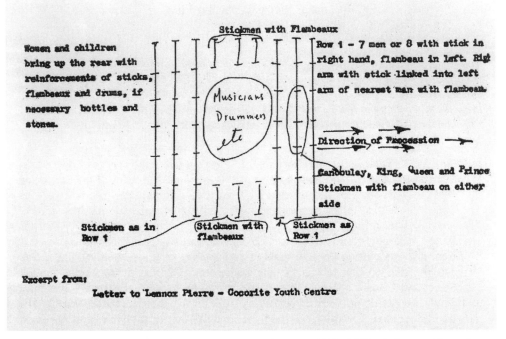

Fig. 2.1 Diagram of Stickmen with flambeaux. Excerpt from unpublished letter to Lennox Pierre from Edric Connor (1953); courtesy of J.D. Elder.

the police. Women's roles included performing first-aid services for wounded fighters and mourning for those killed in action or arrested by police. Females' roles included, as today, the bearing of the banner (flag) of the band. Females were the "out-riders" of the canboulay band. They were the spies who gave the signals of safety from police interferences and harassment of wanted badjohns (e.g. Joe Talmana) and jailbreaks.

On Carriacou island in the Grenadines there is in the Big Drum Dance an "Old People" (ancestors) kalinda played by two women armed with large white towels. They enact a "battle" of Right against Wrong, the steps corresponding to the bois kalinda of Trinidad. The music and drumming are by females (Elder 1966).

This essay is reprinted from Milla Cozart Riggio (ed.), *The Drama Review*, 42 (3): 38–43 (1998), Cambridge, MA: MIT Press.

3

THE TRINIDAD CARNIVAL IN THE LATE NINETEENTH CENTURY[1]

Bridget Brereton

The late nineteenth century was crucial for the development of the Trinidad Carnival. The period opened with carnival taken over almost entirely by the jamettes, the underclass of Port of Spain. The attitude of the upper and middle classes was one of disgust, fear, and hostility, with some exceptions. Between 1879 and 1884 a determined effort was made by the authorities to purge all the features which they considered objectionable, by force if necessary. The climax was reached with the riots at the carnivals of 1881 and 1884. The government succeeded in eliminating the organized band warfare and in suppressing some, though not all, of the obviously obscene masks. Canboulay became illegal. The decade or so after 1884 was a time when many people confidently predicted that carnival would die a natural death, and good riddance too. Finally in the 1890s there appeared signs, small though they were, that carnival was on its way to becoming a festival acceptable to most sectors of the society, including the upper and middle classes.

A study of carnival in this period is of interest for two reasons. First, it was an important means of expression for the mainly Afro-Creole lower classes who participated in it; it provides a window to their values and aspirations. Second, in this period carnival was an arena in which class antagonisms and cultural contestations were worked out. Hardly anything else illustrates so clearly the profound gulf between the "respectable" classes and the jamettes, whose carnival was a reversal of all the values and judgments of society. Reading the interminable editorials, articles, and letters denouncing the festival, one might conclude that there was an almost total lack of understanding and communication between the two groups, though the events of 1881–4 showed otherwise.

Before emancipation carnival had been an elegant social affair of the white Creole upper class. It had involved masked balls, house-to-house visiting, street promenading, small musical bands, and practical jokes. The leaders of society would appear masked in the streets; the masques were mainly European. Emancipation led to a complete change. The ex-slaves and the lower classes in general participated increasingly, and, correspondingly, the upper classes withdrew, and "the comments of their journalistic representatives became increasingly hostile right through till the 1890s" (Pearse 1956a: 184; Hill 1972: 16–21; Cowley 1996: chapter 2; Liverpool 2001: chapters 5 and 7). Masques continued to be mainly European – in 1848 they included Punch, Pirates, Highlanders, Turks, Death, Cavalry and Infantry – but the players were now mostly lower-class persons. Contemporary events were often represented, and the Red Indian band became popular around this time, usually played by "peons" of Spanish-Amerindian descent with a high degree of realism.

In the 1840s there is no mention of organized band fights or of obscenity. But in the 1850s carnival was regarded as increasingly disreputable. In 1858 Governor Keate attempted to forbid public masking; he met with organized resistance which was put down only by troops. No further attempt was made at the time. By the 1850s, too, canboulay had become an established part of the festival, starting at midnight on the Sunday. The withdrawal of the respectable classes was almost complete by the late 1860s. Generally speaking, as L.O. Inniss remembered, "no decent persons" could go about on carnival days in the 1860s and 1870s (Inniss 1932: 9).

Around the 1860s carnival came to have a distinct character: the "jamette" carnival. The festival was almost entirely taken over by the jamettes, who had created in the backyards of Port of Spain their own subculture. Here the urban lower class lived in long barrack ranges situated behind the city blocks, centering on a yard which formed a common living space. At about this time, yard "bands" were formed: groups of men and women, boys and girls, who went around together for singing, fighting, and dancing. Such bands existed all the year round, but were especially active in the weeks before carnival, when they rehearsed their songs, dances, and stickfighting. The yard "chantwelle," or singer, insulted rival yards, and yard stickmen sought out rivals for single combats. The big carnival bands were a combination of several yard bands. The jamettes, who were the band members, were the singers, drummers, dancers, stickmen, prostitutes, pimps, and "bad johns" in general. They boasted their skill and bravery, verbal wit, talent in song, dance, and drumming, their indifference to the law, their sexual prowess, their familiarity with jail, and sometimes their contempt for the church. In short they reversed the canons of respectability, the norms of the superstructure. As one newspaper put it, "the immoral bands of men and women . . . base their right of existence on their power to outrage all that society holds most dear, and all that religion imposes" (Pearse 1956a: 191–3; *New Era*, March 19, 1877).[2]

One need hardly say that the lifestyle of the jamettes outraged respectable Trinidad (Pearse 1956b: 250–62; Brereton 1979: 166–9; Liverpool 2001: 253–92; Franco 2000: 60–76). As the *San Fernando Gazette* reported in 1875:

> There is no gainsaying that year after year adds, in an alarming degree, to the number of these depraved wretches, who . . . band themselves together to the detriment of law and order, and society . . . Hardly anything else is so dangerous to our society . . . Hordes of men and women, youthful in years but matured in every vice that perverts and degrades humanity, dwell together in all the rude licentiousness of barbarian life: men without aim, without occupation and without any recognized mode of existence – women, wanton, perverse, and depraved beyond expression.
>
> (September 18, 1875)

It was these jamette bands which took over carnival in the 1860s and 1870s.

During the 1870s, "pretty" costumes and topical masques became rarer, as the carnival focused more and more on band fighting and on masques involving a sexual theme. The *Port of Spain Gazette* summed up the respectable view when it stated:

> The performances were poorer and more foolish than ever. It is evident that masquerading is dying a natural death . . . In former years there was some amusement to be derived from the exhibitions of the carnival, but each return of the season seems only to render them more thoroughly contemptible.
>
> (February 25, 1871)

In the 1875 carnival there were said to be very few maskers with gorgeous or grotesque costumes, and two years later hardly any fancy masques; Pierrots were almost extinct and the only spectacle was a few masked men in women's clothes. On the other hand, the carnivals of 1878 and 1879 were reported to have featured some attractive representations, including a float showing the capture of Constantinople by Turkish soldiers, with the fort represented by a large box on wheels defended by wooden cannons. In 1879, though there were said to be fewer character groups than usual, among those listed were a Hosay (Muharram) procession, a party of Venezuelan maypole dancers, schoolgirls, a Venezuelan army, a Chinese couple, a squad of Redcoats, Pierrots, and South American Indians (*Fair Play*, February 18, 1875 and March 5, 1878; *Chronicle*, February 13, 1877 and February 26, 1879). Indeed, the frequently mentioned decline in attractive or witty masques may have been chiefly imaginary: commentators may have been so concerned about the fighting and the obscenity that they overlooked, or minimized, the existence of the older kinds of bands.

Probably the most objectionable feature of the jamette carnival was the explicitly sexual dimension, in other words, its "obscenity." Bands of jamettes roamed the streets making indecent gestures and singing "lewd" songs. There were also traditional masques with explicit sexual themes. The most notorious was the Pissenlit – "wet the bed," usually translated as "stinker." It was played by masked men dressed as women in long transparent nightgowns; some carried "menstrual cloths" stained with "blood." Their dance was a rapid shifting of the pelvis from side to side and back and forward, and they sang obscene songs. There was a lot of sexual horseplay, including a poui stick held between the legs. The jamette bands featured both men and women: the women, many of whom might be prostitutes or were ex-prostitutes, in the traditional Martinique dress, often masked. At some times and in some places they exposed their breasts. The men wore trousers, silk shirts, jewelry and chains, panama hats, and fancy waistcoats. They danced and strutted through the streets speaking to bystanders in sexy tones and propositioning women. Newspaper comment was hostile: "the respectable inhabitants are scandalized and outraged by exhibitions which are not only neither amusing nor entertaining, but are decidedly unchaste in character and demoralizing in tendency." And "it were better to deny recreation to outlawed ruffians, than to have pollution and obscenity exhibited naked before the eyes of our wives and daughters" (Crowley 1956: passim; *Port of Spain Gazette*, February 21, 1874 and February 17, 1877).

Transvestism and accompanying horseplay were very common, whether in the Pissenlit or individually: "as for the number of girls masked and in men's clothing, we cannot say how many hundred are flaunting their want of shame. As many men, also generally of the lowest order, are in like manner strutting about in female dress, dashing out their gowns as they go." A few years later: "the saturnalia of this year differed from preceding ones in the enormous proportion of masked men who unsexed themselves to enjoy the strange and silly novelty of wrapping their big frames in a shapeless bundle of female apparel" (*Chronicle*, February 17, 1874 and February 26, 1879).

It seems clear from the reams of press comment that nothing else about the carnival scandalized respectable people as much as the obscenity, real or imagined. Victorian Trinidad was certainly a more prudish and less tolerant society than that of the early nineteenth century, despite the continuation of the traditional "outside" liaisons by upper-class Creole men ("jacketmen"). And of course it was a time when decent women knew, or were supposed to know, nothing about sex, and even married women would have been shocked by any public manifestation. The press made much of the corruption of lower-class youth which was alleged to take place before, during, and after the carnival. Perhaps it did, though in the teeming and squalid backyards where most of the jamettes lived it would have been difficult to remain uncorrupted, carnival or no carnival. The whole business shows very clearly that the ideas of the jamette class about sex and women were poles apart from the notions of respectable people, and that the Afro-Creole urban underclass held very different gender ideologies from those of mainstream society.[3]

Only a degree less objectionable than the obscenity was the organized conflict between bands. The weapons were stones, bits of macadam, bottles, and staves. Serious injury was rare, but there were always broken heads or slashed faces. In the early 1870s the number of bands greatly increased. Bands from Belmont, the Dry River, and the tenements in the center of the city used the days of carnival to pay off old grudges or to increase their prestige at the expense of other bands. In 1871 the names of some of the rival bands were: True Blues, Danois, Maribones, Black Ball, Golden City, Alice, D'jamettres. The Maribones (wasps) were still going strong in 1877, when their carnival outfit consisted of a black hat, obtained from gentlemen friends, red shirts, white trousers with a blue waistband – their colors were red, white, and blue – with a silk foulah band round each knee, in the Neg Jardin style. The women were in trousers reaching the knee, a short red jacket over a blouse, an apron in front, and a sailor hat of white with a blue ribbon. The band leader, the Roi, was on horseback. Each woman carried a wooden hatchet, painted to resemble iron. The Maribones had their own musical ensemble, consisting of a clarinet, two drums, a fiddle, a *beke-nègre* (a fair-skinned black man) with a small drum, a line of tomtoms (keg drums with a goatskin top), and a triangle. The players kept to the center of the band, for protection (*Chronicle*, February 21, 1871 and February 9, 1877; see figure 2.1).

According to an obviously well-informed editorial, in 1877 there were perhaps twelve large bands in the city, formed on a neighborhood basis. Among those named were the Bois d'Inde (allspice tree) from Upper Prince Street; Bakers from east of the market; Danois (Danes) from the Dry River; Peau de Canelle (cinnamon bark) from west of the Royal Jail; Corail (coral) from Newtown; S'Amandes (almonds) from the wharves; Maribones from Belmont Road; and Cerf-Volants (kites) from Duncan Street. The editor concluded:

The band itself seems to be merely the loose, idler, younger members of the floating portion of the populace (it would not be always correct to call them the working class) in a district or neighborhood. In many cases the lads, as men, grow out of this brawling, idle vagabondage but there cannot be a doubt it demoralizes them.

In 1882 Port of Spain was said to be divided into two zones, one belonging to the "English Band," the other to the French Band, alias the Bakers. In one incident three Bakers drove in a cab over the boundary into hostile territory and were stoned by members of the "English Band" (*Chronicle*, February 9, 1877 and *Palladium*, July 1, 1882).

These bands existed the whole year round, but were most active during the carnival, the great opportunity to challenge rivals and show off prowess in song, dance, and stickfighting. Their aggressiveness during the carnival was heightened by liquor, and the result was street fights, often of considerable proportions. Bands would roam about seeking a rival to fight. It seems that firearms or knives were virtually never used; the intention was not to wound seriously, but to establish prestige by skilful use of the stick, though bottles and stones were also used as weapons. Such affrays were, of course, illegal, and numerous arrests were made each carnival. Yet the street fights continued until the early 1880s (*Palladium*, February 3, 1877; Brereton 1979: 166–9; Cowley 1996: 67–84; Liverpool 2001: 253–92).

One notable feature of the jamette carnival was the canboulay. This was a procession of men, usually masked, carrying lighted torches and staves, which started at midnight on Sunday and continued until the Monday morning. It was accompanied by a great deal of drumming, hooting, singing, and shouting, which kept everyone awake. "Canboulay" is said to be a contraction of *cannes brûlées*, or burnt canes. Its origin was probably this: after emancipation (August 1, 1838) the ex-slaves commemorated the First of August each year by a torchlight procession, which looked back to the days of slavery when the slaves had to turn out to fight cane fires on the estates. Carnival was originally held on the Sunday too; this was prohibited in 1841 and so it began at midnight on Sunday. For some reason the torchlight procession formerly held on the First of August, perhaps only for a few years after 1838, was revived as the opening event of the carnival (*Chronicle*, March 26, 1881; Espinet and Pitts 1944: 58; Cowley 1996: 19–21; Liverpool 2001: 220–2). Canboulay was felt to be objectionable on two main grounds, the noise which was kept up all night, and the danger of fire from the torches. A further fear was that the presence of so many men armed with sticks, and in an aggressive mood, was a potential source of riot and disorder. Canboulay was also seen – correctly – as a powerful symbol of Afro-Creole resistance to European cultural norms.

Through most of the 1870s the government's attitude towards the carnival was vacillating. But in 1877 Captain Baker became Inspector-Commandant (Chief of Police). He was altogether a more militant character than his predecessor, and he made it one of his chief objects to control, and if possible to destroy, the organized bands. The carnivals of 1878 and 1879 were strictly controlled, and stickfighting was made almost impossible, by guarding four or five of the chief meeting places of the bands. Instead of waiting until after carnival to make arrests (and since the offenders were masked, they often could not be recognized and found), the police arrested troublemakers on the spot (*Port-of-Spain Gazette*, March 9, 1878 and March 1, 1879).

Two ordinances passed in the 1870s strengthened the hands of the police. In 1875 members of bands convicted of an offense came under the Habitual Criminals Ordinance, which allowed police surveillance of such persons. Usually, a person had to be convicted of three offenses to come under this law, so that band members were being subjected to discriminatory treatment. In 1879 an ordinance amended the law as to the punishment of riot and affray. An ordinance of 1868 allowed the police to stop torch-bearing if it became a public nuisance. In the carnival of 1880 Baker, using this last ordinance, decided to suppress the canboulay. He called on the participants to surrender their torches, sticks, and drums; probably taken by surprise, for Baker's intention had not been announced, they did so without any resistance (*New Era*, February 16, 1880). The carnival passed off quietly, and Baker must have thought that his problems with the festival had been satisfactorily solved.

But the carnival of 1881 was in fact the climax of hostilities between the government and the maskers. Baker's successful suppression of canboulay in 1880 was widely regarded as a step to the total suppression of carnival, and the bands organized to resist police interference in 1881: this time they were prepared. Again without prior notice, Baker tried to seize the torches on Sunday night. He had previously armed the force with special balata clubs. When he struck against the marchers, he met with united opposition from several hundred men armed with sticks, stones, and bottles. A fight ensued in which thirty-eight out of the 150 policemen present were injured; it ended inconclusively. Many street lights were smashed by the mob. Their attitude seemed highly threatening by the Monday morning, and a meeting of the Executive Council decided on drastic preparations to resist a serious riot.

On the Monday afternoon members of the Port of Spain Borough Council, fearing civil disorder, went to the Governor, Sir Samford Freeling, and pleaded with him to make some conciliatory gesture to the people; they argued that the maskers were excited but not riotous and would easily be satisfied by such a move. Freeling, late in the afternoon, went to the Eastern Market and addressed the maskers. He said that the government had no desire to stop carnival; the interference with the torches had only been to prevent fires. They should be peaceful for the rest of Monday and on Tuesday; the police would not be allowed to "molest" them, and would be confined to barracks until the Wednesday morning. After his address, there were one or two incidents; an effigy of Baker was burnt outside the police barracks. But on the whole the Tuesday passed peacefully (*New Era*, March 7, 1881; Brierly 1912: chapter 21; Pearse 1956a: 188; Cowley 1996: 84–90; Liverpool 2001: 306–11).

The reaction of the press to the events of the 1881 carnival is interesting. Without exception, the editors condemned Baker's actions and commended Freeling's. Baker had acted high-handedly and had provoked the maskers into resistance (*New Era*, March 7 and 28, 1881; *Palladium*, March 25, and April 23, 1881; *Port-of-Spain Gazette*, March 26, 1881; *Chronicle*, March 26, 1881; Cowley 1996: 89–90). This unanimous reaction shows one thing clearly. Though the editors, and the people they spoke for, were disgusted by many features of the jamette carnival, and though they looked forward to its natural death, at least in its then form, they strongly resented any attempt by the government to interfere with it by force. In some way carnival was thought of as the "people's" festival, and the government was thought of as alien. If it was a conflict between expatriate officials and the people, the press came down on the side of the latter, even if they disliked the way in which the people chose to amuse themselves. This was especially the view of spokesmen for the French Creole elite and the mixed-race ("coloured") Creoles, who recognized that carnival – for all its objectionable elements as they saw it – was nevertheless a core expression of Trinidad's "creoleness."

The Colonial Office sent a commissioner, Robert Hamilton, to investigate the riots, and he reported in June 1881, having spent exactly one week in Trinidad. Hamilton found that the riots were caused by the people's belief that the police were going to stop the whole carnival, based on their action in 1880, and fomented by certain people who excited the maskers against them. He thought that the carnival should not be abolished, but instead that it should be very strictly regulated. Torch processions should be allowed only in places like the Savannah. Leading citizens should be sworn in as Special Constables in future carnivals and they should impress on the people the need for order and decency. A British warship should be in the harbor during the next carnival. The police should be supported in the execution of their duty, but their very bad relations with the public would need to be improved. Some subordinate officers who were very unpopular should be removed, but Baker, whom the report cleared of charges of provocative conduct, should be retained in his post (The Hamilton Report into the Disturbances in Connection with the Carnival, in *Port of Spain Gazette*, October 22, 1881; Cowley 1996: 90).

After the events of 1881, the carnival of 1882 was the cause of much anxiety. A proclamation issued in November 1881 authorized the canboulay for the next year by allowing the carrying of lighted torches in any street between midnight Sunday and 5:00 a.m. Monday. This was clearly a defeat for Baker. On the other hand, the government took elaborate precautions for the carnival. Two men-of-war were stationed in the harbor; troops and volunteers were on full alert; the fire brigade was ready; the government steam launch was kept under steam and plans for the evacuation of the governor had been concerted; special magistrates were forbidden to leave their posts; government officials armed themselves; and surgeons were ready at the police station to cope with the wounded (*Port-of-Spain Gazette*, February 25, 1882).

It was all quite unnecessary. For the maskers had determined among themselves that there would be no disorder. A deputation of maskers called at the *Port of Spain Gazette* office asking the paper to use its influence for order and peace at the carnival. And a broadsheet entitled "Advice for the Coming Carnival" was circulated, obviously the work of bandleaders, calling on maskers to play peacefully and not to betray the governor's confidence. Canboulay passed off quietly, though celebrated on a larger scale than usual. No fights took place, there were no clashes with the police, and no fires. One band, seeing the approach of a rival, agreed to drop their sticks and refused to "take on" the rival's insults. The other band did the same, and they shook hands fraternally. The bigger bands were led by prominent citizens who had influence with the maskers and who used their prestige to see that order prevailed (*Port-of-Spain Gazette*, February 11 and 25, 1882; *Fair Play*, February 9 and 23, 1882; *Chronicle*, March 4, 1882).

The government still had not made up its mind about the canboulay by the carnival of 1883. No special proclamation was issued and the procession was held as usual. But this carnival was quite as disorderly as before the riots. One band in particular, the Newgates, provoked and attacked other bands with sticks, stones, and bottles. They were apparently mainly from the eastern Caribbean; it was their maxim to beat all French-speaking (Creole) maskers they met. They themselves were not masked, and their only object appeared to be to attack other bands. Private houses were forced open and stoned. One theory was that the police incited and encouraged the Newgates with the object of avenging the reversal of 1881 and discrediting the carnival. Baker was said to have openly promoted disorder by calling on the other bands to beat and arrest Newgates whenever they found them. There were also many individual encounters among maskers (*Fair Play*, February 8, 1883; *New Era*, February 12, 1883; Cowley 1996: 94–5).

Probably the disorder in 1883 strengthened the hand of the anti-carnival faction within the government, and finally brought the governor round to the view that canboulay had to be stopped and carnival rigidly controlled. In 1883 the Peace Preservation Ordinance was passed to give the police wide powers over "riotous bands." Just before the 1884 carnival an amendment was rushed through the Legislative Council. It gave the governor power to prohibit by proclamation public torch processions, drum beating, any dance or procession, and any assembly of ten or more persons armed with sticks or any other weapons; the maximum penalty on summary conviction was a fine of £20 or six months in jail. This, of course, gave the governor authority to abolish canboulay and the large stick bands. Accordingly a proclamation was issued for the coming carnival. It prohibited torch processions, assemblies of more than ten persons carrying sticks, and drumming or the playing of any other instruments except between 6:00 a.m. and 7:00 p.m. Masking was prohibited save between Monday 6:00 a.m. and Tuesday midnight. The provisions of the 1868 police ordinance against assault, drunken and disorderly behavior, riot and affray, and obscene language or songs, would all be rigidly enforced (*Port-of-Spain Gazette*, January 26, 1884: Legislative Council, January 25, 1884; *Review*, January 31, 1884: Proclamation, January 28, 1884; Cowley 1996: 99–102).

All sorts of rumors circulated. It was believed that the government intended to forbid all masking at the eleventh hour. The maskers were said to be rebellious. Someone claimed to have overheard a conversation to the effect that they were planning to retaliate for the prohibition of canboulay by poisoning the Port of Spain reservoir, pulling down the telephone wires, destroying street lamps, and burning down the powder magazine. There was so much resentment at the interference with canboulay and the bands that another proclamation was issued which assured the people that the new ordinance was aimed only at rogues, vagabonds, and prostitutes. This only caused confusion: were people not so classified allowed to do things which would be an offense for people of that description (*Review*, January 23 and 30, and February 14, 1884)? Volunteers were called up, and middle-class persons were sworn in as Special Constables. Everyone waited apprehensively the result of the government's new policy.

In Port of Spain, all was quiet. No attempt was made to stage the canboulay. There were no disturbances and no confrontation with the police. It was, in fact, the quietest carnival in years, though outside the city there was trouble. In San Fernando there was a riot on the Monday morning. A mob armed with bottles and stones and carrying torches was confronted by the police. There was fighting for about fifteen minutes before the mob was dispersed, and several arrests were made. A similar affray took place at Couva. In Princes Town, an attempt by over five hundred persons to hold canboulay ended with firing by the police and two deaths. One newspaper speculated that "ringleaders of some of the most desperate bands" in the capital city tried to stage "in the Naparimas [i.e. south Trinidad] those orgies which were forbidden them in Port of Spain" (*Recorder*, February 27, 1884; *Port-of-Spain Gazette*, March 1 and April 12, 1884; *Review*, February 28, 1884; Cowley 1996: 102–3).

The purging of carnival proceeded slowly in the years after 1884. The general consensus about the government's new policy was that it had succeeded, despite the bloodshed in the south. Canboulay was for ever abolished, and so were the large stick bands and the band fighting. In 1890–1 the control over the festival was extended by a proclamation prohibiting the throwing of missiles, including flour, at onlookers. Another new regulation in 1893 was that persons intending to mask as Pierrots had to register with the police in advance.[4] But in 1890 and 1891 the police were still being accused of doing nothing to stop public indecency. The *Daily News* quoted approvingly the words of the Chief Justice, that the carnival was a disgrace, and that "in two days the whole year's work of the clergy and the schoolmasters was destroyed" (*Port-of-Spain Gazette*, February 6, 1891; *New Era*, February 21, 1890; *Daily News*, January 21, 1893).

In response to this pressure, the carnival regulations for 1895 added a new clause: it was illegal for persons to appear masked "in the dress or costume commonly called and known as Pisse en Lit." As a result there was none of the grosser obscenity in the 1895 carnival, very little transvestism, and only a handful of obscenity arrests (*Port-of-Spain Gazette*, January 22, February 7 and 27, 1895).[5]

The way was clear for the respectable classes to re-enter carnival, and for the festival to develop slowly into a "national" event. Clear signs of this movement can be seen between 1885 and 1900. In the former year a "relatively large number" of respectable persons felt safe enough to mask and play in the streets. Citizens of worth were seeing people they knew playing masked. Three years later there was a small band of courtiers whose "propriety and reserve stamped them gentlemen in the midst of the surging mass of coarser masqueraders. There was a lady among them" (*New Era*, February 23, 1885; *Chronicle*, February 18, 1888).

Upper-class maskers in 1893 revived the pre–1838 tradition of house-to-house visiting, with practical jokes, and music. Another older practice which was revived after 1885 was the holding of fancy dress balls in the weeks before carnival. Governor Sir William Robinson gave one before the 1888 carnival; he was the Earl of Leicester and his wife the Queen of Scots. Two years later a juvenile fancy dress ball was held to aid the All Saints Anglican Church. In 1895 the elite of San Fernando attended a similar affair on carnival Tuesday night. And a paper observed that year that, if masking was to be abolished, then costume balls, much in vogue "of late," would also have to go, for to prohibit street masking for the lower orders, and to allow it in the homes of the wealthy, might cause trouble (*New Era*, February 17, 1888 and February 14, 1890; *Daily News*, February 15, 1893; *Port-of-Spain Gazette*, January 12 and February 27, 1895; Cowley 1996: 104–6, 120–1, 124–33).

By about 1890 businessmen were beginning to realize the commercial benefits of carnival, especially for the dry goods stores. College boys and store clerks began to organize bands. In the late 1890s Ignacio Bodu, a borough councillor and a patron of carnival and calypso, organized competitions for "pretty" bands in Port of

Spain to improve the festival's moral tone (*Daily News*, February 15, 1893; Pearse 1956a: 189–90; Cowley 1996: 132–3; Liverpool 2001: 335–9).

The changing character of carnival was also seen in the development of the calypso. The late nineteenth century was a time when the calypso was emerging in its modern form. Up to about 1898, most calypsos were in Creole, or in a mixture of Creole and English, and they were accompanied by "tamboo-bamboo" bands. By the late 1890s singers were accompanied by the cuatro, guitar, and chac-chac, and Venezuelan or Latin melodies were being used. According to Lord Executor, in 1898 Norman le Blanc sang the first calypso wholly in English, on the abolition of the Borough Council. One verse ran:

> Jerningham the Governor
> Jerningham the Governor,
> I say is fastness in you
> To break the laws of Borough Council.

At about the turn of the century upper-class persons began to attend the "tents," which were made of bamboo, covered with palm branches and with bamboo seats. They soon became better organized and were moved into better districts. The upper- and middle-class patrons were the "jacketmen," the coat being the great symbol of respectability:

> Point for point,
> I prefer a jacketman,
> Jacketman don't beat me with a stick in the street.

Extempore singing was common, and there was often "picong," an exchange of witty insults between rival calypsonians. The last three decades of the century were, in fact, the time when calypso achieved partial acceptance, as a result of the changeover to English, the use of European instruments and melodies for accompaniment, and the organization of better tents (Quevedo 1962: 90; Liverpool 2001: 330–9).

The study of carnival in the late nineteenth century illustrates several aspects of Trinidad society in the period. In the 1870s carnival was essentially confined to the Creole masses, especially those who lived in Port of Spain. In fact the really active participants were a group within a group, for they were members of the jamette society of the city's backyards. It should be emphasized that the majority of the working class were not jamettes themselves, and would not have approved of much of their way of life. But each carnival they came out in their glory and the whole Creole working class probably felt a vicarious pride in their exploits. There was nothing really vicious about the jamette carnival. The fighting rarely resulted in serious injuries, though certainly people got their heads broken and there was a lot of disorder. As for the obscenity, it probably reflects the far more casual approach to sex which characterized the masses as compared to the "respectable" classes. Privacy and delicacy were impossible in the physical conditions under which they lived, and masques such as Pissenlit were probably harmless foolery to them. They also exemplified widely differing gender ideologies held by the jamettes and the strata striving for, or enjoying, acceptance by mainstream society. Carnival as a whole served the function of an escape valve for the masses, whose lives were ordinarily harshly limited, and desperately hard.

The decision to end the two features of the carnival which were most enjoyed by the jamettes, band fighting and canboulay, was taken by the government in response to pressure from the middle class, and their own reaction to the carnival. The decision was carried out by force in 1881 and in 1884, and both times the maskers resisted, in 1884 with fatal results. Once the fighting and the canboulay had been forcibly put down, the middle class turned its attention to public indecency, and this was largely suppressed by 1895, again by police action rather than by a campaign of popular education. It was only then, after carnival had been licked into the shape they wanted, that "respectable" persons began to participate.

At several points in the late nineteenth century, the total suppression of carnival seemed possible. But when it came to a crisis, as in 1881, important sections of the French Creole elite and the mixed-race middle stratum resented what they considered high-handed attempts by British officials to put down a festival which – disgusting though it might be in many ways – was undeniably "Creole." Since carnival could not be persuaded to die a "natural death," forcible suppression of the festival itself was unacceptable to most Trinidadians, with some exceptions such as E.F. Chalamelle who argued in 1897 for outright abolition. Instead, the jamette carnival was purged, controlled, remade, and "social incorporation" of the middle and even upper strata into the festival began (or resumed). The dialectical relationship between carnival's anarchic elements (including violence and obscenity) and the push to control and sanitize it would continue and develop in the twentieth century.

NOTES

1   This is a revised version of my essay, "The Trinidad Carnival 1870–1900" in *Savacou*, 11/12 (September 1975), pp. 46–57. All the newspapers cited were published in Trinidad.

2   "Jamette", a feminine Creole word, means an underclass type, a woman or man whose life centered on fighting, dancing, drinking, promiscuous sex often including prostitution and pimping.

3   For a strongly expressed contemporary argument that carnival corrupted young girls see Chalamelle 1901 (written in 1897).

4   The Pierrot was a champion stickfighter who challenged rivals to combat: see Hill 1972: 28–30.

5   Nevertheless, in 1897 E.F. Chalamelle was still complaining about obscenity in carnival and its role in corrupting youth: see note 3.

4

THE MARTINICAN
Dress and politics in nineteenth-century Trinidad Carnival

Pamela R. Franco

INTRODUCTION

Mary Ellen Roach and Joanne Eicher note that "dress . . . signifies the apparel worn by men and women [and it] also refers to the act of covering the body with clothes and accessories" (1965: 1). John Berger, in *Ways of Seeing*, suggests that women's dress and dressing up allow them to become both object and subject, or what he terms "the surveyed" and "the surveyor" (1972: 46). As objects of the male gaze, women are the surveyed. However, in the act of "watching" themselves, a ritual that is learned at a young age, women become surveyors. Berger, here, introduces the idea of women as subjects or agents (surveyors) capable of constructing and manipulating their self-image. Revisionist scholars, expanding on the concept of women as subjects, emphasize the ways in which women manipulate dress and dressing up – particularly as a strategy to attain visibility and to articulate particular concerns, be they cultural, economical, personal, or political (Hollander 1993 [1975]; Weiner and Schneider 1989; Barnes and Eicher 1993). This body of literature positions women as agents with clearly defined intentions, which they express or communicate through dress and dressing up. Agency, here, is neither fixed nor permanent; it is negotiated at particular historical moments or on specific occasions. Carnival is one such occasion when women use dress and dressing up to create a self-image through which they can "articulate" their opinions.

The effectiveness of dress in such a public space as carnival is dependent on two factors: first, dress as cultural product and, second, dress as sign. As a cultural product, the use-value of dress is dictated by society, what Erving Goffman defines as the "orientational" aspect of dress (1965: 52). In other words, society fashions a system that assigns garments to either a public or a private sphere on the basis of their function.[1] For example, a petticoat worn in a public place would be inappropriate. Even though the apparel covers the wearer's body, its social "orientation" is under an outer garment. Its "dislocation" from the private (invisible) to the public (visible) sphere undermines the extant system thus making the act revolutionary. Or as Stuart Hall posits, "what unsettles culture is matter out of place" (1997, rpt 2001: 236).

Therefore, as a cultural product carnival dress is susceptible to interpretation based on the (dis)"orientational" role of specific garments. As a sign, however, dress achieves some elasticity. Malcolm Barnard, in *Fashion as Communication* (1996), explains that, as a sign, dress can be either denotative or connotative. The former refers to the "literal meaning of a word or image" (Barnard 1996: 80–1), and the latter is "the word or image [that] makes a person think or feel" (ibid.). In other words, the meaning of a denotative sign is fixed; it is literally what one sees or what is conventional. Conversely, the meaning of the connotative sign is dynamic because it is context-driven. Therefore, the connotative aspect of the sign permits multiple, sometimes conflicting, readings. In actuality, both aspects are present in dress; however, it is the connotative that better facilitates analysis of carnival dress. In the context of carnival, new meaning(s) is (are) further negotiated within a performance frame. Barnard's connotative factor permits the constitution of the author and meaning within performance.

In this chapter, I will discuss how nineteenth-century black women constructed a new self-image through the creation of the Martinican dress. As the authors of this sartorial ensemble, they controlled much of its meaning. However, in carnival the Martinican dress took on several meanings that were based on social, cultural, and legal issues framed within the contemporary politics.

MARTINICAN DRESS: ANALYSIS OF A CREOLE STYLE

In nineteenth-century Trinidad, the term "Martinican" was a popular designation for black women's fancy dress: specifically the *à la jupe* and *la grande robe*. The *à la jupe*, or *chemisette et jupe* (figure 4.1), was a bodice and skirt ensemble. Draped to the side and tucked into the waist, the skirt revealed a *jupon*, an underskirt. The more formal *la grande robe* (figures 4.2 & 4.3), an all-in-one gown or *douillette*, was secured at the waist. Like the *à la jupe*, the skirt was often draped, rolled, and tucked into the waist, revealing an elaborately decorated underskirt. Both styles incorporated a *foulard*, which was draped around the shoulders, and a calendered, or painted, headtie, adorned with brooches. Gold chains, rings, and bracelets completed both costumes.

In the late eighteenth century, immigrants from the francophone islands – Grenada, Guadeloupe, Martinique, and St Vincent – brought the Martinican dress to then Spanish Trinidad. Many were fleeing the French Revolution and its effects on France's Caribbean colonies. The Spanish government, through the Royal Cedula of Population (1783), offered refuge to the region's French Creoles whom they expected to develop the island. Therefore, they offered them plots of arable land, and additional acreage was given to those planters who brought their slaves with them (Borde 1982 [1876]: 185–93). The immigrant population included white, free coloured and black families, and slaves. It is during this period that black French-Creole women introduced their unique style of dress to Trinidad. Since Martiniquians constituted the numerical majority of the immigrant population, the dress became identified almost exclusively with them, hence the appellation, Martinican dress.

The Martinican ensemble was a veritable Creole invention. Using an assemblage technique, black women combined European-manufactured cloth with a West

Fig. 4.1 *Mulatresse de la Martinique.* Late nineteenth century. Published by permission of Musée Regional d'Histoire et Ethnographie, Maison de la Canne du Conseil Regional de la Martinique, Fort-de-France, Martinique. no. 88–56–14.

African dress aesthetic. They chose colorful cloth – scotch plaid, madras and printed cotton – and/or sumptuous materials such as silk, damask, muslin, and lace, which they draped, rolled, and tied in a West African style. Forgoing the European-styled dress handed down by the planter's wife, black Caribbean women created their own version of fancy dress. They fused bits and pieces from the region's major ethnic and cultural groups and created a novel and distinct dress style and aesthetic. This process can be interpreted as an "act of cultural *bricolage*" (White and White 1998: 19).

Fig. 4.2 Jean Michel Cazabon, *Old Negress, French, in Gala Dress.* Published by permission of the Trustees of the Harris Belmont Charity.

The colorful and sumptuous materials were further enhanced by a brilliance that emanated from the women's jewelry. In Martinique M. Granier de Cassagnac was amazed at the profusion of jewelry that the members of "Les Roses" association wore at an 1840 carnival ball.[2] He remarked "du reste jamais de ma vie je n'ai vu autant de bijoux, de turquoises, d'emeraudes et de perles" (quoted in Rosemain 1986: 100–1) ("never in all my life have I seen so many jewels, turquoises, emeralds and pearls," my translation). In nineteenth-century Jamaica, an observer of the *Set Girls* (similarly dressed women who paraded during the Christmas/Jonkonnu festivities) also remarked on the quantity and diversity of jewels worn by black

Fig. 4.3 Fashionable young lady, 1880s. Published by permission of Paria Publishing.

women. "I was astonished to see such a display of valuable trinkets – coral and cornelian Necklaces, Bracelets, etc." (quoted in Bettelheim 1979: 23). Sometimes the planter or his wife provided pieces of jewelry, but black women purchased most items.[3] The overall brilliant and dazzling effect of colorful dress and jewelry "transliterated" the women from a life of hardship and drudgery to one of implied affluence, which they successfully displayed using the conventional signs of wealth – jewelry and sumptuous dress.[4]

Although jewelry helped to create a dazzling image of the black woman, the headtie was her crowning glory. "The making-up of . . . a turban [was] called 'tying a head' (*marre yon tête*), and a pretty folded turban was spoken of as 'a head well tied' (*yon tête bien marre*)" (Hearn 1923 [1890]: 226). Mary Jo Arnoldi explains: "in the thought and moral imagination of many African and African diaspora societies, the head, itself, is a potent image that plays a central role in how the person is conceptualized" (Arnoldi and Kreamer 1995: 11). For example, in Yoruba philosophical thought each person possesses two heads, the outer and the inner head. The more important is the inner head or the *ori-inu*. Art historian Rowland Abiodun defines the *ori-inu* as one's "essential nature and personal destiny" (1994: 74). Wande Abimbola states that "Ori is the essence of luck and the most important force responsible for human success or failure" (1975: 390). Piggybacking on Abiodun and Abimbola's explication of *ori*, it is feasible to suggest that many black women would have been familiar with this concept of the head, as a critical component in the process of self-identification and in determining one's destiny. Thus, the elaborate tying of the head may have been a way of acknowledging the head's significance and its sacredness.

The headtie served many functions. In the nineteenth-century American South, African-American women "completely covered the hair and held [it] in place either by tucking the ends of fabric into the wrap or by tying the ends into knots close to the skull" (Foster 1997: 272). Basically, it was used to protect the head from the sun and to keep one's hair in a neat fashion. In nineteenth-century Trinidad, Mrs Carmichael observed that black women were not well dressed without their headties. Prior to a dance or special event her female slaves "came up not an hour before the dance commenced to have their 'hats drest'" (Carmichael 1961 [1833]: 292). In late eighteenth-century Louisiana, sumptuary laws were enacted as a strategy to publicly demoralize and humiliate women of color. Both free and enslaved women were forced to wear headties which, according to Helen Foster, "became a badge of servitude and inferior status for Black women" (1997: 272). In an ironic twist, the women wore the headtie, as the law dictated, but they fashioned it in elaborate sculptural designs, thus remodeling the garment from a sign of their servitude to one of personal agency. In essence, they "played with the white 'code' by convert[ing] it [headwrap] from something which might be construed as shameful into something uniquely their own" (ibid.: 292).

The headtie functioned also as a marker of the wearer's occupation, age, marital status, and ethnicity. In the American South, for example, headwraps were used "as a signifier denoting religious beliefs and age, sex, marital, gender and class status" (Foster 1997: 284). In many parts of West Africa, hairstyles and special cloths have been integral aspects of young girls' coming-of-age ceremonies. Similarly, in nineteenth-century Nigeria the Ejagham women wore elaborate hairstyles in "coming out" ceremonies (Arnoldi and Kreamer 1995: 55). Lisa Aronson, in her work on the Kalabari region, observed the significance of cloth in a young girl's coming-of-age ceremony or *bitite*. In the "cloth-tying ceremony," which follows her seclusion in the "fatting house," the young woman ties several types of cloth around her body, transforming herself into a site/sight of abundance. "The most highly regarded cloth throughout the eastern delta is now the Indian madras, the tying of which constitutes the last phase of the ceremony, the *bitite*" (Aronson 1980: 63).[5] In Kalabari, the madras marks the crossing of the threshold from childhood to adulthood.

In nineteenth-century Martinique the madras also signified female adulthood and a young woman's marriageability. According to Louis Garaud, in *Trois Ans à La Martinique* (1895: 200), "Vers dix huit ans, la jeune fille prend tête, c'est-à-dire, en langue du pays, echange le foulard contre le madras" ("At about eighteen years of age, a young girl takes/gets a [new] head, in other words, in the local parlance, she exchanges the [regular] scarf for the madras", my translation). The "taking of a new head" appears to have been a coming-of-age ceremony, with the madras signifying the transition from childhood to adulthood. On "taking a new head," the young Martiniquaise also had a choice of several headtie designs, which were centered on the points (*pwen*) or bouts (*boo*). For example, the headtie design with one point or bout signifies "My heart is free – not taken by anyone"; the head with two points, "My heart is taken, but you can take a chance"; a head with three points, "I am taken – nothing doing"; and a head with four points, which was extremely rare, "There is place for those who want it" (Aumis *et al.* 1992: 60). Thus, the design of the headtie "communicated" the young wearer's betrothal status.

The elaborate and complex headtie designs were enhanced with jewelry (figure 4.4) – gold pins and brooches – that enhanced an already radiant image. Frequently, they were given such names as *Dahlia*, *Chenille* (Caterpillar), *Les Hisbiscus*, and *Le Nid abeille* (Wasp's Nest). The significance of these names is not clear; some (*Dahlia* and *Hisbiscus*) appear to be descriptions of specific floral designs. Other jewelry pieces with such names as *Louis XVI* and *Fleurs de Champs* seem to have had some political ramifications. Louis XVI was dethroned during the French Revolution. His ouster ushered in a republican government whose ideology was based on *liberté, égalité et fraternité* or freedom, equality, and brotherhood. Without a description of this piece of jewelry, it is difficult to ascertain the full meaning of the object. Hypothetically, for royalists the Louis XVI brooch would have been a commemorative emblem. For republicans, most likely, it would have been a satirical or parodic commemoration of a once-royalist France. Placed on black women's headties as a decorative element, Louis XVI is reduced to a trinket[6] that the women controlled. There is ambiguity and uncertainty in my rudimentary attempt to determine the true meaning of the brooch designs, and further research is needed. Despite this shortcoming, this example suggests that the headtie and jewelry may have been part of a complex sign system for which black women inscribed the referential meanings. Colorful dress, dazzling jewelry, and sculptural headtie designs enabled black women to create a new self-image that veered significantly from the racialized picture painted by members of the planter class.

THE MARTINICAN DRESS: POLITICS AND CARNIVAL

Traditionally, the Martinican dress was worn throughout the year to celebrate such events as baptisms and weddings. However, it was at the drum dance, specifically the belair, that black women showcased their sartorial creativity. The term "belair" describes a Creole dance and song style from the French-speaking Caribbean. It was black women's premier performative domain. They constituted the major and majority participants; they were the dancers and singers, and men were often the drummers. Women choreographed belair dances, and frequently composed songs in French Creole or patois. Some made reference to the island's contemporary

Fig. 4.4 Camille Dedierre, a Martiniquian mulatto, photograph c. 1900.
Published by permission of Paria Publishing.

politics. For example, an 1805 belair song conjures up images of the Haitian revolution, an event that the British hoped to arrest in Trinidad.

> The bread we eat
> Is the white man's flesh
> The wine we drink
> Is the white man's blood
> He St. Domingo,
> remember St. Domingo

(quoted in Cowley 1996: 14)

Songs and dance were enhanced by the women's elaborate toilette. Dressed in the most beautiful *chemisette et jupe* or *la grande robe*, black women appropriated the dominant culture's material icons of wealth, social status and power – fancy dress, jewelry, shoes and silk stockings – and reinterpreted them. They reworked the "borrowed" European elements to reconstitute a social order that they controlled, a practice that resonates of James Scott's "hidden transcript," a private, often subversive, response to societal norms (Scott 1990: 25). The belair performance was structured around a hierarchical "society" that included " 'royal' leadership by Kings and Queens, and a Dauphin (or Prince), 'royal' households, and political, legal, and military personnel – for example Ambassadors, a Prime Minister, Grand Judges, an Admiral, Colonels" (Cowley 1996: 13). These events were held in "neatly built edifices . . . [with] an elevated platform . . . where the King with his gorgeously apparelled [*sic*] Queen sat surrounded by her almost equally dressed attendants . . . the Chorus and Dancers [were] all gaily dressed females, with bright colored head dresses and sparkling with jewelry" (ibid.: 45). Thus it is reasonable to say that at the belair blacks constructed a world in which they held all hegemonic roles and they dressed up for their parts.

Belairs were performed also throughout the Christmas-carnival season when slaves were "given considerable freedom for dancing, pageantry, parades and traditional good strife between plantation bands" (Pearse 1956a: 13). The highlights of the season's performances were private masquerade balls and street-processioning either on foot or in carriages. The coloured middle class generally adhered to this tradition; they hosted balls and paraded, probably in a limited capacity, in the street. Slaves rarely participated in the public festival. But Friedrich Urich, a German store clerk, recorded the extent of black festive activities in the pre-emancipation era. For example, on carnival Sunday, 1831, "After dinner we went to see the negroes dance" (quoted in De Verteuil 1984: 12).[7] The "negroes dance" most likely was a drum dance, probably the belair. Since the slaves did not host European-styled masquerade balls, the belair, being their most extravagant performance, would have functioned as a comparable alternative to the upper classes' elaborate dressing up and disguises.

On carnival Monday Urich "follow[ed] various masked bands. The dances [were] usually African dances, and the enthusiasm of the negroes and negresses amuse us very much, for these dances [were] stupendous" (ibid.).[8] Similarly, in 1832, he wrote of "coloureds and negroes" being very active in the street parade. So blacks, free and enslaved, were part of the pre-emancipation street carnival. Since there is no description of the costumes, it is difficult to ascertain whether or not the women wore the Martinican dress. However, at the "negroes dance" on carnival Sunday, black women would have worn the Martinican dress creating a spectacle of dancing black female bodies radiant in jewels that shone brighter in the glow of the candle-light or flambeaux. From Urich's account it is reasonable to suggest that the "negroes dance," or belair, was an integral part of the early nineteenth-century carnival, and consequently black women, as its premier performers, were active participants in the festival.

The Martinican dress connoted many things. For black women, it allowed them a certain visibility and an opportunity for self-identification. They may have also used the dress as "an ideological weapon" in the constant power struggle with the local white authorities. Inter-island travel and migration not only facilitated the movement of dress from one island to another; it also permitted the movement of political ideology. Fallout from the 1789 French Revolution impacted the politics of the Caribbean region. Supporters of the Revolution, who called for *liberté, égalité et fraternité*, were labeled republicans, and the supporters of the monarchy and a court tradition were royalists. This ideological division became part of the political landscape of the francophone Caribbean with the elites generally favoring the royalists, and the lower classes the republicans. Trinidad's French elite community was also "royalist in politics, [and] bitterly hostile to the revolutionary and republican movements" (Brereton 1979: 37). Blacks generally were more sympathetic to the republicans because, theoretically, they were fighting for freedom and equality, social and moral conditions that had great resonance for them. As part of the middle class, free blacks had lost the privileges that were gained under Spanish rule. Many blacks also had enslaved kin whose freedom they were trying to secure. Republicanism, with its emphasis on freedom and equality, seemingly echoed the plight of this community. Thus it was adopted as a rallying cry for the freedom of enslaved blacks and for the colored middle class, the recovery of lost privileges.

In the 1790s, prior to the capitulation of Spanish Trinidad to the British in 1797, French republican supporters, many from a rapidly declining francophone Caribbean,[9] traveled throughout the region enlisting the help of the free coloured and black middle class, in an attempt to gain support for a republican France, the overturn of Britain's fortunes in the region, and "the abolition of slavery everywhere" (Brereton 1981: 29–30). In Trinidad, reportedly, they organized meetings and distributed anti-English and anti-royalist literature. The propagandistic rhetoric so unnerved then Governor Chacon that he remarked, "the contact which our coloured people and our Negro slaves have had with the French Republicans, has made them dream of liberty and equality" (ibid.). They did not only dream of freedom; they also acted upon it. "The slaves . . . adopt[ed] the revolutionary tri-colored cockade introduced by the French republicans" (ibid.).

The cockade was a recognizable sign of French republicanism. To wear it in a Spanish colony, with strong royalist support, was a bold and daring act. Moreover, the slaves' public display of the cockade suggests a growing militancy among this group. In 1797, General Abercromby attempted to arrest the island's revolutionary climate. He quickly issued a proclamation with instructions for evacuation: "all such Frenchmen as consider themselves to be citizens of the French Republic were to be allowed to leave and were to be given safe conduct to some French, Dutch or Spanish Colony" (ibid.: 33). Some left voluntarily and others were deported. The events of the recent Haitian war of independence coupled with a growing militancy among the slaves increased the British fear of insurrection on the island. Subsequent governors undertook steps, sometimes brutal and violent, to suppress black militancy and to curtail revolution on the island (Campbell 1992: 129–39, 145–8).

In this highly charged political climate, black women, many of whom would have been Martiniquaises, may have sought ways to distance themselves from the British and their racist attitude toward slavery and social inequality. They accomplished this goal by constructing a distinct Creole cultural identity through their manipulation of dress. As cultural historian Elizabeth Wilson notes, "in a fragmenting world people . . . rework their identities, and [they] use dress and style as a substitute for identity" (quoted in Tulloch 1997–8: 48). Using the seemingly benign Martinican dress the women constructed visually a cohesive communal identity, an act that resonates of Frantz Fanon's writing on the role of the veil in the creation of Algerian women's identity. As he explains it, "the fact of belonging to a given cultural group is usually revealed by clothing traditions" (1967: 35). In other words, the cultural or ethnic orientation of clothes allows for easy recognition of a group or community. Similarly, the idiosyncratic Creole dress stressed the women's cultural identity while simultaneously distinguishing them from their white counterparts.

The Martinican dress remained part of the nineteenth-century carnival landscape, but the colorful and radiant image would be greatly diminished. By the 1820s the "mulatresse"[10] was a popular street disguise among white women. Donning a simplified version of the *chemisette et jupe*, they paraded with their male counterparts, who were disguised as the *Nègre Jardin* or field laborer. Their performance was a parody of the quelling of estate fires. Later, blacks would appropriate and reinterpret this carnivalesque performance, which would be called the canboulay. By the 1840s white women would also use the mulatresse costume while parading in all-women's bands, as Charles Day observed in the 1848 carnival when he encountered a group of young girls dressed in the "à la jupe, the vrai creole negro costume" (1852: 316). In a typical carnivalesque manner, upper-class white women, by appropriating lower-class black women's dress, symbolically inverted both race and social status. Black women would continue to wear the dress in carnival but its sartorial splendor would be greatly compromised. In 1841, they choreographed a *Coq d'Inde ponde* dance, still projecting a republican ideology, but there's little reference to the colorful Martinican dress. While contemporary accounts identify black women as maskers in the street carnival, their dress style may have changed (see Day 1852: 313–14). By the 1860s, jamette[11] women would remodel the garment to allow them ease in unstringing the bodice to reveal their breasts. Recalling Goffman's "orientational" aspect of dress, this public behavior undermined the Victorian code of moral ethics. Allegedly, the bared breasts were so shocking that the sight did not "permit our [white] mothers, wives and sisters to walk the streets and promenades without having their senses shocked" (quoted in Pearse 1956a: 31) by such disgusting behavior.

The carnival climate had changed. According to the newspapers, there was a marked increase in violence and sexual obscenity, only among black maskers. The authorities would issue proclamations and activate the police force in an attempt to suppress the festival's reputed degenerate elements. Reportedly, the once-elegant belair had become "one of the most fruitful and common sources of Trinidad demoralization" (quoted in Cowley 1996: 72). And by the 1880s the performers were "a few dirtily dressed women who serve[d] as Chorus, a mixed crowd of dirtily dressed men and women who dance to the sound of the drum independently of each other" (ibid.: 96). Gone was the splendor of a court with its royalty in attendance. Supplanting this style of performance was a seemingly unstructured and slightly chaotic event. The sumptuous Martinican dress would be seen less and less in carnival. Finally, in the late 1880s, batonniers or stickfighters appropriated this special dress. After the banning of sticks on the streets on carnival days, black male maskers sought ingenious ways to carry their sticks unnoticed into the street. To circumvent the prohibition they donned the Martinican-styled dress as a disguise.

The voluminous skirt allowed them to hide their sticks. It is evident that the Martinican dress was a staple in nineteenth-century carnival; however, it underwent several changes, and its meaning was derived from the particular performers and the historical period and situation in which the garment was used.

In sum, I am suggesting that the Martinican dress, with its dazzling and spectacular aura, may not have been simply a sartorial strategy for black women to become visible or temporarily invert the extant social order. From very early, it appears that the women may have transformed the garment into a discursive site of resistance. With limited economic resources and little political power, they used their brightly colored and dazzling Creole dress and the tricolor cockade to "transliterate" themselves from the realm of the exotic (the surveyed) into the political arena (the surveyor). This seemingly "innocent" dress connoted black women's construction of a cultural or communal identity and a unique protest strategy. The sartorial display of self-affirmation and anti-slavery protest was probably one of many elements that threatened the British sense of political stability and the continued success of slavery. Despite its varied and "deteriorated" representation in the later decades of the nineteenth century, the dazzling and sumptuous Martinican dress provided a "voice" to black women at a time when they were expected to be silent.

NOTES

1 Since diverse communities constitute a complex society, the garment's meaning can differ from one community to another.

2 According to de Cassagnac, this was an association of domestic workers.

3 Black women earned money through a variety of endeavors. Many used the profits earned from selling the produce from their plots of land. Some ran huckster shops, organized dances for which they charged an entrance fee, or managed boarding houses.

4 Cloth, fancy dress, and jewelry were signs of wealth and social status in Africa and Europe.

5 I am not suggesting that the Martiniquian and Kalabari women were aware of each other's usage of the madras. The madras probably entered Martinique in the early nineteenth century. In the Kalabari, the madras was introduced into the area in the early twentieth century.

6 This style of decoration seems to replicate the Bini's Queen Idia's ivory pendant, with its stylized images of the Portuguese men arranged in a semicircular design at the top of the head.

7 In Urich's diary, the term *negroes* is a synonym for slaves.

8 Urich obviously believed that the Negro dances would have been African. Some were probably creolized dances.

9 In the late eighteenth century, Britain captured several French colonies including Grenada, Tobago, and St Lucia. They also occupied Martinique in the late eighteenth century. Victor Hugues, a professional soldier and a republican, fought off the British to regain control of Guadeloupe.

10 "Mulatresse" is a synonym for the Martinican dress.

11 "Jamette" is a creolization of the French *diametre*. Translated it describes those at the periphery of society, who sometimes engage in petty criminal behavior.

5

INDIAN PRESENCE IN CARNIVAL

Burton Sankeralli

Trinidad's carnival is alive. It grows organically out of a rich culture, a tortuous history. The event is a space where the entire range of our cultural expression and ethnic diversity emerges. It is in terms of this, the fundamental nature of carnival, that we are to understand the Indian presence in it.

Indian indentured immigrants arrived in Trinidad from 1845 to 1917. The conditions on the sugar plantations, where they labored during their contract period of at least five years, were like the slavery which indentureship replaced. The conditions were oppressive in the extreme: a number of families shared a single barracks; the Indians were strangers to each other, often speaking different languages. They came from Uttar Pradesh, Bihar, and Tamil Nadu. Men outnumbered women by up to three to one – making the women targets of male violence despite the potentially strong position that imbalance gave women. Despite all these troubles, a communal dynamic emerged. The dominant language was a Trinidadian version of Bhojpuri-Hindi, common in Uttar Pradesh. And as the Indians moved off the plantations, a basic pattern of Indo-Trinidadian community – the rural village – came into being. Life in the villages centered on the extended family and a reformulated sense of caste.[1] Village life was regulated by the rhythm of cane and rice farming. It is not coincidental that the major Indian settlements were around the Caroni and Nariva swamps where rice flourished. Beyond farming, some Indians became involved in family-based businesses. Hinduism and Islam were practiced in the villages by most people, though some converted to Christianity, especially Presbyterianism, which is viewed in Trinidad as an "Indian church." For all this diversity, the core of East Indian spirituality is Hinduism, especially as disclosed in the notion of leela (also spelled lila), or play.[2]

The entire cosmos is a leela, a dance of energy, a drama staged by Brahman, the Absolute. Leelas are also specific celebrations, the most important in Trinidad being Ramlila, the story of Ram (Rama), the god-warrior-king as told in Valmiki's Sanskrit *Ramayana* and retold in Hindi by the seventeenth-century poet Tulsidas. The celebratory feeling of Ramlila and other Indian festivals was countered by more than a century of severe oppression. During this period, the Indian community was ghettoized, and responded by adopting a siege mentality. The Indian engagement with the Trinidad landscape is awkward: a *kelapani*, the "black water," from India to Trinidad was a one-way trip. Within the Trinidad landscape, Indianness had to be redefined.

The Indian celebration most like carnival is Hosay, derived from Shiite Islam.[3] Celebrated during the first ten days of the Islamic month of Muharram, with processions on the seventh, eighth, and ninth nights and the tenth day, Hosay commemorates the martyrdom of the grandsons of the Prophet Muhammad, the brothers Hassan and Hussein. The former was poisoned and the latter was killed in the seventh-century battle of Kerbala (in modern-day Iraq). In its Trinidad form Hosay is rooted in leela. The martyrdom and particularly the funeral of the brothers are re-enacted. The ritual drama culminates on Ashura, the tenth of Muharram, the day when Hussein was killed. The centerpieces of the performances are the parades through the streets, on three successive nights, of, first, flags, then small tadjahs, then the tadjahs (or Hosays) – massive, beautifully constructed tombs of Hussein which, these days, reach a height now limited to 15 feet (it used to be 25 feet). The tadjahs are carried in the streets the night before Ashura and again on Ashura Day. In years gone by the tadjahs were illuminated by blazing torches, accompanied by armed men engaged in dramatized stickfights, weeping women singing funeral songs, and (as is still current today) the music of *tassa* drums, huge bass drums, and *jahlls* (cymbals).

This Muharram festival, as Hosay was also called, was the major Indian celebration in nineteenth-century Trinidad. The procession took place throughout the center and south of the island in the "sugar belt" and even in St James, from where it entered Port of Spain. Every plantation where the "coolies"[4] worked produced its tadjah, but the center was San Fernando, where over a hundred tadjahs extended for more than a mile. Hosay included Indians who were Hindus as well as Muslims: it was the island's major source of Indian cultural affirmation and pride. It took on proportions of an "Indian Carnival," in which many thousands participated and watched. Today those building tadjahs commit themselves to a period of "clean" living – abstaining from sex and alcohol, following a prescribed diet. On the streets in the nineteenth century people danced, drank, smoked opium and ganja (marijuana), and ingested bhang (marijuana boiled in cow's milk) – as in India itself.

Hosay also broke the ethnic barrier separating the Indian and African communities. There still is significant African involvement in Hosay. Africans have always been able to connect with the vital rhythm of the drums of Hosay. Indeed, there are accounts of tadjahs appearing in carnival itself (see Cowley 1996: 83).

The late nineteenth century was a turbulent time, as the colonial masters tried to suppress local cultural expressions (see Singh 1988). This oppression was at the root of the 1881 Canboulay riots (see Elder and Brereton in this volume). The authorities were particularly concerned about Hosay because it was a source of Indocentric self-affirmation at a time when the "coolies" were resisting plantation conditions and because Hosay was a bridge connecting Indians to Africans which undermined the key colonial policy of isolating the Indians. Additionally, Afro-Creoles resented Indian economic competition which broke the hold of Africans on the labor market. Hence, the question was raised: If canboulay was restricted, why not Hosay?

Thus on 30 October 1884 the police and the military opened fire at close range on the Hosay procession. At least twenty-two people (of whom eighteen had recognizable Hindu names) – and probably many more – died. Well over a hundred were wounded. The "Hosay riots" represent the bloodiest confrontation of its kind in the history of Trinidad. But though initially suppressed, Hosay was accepted by the Victorian British government, which, for the first time, authorized a public gathering place for such a religious observance on the grounds of the Queen's Royal College in Port of Spain. Hosay has today survived in some parts of the south such as Cedros and in St James, a Port of Spain suburb, which became the new centers of the festival.

In Hosay one may see the cultural confluences of Persia, Arabia, India, Africa, and Europe: the fusion of sacred and secular, of funeral and fete.[5] St James itself was to become a major center for a cultural sharing and crossing-over between Indian and African. Both communities struggled against the same Eurocentric hegemony, though in different ways. The Africans were oppressed within the Creole mainstream, while the Indians were alienated from the mainstream. The dominant Creole structure established a relation of contestation between the African and Indian communities even as they both shared the same foundation of "folk culture" which vitally defined the Trinidad landscape. This sharing took place despite the fact that the African community was largely urban and the Indian largely rural.

How is one to articulate the structure of the encounter? The engagement is defined by three simultaneously occurring aspects: assimilation, contestation, and communion. There is assimilation as each community appropriates cultural elements of the other, defining them in terms of its own center; there is contestation as each community establishes itself in defined spaces which the other community also wants to occupy; there is communion as each community participates with the other in a shared cultural space. The best way to get at this sense of shared space is to examine the distinct Indian presence in carnival.

Solo Girdharrie (interview, 1997) has described carnival in San Fernando and central Trinidad in the 1950s:

> In the 1950s, it was a rare thing for anyone from outside San Fernando to go to the city. You had to go by cart and that took a long time. People from central and south Trinidad would go to San Fernando maybe twice a year. At carnival, they came to have a meal in a "cook shop," then go to the cinema to see an Indian movie, and finally to watch some mas. Performers gathered behind the library near the big salmon tree. From there minstrels emerged, musicians sat on the steps of the library and played the harmonium and dholak, and there was singing and dancing by a male dancer in a very dressy gown. One was to dress up like colonial officers – khaki pants, cork hat, and white shirt – and pretend to be measuring or surveying land. This came from the time when indentured servants, having decided to stay in the country after their contracts ended, were allocated plots of land by the colonial authorities.

Costumes in the primarily Indian villages were very basic: Ravi Ji describes them as being of the old mas type: "Indians played in steelbands and, before steelbands, Indians beat biscuit tins with two sticks as if they were tassa drums" (Interview, 1997). The Jab Jabs, with their fancy clothes, whips, and bells, had a particular Indian involvement – the Indians would have understood the bells as *gunghroos* (shunghroos), bells Indian dancers attach to their ankles. Jab Jabs were indeed referred to as "coolie devils" (Crowley 1956: 74). Indians were attracted to the Devils because they evoke images from Indian mythology. Indians also played Red or Wild Indian (Amerindian), with a creative "confusion" both by Indians and Afro-Creoles of the very word "Indian."[6]

Carnival in the villages involved music, dancing, and the little skits, leelas. This kind of celebration forms the basis for today's carnivals in central Trinidad in towns such as Chaguanas, Couva, and Carapichaima where traditional characters – Jab Jab, Jab Molassie, Blue Devils, Midnight Robbers, Sailors, Wild/Red Indians, "Arabian" dancers, Moko Jumbies, Bats, and Burroquites – come out on carnival Monday. There is a distinct Indian version of Burroquite taken from the leela of the Hindu goddess Durga and played in the villages, referred to as the *harichand* dance. The mas is called Sumari:

> The costume consists of an ornately decorated bamboo frame in the shape of a horse with a hole in the "horse's" back. The masquerader enters this hole and is attached to the frame by a series of straps. He holds the reins of the "horse" and dances. He moves the "horse" forward and backward to give the illusion of riding on horseback. Drums and singing in Hindi usually accompany the dancing.
>
> (J. Singh 1997: 18)

We are at this point in a position to make some preliminary reflections on the Indian presence and influence on the three key components of carnival: steelband, mas, and calypso. In steelband there has been, and continues to be, a very strong Indian presence, particularly around San Fernando. The most famous name here is Bobby Mohammed, who played the cowbell,[7] his name immortalized in David Rudder's calypso "The Engine Room." However, by far the most celebrated Indo-Trinidadian is the legendary Jit Samaroo, arranger of the Renegades, one of the oldest steelbands. Jit, the most successful Panorama arranger in the history of the competition, is closely associated with the music of Kitchener, the calypsonian. Jit also leads his own very successful family pan ensemble, the Samaroo Jets. Perhaps even more fundamental than the outstanding Indian arrangers and performers is the influence of tassa drums on the very creation of pan. Solo Girdharrie intimates this connection in his account of San Fernando (Interview, 1997). A case has been made that tassa also influenced the development of pan in Port of Spain.

In mas the Jab Jab with its bright colors and mirrors and glitter is significantly rooted in an Indian aesthetic. Mirrors and glitter are also prominent in such characters as the Fancy Sailor, Midnight Robber, and Neg Jardin. The Indian aesthetic is very strong in mas, as, for instance, in the color schemes of Peter Minshall's *River* (1983), *Carnival Is Colour* (1987), and *Tantana* (1991). Following the lead of Carlisle Chang, designer for Lee Huang in the late 1960s, Minshall introduced the tassa into Port of Spain mas in the 1980s. In his works, Minshall weaves together the African, Indian, and European. From 1995 to 1997, Minshall's music was mixed by Indo-Trinidadian Anil Harditsingh. Indians have also been band leaders. Ivan Kallicharan was for years the leading mas man in San Fernando, and Raul Garib was prominent in Port of Spain. Garib brought his band to Tobago in 1997.

Formal Indian involvement in calypso can be traced back at least to the 1920s (Constance, interview, 1997). In the 1970s and 1980s, Indian calypsonians included

Shah (who raised issues of ethnic identity), Raja, and Hindu Prince. While the point of departure for calypso is African, it engages the entire society, including Indians. There are community calypso competitions in Indian areas. But of more fundamental significance is the Indian influence since the 1970s on the form of calypso itself. Lord Shorty (now Ras Shorty I, one of the key architects of soca) lived many of his formative years in an Indian community. Shorty infused Indian musical patterns into such soca songs as "Indrani" and "Om Shanti." Another key moment surrounded the controversial calypso by the Mighty Sparrow, "Maharajin" (1982). The word refers to a Brahmin's wife, though this meaning does not carry into the song, where it refers to any Indian woman. The song is constructed from Indian melodic patterns. In the song, Sparrow confesses his love for an Indian woman, the Maharajin. This calypso represents a desire by the Afro-Creole to appropriate the Indian musicality. But it can allow itself to do so only through the Trinidadian tradition of humor known as "fatigue" and "stereotyping." Hence, "Maharajin" simultaneously pokes fun at and expresses appreciation for Indian music. This process must not be understood only as the use of Indian music by Africans, which of course is taking place, but also as further establishment of the Indian presence in carnival. This process reached a climax with Indo-Trinidadians such as the female Drupatee Ramgoonai in the late 1980s and Rikki Jai in the 1990s and 2000s competing as calypsonians in carnival.

Carnival is an arena of cultural affirmation – different for Indians and Africans. Africans experienced oppression while Indians experienced alienation, experiences which, within the Creole framework, created contestation between these two groups. By putting each community in its "place," the dominant colonial authorities suppressed this contestation. After independence, the oil boom of the mid-1970s created an influx of wealth. The centrality of the folk-community structure was undermined as Trinidad society came to be defined by a new Americanized middle-class culture, representing a new stage of Eurocentric hegemony. The various ethnic centers – Indian, African, European – are no longer held each in its own place. These centers now contest the space which is the society's mainstream.

Today three "tribes" (a term used in Trinidad) are now clearly demarcated. The first is the Eurocentric elite, the core of whom are the "local whites" (often referred to as the French Creoles but who are actually by now racially mixed, hence the term "neo-Europeans"); the neo-Europeans are culturally middle-class. The second tribe is the Indian community with its center moving away from alienation and into the mainstream where the Indians are challenging Eurocentric hegemony. A critical point in this emergence was the election in 1995 of an "Indian" government led by Prime Minister Basdeo Panday. This radical shift has implications for the carnival. The third tribe remains the Afro-descended Trinidadians.

The older community structures must now be understood in terms of a radical new frame of reference. Previously, Indian participation in carnival took place within the Creole framework. Indians participated but were alienated from the carnival mainstream itself. Currently, Indian participation expresses the very center of this community, claiming its space in the post-Creole mainstream. In this context, the town of Carapichaima celebrated fifty years of formally staging carnival in 1997 with a large celebration attended by Prime Minster Panday. A crowd of about twenty thousand gathered to listen to speeches and enjoy the trademark traditional characters, calypso and steelband contests, and a mas of thirty bands who reached Carapichaima on carnival Monday from around the island. (Carapichaima Carnival is on Monday only, leaving the bands free to go to the "big show" in Port of Spain on Tuesday.) In Carapichaima, in the midst of the traditions one associates with Creole carnival, there is a distinct Indian aesthetic in the dancers, the Sumaris, and other performers, some of whom reappeared for the Energy and Sugar Festival in Couva in June 1997. Also, recently, there has been a major Indian participation "on the road" at carnival time. A number of young Indo-Trinidadians play mas in one of the neo-European bands, Poison. Indians are claiming carnival space as Indians.

The flagship of this Indocentric presence and contestation for space is chutney, which originated as a distinct form in the 1970s and bloomed in the 1980s. Chutney is the confluence of the folk-songs of women (particularly those associated with the matikhor and cooking nights of the Hindu wedding), the raw celebratory music of the menfolk, Hindu religious music, and Indian film songs. The pivotal erotic energy is that of the female matikhor, where, for women, dancing onstage, both planned and spontaneous, is essential. In chutney, "grassroots women" (a term which in local parlance refers to the poorer classes) claim their space, even as men and women spectators dance and wine. Traditional instruments have given way to electronic keyboards and guitars. Chutney shows occur throughout the year. It is in this context that Drupatee Ramgoonai's successful break into the calypso arena in the 1988 season must be understood. She was followed by Rikki Jai – calypso and chutney intersecting. Chutney now struggles with calypso for dominance. Drupatee symbolizes this contest for control of the carnival mainstream by Indians.

The move of chutney into calypso space climaxed in 1996 when Indo-Trinidadian Sonny Mann's chutney "Lotay La" was a major hit during the carnival season. However, while "Lotay La" was a hit with non-Indians, ethnic tension was not far beneath the surface. In this context, and in retrospect, there was an unsurprising backlash in the pelting of Sonny Mann at the Soca Monarch final in 1996.[8]

This incident, which arose over a controversy surrounding Mann's qualifications to be in the Calypso Monarch finals, may be understood as an Afro-Trinidadian reaction to the emergence of Indians. Mann's near-disqualification rested not on his abilities as a singer but on the fact that his calypso had been written and recorded before the previous Ash Wednesday. Nevertheless, the Indo-Trinidad community reacted fiercely to his initial disqualification, which was rescinded before the final competition on the technicality that a new version of his calypso had been recorded within the permitted time frame, i.e. after the previous Ash Wednesday. This pattern of racial divisiveness in calypsos was first evidenced in the calypsos of the late 1980s, grew more intense after the elections of 1995, and reached highly controversial and possibly explosive proportions after the 1997 carnival, with the Prime Minister threatening to censor calypsos if they are deemed to be racially offensive. While many calypsonians have been involved in this process, the major ones are Cro Cro, Sugar Aloes, and, in 1997, Watchman, who sang a calypso that was a blatant attack on Prime Minister Panday. In this light, the "Indian" Prime Minister threatened to take measures against the "African" calypsonians. The proposed measures involve the withdrawing of state funding for calypso shows.

Secondly, there is the "Jahaaji Bhai" controversy. In 1996, Afro-Trinidadian Brother Marvin sang the calypso "Jahaaji Bhai" on the 150th anniversary of the Indian arrival, which was celebrated the previous year. "Jahaaji Bhai" is about the bond between African and Indian. The phrase itself, as the calypso says, originally refers to the "brotherhood of the boat" established between indentured immigrants who traveled together; "Jahaaji Bhai," rich with Indian musical patterns, was the outstanding calypso of 1996. It was strongly endorsed, indeed taken over, by the Indian community. Nevertheless, there was an objection raised in some Afro-Trinidadian quarters. In the 1997 season several calypsonians (Marvin himself counted nine) attacked the song. The reason given for the reaction was an objection to one line in the calypso which was considered offensive. While there may well be some legitimacy to the charge, it would appear that the real concern runs deeper. There is a perception that the Indian presence is being glorified at the expense of the African. By 1997 the soca-chutney space had "parallel mainstreams" – the African and the Indian, each having its own artists, its own shows, and its own radio stations.

The designations "chutney soca" and "soca chutney" are employed to denote a fusion of the artforms, though such fusion has not essentially taken place. It may be said that "chutney soca" refers to soca which has assimilated patterns from chutney. "Soca chutney" refers to chutney which has done likewise in regard to soca. Judging from the 1997 season and the general trend in the society, the Afrocentric soca space is not particularly open to such experimentation – while in the chutney space, it is the "Indian" soca chutney that will predominate; it is this which has more of a future, at least in the short run.

In Afrocentric soca there was no chutney or Indian-oriented song in 1997. Contrast this with "Lotay La," "Jahaaji Bhai," and even Chris Garcia's very popular "Chutney Bacchanal" of the previous season. Some artists effectively function in both mainstreams, but to a large extent they allocate different songs to each. In this regard, the most significant was the very successful soca singer Crazy (of part-Chinese ancestry), who fully embraced the challenge and sang two songs which may fairly be described as "raw" chutney. In terms of participation, soca, being more directly descended from the old Creole culture, is ethnically more diverse, though often overwhelmingly Afro-Trinidadian. However, there are as well neo-European and even Indian-dominated soca fetes. On the other hand, chutney shows are musically more assimilative – an indication of the Indian community's vitality in this period of its expansion. It is also manifest in the proliferation of Indian radio stations, which have further sustained the chutney space.

Since the 1980s there has been a Hindu renaissance, a resurgence of Hinduism, marked also by some Hindu fundamentalism. Take, for example, the Divali celebration in the Hindu month of Kartik (October or November, according to a seasonal lunar calendar) which has taken on truly national proportions. "Divali Nagar" is an open "village," running for a week before Divali, full of religious and commercial booths and cultural presentations – storytelling, skits, *bhajans* (Hindu hymns), devotions. From the large stage come musical shows that are broadcast over the radio. Food and drink are in abundance, but no alcohol or meat. Estimates have put annual attendance in the hundreds of thousands.

The Hindu renaissance has also provided the basis for the successful 150th Indian Arrival Day celebrations and its declaration as a public holiday. Much of

Arrival Day took place "on the road." The renaissance has also led to the Phagwa festival, which includes the pichakaaree competition. The pichakaaree is an Indian song sung mostly in English. It utilizes traditional instruments and music as well as some film and Indian pop tunes. What is most significant about the Phagwa pichakaaree is that it deals with social issues confronting the Indo-Trinidadian community. Pichakaaree parallels Afro-Trinidadian "social commentary" calypso. Mukesh Baburam is an exponent of a strand of pichakaaree which may be called "Indocentric calypso." Baburam challenges Cro Cro and Sugar Aloes.

Pichakaaree is broadcast on radio and television. Though funding the pichakaaree competition is always an uphill struggle, the finals have in recent years drawn large and enthusiastic crowds. I predict that in time this or its equivalent will become more central. What is evident is that the very definition of what constitutes "carnival space" is being radically redefined by the Indian entry into the Trinidad mainstream. The question is whether such contestation will lead to increasing fragmentation and the disintegration of Trinidadian society or whether there is a possibility of unity.[9]

Carnival is not only a reflection of Trinidadian society, it is the essence of the society. The "road" is the gathering, the concentration, the intense focus of the earth. It is a place of dwelling and journeying, a space of play and struggle. It is here that the energies of our people are focused. However, carnival does not disclose abstract "cultural expressions" or "artifacts." The space is engaged by living communities, who assimilate, contest, and participate. It is out of this that real communion emerges.

When we speak of Indian, African, and European groups, we do not mean that they are any less Trinidadian. What are disclosed are phenomenologically distinct ethnic centers, living communities constituted by ancestral patterns which in terms of the present global frame of reference are recognized as being "Indian," "African," and "European." However, these centers are all "Trinidadian." The communities are grounded in the same earth, they play on the same road where they engage each other. What is often overlooked is that the Indian community has long been a key "audience" for carnival (Ravi Ji, interview, 1997). At present, Indians are claiming their rightful place in the "center." This raises the question of ethnic fragmentation. The Afro-Creole celebration of life bore witness to the possibility of unity. But the "Creole structure" carried with it the inherent violence of oppression for the African and alienation for the Indian. With the collapse of the hegemony, ethnic contest began in earnest. Contestation need not lead to disintegration; such chaos may be both violent and creative, yielding new possibility. To Hindus, chaos really means transformation and regeneration. Such is the nature of leela. Is this not the essence of carnival?

NOTES

This chapter is reprinted from Milla Cozart Riggio (ed.), *The Drama Review*, 42 (3): 203–12 (1998), Cambridge, MA: MIT Press.

1   The system was not as complex as in India. The most significant caste designation was *Brahmin* (Brahman). But in Trinidad this was often acquired during or after the boat trip.

2   [Editor's note]. There is also in Trinidad a vibrant Indian-Trinidad muslim community.

3   Also known as Hosein, the festival is named after the brother martyred on the plain of Karbala

on Ashura. The account given here of the festival is based on my own experience and written sources. It should be noted that there must have been variations over time and location. This account is not presented as definitive; it is suggestive only of certain traditions and trends in Hosay.

4   At the time "coolie" was a term for an Asiatic laborer, including the Indian. It is today a derogatory ethnic term, roughly equivalent to "nigger."

5   Those who create Hosay as a sacred religious, funereal re-enactment themselves resist the idea of this event as having any link to the "fete," though they of course acknowledge the ribaldry among the gathered crowds on the street. This is especially true in St James, where the Hosay camps are controlled primarily by Muslims. In the southern fishing village of Cedros, however, where Hosay is the biggest celebration of the year, celebrants themselves on Ashura day – after they have broken their strict fasting the night before – tend to be more carnivalesque in their own exuberance, sometimes drinking beer as they process, with a tendency to jump up and wave to the beating of the tassa drums. This adds a note of gaiety and some might claim profanity to Ashura day in the south. Moreover, orthodox Muslims throughout the island have at best an ambivalent relationship to Hosay. Many reject it, though not all. The prayers in both St James and Cedros (where it is celebrated primarily by Hindus and some Christians) are fervent, and the fasting strict. [Editor's note.]

6   An Indian form of stickfighting was called *gadka* (or *gatka*), with shield and drumming. According to Ravi Ji, the Indian attraction to Native American (AmeriIndian) rituals and customs extends beyond carnival masquerading and even beyond Trinidad, back to India. There is much to be studied here. [Editor's note: Interview, 2004].

7   A cowbell is a percussion instrument in the rhythm section, or engine room, of a steelband. The song is found on David Rudder's album *Haiti* (1988).

8   The pelting of calypsonians with toilet paper and bottles is by no means unknown. The reasons behind this particular incident were complex, but ethnic considerations were a factor.

9   Since this chapter was first published in 1998, the Hindu festivals have increased both in number and in intensity under the direction of Pundit Ravi Ji, with a commemoration of Holika Dahan being added to Phagwa in the Spring and Ganga Dhaara (or the River festival) celebrated in June. Plans exist to further develop Ramlila, already arguably the most extensive celebration of this Fall festival outside India itself. [Editor's note.]

6

CHINESE IN TRINIDAD CARNIVAL

Carlisle Chang

Ten years after the British took over the island of Trinidad, the first British census of 1808 records the presence of twenty-two Chinese among a mixed population of English, Spanish, French, German, and Corsican whites, Amerindians, mainly French-speaking free coloureds, and enslaved Africans. The Chinese were probably part of a British experiment to find a source of free labor that could replace the uneconomical slave system. The Chinese experiment was unsuccessful; beginning in 1845, it was replaced with indentured labor from India.

Chinese immigrants came to the island after an often hazardous six-month voyage from the province of Canton. The men were not usually accompanied by their womenfolk; interracial marriages required registration and religious conversions for the Chinese. Over the years, ignorance of the Chinese custom of stating the clan or family name first has produced a number of pseudo-Chinese (or newly created Chinese) family names. Thus, a Mr Chin Lo-sin could become Mr Chin, Mr Chin-sing, Assing, or Alowsing. Moreover, the converted Chinese spouse often assumed the name of the parish priest or the sponsor at his baptism, a practice resulting in Chinese families named Johnson, Richards, Isaac, and Scott. With counterparts throughout the southern Caribbean, these anomalies must be noted in any study of Chinese involvement in the social development of Trinidad, in which carnival forms a unique cultural expression.

The Chinese soon became known not only as good providers in a marriage partnership but also as possessors of acute business acumen. Before long they controlled a network of variety shops throughout the island. Their entrepreneurial skills made them one of the most upwardly mobile social groups in the country.

The earliest evidence of Chinese participation in the street carnival – from 1927 – appears to point to the brothers Christopher: Choy-yin, Chin-yu, and Con-chin (the youngest), also known as "Bolo." These were the children of a very successful merchant from Canton and a Venezuelan mother. The family lived at 7 Nelson Street, less than a hundred yards from the Roman Catholic Cathedral and the splendid twelve-block esplanade then known as Marine Square. Their home was a large two-storeyed building with a Spanish-style courtyard. The living quarters

Fig. 6.1 Carlisle Chang at work in his living room in Woodbrook, a suburb of Port of Spain, Trinidad. Photograph by Jeffrey Chock.

were above with a wide veranda overhanging the sidewalk; on the ground floor the family had a musical-instruments business. Later they would import gramophone records and eventually make their own.

All the children were taught music, as befitted a well-established middle-class family, studying the four-stringed cuatro from Venezuela, the Spanish guitar, and all the instruments of the *'pagnol parandero* orchestras. But they were becoming increasingly interested in the latest jazz instruments from America – clarinet, saxophone, banjo, and trombone.

The Christophers lived on the east side of Port of Spain's business district; farther east, beyond the dry river, in the hills of John-John, Laventille, and Belmont, were the shanties and cottages of the working class whence nightly sounded the drums of Orisha and the Rada people. From these hills at carnival time the traditional mummers descended into the city – Moko Jumbies on stilts, Warrahouns speaking Amerindian tongues, Pierrot Grenade in rags, Jab Jabs with whips, Jab-Molassi painted blue – moving to the beat of African drums or tambour-bamboo.

The Christophers were a different breed. Theirs was the world of resurgence following World War I. Oil had been discovered as early as 1857, but, following the Great War, a major influx of investment in petroleum drilling came from the United States, Britain, the Netherlands, and Switzerland. The country could boast of water piped to every district, free health care and education, a network of asphalted or graveled roads, and a grand new railway terminus as fine as the governor's mansion. In roared the 1920s with the latest products and influences from Europe and America. It was the era of the Charleston, one-piece bathing costumes, flappers, movie theatres, visits by Lindberg and the Graf Zeppelin, and new air connections to Miami to begin by the 1940s.

The Christophers' trading emporium and their interest in music brought the family directly into the world of the street carnival. In those days bands of musicians roamed the streets of the city nightly, dancing and visiting friends in the Italian tradition (which arrived in Trinidad via Corsican immigrants). Accompanied by costumed revelers, everyone wore masks of papier-mâché or molded wire, well-covered to ensure anonymity. This enabled the women to join in the revelry without being recognized and branded as "immoral." The season extended from January 1 to jour ouvert (jouvay), the dawn of the last Monday before Lent when all forms of satirical costumes or old clothing are worn. This was followed later by more sumptuous costumes culminating at midnight on Tuesday.

Like many other established families that subscribed to this Creole custom, the Christophers and their musical friends inevitably were drawn into the main costume parade. They began organizing bands, as they were called, in 1927 and continued annually until 1939 when another world war began to loom. As Bolo tells it, the brothers played "every type of costume imaginable" reflecting the expanding world of the 1920s and 1930s – Arabs of the desert, Mexicans of the haciendas, Gauchos of the pampas, French Pierrots, Spanish Toreadors and Caribbean Pirates – all lavishly decorated with the latest haberdashery from Paris, the newest rayon satins and cotton velvets from London, wire masks from Germany, and ostrich and swans' down, spangles, and braid from everywhere else (Christopher, interview, 1997).

The brothers decided to retire after twelve years, but another Chinese stepped into the breech, a young salesman named Manzie Lai, the son of a Cantonese artist and his Venezuelan wife. Drawing his main support from members of the Chinese community, Manzie first appeared on the scene with the masquerade band entitled *The Moors* in 1939 and followed with the *Knights of the Round Table* the next year. But the war in Europe was now a reality and would be followed shortly by the Pacific war. Carnival was halted for the duration, and the wearing of face masks or any garment too closely resembling military uniform was forbidden.

Manzie reappeared in 1946 with *Apaches*, and the following year he produced *Daniel Boone*, evidence of the increased influence on carnival of American films and the large US naval and army bases set up under the US Lend-Lease Agreement with Britain. Manzie's final carnival appearance was with *Leopard Men* – one of the largest groups of the day, its costumes simple, inexpensive, and lighter, suited to the interests of a comic-book generation. Since VE Day, the wearing of masks had been abandoned and the bands showed an increasing female participation which would continue annually up to the present.

Manzie Lai was replaced by Lyle Ackrill, a manufacturer's representative who created bands from 1951 to 1954. His major bands were *Ghenghis Khan* and *The Greatest Show on Earth*. About this time Dr Robert Ammon, a dentist, entered the competition arena. He developed several presentations reflecting his wide-ranging interests and an intellectual turn of mind, but also the growing affluence of Port of Spain. *Gods of Olympus* appeared in 1954, the first time that hand-tooled metal breastplates were worn. These were done in aluminum, copper repoussé, and gold plate, and were executed by the celebrated silversmith Ken Morris. Ammon created several notable bands – *Richard II* (1955); *La Fiesta Brava* (1956), a tribute to the famous Spanish bullfighter Manolete, in which each costume was individually decorated; *Atlantis* (1958); *Conquistadors* (1959); and *China in Peace and War* (1960). His triumph was the *Flagwavers of Sienna* (1962), introducing flags as an effective hand prop.

Up to the mid-1950s the street carnival parade still reflected the ideas and aspirations of the predominant Afro-Trinidadian groups. Costumes tended to be "traditional" or folkloric, such as Wild Indians, Jab Jabs (devils), Fancy Clowns with wired collars, etc.; sailors of various types and uniformed groups depicting World War II Pacific theatre operations copied from American movies and produced by the burgeoning steelbands; African tribal themes, commonly referred to as Ju Ju Warriors; and Old Testament biblical stories of Assyrians, Egyptians, and Philistines, reflecting the extensive missionary work of the African Methodist church among the African-derived working class.

Ammon's organization represented the broader interracial mix of the younger professional, business-oriented, or gainfully employed and educated middle class. By the time he withdrew from active production, several spinoff groups were emerging under non-Chinese leadership: Harold Saldenah out of Lai, who made excellent use of Ken Morris's metal skills in a series based on Roman history; and Edmond Hart, a customs broker, out of Ammon. Hart developed his band into a family business which continues today as Hart's New Generation, now several thousand strong and already parlayed into two separate groups for more effective control.

By the 1960s the entire carnival celebration began to come under greater governmental regulation. A new Carnival Development Committee was established to manage the undertaking – to advise on policy, to codify rules and regulations, and to generally promote carnival as both a national event and a tourism investment. The organization of individual bands became more complicated and expensive, and keen rivalries grew for the prestigious awards and money prizes.

In 1963, Archie Yee-Foon, a young commercial artist, won the first Band of the Year award for his production *The Field of the Cloth of Gold*. It recreated the meeting between Henry VIII of England and Francis I of France, which was celebrated for its opulent display. That was Archie's only contribution to carnival history. Participation in the now government-regulated competitions with the main venue at the Queen's Park Race Course (i.e. Queen's Park Savannah) was becoming more expensive to produce and more complicated to manage. Volunteer helpers were being replaced by hired labor, orchestras grew larger and pricier as band membership increased, and making costumes for fun was quickly becoming obsolete. Carnival was now a critical business investment demanding entrepreneurial skills.

Thus it was that Stephen and Elsie Lee Heung, after several years of organizing old mas bands – a particular style of satirical performance presented at private clubs – decided to enter the larger arena of the Monday and Tuesday parades. I was invited to create their first presentation in 1964. *Japan, Land of the Kabuki* was a small group but it earned the fourth prize and high praise for elaborately embroidered costumes, traditional *kabuki* theatre characters, and an innovative presentation in mime. Thereafter my association with the Lee Heungs lasted eleven years until we parted company after carnival in 1975. In that time I was able to introduce more esoteric concepts and new innovations into the street parade.

Themes ranged from *Crete* (1966), to *Yucatan* (1971), and *East of Java* (1973). *Les Fêtes Galantes de Versailles* suggested a correlation between the entertainments at the French court of Louis XIV and XV and the structure of bands in the Trinidad Carnival. There was make-believe and childlike fantasy in the *1001 Nights* (1969) and *Russian Fairy Tales* (1972). *Primeval* (1968) postulated the notion of the universality of tribal beliefs, while *Terra Firma* (1974) explored the molecular structure of matter. *Conquest of Space* (1970) saluted the US space program and *We Kinda People* expressed the vernacular paraphase of our national motto, "All ah we is one!" The band won the Band of the Year title three times, produced four Queens of Carnival and two Kings, and I won the Designer's Prize several times. We were always ranked among the first three prizes and were depicted on at least three national postage stamps.

Annually, however, surprise elements were injected into our presentations. We are regarded as having developed hand props into a fine art. We first introduced Chinese drums in *China: The Forbidden City* (1967) and East Indian tassa drummers every year thereafter, and that has become almost universal among large bands. In *Versailles* I transposed the Burroquite hobbyhorse costume into caparisoned horses for the *Horse Ballet of Louis XIV*, and traditional Bat costumes became pterodactyls in *Primeval*. We tried everything and anything to gain a competitive edge, from battery-powered gears in the *Magic Horse (1001 Nights)* to pinwheels in *Yucatan*.

Stephen Lee Heung was the first president of the Carnival Bands Association, formed to ensure representation for costume bands on the controlling Carnival Development Committee. As bands were becoming larger and more expensive, requiring upwards of a half-million dollars to underwrite, there were few new organizers with the capital or the production capabilities required. Lee Heung was among the top three producers whose works were annually showcased in Madison Square Garden, New York, during the late 1960s and early 1970s in shows that paved the way for the establishment of the present Labor Day Parade in Brooklyn.

In 1989, as the Lee Heung star faded, another Chinese producer, Richard Afong, broke away from his apprenticeship in Edmond Hart's band to form a partnership under the name Savage. This was the first of the truly large bands, growing larger each year with the inflow of new teenagers. Afong again separated and formed Barbarossa in 1992. He was an immediate success and produced *Cipango* (1993), *Picasso* (1994), *East of Sumatra* (1995), *Comanchero* (1996), *Sarragossa* (1997), *Botay* (1998), *Jewels of the Nile* (1999), *Xtassy* (2000), *Arena* (2001), and *Untamed* (2002). Another Chinese of mixed ancestry, Afong rehabilitated the almost-defunct Carnival Bands Association, presiding as president from the inception of Barbarossa to the present. Afong has shown astute managerial skills and an unusual turn of mind. He produced the first international King and Queen of Carnival show (in the Fall of 1994) and has developed the organization into a powerful bargaining group, on a par with the much older calypsonian and steelband organizations.

The third and fourth generations of Chinese, more fully integrated into the festival, have found other ways to participate. Dr John D'Arcy Lee, for instance, brought out a jouvay band of Blue Devils – with some interruption – for more than a decade (resuming this band in 1995 after a hiatus and ending in 2000). There have also been tentative attempts to enter the world of calypso, the chief exponents being Rex West (a medical doctor) and Chinese Laundry, already a DJ popular with the young. In addition, there has been steelband sponsorship, such as the Lee Chong Serenaders of San Fernando. A Chinese-Jamaican bandleader, Byron Lee, who regularly plays for one of the biggest and best masquerade bands in Trinidad, has been an instrumental factor in developing carnival in Jamaica. It is too early to surmise the degree to which the Chinese will participate in the performance aspects of carnival because of their characteristic reticence, but one will readily find them wherever they can express their creative and organizational skills. The Chinese have manifested their presence in unexpected places. They will continue to do so as Trinidad and Tobago Carnival evolves.

This chapter is reprinted from Milla Cozart Riggio (ed.), *The Drama Review*, 42 (3): 213–19 (1998), Cambridge, MA: MIT Press.

Part II

PLAYIN' YUHSELF – MASKING THE OTHER

Tradition and change in carnival masquerades

7

"PLAY MAS" – PLAY ME, PLAY WE
Introduction to Part II

Milla Cozart Riggio

"You feel I should play a princess or a slave girl?"
He smiled. "You is a princess already," he said, "Play a slave girl."
Earl Lovelace, *The Dragon Can't Dance*

The apt description of the typical Caribbean person is that he/she is part-African, part-European, part-Asian, part-Native-American but totally Caribbean. To perceive this is to understand the creative diversity which is at once cause and occasion, result and defining point of Caribbean cultural life.
Rex Nettleford, *Texture and Diversity: The Cultural Life of the Caribbean*

Contemporary Trinidad Carnival has three major divisions: pan, calypso, and masquerading – collectively, the music and the masks of carnival. Separating carnival masquerades from carnival music belies the reality of the event itself. But in an island in which "playing mas"[1] has for many come to define a way of life, where to "play your mas" can mean to "do your thing," carnival masking has a mystique that both manifests and calls into question varying senses of identity and processes of cultural memory. Ultimately, the assimilation that is the lifeblood of the Caribbean – "part-African, part-European, part-Asian, part-Native-American but totally Caribbean" – is interwoven into the process through which the carnival masquerades of the "hoi polloi" have become the identifying signifier of a nation, transforming carnival into something that is neither European nor African nor Asian, but a unique Trinidadian spectacle newly created in this so-called "new world."[2]

IDENTITY AND DISGUISE

In Trinidad, as in any of the plantation cultures developed by enforced labor to supply leisured foodstuffs – sugar, rum, coffee, cocoa – to the ironically designated "mother" countries of Europe, identity and disguise often merge. Subjugated peoples living under laws they do not make themselves tend to develop a Janus-like double face, looking outward with impassive expressions, often accompanied by a deceptive "yes massa" cooperativeness, while their vital lives are turned inward, to their own enclosed community. The face that points outward becomes a mask, disguising and hiding the personality beneath. In their own space – their homes or the yards or huts they inhabit – the people free up, manifesting independence of spirit, pride, and a hard-won distrust of outsiders. Masking yourself and playing the "other" that one is expected to be becomes a daily survival mechanism: be a "princess"; play a "slave girl."

The issue, of course, is not so simple. How does one sustain a sense of self when all the public measures of beauty, intelligence, strength, and wisdom work against you? How to keep the physical chains from becoming "mind forg'd manacles" that cripple the spirit and destroy the soul (quotation from William Blake, "London")? How to be "enslaved" without becoming a "slave"? One solution is to disguise forbidden customs or religions, hiding outlawed traditions behind allowed rituals. Africans transplanted to the Americas, for instance, often subsumed their some-times diverse African religious systems under the Yoruba Orisha banner, first by identifying their own deities with the Yoruba Orishas and then masking the Orishas (or gods) in the acceptable figures of Catholic saints, such as St Michael, John the Baptist, St Barbara or others. Cultural and religious rituals thus transplanted do not remain the same. They are inevitably altered by collisions with other traditions. Thus, no matter how strongly he continues to wield his African ax, the Shango that peers through the eyes of John the Baptist on a Caribbean plantation is not pre-cisely the figure he would have been in a Nigerian tribal setting.[3] Similarly, the "princess" who in her daily life "plays" a "slave girl" cannot so easily separate the self from the mask.

Such syncretism works both ways. If the African Orishas are altered by the Catholic masks they are made to wear, they also leave their own imprint. This is true throughout the Caribbean. The particular Trinidad story is even more com-plex. Despite the horrors of genocide and enslavement that remain the foundation stones of Trinidad cultural history, there was never a simple opposition between a hegemonic authority and an oppressed people. Ruling elites (British and French Creole, with a strong Spanish residue) conflicted over religion, language, and con-cepts of power, each with its own Afro-Creole underclass or, in the case of English-speaking Barbadians, sometimes middle class; a population of often well-educated, sometimes wealthy "free persons of color" had its privileges restricted; African Creoles owned slaves; Chinese indentured laborers, Germans and other Europeans, and many more filled in a social picture further complicated by a continuous process of interracial mating and creolized miscegenation.

In this situation, carnival – with its "inherent capacity to appropriate spaces and transgress boundaries in order to manifest and celebrate aspects of human com-munity" (see Riggio 2003) – emerged as the festive arena in which classes, races, and finally genders and even religions would most naturally mix with, resist, and finally accommodate each other. In a culture of multiple identities, to "play yuhself," as the carnival cliché suggests, may be best achieved in fantasies of the so-called "other." This reality complicates our understanding of carnival masking in a situation in which "dressing up" and "dressing down" in the carnival season mean more than temporary release or momentary social inversion.

MIXING AND MASKING

Often histories of carnival masking in Trinidad are reduced to questions of origins: What is African? What is European? Which came first? Which is most basic? Most dominant? This debate may be a necessary corollary to reclaiming cultural space denied to a subjugated people. But it also tears at the fabric of a festival in which the individual threads are indistinguishable parts of a whole cultural tapestry. Certainly, Africans brought with them basic festive customs still evident in today's carnival – not the least of which is the habit of "playing royal," of crowning festive Kings and Queens for their beauty rather than their grotesque comedic functions. African concepts of masking are abundantly reflected in carnival, just as the history of resistance and rebellion is encoded in the evolution of canboulay, the territorial street bands of stickfighters that collectively produced the pre-dawn rituals of jouvay, and many of the traditional characters of carnival. But in each of these cases – as in the influx of Chinese, Indo-Trinidadian, and many other cultural influences – the product is finally a uniquely Caribbean hybrid.

Equally as important as the threads of origin are the parallels between different masking traditions: between the European hobbyhorse, the Indian Soumarie, and the Trinidadian Burroquite; the African martial game of stickfighting and European fencing; African Moko Jumbies and European stilt walkers. Just as the character of Catholic saints made it easy for Yoruba Orishas to take refuge behind Catholic masks, so too these parallels facilitated the creation of carnival as a Trinidadian phenomenon, merging and mixing many traditions.

When and how this merger first began is impossible to say. As early as 1827 – a full decade before emancipation – the "high and the low, rich and poor, learned and unlearned Catholics of Trinidad" are described by a visiting British officer as "masking" for carnival in a display of gaiety and transformation on the streets of Port of Spain compared to which "Ovid's Metamorphoses were nothing" (Bayley 1833: 214). Do the "low," the "poor," and the "unlearned" include Africans? It is not clear. But Mrs Carmichael, a British matron newly arrived from St Vincent with her husband, describes a Christmas spent partly with slaves, first attending a dance held in the slave quarters, characterized by its decorum as well as the elegant sense of clothing styles, and then welcoming the enslaved Africans outside the big house the following morning in a celebration of the season, to which the slaves brought "good wishes for a good crop and good sugar" – in a show of solidarity or hiding behind a festive mask (Carmichael 1833: 288–97, quoted in Cowley 1996: 17). Who is to say? The significant point is the early evidence of festive intermingling. Christmas was, of course, a time of gift-giving when the rules of the plantation would be somewhat more lax. But one cannot help wondering what better documentation might also reveal about interactive patterns of celebration extending into the carnival season. Even in this case, the Africans were invited to return on New Year's Day (Carmichael 1833: 288–97, quoted in Cowley 1996: 17).[4]

We do not know when European and African masking traditions began to impact each other directly. What we do know – and what continues to be true today – is that costume styles were less codified than we often imagine. Today we think of the stickfighters and the Neg Jardins (field Negroes) as separate carnival characters, with the latter often described as a costume favored by French Creole planters, in a display of carnival inversion. But the costume was also favored by Afro-Trinidadians. Stickfighting bands were once known as "Neg Jardin stickband[s]" (Lennox Pierre, interviewed by Hall, 1998b; see p. 51 in this volume; see also *Port-of-Spain Gazette*, 1908, quoted in Cowley 1996: 164). Like the earlier stickfighting costume, the Neg Jardin is a fancy dresser; he wears European-style knee-length breeches and satin shirts, on which is sewn a heart-shaped "fol" (the name is French) decorated with small mirrors. There are at least four characters in today's carnival who wear this fol: the Neg Jardin, the Pierrot, the Jab Jab, and the traditional stickfighter (see figure 7.1). In their origins and early development, these characters – the well-dressed field slave, the clown, the fancy devil, and the stickfighter – were neither as separate nor as ethnically specific as they now may seem. Moreover, the fol, which resembles a similarly heart-shaped decoration on (East) Indian clothing, also decorated with mirrors, may have helped to encourage *gatka*, or Indo-Trinidadian stickfighting, to develop alongside the African form. As we

Fig. 7.1 Traditional Jab Jab carnival character, with fol breastplate covered with mirrors. Carapichaima, carnival Monday, 2002. Photograph by Pablo Delano.

review the history of masquerading and the development of traditional characters, it is good to be reminded that the taxonomy of costuming is as fluid and changing as language itself.

MAS AND CLASS

From at least the mid-nineteenth century on, there were multiple middle classes in Trinidad: African Creole, French Creole, free colored, and British. Ordinarily, the history of the festival in the latter half of the nineteenth century is described as an African Creole middle-class takeover of carnival (see Brereton in this volume). In essence, though carnival is now a festival that involves all the classes of the island and throughout the Caribbean diaspora, the values of the middle class, created as a function of the Industrial Revolution in capitalist economies, are intrinsically opposed to the values of carnival. This has resulted in a dialectical tension that has remained much more constant through the history of carnival than is ordinarily recognized.

The British brought a stern sense of ethics and a code of acceptable behavior to the event, which was from a very early period commercialized (costumes were advertised as early as 1829; see Cowley 1996: 23), subjected to restrictions based on notions of gentility and morality, feared for the possibilities of insurrection that might be created by allowing a majority dark population to gather even for festive purposes, and repeatedly thought to be dying out. At the heart of much of the conflict was the basically middle-class notion of decency. In 1895, cross-dressing was forbidden, with the result, it was said, of much less vibrance on the streets. Pierrots were required to be licensed from 1891, and Neg Jardins were frequently arrested for disturbing the peace, particularly in the decade before and after the turn of the century. In 1919, the rules for the so-called "Victory Carnival" sponsored by the *Trinidad Guardian* newspaper after World War I stressed decorum, threatening to take away prizes from anyone for vulgar behavior *subsequent* to the competition.

This Victory Carnival also featured a "Grand Illuminated Parade of Decorated Motor Cars and Other Vehicles" that would on Tuesday night circle the Queen's Park Savannah three times. These decorated cars and, especially, the "other vehicles" are important milestones in the history of carnival. They are the proto-type of the lorries that in the 1930s, 1940s, and into the 1950s would be the bastion of the white middle class in carnival, allowing them to participate in the street event without actually mingling on the streets. These lorries in their turn provided the origin of the massive semi-trailer sound-trucks that now provide music for masqueraders of all classes who mingle on the streets.

Even when middle-class, mainly white, masqueraders played on trucks, safely above the street fray, the mas they played and their costumes were no more neces-sarily distinctive from those of the working-class street festival than they had been when nineteenth-century Creole planters and stickfighters both favored the Neg Jardin. See, for instance, figure 7.2, which shows a truckload of white masqueraders playing "prison mas" in 1935, compared to photographs of Afro-Trinidadian, plebian traditional masqueraders playing prison mas on the streets of Port of Spain in the 1940s and a middle-class steel band in 2003 (figures 7.3 and 7.4). The similarity of costuming bridges the divide between the masqueraders, emphasizing

Fig. 7.2 Prison mas played by middle-class masqueraders on a lorry or truck, 1935.
Photograph from the collection of Pablo Delano. Used with permission.

Fig. 7.3 Prison mas played on the street by traditional masqueraders, 1940s. Photograph courtesy of Narrie Approo.

the crossing of boundaries, which is one of the most basic characteristics of carnival.

CATALOGING CARNIVAL

Although contemporary Trinidad Carnival defies all attempts to contain or restrain it, it does now have a plethora of categories and rules that purport to govern its many competitions, prizes, and levels of production (there are more than a hundred different kinds of prizes given for traditional characters alone each year, with at least two dozen of them for varieties of Amerindian masquerading). Thus, it can at times appear to be a conglomerate of criss-crossing separate tracks and paths. Such definition, of course, is a recent innovation, belied by the actuality of the festival that grows from the streets and city squares as if by magic. Mas itself, though only

Fig. 7.4 Prison mas played on the streets of Port of Spain. Christopher Laird (in center with flag) leads masqueraders with Phase II Steel Orchestra, carnival Monday, 2003. Photograph by Pablo Delano.

one part of carnival, is a many-headed hydra that resists definition: on the one hand, it is topical; each year's mas reflects local and international events of the months preceding, often satirically but also with an edge of glorification – with, for instance, many representations of Osama bin Laden in 2002; in 1907 the USS *Alabama* arrived as part of Teddy Roosevelt's "Great White Fleet" and was represented in carnival in 1908. On the other hand, mas can be entirely fantastic – given to representing insects, animals, bugs, abstract symbolic ideas, historical recreations, mythology, and much, much more.

The chapters that follow in this section do not aim at inclusivity. Therefore, it may serve us to identify some of the basic types of masquerading. Please see the glossary for specific definitions:

- Ole mas – now often called traditional mas, basically a satirical form, usually involving skits with much wordplay and many puns.
- Jouvay, including the low-keyed jouvay king and queen competitions held at the downtown Port of Spain venue in the early hours of carnival Monday, as well as the mud bands that are now among the favored forms of mas for all classes.
- Traditional "culture-bearing" characters. These are the characters who play singly or in bands whose evolution is enmeshed in the history of carnival as a resistance festival. Daniel Crowley defined many of the traditional categories in 1956. They play throughout the carnival season.
- Military and sailor mas – special categories of mas, often associated with the history of the steelband in the twentieth century. The earliest street mas recorded was a military band in 1834, mimicking the artillery of Christmas militia forces. Military and sailor mas illustrate the dialectic through which masqueraders often satirize behavior they also wish to appropriate, and which they sometimes more simply glorify. (See, for instance, figure 7.5, in which a living tableau created by Wilfrid Strasser, a third-generation Trinidadian of Martiniquian and German ancestry and one of the legendary innovators of mas, portrays the newly elected President Eisenhower imbedded in a globe, in the process advertising Esso Oil Company.[5])
- Pretty mas or fancy mas. The legacy of carnival designers such as Strasser or George Bailey, who helped to develop both European and African history mas bands, and Carlisle Chang, an artist who designed the Trinidad flag and coat of arms and who designed mas bands mainly in the 1960s and 1970s (see Chang in this volume), has helped to create the mystique of masquerading, and to link the sense of beauty and the idea of royalty to carnival costuming and cultural history, to some extent in opposition to the ballgown Carnival Queen contest once sponsored by the *Trinidad Guardian*, later by the Jaycees, and revived in the 1990s by Wayne Berkeley, another distinguished masman. Pretty mas dominates the streets on carnival Tuesday; in Port of Spain on carnival Monday afternoon, fancy mas bands will move through the city, with masqueraders wearing part of their Tuesday costumes, or perhaps only band-issued tee shirts, in a preview of what is to come on Tuesday. Carnival in San Fernando and other towns throughout Trinidad may also include fancy mas costumes on both Monday and Tuesday.
- Children's carnival. In a typical carnival season, there are more occasions for children to masquerade in fancy costumes in the street than for adults.

Fig. 7.5 Living carnival tableau, US President Eisenhower behind a globe of the world, advertising Esso gasoline, Wilfrid Strasser mas, carnival Monday, 1952. Photograph from the collection of Pablo Delano. Used with permission.

Beginning several weeks before carnival Tuesday, children may appear in their disguises in at least four recognized major competitions (along with other events, such as school carnivals or private parties): PSA (Public Services Association), children's carnival organized by the St James street community, Red Cross Carnival at the Queen's Park Savannah, and the NCC children's carnival. The final and official "children's carnival," traditionally on the Saturday before carnival, is a massive affair, rivaling carnival Tuesday in diversity and grandeur. Watching the parents guide their children through the streets on their way to or from the Queen's Park Savannah, one quickly understands that these children – ostensibly at play – are also in school, being trained and disciplined to participate in the ritual of masking that helps to define identity in Trinidad (see figures 7.6 and 7.7). To this end, children are increasingly participating in the traditional character festivals, also organized by the NCC, particularly on the Friday before carnival.

- Regional variations. Port of Spain is regarded as the Mecca of carnival, but there are carnivals throughout the island, on both Monday and Tuesday. Sometimes the carnivals in places such as Arima, Arouca, or Carapichaima (which hosts only Monday mas) may encompass aspects of cultural and religious life in Trinidad not seen in Port of Spain, reflecting the eclectic inclusivity of carnival throughout the island. See, for instance, the figure of Buddha carried in Carapichaima in 2000, preceding a carnival dragon (figure 7.8).

CARNIVAL PEOPLE: PRESERVING AND TRANSMITTING CULTURE

One of the offshoots of defining carnival as a national festival is its increasing link

Fig. 7.6 Children's carnival on the stage at the Queen's Park Savannah. Photograph by Jeffrey Chock.

Fig. 7.7 Sheynenne Hazell, Junior Calypso Monarch, Dimanche Gras show, carnival Sunday night, February 29, 2004. On the stage at the Queen's Park Savannah, 10-year-old Sheynenne, one of the youngest Calypsonians to win the title, was co-winner also in 2003. With thanks to Gemma Jordan. Photograph by Pablo Delano.

to education. Even among those who continue to believe that the carnival of the streets is a vulgar and decadent affair, it is sometimes thought to be a good teacher of cultural history.[6] Many schools have their own in-school carnival jump-ups, sometimes with their own steelbands, often with their own calypso contests. Children study carnival as an essential component of the history of resistance, rebellion, and cultural self-determination in Trinidad whether they design and wear their own costumes or not. And in the Lady Hochoy School for physically challenged students, steel pan is used as a teaching tool, while young men with severe physical disabilities produce carnival staffs for major mas bands, such as Stephen Derek's D'Midas. In addition to the emphasis given to carnival in the formal school system, the National Carnival Commission, in an impetus guided by John Cupid, has established camps across the island that teach children traditional character dances and chants (see Hall in this section).

Though Trinidad Carnival mas is known internationally mainly for its grand costumes and massive celebrations in Port of Spain, there are also those that still produce the traditional masquerades in a more conventional way, often outside the capital city. In Carapichaima, a traditionally (East) Indian area in the center of the island, B.M. Singh and his daughters Jill and Sue have, with the assistance of an outstanding carnival committee, presented a Monday carnival every year since 1947 that is now the largest carnival Monday festival on the island (see Sankeralli in this volume; see also figures 7.1 and 7.8). In this section of the book, Puerto Rican photographer Pablo Delano captures the essence of some "carnival people" from

Fig. 7.8 Buddha carnival float preceding dragon in parade of bands. Note kitchen sponges on sticks as props. Carapichaima, carnival Monday, 2000. Photograph by Pablo Delano.

Caripichaima to Port of Spain. Other chapters further highlight two specific traditions associated with regions outside Port of Spain. Hélène Bellour and Samuel Kinser focus on Amerindian masquerading in the House of Black Elk in San Fernando, Trinidad's second city. Theater director and scholar Martin Walsh describes and Trinidadian photographer Jeffrey Chock sensitively illustrates the continuing legacy of Blue Devils in the nine-village area atop Paramin Mountain, abutting Maraval in the environs of Port of Spain. Like the children's camps, those who preserve these cultural traditions do so partly by passing them on to their children.

The other route to preservation and transmission highlighted in this section is that of assimilating traditional styles into contemporary masquerades. Many of the large mas bands, as for instance NCBA President Richard Afong's 1998 Barbarossa Band *Botay*, have begun to pay homage to jouvay and to incorporate representative symbols from traditional masquerades into their "fancy mas"

Fig. 7.9 The late Theresa Morilla Montano. Morilla, then 84 years old, prepares for her role as leader of the The Minstrel Boys, a white-faced traditional masquerade group, carnival 2001. Photograph by Pablo Delano.

Tuesday bands. Carnival designer and artist Peter Minshall – as illustrated in an interview edited for this volume – has enshrined the idea of "playing mas" as a marker of uniquely Trinidadian identity, evolving new artistic forms from traditional carnival characters, particularly the Bat, always with an eye to a vitally evolving carnival dynamic.

And then the carnival plays: beginning with references as early as 1827 to plays such as *The Tragedy of the Orphan* or *The French Farce of "George Daudin"* (Cowley 1996: 22), formal and informal plays have been part of the carnival scene. Concluding this section, award-winning filmmaker, director, and playwright Tony Hall tracks carnival mas from the streets to the stage, ending with a description of the process through which he uses traditional character archetypes, such as the Sailor, Baby Doll, or Midnight Robber as dramatic vehicles.

Carnival masquerading in Trinidad is prolific, varied, historically resonant, and contemporary. Traditional masqueraders – such as the elegant and talented Narrie Approo of Arima, who plays many characters including Black Indian, Midnight Robber, and more; the late Theresa Morilla Montano, crowned sixteen times as Jouvay Queen and leader of the white-faced Minstrel Boys before her death in 2001 at age 84 (figure 7.9); Felix Edinborough, a Belmont principal who has almost singlehandedly revived the Pierrot Grenade; Brian Honoré, who keeps the Midnight Robber tradition alive in the spirit of his mentor Puggy Joseph – carry the traditions of past decades into the present, supplemented by many others, including the children in the NCC training camps. Among the older traditional characters bands, men continue to outnumber women (though this is changing). However, more than 80 percent of those playing mas on carnival Tuesday are now women. Empowered by the beauty and sexuality made visible by the bikini costumes that are the bane of carnival purists and traditionalists, women who decades ago might have taken refuge in a decorated lorry now mingle with others on the street, proudly displaying bodies often honed for the occasion in the gymnasia of Trinidad or their home cities in North America or Europe. On the surface, it might seem that the carnival beast has been tamed by its own success. But beneath the glitter, the glamor, and the increasingly banal surface of the large-scale annual carnival shows, there is no doubt some rough beast even now slouching his – or perhaps her – way to Port of Spain to be born.[7]

NOTES

1   Formerly, "playing mask," literally, masquerading for carnival; see Glossary.

2   I am aware that the concentration on Trinidad appears to diminish the significance of Tobago. The history of carnival in Tobago is a vital part of the overall Trinidad Carnival story. It began in the 1920s with the early innovations of transplanted Trinidadians such as George Leacock but was developed mainly after World War II. Please see Hall and Eddie Hernandez in Riggio 1998a for a fuller sense of that story. Tobago's own cultural history is much more deeply invested in the Tobago Heritage Festival, re-created each July. Nevertheless, the story of carnival in Tobago is a rich one that needs to be explored in detail.

3   Shango was identified with John the Baptist in many areas including Trinidad, but with St Barbara in the evolution of Santería in Latin American countries, particularly in Cuba. There is a continuing debate over the extent and nature of syncretism in "New World" adaptations of African religions (see, for instance, Houk 1995 or Lawson 1985). The point here is not to

engage in that debate but more simply to link the notion of disguise that emerged from social and religious customs with festive masquerading.

4   I am indebted to Cowley's masterful study (1996) for the idea of using Christmas revels as one key to understanding carnival celebrations. This is but one of many ways in which I, and all other researchers following Cowley, owe much to his extraordinary archival work.

5   Strasser's great-grandmother's parents (née Capet) fled the French Revolution to Martinique. His grandfather (Strasser) came from Germany to Panama to work on the Canal. He met great-grandmother Capet in Martinique and they came to Trinidad about the middle of the nineteenth century. This information, provided by Hadyn Strasser, nephew of Wilfred Strasser, illustrates the complex pattern of ethnic intermixing that underlies the history of the entire Caribbean region.

6   Of course, this is not uniformly true. There remain many who feel that the history of the island is trivialized by the emphasis placed on carnival. This, too, is in a larger sense part of the carnival story and must not be forgotten.

7   Cf. "And what rough beast, its hour come round at last, / Slouches towards Bethlehem to be born?" William Butler Yeats, "The Second Coming."

8

PETER MINSHALL
A voice to add to the song of the universe

An interview by Richard Schechner and Milla Cozart Riggio

February 14, 1997, Port of Spain, Trinidad

Minshall: The other day just outside the mas' camp I was talking to someone who had come down from Jamaica, and in the middle of a very relaxed conversation she said, "But your accent doesn't sound Trinidadian." And I said, "I have two languages. The one in which I am expressing myself now – and my native language." I think in both these languages. Though, when I am most excited, I revert to my native tongue both in thought and in speech.

In 1974, a year of revelation and change for me, with a colleague of mine [Arnold Rampersad] up near Maracas [Beach], we met by chance a 92-year-old woman, Elise Rondon, who sold sugar cakes and pickled pomseetay [a tropical fruit]. There in a little rum shop, sheltering from the rain, drinking a beer – this lady, brightly garbed, golden earrings, with her tray of fruit. I became fascinated with her. In the meantime, TTT [Trinidad & Tobago Television] asked me to do a half-an-hour program on a subject of my choice, and my mind went, Ping! Idea! I visited Elise Rondon about four or five times – and she started to tell me stories. She had an extraordinary presence and sense of theatre. The reason why? She had been a bélé queen all her life. The dance called bélé is like a minuet to African drums, mainly a women's dance, utterly Caribbean. Here is a young man who had gone away in 1963, believing his life lay abroad, coming back in '74, understanding that this woman knew "attitude" in her way as much as Olivier did in his.

Schechner: Did you play mas' when you were a kid, and if so, who did you play with? I ask because clearly you've lived several lives. Your early life, then your life abroad, then your life as a person who chose to return to Trinidad – but who lives also an international/intercultural life.

Minshall: It starts when you're a child, mindless, you don't know why you're doing what you do. But at the age of 13, with cardboard box and Christmas tree bells turned inside out as eyes, and some silver and some green paint that I begged from the Chinese man who ran the grocery at the bottom of the hill, and some grasses from San-San, which was the name of that very hill behind the house, and bits of wire, and bones the dogs had left around the yard dried in the sun and bleached, I prepared all by my precocious little self a costume for the Saturday afternoon children's competition.

I called my mother to the balcony. "Mummy, mummy, mummy! Come see my costume!" "Oh, very nice, darling! Tell me, what is it?" "But, mummy, I'm an African witch doctor." "Oh, but darling, you're the wrong color. Here, come." And she gives me a dollar, sends me down to Ross's drugstore on Frederick Street for eight ounces of "animal's charcoal." That's all I remember. To this day I don't know what "animal's charcoal" is. So I get the stuff, and I am transformed into a black that is as deep as velvet. Then I go down to the Savannah and dance my mas' and I am awarded the prize in my age group for "the most original." So I suppose the die was cast there and then.

Now, three years later, at age 16, still a schoolboy, I do something which was then commonplace. In those days, prominent figures in society – lawyers, doctors – would be seen in the jouvay in their wives' nighties or in corsets. Jouvay was about the ridiculous. It was also about Jab Molassie – Blue Devil as I knew him – in all my experience of theatre, one of the most powerful pieces of theatre ever!

And another thing about the jouvay then was the mud. Sometimes when I think of people putting mud on their bodies in the predawn, when I try on my own to figure out what the carnival's about, I say: The ritual of putting mud onto the body for jouvay is about the myth of man being made from that mud. It is returning to the source, it is being one with the universe. That mud is of the earth, but it is also of the Milky Way. That river of people is a river of stars, it is not your everyday.

OK. Into that jouvay this schoolboy, having tied a pillow to his backside, and having stockinged every inch of his body, including his head with the tee shirt, over which there is a mask, over which there is a hat, in one of his sister's discarded dresses and a pair of old slippers, goes into town quite unconsciously as a Dame Lorraine – but totally disguised. To be disguised is not to be hidden or submerged. On that jouvay morning that schoolboy was liberated from race, from age, from gender. It was total liberation.

And then a Mrs Burnett, a good friend of my mother, a black Trinidadian, while visiting said, "Jean [Minshall's mother], why doesn't Peter design a costume for my daughter?" Now this is the unconsciousness of a young growing-up-person; you don't know what you are doing or why. But as I look back I find it plain to see. His first costume as an African witch doctor is for his white self, and then I take this black girl and send her up as a Gothic stained-glass window. So I think the business of playing mas' is about being other than yourself.

Schechner: What made you want to go to the UK – what drew you away, and what then drew you back?

Minshall: My parents were divorced, I was living with my mother, but my father made sure I had at my disposal an easel, oils, and canvases at age 12. I was painting, I was making costumes for carnival, I got involved with the Light Operatic Company's yearly Gilbert and Sullivan. This flair for set design emerged. Having left Queen's Royal College, I went straight into a job at Radio Trinidad – and so here am I, a household name on radio on an island. Television ain't come yet. And in the meantime, some of my schoolmates are going away and coming back saying, "Minsh, boy, you really have to come up there, you know." And not only that, this artist thing is niggling at me. So it enters into my head that I am going to go away and be a painter. But my father takes me aside and advises, "It would be saner to go away and be a designer for theatre." Well, I was admitted to the Central in London [The Central School of Art and Design, now associated with St Martin's]. At Central I was taught by the likes of Ralph Koltai. To see London fresh and new at the age of 21! I arrived at a most extraordinary time, the beginning of the '60s, the year of the Beatles, I saw Olivier's *Othello*, went to the National Gallery and saw that sepia-tinted cartoon of the Virgin of the Rocks done by Leonardo himself. Any art I had seen before had only been in books.

And the World Theatre season! A Zulu *Macbeth*, *Umabatha*, with this army, this wall of warriors, coming from the furthest back wall of the theatre down to the edge of the audience. That awesome production of *A Midsummer's Night's Dream* by [Peter] Brook. And then his *Marat/Sade*. In London I saw my first opera, a baptism of fire, *Götterdämmerung*.

Bit by bit I learned – without sounding too grand – what art is. And amidst all of this, for reasons that should need no explanation, my thesis at the end of three years is on the Trinidad Carnival. The more my eyes were being opened the more I was able to see. My thesis deals with the Bat, and with the Fancy Sailor – which, in its time, in my knowledge of world costume, was the most surreal statement I have experienced. Imagine a man coming down the street in Port of Spain, and where his head should be is a giant slice of paw-paw [papaya], or a cash register with a drawer that actually works, or a headpiece with three barking dogs on it, or made out of cottonwool and swan's down and little bits of silver paper, a great delta-winged warplane – utterly surreal. But surreal with that kind of basenote truth of Magritte. So honest yet so fantastic. And then, I can't remember how it happens, somebody says, "Get off your ass, child," and I take my portfolio to a producer who says, "I know who you ought to see, Peter Darrell." It just so happens that Peter Darrell and Colin Graham are collaborating on *Beauty and the Beast* for the inauguration of the Scottish Theatre Ballet. As I am showing them my work from Central, I turn the page and there is a costume for the now-defunct J.C.'s Carnival Queen Show called *Once Upon a Time* – and Darrell looks at this thing and says, "You're the person we're looking for." That was 1969. So I designed the set and costumes. *Beauty and the Beast* premiered at Sadler's Wells.

Four years later my mother is in London and says, "Now Mr Designer, I want you to design a costume for your little adopted sister." The heart skips a beat. "Furthermore, I want it to be a hummingbird." Oh dear. The happening young London designer returns to the island to design for the children's carnival. And of course there is no way out. So I must make the best of it. I must've spent off and on about five months just fiddling – in between whatever jobs I was doing – putting into this diminutive little work all my theories about playing the mas' and its energy: it's about performance, it's about mobility. It was Christmas Eve night I came [home to Trinidad] with £100 worth of fabric, which was a lot of money back then. On New Year's Day we start to construct the costume. It took five weeks, twelve people. It was totally meticulous, 104 feathers, each one made of 150 different pieces of fabric, the blue to the purple to the green, stuck with transparent nail varnish over bits of plastic over a pattern. All pinned up, then finally assembled. It has to be finished. We haven't slept for three nights. One person is holding the thing onto Sherry standing there like a little girl crucifix – there's not time for zips [zippers] – while we sew her into it.

We lift her up onto the jitney, drive to the Savannah in a dream, in a daze, mindless. This little 12-year-old girl is going up the path. I've rehearsed with her with canes and an old sheet and told her, "Forget you're a bird. You're a flag woman. Wave your flag, dance, you're not flying, these are not wings, you're a little girl enjoying yourself." This little thing exploded like a joyful sapphire on that stage, and ten thousand people exploded with her. On that afternoon, a moment of revelation. "Christ, so this too is art!" I did not choose the mas' – it held me by the foot and pulled me in. Three weeks after that experience I met Elise Rondon. Put those two things together. I was finding myself. I was so proud to be from where I was. There was an art that we knew how to make. We have a voice to add to the song of the universe.

Fig. 8.1 Peter Minshall drawing for the *Hummingbird* costume, whose movable wings Minshall combined with the fixed wings to create later costumes (see figure 8.3), costume 1974. Courtesy of Peter Minshall and Callaloo Company.

So back to London, I started doing things in the Notting Hill Carnival. In '75, because of the Hummingbird and because he has fallen out with one of my first gurus of the mas', a great artist, Carlisle Chang, Lee Heung rings me up in London and says, "How would you like to design my next band?" At the time in Notting Hill I am doing a band of devils called *To Hell with You*. It just comes to me. While Braf [Hope Braithwaite, one of Minshall's teachers at Queen's Royal College, Port of Spain] was teaching me all about *The Tempest* and *Othello*, my other English teacher, Mr Laltoo, was teaching me about Mr Milton and his *Paradise Lost*. So these many years later, I think, "Mr Lee Heung wants me to do his band . . . what do I do? PARADISE LOST!!! I'm already makin' devils, all those fallen angels!"

Paradise Lost was a watershed in the context of carnival; it was epic. It was a visual thesis of many of the things I would do in years to come. A band? How do I do a band? What is a band? A band is the closest I know to live visual art, a band is symphonic, you can't see the whole of it all at once. I approached *Paradise Lost* as a symphony in four parts.

Schechner: What year was it?

Minshall: *Paradise Lost*? 1976. *Hummingbird*, '74.

And then there is another family falling-out, and as a result a group assembles itself and says, "OK, Minshall, come. You're not going to be working for any other bandleader. You're going to bring your own band." So 1978, I return to Port of Spain to do *Zodiac*.

Discipline, not a damn sequin, not a piece of braid! Primary colors – red, blue, yellow, black, and white – spinnaker nylon. It's incredible how things happen. Sitting in the Tube in London, trundling through the Underground, all these Americans on tour with their great backpacks. I'm sitting there: "Mas', mas' " – it's never far away – I go into the sporting goods shops, lookin' at all the backpacks. *Zodiac* was aluminum backpacks, extensions here, spring-steel wires there, and great shapes attached to the ankles. As [George] Balanchine said, "I want you to 'see' the music and 'hear' the dance." So the whole band is coming down, and every step to the music moves the fabric ten feet in the air and you get this kinetic madness. And *Zodiac* amazingly came second, unheard of for first timers. You're challenging people. You're saying, "Come on, let's stop being so quaint."

Riggio: How many people in the band?

Minshall: About fifteen hundred.

Schechner: What finally got you to move back to Trinidad?

Minshall: You begin to feel homeless. Around this time, [the late] Errol Hill, a professor [of theatre] at Dartmouth [and a Trinidadian], who I knew since I was a little boy, gets in touch with me in London to design his [play] *Man Better Man*. A bright Caribbean island is going to be set down in the middle of White Winter, in Hanover, New Hampshire, and this island is going to be populated mainly by whites. This is a problem I am trying to solve.

White linoleum on the floor, mirrors on either side, I create a Barbados beach, a white gingerbready cottagey thing, and white fucking costumes on everybody. All of these ladies with great white cotton skirts, and it's as though bits of the scenery, and the gingerbread, and hibiscus had bits of color printed on them as differentiation. And one character, Minnie, had a black silk

Fig. 8.2 Peter Minshall drawing of figure with fixed wings, the Imp of *Paradise Lost* (1976 mas band). Courtesy of Peter Minshall and Callaloo Company.

headtie ... a contemporary Broadway set, not condescending West Indian charm. Errol, his heart in hand, unwillingly says, "OK, do it." I shall never forget at the dress rehearsal, Errol Hill dancing like a child, bubbling over with joy. It worked! Errol asked me to give the first lecture I ever have on the mas'. The success of *Man Better Man* led to an invitation to return to Dartmouth to design *Blood Wedding* – the nearest thing to Greek ritual that I know.

Schechner: After that you came back to Trinidad for good?

Minshall: I don't remember the exact date. At a certain point, I thought, "Enough is enough." I rented out my London apartment and decided Trinidad is where I am going to be.

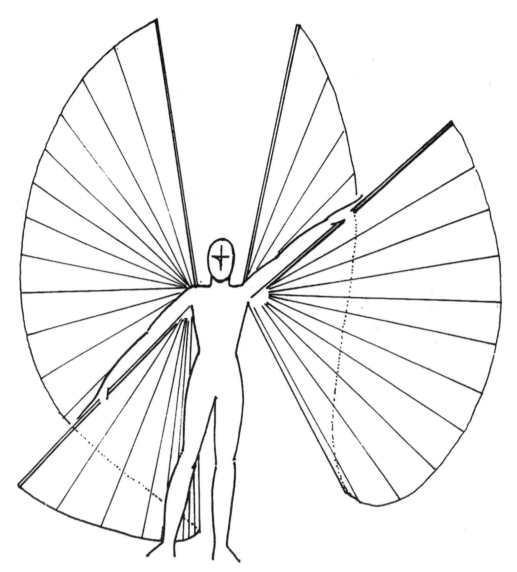

Fig. 8.3 Drawing of Sweet Oil Butterflies of *Paradise Lost* (1976 mas band), showing fixed wings attached to a back-pack and movable wings on the arms. A mobile Minshall signature style allowing for a maximum of graceful movement. Courtesy of Peter Minshall and Callaloo Company.

I start doing the mas', even as the mas' is undergoing certain social changes. It used to be very much a male thing, but at the point of my return it was becoming what you now see, very much a female thing. It was also going through all kinds of visual changes. At this point, I really come into it saying, "This is a theatre of the streets." Which is obvious to me, but no one here understands the terminology. "Oh, you're trying to turn it into theatre." "Oh my God, don't you realize it's always been that?" When the Midnight Robber makes a speech, when I run away from a Blue Devil, when George Bailey brings a black Queen Elizabeth in a golden coach drawn by white horses. All of this happened when I was small.

It's not easy. I suppose that not-easiness came to a mighty crescendo with the experience of *Hallelujah* [1995], where nothing I had done in my life had prepared me for two and a half months of daily diatribe in the newspapers, every single day, the most extreme Pentecostals saying it is sacrilege to use the word "hallelujah" in carnival – "the mother of all rot," they called it – and columnists, editorials, politicians, bandleaders, priests debating the pros and cons. But of course you can call a band "Hallelujah" – Ella Fitzgerald sings, "Hallelujah, come on, get happy!" What are you talking about? But not just the Pentecostal point of view, but others too. "Why don't you change the name of the band?"

I went through my own spiritual transformation. I am sitting right here one day, I hear a rustle over there in the heliconias, and I look: there is the cat, Missy, having just missed the hummingbird that was about to touch the heliconia flower. In a flash, I understand that the cat, the hummingbird, the heliconia, and myself are one. I can explain it no other way. And I was paralyzed. This is my life's work, I want to bring celebration into the mas'. This is the only way I know. Hallelujah! Curses were heaped on people. "If you play in this band, the island will be cursed." And so people began to pull away, and the band became smaller. Then carnival came. The people had a joyful, transcendent experience. The people who played in the band and the people who watched it. *Hallelujah* was the Band of the Year. It is a week after the *Hallelujah*, and I am on the north coast, by the sea, alone. The rocks, the crashing waves, the horizon. Everybody has their version of communication with the higher self. Mr God says to me, "It was a beautiful *Hallelujah*. But what ever made you think it would be easy?"

It is not easy. In dealing with the mas', I and other people have had to deal with my whiteness. It is not easy. [Silence] It has not been easy.

It is not easy when the fear of AIDS seizes the place, and you read in one of the weeklies, "Don't join the Minshall band, you'll get AIDS." It is not easy. [Long silence]

The first trilogy [*River* (1983), *Callaloo* (1984), and *The Golden Calabash: Princes of Darkness and Lords of Light* (1985)]. Derek Walcott has always been a champion of my work. Himself having received a Guggenheim Fellowship, he recommended me. There was this great battle. Derek saying, "They'll only give it to you if you apply for theatre." And I said, "No, it has to be for the mas'." The difficulty being in making the application, you have to say both what you want to do and explain what the mas' is. Miracle of miracles, I am awarded a Guggenheim on the basis of the mas'. My work is not to make pretty pictures but to make you shed your self-contempt. The Guggenheim people are treating me seriously, well let me treat the mas' seriously now I have a little money. *River* flowed out of that, and *Mancrab* came into being.

Now all of these connections – *Paradise Lost, Zodiac* – the thing coming from the feet, [and most of all finding the phrase] "to make the cloth dance." The other thing, too: Yes, I adore the Robber, the Bat. But the Bat was right for the '50s, he's quaint now because his competition really is Darth Vader. Today it's movies, television. So we have to learn what the Bat or Robber teach us – about dancing the mas', about mobility – and not just re-create them, but find their contemporary equivalents.

Mancrab [the principal male character, the king, of the mas' *River*, 1983; see Figure 8.4]. I actually constructed the model, then realized that a man normally stands like this [demonstrates feet together], but you play mas' like this [demonstrates feet apart] – considering the distance between the ankles. Therefore, extending a man's shoulders into a kind of rectangular armature with arms going out at each corner perfectly angled and fiberglass fishing rods coming into the angles so that one is going there, one there, one there – as he rocks his shoulders all of those rods move. At the tip of each rod the corner of a 25-square-foot piece of silk, so that the dancing steps of the feet move the rods which give life to the canopy of silk, a turbulent, billowing cloud. Yes, "to make the cloth dance." This is contemporary. This is our equivalent of what you see now at the Museum of Modern Art. I feel comfortable with this.

Then a story begins to build. And you don't get the final line in the story until a week before the carnival, because that's how it happens. You put parts into place, you don't know – then suddenly, "Oh, that's the story, 'Mancrab and Washerwoman.' " He, a master of technology, all of man's genius, all the more powerful now because he has technology. She, simple love and beauty. She representing Blanchisseuse, the pureness of the clear river water, also the pureness of true love. She, dressed in white cotton organza, the simplest little costume, carrying two poles, and lines of silk washing just hanging down, and a laundry basket in her hand, so simple. He, Mancrab, the claws of the crab turned this way [gestures upward] like so many arms, and the two gundees [main claws, pincers] like something coming out of a military tank. He's metal with a great crab's head with little lights and things flashing, a compressed-air canister on his back. He comes onstage moving to the sound of East Indian tassa drums. I had seen kathakali in London – so I go up to an Indian village with Peter Samuel [Minshall spreads his legs into the wide, bent-knee stance of kathakali and stamps the ground with high, violent steps to an imagined drumbeat].

Schechner: They do kathakali here?

Minshall: No. And there's a bicycle chain and gear thing, and you know it has to be exposed, because you don't hide de innards and de workings. And there are levers and cantilevers, the claws are going up and down. There's a moment he just settles center stage and breathes. And at that moment, the cloth begins to bleed in front of your eyes. This is the beauty of mas'.

The thing about the mas' in a push-button television age, it's about human energy. There are no electric wires, it's me doing this, it's me making it work. It really is a chilling thing, in a carnival, full of all its many parts, its sequins, its feathers, to see this piece of white silk undulating, and suddenly rivers of red starting to run. At that point, with due respect, because it was so good, stolen from kathakali, a performance that left me limp, he exits pulling from his gut –

Schechner: Yes, yes, the revenge Bhima takes on Dusassana at the end of *The Mahabharata* –

Minshall: – he just leaves this 30-yard trail of red silk as he exits.

On his first appearance, half the audience, I tell you, as an artist, it was as though there were two prize fighters onstage. Half the audience was booing, half the audience was clapping. It was a moment of terror.

Another designer comes up to me after and says, "How could you do that! That is my daughter being raped!" I thought – once more this is the Hummingbird – yes! Mas' when it works is as grand and as great as opera when it works. When it jumps you have no defense!

River. [Each section was called by the name of a river of Trinidad.] I used the clothes of our island ancestors – African, Indian, some European; turbans with pearls, two thousand people, men and women – all in white cotton. Of course, controversies rip. How I could bring a band all in white, carnival is colour! This is madness. In fact, the colour scheme of the band was this skin tone and that skin tone and all the many others. And the white just framed it. The people looked beautiful. So on Monday, as the band hits the stage, there is Mancrab, crowned King the Sunday night before, challenging Washerwoman. And with a symbolic square of white cloth, she dismisses him. But the story goes that that carnival Monday night, Mancrab, using all his technological magic, fashioned an illusory rainbow. All those little gadgets of the twentieth century, that are so dear to us, that make our lives so comfortable, offering all these pretty colours to the people, a rainbow of colours.

Tuesday morning. Every single person in the band has been supplied with a white cotton pouch and in it is a white squeezy bottle [plastic squeeze bottle, such as is used for dishwashing liquid] loaded with colored dye. Ha! Red, orange, yellow, green, blue, purple. Now this is where the people take the art over from the mas' man. You have to understand the thing.

Carnival Monday. A river of people. A river of cloth. A single piece of white cloth as wide as the road, one mile long, held aloft on poles. One cloth. One river. One people.

Carnival Tuesday. We have folded up the white cloth, put it away. We have made exactly the same size, exactly the same length a cloth that is a rainbow. Suddenly on Tuesday the people are under Mancrab's rainbow. The ritual begins. Charlie's Roots is playing the most painful funeral version of "River of Babylon," a reggae. Thirty priestesses, women in white, with white headties, holding calabashes. Fifteen faced the grand stand, fifteen faced the north stands. They go through the ritual. Then all of a sudden they tip the calabashes down the fronts of their white dresses. The poor announcer, "And it looks like – blood!" Red, and they go into a Shango frenzy.

Mancrab comes on under his canopy, but it's not attached to his feet; four men are holding it, thank goodness, because the wind is raging. Washerwoman's washing has been slashed overnight and splattered with red, the red of his silk. Washerwoman, the queen of the band, in the middle of carnival is brought over the stage lifeless, on the shoulders of three bearers. And then, the best laid plans. [. . .] The band is waiting at Frederick Street by the jail and down at the tail end, Patrick Raymond, who heads the last section, puts his bag of squeezy bottles [of colored vegetable dye] which he is about to give to his group onto the ground and a car wheel mashes the bag, a bottle bust, color splashes onto a lady's nice white costume. Well, is to know, color spread like fire through the band. My friends, do you know about theatre? Do you think I

Fig. 8.4 Mancrab (on left of photo) from *River* (1983 carnival mas created by Peter Minshall). Photograph by Jeffrey Chock.

know about theatre? Those people start to paint each other. Talk about action painting! Two thousand people on the day of the carnival going through this ritual of ablution, see their shining faces – but it happened before its time. [. . .] This rainbow thing starts to stretch and haul itself over the stage and the calypso music breaks out. All those people who said, "Oh God, it's white!" on Monday, but then realized it looked so beautiful! On Tuesday, Jesus, the country is in disbelief. How we could spoil it so! Because the river now – the story is coming to completion – is polluted.

We had parked up by the side of de stage six 500-gallon barrels of these same colors, hooked up to power hoses. Yellow went 30 feet up into the air like an arc of pee, and look at the people: "Oh, God, wet me down!" And they came with the blue, and as it came up the people are shouting, "Wet me dowwnn!" This baptism, this ritual, this total madness onstage! This was pure, living theatre, pure ritual! I've never experienced anything like it.

So much for my artistic ideas of neatly coloring each section. This was a chaos of color, a madness, all the colors running together till they got to a deep purplish muddiness. But it was so much better than what I had planned – the people played the art profoundly. They played pollution better than any artist could have painted. They played the mas.

Two days later, the results are announced. And in those days it was grandly and publicly done, there was an audience, and the envelope was opened. And as you know, when they make these announcements they start at the bottom and work their way up. "Ladies and Gentlemen, we will now announce the Band of the Year results. Tenth, *River*." The audience is of the mas' fraternity, and my brothers went up in a roar of approval. Yes! Tenth and last! I in my heart knew that I had been part of an extraordinary experience, a statement that could only have been made in the mas'. The simplicity of it, the power of it. And – dare I say it? – my own humility, in learning once more from those people, that this *River* was truly a river polluted. Two days afterwards, they count up the votes for the "People's Choice" [determined by the audience marking their ticket stubs and putting them into a ballot box on their way out]. And by a vast majority, and I'm speaking about thousands, *River* was the People's Choice.

Schechner: Do they do that any more?

Minshall: They don't, and the reason that's generally believed is that one person, one band, was winning the People's Choice too often. The band-leaders recommended to the officials to stop the People's Choice. The People's Choice was introduced for the very reason that the judges' decisions were often very unpopular. And so the first Prime Minister of independent Trinidad and Tobago, Eric Williams, instituted the People's Choice. And the bandleaders de-instituted it.

I've taken the time to tell this story not without reason. Often I am asked, "Which was your favorite, or most important?" In fact, in its entirety, the Mancrab, the Washerwoman, the River People, the mas' played in two acts, Monday and Tuesday, the mile long ribbon of cloth. Words, paintings, a movie can't convey this. On New Year's Day [1997] when I was asked to say a few words. "Ladies and Gentlemen, our carnival is going to grow when you start awarding prizes to those works that can truly be called 'works of art.' "

And *River* was one such powerful work. Having done *River*, we knew there was more. The next step was the band *Callaloo* in 1984, and the climax was *The Golden Calabash: Princes of Darkness and Lords of Light* in '85. We didn't know that *Hallelujah* [1995] was leading to a trilogy – it just naturally led into *The Song of the Earth* [1996], which carried the theme on, and *Tapestry* [1997] which just finished it.

Schechner: One of the most impressive things about carnival is that it's both very local and enormous. Members of bands know each other, people on the island know each other, but the scale of carnival is vast. Between the people watching and the people doing, who's left inside?

It is ritual, definitely. How else can people go hour after hour repeating the same movements to the same music? It's a kind of religious service. A celebration, certainly, but a playing out of belief also. They also immensely enjoy seeing themselves enact themselves. To put it in Clifford Geertz's words, the carnival is a story Trinidadians tell themselves.

Minshall: I have this observation. Here's a little island that needs catharsis like anybody anywhere else. We don't have either the resources or the audiences for a Broadway season or a West End. But we have the same needs. So what do we do? Carnival. That it goes back to the most ancient times, that it really is a celebration of life – is almost neither here nor there. What matters is that we are here now, and we have this festival of the arts. We sing songs, we compose tunes, we dance. And it involves the whole society. It is not just the few days. The band is launched the year before, there is a build, a build, a build. There are calypso tents, steelband yards, mas' camps.

Schechner: And there are people designing, people sewing, people preparing all over the island – and in New York, Toronto, London, too.

Minshall: There is much creative activity, it's our Broadway.

Schechner: It's both more and different than Broadway. Broadway is a very expensive veneer entertaining relatively few people. Carnival is more like the Elizabethan or Greek theatre – such a large proportion of the whole population participates. At Broadway there is an absolute separation segregating the audience from the stage. In carnival, at many decisive points and times, all separation dissolves into a scene of total participation. Even if you're not in the band now in front of you, you have been in some band, you have danced across the Savannah stage, in the streets, at any number of venues. Or you've sung calypso, beaten pan. The people who watch are experts through their own experiences, that's why the People's Choice was so important: it was the collective opinion of experts. Brecht would have loved the carnival audience – active, involved, knowledgeable, and critical. The Broadway audience is an extension of the TV audience – passive and receptive.

Minshall: Boss, you make me want to cry. Because I know the absolute truth of what you saying. But I do not think that there are many people on this island who would understand your language. Perhaps the reason I choose to explain as I do, if I say "Broadway" they understand.

I squirm when the announcer or commentator says, "This 'costume'. [. . .]" Please learn to say "mas'," or "this dancing mobile," or "this walking sculpture." This is not a costume. I like the word "mas'," it is our word: m-a-s apostrophe.

I have the knowledge through the mas', having watched it ever since I was a little boy, that if you give a person a cloth, a robe, that extends from wrist to wrist, and you play the music, look at me [Minshall extends his arms as if to show off his "robes"], this is going to happen. If you give a person another piece of cloth with two sticks on it, then this is going to happen. [Minshall waves his arms as though they are wings]. We have our own body language here, our own rhythm. One of the fears in Barcelona [1992 Olympics], expressed fairly early on, was, "We are not Caribbean people here." And I hastened to assure my hosts, "No, there is something else my work tries to be at its best – to inspire the ordinary man to say, 'Look at me, look how much bigger I am than I was before I went into this thing!' " And though the Olympic stadium is a vast arena, a huge space, I remember when I first got to Barcelona they thought it was going to take seven thousand people to make the Mediterranean Sea, but with the things I knew from mas', it took one thousand.

Schechner: What was the development from Barcelona to Atlanta?

Minshall: I had no expectation that there would be an Atlanta after Barcelona. I am the servant of my master. I went to Barcelona to serve Barcelona. Likewise Atlanta. What is "the South"? I was able to draw on many experiences from Trinidad to decipher the riddle of the [American] "South," and I am happy to say that every Southerner I have met so far has been very pleased with our representation of the South.

Even as the *Hallelujah* controversy was raging, I knew that three weeks after carnival I was due to present first sketches, notes, and ideas for *The South*. So all through the working of *Hallelujah* I am supposed to be doing *The South*, all these other wheels are turning. But up till that time, *The South* had not resolved itself, no one knew what it was. I didn't know where I was going, left, right, or what. I remember one afternoon seeking the counsel of a man of the cloth. And he said, "You're an artist. Go into the studio and work. Your work is your prayer."

After that, at the eleventh hour, I got the silk, I knew I was going to do a costume because I had promised somebody, a girl from London, who had come to dye silk, that "It's all right, I will design a costume for you to dye." That's all I knew. And out of this came a work called *Joy to the World* that appeared at the preliminaries all in white because we didn't have time to dye it. And after the semifinals, all day Saturday into Sunday morning, under a light specially set up in the abandoned warehouse next door, the girl with the dyes puts water colors onto the white silk wings. And Alyson Brown floats onto the stage like some Southern angel. [After having come second in the prelims and semifinals, Alyson Brown as *Joy to the World*] is the Queen of the Carnival, the most graceful, most feminine Queen ever to earn that title.

The carnival was over, I come back to town. We laid [Gershwin's] "Summertime" music over the soundtrack of a videotape of *Joy* in performance. And so, from a real-life experience of preliminaries to the Dimanche Gras, I was given the tale of *The South*. It was called "Summertime." And the Spirit of the South is actually created as part of the drama. The Sun and the Moon come with their attendants and in a sort of ritual they put her wings in place, and the Southern Spirit is born. She is dressed all in white, and she brings alive the Garden of the South as she leads the River of History through it. And a great storm, a Thunderbird, comes to attack her. The storm sweeps everything in its path, but out of the storm there is rebirth. She hangs by that

Fig. 8.5 Gilded Pieta living tableau, following the style of Wilfrid Strasser, from *Tapestry*, carnival mas created by Peter Minshall, 1999, which included tableaux representations of figures from many different religions. Photograph by Jeffrey Chock.

Fig. 8.6 Peter Minshall follows in the tradition of masman George Bailey. *Tears of the Indies* **was Bailey's last mas band before his death in 1970. The woman on the right won Best Female Individual of the Year in this mas. Photo courtesy of Norton Studios Ltd, Trinidad.**

one thread of hope. There is a note in the music – such a beautiful blues sound! – and her Southern Spirits come to give her good cheer – and they, all forty of them, have the colors of the Dimanche "Joy to the World" on their wings.

The folks in Atlanta wanted a feeling of church, so it seemed correct to end the piece with a great Southern-gospel *Hallelujah Chorus*. And "Summertime" had many makers: composers, choreographers, and people making huge puppets – each one bringing their own love and skill and inventiveness. Sometimes I wonder, "Did I have anything to do with any of this, or did it just happen to me?" Do you know what I mean?

Schechner: Of course. When you do your best work, you are animated, energy passes through and literally takes you with it. You sign your name to it, but when you are doing your best work, it's objective, like a piece of rock on the ground, not really yours. You can never own it, you can only receive it and give it.

Minshall: Absolutely. And share it.

Riggio: Of your two trilogies, the most recent comes when you feel danger, threat, and rage among your people. Yet you celebrate beauty and union and wholeness, a swirling kind of coming together – out of the *Tapestry* of the world and out of the *Song of the Earth* and *Hallelujah*, with its *Joy to the World*. The earlier trilogy – Mancrab was allied to – ?

Minshall: *River* followed by *Callaloo*. Throughout my work is this duality. The very structure of Mancrab, the four poles, the structure of evil became the structure of goodness for the king of the following year [with two enormous diaphanous splashes one from each ankle], called "Callaloo Dancing Tic-Tac-Toe Down the River." Callaloo is the son of the Washer-woman from *River* and Papa Bois – who is the father of the forest. Because he was son of the water, the water taught him how to dance tic-tac-toe, like a stone skipping down the river. The king of the first band, the same structure, is the king of the second band. And it says in the story that "Callaloo, besides being good was also very wise. He had brains as tall as any skyscraper." So his headpiece made of balsa wood, 16 foot, a shaft, very African – a vertical line like the stamen of a flower rising up between these two huge dancing splashes. So every time he stamps his foot, the water splashes. And in *Papillon* [1982], which was as much about social structure as about butterflies – here today, gone tomorrow – the king of that was called The Sacred and The Profane.

Riggio: And the third year?

Minshall: There's an old calypso, "And when de two bands clash, partner / If you see cutlass / Never me again / Jump up in a steel band in Port of Spain." There used to be steelband clashes. Taking this theme, I wanted to bring a mas' that was actually two bands. So, the third in the *River* trilogy was called *The Golden Calabash*. Whoever owns the Golden Calabash is given great power. Two bands fought for this Golden Calabash – one called *Princes of Darkness*, the other, *Lords of Light*. I would simply leave it up to the judges to decide who should win. But, ironically, neither of them won.

Schechner: Any final words?

Minshall: I'm visiting San Francisco doing the tourist thing, and I pass a corner shop just bright with kites. I've always loved kites, so I go in to look and touch and I discover – I forget the year, I always forget the year [1981] – the fiberglass rod. In carnival we have used wire, cane. Immediately I think, mas'! mas'! The first time I use it to simply make long, long feathers for the band *Jungle Fever*, like grasses, forests of feathers quivering across the stage. Then one day, this is how it happens, we've done the Mancrab thing, I'm working on the band *Callaloo*, and I am thinking, how does this band work? Instinct takes over. I'm wearing an ordinary tee shirt, the fiberglass rod is there. The mind doesn't think it, the hand does it. The hand picks up a scissors, cuts into the hem of the tee shirt and pushes the fiberglass through. And suddenly this [Minshall describes a circular shape around his waist] happens all around me. "Todd, please, run into town, get me a bolt of cotton jersey, and buy a sewing machine." I start to make shapes and cones. Talk about making a person's energy bigger! That price of fiberglass has gone right through the hem and into the carnival. It went straight into the Atlanta Olympics. The opening number, the tribal "Call to the Nations," all of those jumping and dancing hoops, it started off one day with a fellow in a studio with a tee shirt and a piece of fiberglass. Two years later, it's fashion. Well I'm not Cecil Beaton, and this isn't *My Fair Lady*. Nobody knows it, but Trinidad put a little thumbprint out there, our little mark on the universe.

A longer version of this chapter is printed in Milla Cozart Riggio (ed.), *The Drama Review*, 42 (3): 170–93 (1998), Cambridge, MA: MIT Press. This version was orally edited by Minshall, June 2004.

A TIMELINE OF SOME OF PETER MINSHALL'S MAS' AND OTHER WORKS

Mas' for Trinidad Carnival

1972	*Josephine Baker*, individual mas'
1974	*From the Land of the Hummingbird* and *The Little Carib*, individual mas'
1976	*Paradise Lost*
1978	*Zodiac*
1979	*Carnival of the Sea*
1980	*Danse Macabre*
1981	*Jungle Fever*
1982	*Papillon*
1983	*River*
1984	*Callaloo*
1985	*The Golden Calabash*
1986	*Ratrace*
1987	*Carnival Is Colour*
1988	*Jumbie*
1989	*Santimanitay*
1991	*Tantana*
1993	*Donkey Derby*
1994	*The Odyssey*
1995	*Hallelujah*
1996	*Song of the Earth*
1997	*Tapestry*
1998	*RED*
1999	*The Lost Tribe*
2000	*M2K*
2001	*This is Hell*
2002	*Picoplat*
2003	*Ship of Fools*

Mas' for other carnivals

1973	*Mas' in the Ghetto*, Notting Hill, London
1974	*Play Mas', Pierrot*, Notting Hill, London
1975	*To Hell with You*, Notting Hill, London
1976	*Skytribe*, Notting Hill, London

1986   *Drums & Colours*, St Paul's Carnival, Bristol
1989   *Caribbean Baroque*, Brooklyn Labor Day Carnival
1990   *Tan Tan* and *Saga Boy*, individual mas' guest performances, Miami, Toronto, Jamaica
1991   *Tan Tan, Saga Boy*, and *Mr and Mrs Merry Monarch*, individual mas' guest performances, Jamaica
1998   *RED NY*, Brooklyn Labor Day Carnival
2001   *Tan Tan* and *Saga Boy*, guest performance, Brooklyn Labor Day Carnival

Stadium events, concert-spectacles, and festival performances

1987   Segment of the Opening Ceremonies, Xth Pan American Games, Indianapolis
1990   Part of *Paris in Concert*, a Bastille Day Spectacle, Paris
1992   *L'Homme et Le Toro*, a group mas' work for the opening procession of the Feria de Musique de Rue, Nîmes, France
1992   The *Hola* segment of the Opening Ceremony of the 1992 Barcelona Olympic Games; the massed-group elements of the *Mer Mediterrani* segment
1994   *The Dance of the Nations* segment of the Opening Ceremony of the World Cup Finals (soccer), Chicago
1995   Theatrical characters for *Concert for Tolerance*, a citywide event for UNESCO, Paris
1996   Opening and Closing Ceremonies of the 1996 Olympic Games, Atlanta, including *Summertime: A Song of the South*
1997   *Oxygen in Moscow*, produced by Jean-Michel Jarre, Moscow; dancing mobile characters for citywide concert-spectacle
1999   The Miss Universe Pageant, broadcast on CBS from Port of Spain, Trinidad. The opening segment and other performance elements were conceived and designed by Minshall
2002   Mas' costume designs for *The Fire Within* segment, and member of overall creative team, for the Opening and Closing Ceremonies of the Salt Lake City Winter Olympics

Theatre and visual art

1969   Sets and costumes for *Beauty and the Beast*, full-length ballet, world premiere by the Scottish Ballet, Sadler's Wells Theatre, London
1970   Sets and costumes for Molière's *Sganarelle*, Theatre of the Deaf, Toynbee Theatre, London
1971   Set and costumes for *Cannes Brûlées* by Trinidadian director/choreographer Beryl McBurnie, Commonwealth Institute, London
1972   Sets and costumes for Edward Albee's *Who's Afraid of Virginia Woolf?*, Crewe Theatre, England
1973   Sets and costumes for *The Adventures of Robin Hood*, Birmingham Repertory Theatre, England
1974   Costumes for *Play Mas'* by Mustapha Matura, Brighton Festival, Royal Court and Phoenix Theatres, London
1974/5   Set and costumes for *Man Better Man*, written and directed by Errol Hill, Dartmouth College
1976   Sets and costumes for Lorca's *Blood Wedding*, costumes for Aristophanes' *The Birds*, Dartmouth College
1979   Sets and costumes for Lorca's *The House of Bernardo Alba*, the Ballet Metropolitan, Ohio Theatre, Columbus

1985   *The Adoration of Hiroshima*, Washington, DC, mas'-style street theatre anti-nuclear presentation, performed on the fortieth anniversary of the bombing of Hiroshima

1987   *Peter Minshall: Callaloo, an Exhibition of Works from the Carnival of Trinidad*, 19th International Biennial of Sâo Paulo

1989   *The Coloured Man*, painting, drawings, and renderings, Gallery 1 2 3 4, Port of Spain

1990   *Minshall: The Early Years*, an exhibition of theatre designs from productions in England and the US, 1996–80, On Location Art Gallery, Port of Spain

1990   Part of *Zeitgenössische Künste aus Trinidad und Tobago* (Seven Artists from Trinidad and Tobago), IFA Gallery, Bonn, Germany

1991   *The Spirit of the Savannah: J'ouvert – The Rising Sun*, mural, 18 feet by 15 feet, for The Mutual Centre, Port of Spain

1993   Section in show, *The Power of the Mask*, National Museums of Scotland, Edinburgh

1995   Part of *Caribbean Visions: Contemporary Painting and Sculpture*, traveling exhibition

1998   *Caribe Insular: Exclusion, Fragmentacion, Paraiso* – an exhibition of Caribbean Art presented by MEIAC (Museo Extremeno e Iberamericano de Arte Contemporaneo) and Casa de America (Madrid). Works from Minshall's mas' *RED* were featured in the exhibition

1999   Minshall and the Mas (Brooklyn Museum of Art) – mas' performance works *MonkeyBird* and *The Dance of the Cloth*, accompanying a lecture-performance by Minshall on his life and work in the mas'

2000   7th Biennial of Havana – *RED* by Minshall, an exhibition of works from the mas' *RED* presented by Minshall in the 1998 Trinidad Carnival, and the presentation of the mas' performance work *The Dance of the Cloth*

2001   *Leonardo's Man*, Prince Claus Awards Ceremony, Amsterdam; a multimedia performance work combining costumed mas' performers, live drums and violin, and computer-projected images

2004   *Play mas'* festival collaboration, Hamburg, Germany

9

AMERINDIAN MASKING IN TRINIDAD'S CARNIVAL
The House of Black Elk[1] in San Fernando

Hélène Bellour and Samuel Kinser

In 1498 Columbus, coming upon this island about the size of the US state of Delaware, observed what to him and a long series of reporters after him seemed to be "wildmen," naked beings living in the "wilderness" with no fixed abode. Such beings had been emblematized in European festive performances for several centuries prior to their discovery in the West Indies. They had existed in Greco-Roman and Christian imaginations for a much longer period – consider the Scythians or hairy, disheveled John the Baptist. Since the voyages of Columbus, most Europeans and Euro-Americans have reduced Amerindians to their pre-conceptions of wild people and wilderness, finding in the stereotype a convenient cipher for one of those dualisms which seem almost intrinsic to human reasoning: us and the others; we who are civilized and you who are not. Since carnival is, among other things, a festival of inversion, we who are civilized can play at being you who are not. But what if the "we" in question is *also* not considered civilized by the dominant culture into which "we" are born? Then "we" may play back and forth, ambivalently, across this line of division, momentarily placed in question. How this option has been drawn upon in Trinidad, how the tradition of Amerindian masking is today pursued by a small neighborhood band in San Fernando, is our subject here.

Unlike the case in most Caribbean islands, Trinidad's aboriginal population was not quickly eradicated by war, enslavement and disease after the Spanish arrived. Aborigines maintained their diminishing tribal independence in the southerly areas of Trinidad until the mid eighteenth century. By 1797, when the British conquered the island, Amerindians no longer existed in any significant way as self-sustaining communities. But they had waned slowly, leaving behind groups of mixed Spanish-Amerindian-African descent in several parts of the island.

San Fernando has a particular connection to the Amerindian world. The hill around which the town is built plays its part in the cosmology of a large tribe (twenty thousand in 1980) who still inhabit the swampy Orinoco delta opposite to the southern shore of Trinidad. The distance is small across the intervening gulf and the Warao are skilled in canoeing. For untold centuries they came to "the abode of the northern earth-god known as Nabarima or 'Father of the Waves,' "that is, to San Fernando Hill. After the town was established, they continued to come for trading purposes (Wilbert 1993: 11, 58–61).

On February 23, 1879, the Sunday before carnival, Father Armand Massé, a Catholic priest, observed thirty "Guaraoon" Indians – men and women with babies at the breast, naked except for "belts" – who had come to trade for fish hooks, tobacco, mirrors, and salt (De Verteuil 1984: 1). Those who grew up in San Fernando in the 1930s can still recall these traders, male and female, bartering hammocks, parrots, dogs, and basketry in the large marketplace. By the 1950s these trading expeditions had become a thing of the past (Wilbert 1993: 58n). Another kind of Indian, however, had at an undeterminable epoch emerged to become a familiar sight during carnival. The following account, paraphrased from a local newspaper, describes a Warahoon performance in San Fernando in 1923 (Anthony 1989: 34):

> Then there were the groups of fierce-looking Wild Indians, with their roucou-red faces, their costumes of bodice-and-skirt stained in red, with rings in their noses and ears, and shrieking with the crowds surging round them, "killing" with their staves the pennies thrown at their feet by people, and hopping and dancing down High Street, with the chant:
>
> > Gran failya, Katuama,
> > Kat, Kat, Katai Kobie,
> > Gran failya, Katuama . . .

What would the naked Warao think of all this, so little consonant with their appearance and customs? "Red Indians" in carnival in the 1950s, according to a contemporary report and sketch, wore long underwear dyed red and a wig of tangled hemp rope. In keeping with the report of 1923 just cited, a red skirt reaching to the knees was usually added (Crowley 1956: 205).

An elderly masquerader interviewed at San Fernando in 1996 remembered bands of Red Indians whom he also called "Warahoons." We showed him and one of his friends a sketch of a Red Indian accompanying Daniel Crowley's 1956 article. The sketch shows something similar to a peacock on the warrior's head (Crowley 1956: 208). "Yes," the two agreed, Red Indians "made funny things." They wore headgear of "airplanes" and "ducks." They came "from the country" south of San Fernando at Fyzabad and at Moruga on the southern coast. People living along the rivers down there also wore "boatheads," that is, little models of canoes. Different bands had different headgear. Some people in San Fernando also wore such costumes, they added (interview, December, 1996).

These two informants, Afro-Trinidadians, focused on the features of Red Indian costumes which were least probably Amerindian and most probably African in derivation. Headdresses modeling elements of everyday life are common festive paraphernalia in large areas of West Africa, particularly in the Yoruba area of Nigeria from which many Trinidadian slaves seem to have been taken (Drewal 1977).

Did Spanish colonial dress, on the other hand, inspire the graceful short red skirt and petticoat with lacy leggings reaching just below the knees also shown in the sketch? (In today's northern Spanish carnivals similar costuming is traditional

(Regalado and Regalado 2004).) Crowley reported that Red Indians shouted "Mate" when encountering another Red Indian band, an exclamation plausibly derived from Spanish *matar*, to kill (Crowley 1956: 205), and in 1905 and 1913 the newspaper noted "wild Indians" incongruously carrying "swords" (Cowley 1996: 166, 188) (see figure 9.1).

The connotations just mentioned point toward Spanish and African inspiration. But the name "Warahoon" and the roucou on the clothes and body also connect

Fig. 9.1 Red Indian in old time masquerade (*Viey le Cou*), Port of Spain, 1996. Photograph by Gordon Means.

this character to the Waraos of the Orinoco. Whatever the sources and precise iconography of this costume, it suggests the mingling minds as well as bodies, during three long centuries, of Spanish colonials and native Americans – and the similarly mingling body-minds of the Africans who observed them and eventually played with these observations by means of carnival.

Sometime in the late nineteenth or early twentieth century another kind of Indian masquerade made its appearance. The masqueraders in the group which calls itself the House of Black Elk (figure 9.2) follow that other tradition. Predominantly Afro-Trinidadian in ethnicity, they exhibit North American Plains Indian costuming in their merry-making. In 1978 the band won a prize in San Fernando's carnival competition for the best masking group or "mas band" in the category "Authentic Indian." The band celebrated its victory by posing with panache in the one place in the middle of the city which is *not* urban: the naked rocks of San Fernando Hill.

Why did the Black Elk group choose to portray North American Plains Indians? Why didn't they choose to depict Amerindians of their own past, in their own geographical area at the foot of the sacred hill? Why did they choose to mask themselves as Indians at all? And why in any case did the Plains Indian costuming become so popular in Trinidad in the decades just before and after World War II?

Questions such as these demand pursuit of several analytical avenues – historical, sociological, cultural, and political. They cannot all be delineated properly within the framework of a chapter. But some initial results can be reported.

Fig. 9.2 Black Elk crosses the Grandstand stage on carnival Tuesday, Port of Spain, 1998. Lately the band has begun to compete on Tuesday in the capital and on Monday in San Fernando. Photograph by Jeffrey Chock.

HISTORICAL AVENUES

The first description of Amerindian masqueraders in carnival is by Charles Day, an English visitor to the West Indies between 1846 and 1851. He witnessed a carnival parade in Port of Spain in 1848 which included masqueraders portraying "Indians from South America." These masqueraders were "Spanish peons from the Main, themselves half Indian." "Daubed with red ochre" and proceeding in parade, they carried "real Indian quivers and bows, as well as baskets; and, doubtless, were very fair representatives of the characters they assumed. In this costume children were very pretty" (Day 1852: I, 315). That Venezuelan peons would have played a role in the development of Amerindian masking is consonant with the Spanish/ Amerindian references found in the twentieth-century Warahoon costume and with the regular flow of immigrants from Venezuela during the nineteenth century. Day's description is not very detailed but his account, coupled with a few other references relating to the same period (Cowley 1996: 36, 42), indicates in any case that by the 1840s Amerindian masking was an established part of carnival.

At the time of Day's visit to Trinidad in 1848, fourteen years after the abolition of slavery, carnival revelers were mostly Afro-Trinidadians. This was also the case at the time of a second representation of Amerindian masking, found in the engraving of a Port of Spain parade published by the *Illustrated London News* in 1888 (figure 9.3). The scene is structured by the contrast between excited masqueraders front and center, and the spectators looking on from above or at the sides of the street. To the right a white clergyman observes the festive crowd superciliously. Although many are disguised in white-face, all the leaders of the carnival throng show some dark-colored flesh. The head of an Indian masquerader bobs up behind the procession's leader who is masking as a giant devil figure. The headdress, round in shape, can be linked to so many different contexts, North and South American alike, that it provides few indications. But what is the significance of the three points appearing at the top of the masquerader's weapon? Could they represent a decorated lance like those carried by North American Plains Indians? One can also not rule out the possibility that the masquerader's headdress is not simply round but has feathers trailing down the back in Plains Indian style, similar to those of a masquerader shown in an illustration of New Orleans's carnival in 1873 (Kinser 1990: 139).

From the beginning of the nineteenth century more precise ethnographic representations displaced generic allegorical models for Amerindian illustrations. After the 1860s popular monthlies such as the *Illustrated London News*, *Scribner's Monthly*, and *The Century Magazine* began to include engravings of subjects such as Custer's Last Stand, Buffalo Bill, Sitting Bull, and the Wild West shows which became a vogue in the 1880s. Were these media sufficiently disseminated in Trinidad to influence the popular imagination by 1888, or did images of North American Indians become familiar only later? By the 1920s in any case, when more detailed reports of Trinidad Carnival began to be published in newspapers, such influences were clearly at work. Michael Anthony, paraphrasing newspaper reports, mentions Indian masqueraders around their "wigwams" in 1919 and portrayals of "Indian Braves and Squaws" in 1920 (Anthony 1989: 20, 26).

The taste for novelty and exoticism has always played a major role in carnival. At the same time, in the late nineteenth- and early twentieth-century context of colonial inferiority imposed upon non-white Trinidadians, to imitate one of these grand

Fig. 9.3 M. Prior engraving, carnival parade, Port of Spain, 1888. From *Illustrated London News*, photograph by Gordon Means.

warriors of the north was to adopt a deliciously ambivalent position: "Yes, we are 'wild men,' just as everybody thinks we are, just as Africans and Indians have always been known to be; but no, we are just fooling around – and fooling you, who confess by your reticent yet fascinated staring that this heroic persona adds to our stature." At the same time the superbly decorative style of the Plains Indians was a new source of inspiration for those whose energy was increasingly focused on creating spectacular costumes and winning public approval at carnival competitions.

This dual theatrical leverage was the more effective because it involved another ingredient in Plains Indian attractiveness, an ingredient formed at a deeper chronological level and attracting all ethnicities and classes, privileged and exploited. All of us, wherever Western popular culture has penetrated, feel the pull by such wildly free warriors on the strings of our fantasy life. The pull comes from the slow European construction, from the Renaissance to the Enlightenment, of aboriginal people as noble as well as barbarous savages. This construction generated sometimes competing, sometimes complementary images. On the one hand, each European nation as well as each region in the United States created a special version of the white man's burden. On the other hand, the opposition shifted its vectors to look less like the uncivilized versus the civilized and more like the natural versus the superfluous, or like honesty and forthrightness versus corruption. Chateaubriand, James Fennimore Cooper, and a hundred authors of lesser fame infused such Enlightenment revisionism with the enthusiasms of Romantic humanism. New World aborigines became nature's noblemen, wildly free and, however cruel, also grandly brave.

The American West was the main stage where this refiguration was acted out, at least in the popular media. The Plains Indian warrior, with his freedom and his courage to resist, became the ultimate empowering figure because he embodied, and still embodies, a dream recognized by everyone: the dream of a heroic and natural life, untainted by the constraints of society. For Afro-Trinidadians or African-Americans, masking as an Indian had an added appeal: it expressed independence from European-initiated dominance at the very least and outright resistance and defiance at another extreme; yet all this was represented in a context, carnival, understood not to be serious.

Such ideological and social contexts help explain the growing popularity of Plains Indian masking. The role of the media in that process should not be underestimated. The influence of American popular culture began to be felt in Trinidad as early as the 1840s. In the 1940s and 1950s, the decades of North American Indian bands' greatest popularity, this influence was massively disseminated not only by the growing saturation of the island with American newspapers, radio broadcasts, and movies but also through interaction with the large number of US sailors stationed in Trinidad during World War II. Movies in particular generated tremendous excitement. Not only did they shape Indian masking generally during this period; they also regularly restimulated the desire to diversify Indian costumes in colors and accoutrements.

"THE HOUSE OF BLACK ELK PRESENTS: THEN AND NOW"

It is time now to turn out of the historical avenue into the busy main street of today's performances. The mas camps of San Fernando are smaller versions of those found in Port of Spain. For the past five years the Black Elk group has rented a wood and half-corrugated tin structure with earthen floor, located in a working-class residential area in the central part of the city. One evening shortly before carnival's climax on February 20, 1996, the place hummed with music from a radio cassette deck, playing soca and also something resembling a North American Indian idiom, which somebody in the shop accompanied by beating on a can with a spoon. Eight or ten people, gathered around a long table, were cutting, pasting, and measuring costumes, and others came in and out for short conversations, bringing food and beer and pop and taking care of assorted children's needs (five of them, aged 4 to 10, ran about). The atmosphere was easy and pleasant and yet busy and purposeful. We outsiders were quickly accepted and absorbed into the rhythm of the evening without much disruption for the following two hours. Several Black Elk mentioned that they would in any case be working all night. Five or six nearly finished costumes hung on the walls.

Thirteen people living nearby were pointed out to us as the organizing committee of the group. These organizers range in age from 31 to 51 and four are related by marriage or kinship; all are close friends of long standing. After a half-hour of desultory talk one of them produced an album of the group's past parades with forty to fifty photographs dating between 1968 and the present. It was a folklorist's dream – a neighborly group that had been around for more than a generation, and with documents to prove it; a group fabricating costumes of esthetic and historically intriguing quality, while having a good time, going at it in that relaxed and open-to-outsiders way of Trinidad.

Success! On carnival Tuesday the group carried off a flock of first prizes with their band, *Then and Now*. In San Fernando as in Port of Spain it is customary for performances to take place on both Monday and Tuesday. We did not see carnival Tuesday, but we were there for their performance the day before. Between 12:30 and 3:45 p.m. people slowly assembled. At the head of the group two children in Indian costume carried the group's banner. Because of the number of years that the organizers had been working together, there was no need for a hierarchy or a boss to indicate what had to be done. The same agreeable, convivial busyness noticed during our first visit took place, and as if by magic the masqueraders grouped themselves near the sound-truck blaring socas at a quarter to four.

Matotope, White Bear, Medicine Man, Chief Pigeon Head, Indian Policeman, characters from the 1870s and 1880s indicated to us the week before, appeared in full regalia and generally accurate dress. The Black Elks' sources included sumptuous and well-illustrated books such as Thomas Mails's 1972 volume *Mystic Warriors of the Plains*, and others which reproduced George Catlin's famous early nineteenth-century sketches of Plains Indians. Adaptations from the sources had been made in the colors and in the way feathers extended out from the body. The colors tended toward pastel brightness and vivacity. These preferences accorded with those observed generally among mas bands in Trinidad. Mas players seek an exoticism that is gaily bright. "Pretty mas" is an accurate phrase for the coloristic effect of the costumes.

Masquerades get prettier and prettier, not least because middle-class women have come to dominate them. Eighty to ninety percent of the masqueraders in Port of Spain's large carnival bands today are women. But only three or four women over the age of 15 were with the Black Elk on February 19, and their costumes were not elaborate. The extravagant headdresses and bustles, the densely figured pastel costumes, and the soca dancing around the huge sound-truck were largely male preserves. We had been told that the group had a "queen." She did not participate, and there was no picture of her or of any other women in the group's album. It is possible that the amount of gendering in the costumes and performance differs from year to year. In a videotape we saw of the 1995 Black Elks' carnival Tuesday performance at the Skinner Park Grandstand, half a dozen women wore quite individualized costumes. But male-oriented display is probably an enduring characteristic of this group.

On the other hand, it is a woman who maintains the books and archives for the group; she and another female member of the committee occasionally join the masquerades, and their children take part. At all levels the activities of the band are embedded in the family life of the neighborhood. Children of both sexes and all ages play with the group and are present in all its activities. On that Monday three or four families living close to the mas camp had participating children and in-laws as well as parents. Two café-restaurants a few houses away were involved and eager for patronage. It was a neighborly affair in the historically oldest section of San Fernando, a working-class residential area near San Fernando Hill, only three blocks from the store-lined High Street and about a kilometer from San Fernando's center.

We were told that the Black Elk on carnival Tuesday moved in a certain order across Skinner Park stage, so that the grandstand announcer could indicate who was who in their group. But on Monday they moved down the street in a random way, changing places and moving to the sides with freewheeling looseness. Some, like a masquerader swirling in front of the sound-truck, used the long tail extensions of their costumes to create colorful effects as they moved. But few made attempts to create dance steps characteristic of Plains tribes. For the competition at Skinner Park a few masqueraders probably imitated Plains-tribe dancing very well, to judge from the videotape of their grandstand performance in 1995. But the music accompanying them was and is always soca, and the vast majority of the dancers "jump-up" and "wine" if their elaborate costumes allow for it. The larger and more thickly elaborated costumes are presumably designed less for dancing than for slow-moving, straight forward or circular movement with outstretched arms, which in the culture is called "dancing the costume" (figure 9.4).

Black Elk masqueraders occasionally whoop and chant in call-and-response style, using French patois and words designated as "Indian language," and they may imitate Indian dancing for a moment in the street or on stage. They even sometimes use a peace pipe. But their focus is not on achieving a tightly woven ritual ensemble of visual, verbal, melodic, percussive, dramatic elements. Participation in the band is not based, as in the case of the Mardi Gras Indians in New Orleans, on acquiring a repertory of some dozen songs which are known by all masking groups, with each group, or rather the lead singer in each group, creating competitive variations. It is not based on working out extended dance competitions and verbal boasting routines, learned collectively, in repetitive tavern-located Sunday-night practices. New Orleans Mardi Gras Indian parades are ritualized versions of intertribal war. In the old days the rituals nearly always led to knife- and hatchet-wielding mayhem. Now they nearly always issue in battles of gestural and verbal-musical virtuosity. But today as yesterday carnival unfolds

Fig. 9.4 Black Elk warrior, San Fernando, carnival Monday, 1996. Photograph by Gordon Means.

in New Orleans as a long series of ritual actions, each one repeated in different circumstances, each one carrying the possibility of a confrontation. These confrontations are numerous and cumulative. There are no judges, no grandstand, and no particular prize to be gained at any one moment. The prize is reputation, collectively engendered among onlookers and collectively maintained by the ritualized cohesion of the Indian troupe (Smith 1994; Kinser 1990: 165–93).

Sixty or eighty years ago Indian bands in Trinidad acted very much like their New Orleans counterparts. Routines were learned through weeks of practice and ritual confrontations easily led to physical battles. "If you was a Red Indian, and you don't know the [other group's special language], then they gonna hit you. They gonna be a fight" (interview, San Fernando, December, 1996). In Trinidad as in New Orleans Amerindian figures were crafted to inspire fear. During the weeks preceding the 1919 carnival in Port of Spain, "in Bedford Lane, home of the Wild Indians, ghastly shrieks pierced the night, in the area of the wigwams" (Anthony 1989: 20); three years later a fierce fight between two Wild Indian bands in carnival led to a fatal stabbing (Anthony 1989: 20, 38). By that time, however, social perception of ethnicity in Trinidad was moving not towards caste-like black and white bifurcation but towards the shading-in of many small distinctions of social, cultural, and economic prejudice. Indian masqueraders did not raise the same fears in Port of Spain as in New Orleans. When a local business offered a prize in May 1909 for the "best-dressed Wild Indian band," it was won by a group from the same Belmont which produced shrieks and stabbings some years later (Anthony 1989: 17). In New Orleans no civic or business prize has ever been offered to Mardi Gras Indians for their carnival performances.

In the first part of the twentieth century Trinidad Carnival was progressively made safe and even attractive to the middle classes through a combination of police action, business sponsorship of prize competitions and direct advertisement of consumer goods. Simultaneously the role of the festival as a vehicle for social protest diminished. The evolution was slow and non-linear. Ritualized aggression remained a defining feature for many lower-class groups, including Indian bands, as late as the 1940s and 1950s, and it manifested itself with renewed force in the battles that steelbands fought against each other. But over the long term violent incidents decreased. Costumes became more elaborate, in keeping with the progressive investment of the middle classes in the holiday. In the 1950s a new form of Amerindian masking appeared, devoted to spectacular effects that increasingly immobilized the costume-bearer; these costumes were called "Fancy Indian," and were better adapted to grandstand competition than to street-parading, let alone fighting. As the country moved toward independence and non-whites expanded their role in the public arena, Trinidad's ethnic and cultural diversity could begin to be celebrated as something positive. Carnival acquired generalized political meaning as a festival of the whole, a celebration of the nation's pluralism, a gigantic advertisement directed first to the country's own citizens and increasingly to the world.

Today at the House of Black Elk a core group of ten to fifteen people imagines next year's performance and then advertises it to the public, so that anyone, young or old, Trinidadian or foreigner, can come to buy a costume, whether they know or don't know the steps. The focus is not on ritual but on pleasure, on creating historically precise, but above all spectacularly accented visual effects. "First we think about the colors, then we choose a theme, then we get the artist," the person serving as the Black Elks' secretary informed us. *Do you like the way this costume looks? This one here, the third from the left on the placard at the mas camp door. Buy it, get inside it, and have fun with it, whooping and jumping, passing the bottle, maybe smoking a little, 'playin' mas' and enjoying yourself.*"

The Black Elk are proud of the historicist purity of their costume themes ("we do research . . . we choose our costumes from books . . . we have a lot of books, all the books about Indians"). But they combine exactitude with eclecticism in colors (using modern pastel colors) and in performance (swirling in time with the costumes and soca). And they offer social openness, distributing membership in the band to anyone who wishes to costume themselves in the same thematic way, without sacrificing thereby a highly developed sense of individuality. Asked some months after the 1996 performance about what costume he was planning for 1997, one member of the organizing group said: "I'll be a Cheyenne warrior returned from the dead. I always try to do something original." Thinking of the costume he had made in 1996, we asked: "You mean, something different from last year?" "No, not just that," he replied, "I want to stand out, apart from the others."

Historicity and eclecticism, openness and individuality: the combination is well suited to the ordering of carnival in San Fernando, which carries you out of the mas camps, into the High Street, up through the center of town and out to the climactic moment at Skinner Park. You move together, interacting with your friends in the group, acknowledging acquaintances among the spectators along the route. But during those final decisive few moments on stage when your small subsection of the mas band moves forward to impress the top judges in the city, you're on your own, "apart from the others."

CONTEXTS

New Orleans's million and more people are all urban, and New Orleans's central-city blacks are hyper-urban, pressed together in broken-down housing and given few of the public services to which all citizens have supposedly equal rights and access. Black Elk masqueraders are not necessarily better off economically than most New Orleans Mardi Gras Indians. Most of them engage in manual and semi-skilled labor as carpenters, masons, mechanics, offshore-oil workers, and security guards. They too are often unemployed. In that small island which most economists would qualify as a "Third World" or "developing" country, the standard of living is lower overall than in the United States. As limited as income and opportunities may be, however, Black Elk masqueraders are not surrounded by mostly hostile white economic and mass-media structures. And Trinidadians today possess almost as a birthright what New Orleans black people enjoy only in limited, neighborhood terms: sociocultural receptiveness to the way they play mas.

Another significant contextual dimension is geographic and environmental. Trinidadians live in a small island, far from the centers of wealth and power. The relatively limited level of economic development seems to pull every settlement, and until recently even most neighborhoods in the Port of Spain urban strip, back toward isolated provincial particularity. San Fernando is not exempt from this atmosphere of isolation.

Isolation and yet openness: Trinidad's population was very small in the eighteenth century and it grew slowly, leaving large parts of the island unoccupied. This excess space, left untamed for so long and so late, through the early twentieth century when the canoes came from Venezuela, and still wild today along the flank of many unexpected hills and valleys throughout the island: this presence of physically available opportunity for runaway slaves and then former slaves, for indentured servants, illegal immigrants, half-breed Indians and Grenadians and

Haitians and Venezuelans – and those other more mysterious beings of the forests, Lougawou, Papa-Bois, Ladjabless, Soukouyan – played a never exhausted role in creating a horizon of possibilities, a horizon of otherness.

The scenes that this former Wild Indian masquerader from San Fernando described to us as his boyhood joy in the 1940s do not even today seem out of tune with the small-town flavor of the place:

> All through the week, we'd go to the stores up n'down the Coffee [Street], an' in each one say gimme a l'il flour, jes' a l'il, an' another day jes' a little sausage, an' another day a l'il sugar . . . like that, you know. We all would do that, me an' my friends, we'd put it all together in cans. Them store-keeper was nice, we was l'il kids an' it all wasn't worth nothin', we jus' ask a l'il each time. Then we take all that stuff Friday an' go up on the Hill, an' we camp there an' cook with that stuff all the weekend, jes' like Indians. That's what we always used to do.
>
> (interview, San Fernando, December, 1996)

What did this man know about the Warao and the sacredness of the hill where he and his friends used to play? He vaguely knew about them, relating them to the Red Indian costume. But the hill for him was a wild space, not a Warao place. It was a place for freedom and a place of separateness where boys could play "just like Indians," and educate themselves subconsciously for the carnival masking that would come.

The mind works both with and against people's immediate experience. It does seem paradoxical that the Warao, once the actual inhabitants and still until the 1930s and 1940s actual practitioners of nobly envisioned natural freedom, could not in the end directly embody these values. They were too actual, as silent traders in San Fernando and other marketplaces. They had to be reinvented as Warahoons, with red skirts, nose- and earrings and incomprehensible language. Then they could become imaginatively wild, and in this guise they circulated in San Fernando in 1923 and later. Similarly Trinidadians' remoteness from the noble savages who valiantly resisted white hegemony, far to the north, made them all the nearer in spirit. Like other heroes and anti-heroes – cowboys and gangsters, English kings and queens, African warriors, biblical figures – North American Indians were emphasized in their appeal by the isolation of local contexts. The ever-present lush nature just outside the door, down the street, just over the hill gave space to the imagination to develop a distant generalized appeal.

MAS

Even at the time of its greatest popularity in the 1950s, the Plains Indian model never entirely displaced other sources of inspiration. From the 1920s to the 1950s newspaper reports mention Black, Red, Blue, Yellow, Green, and White Wild Indians (Anthony 1989: 85ff). The most popular forms during this period were the Red and the Black Indians. It is a testimony to the popularity of the North American paradigm (and the eclecticism of masking categories) that the term "Red Indian" ended up being used, depending on the context, for Plains Indian masqueraders as well as for the Warahoons. White Indians also portrayed North American (Canadian) Indians. But Blue Indians were said to be "from the Orinoco" (unfortunately we have no details about their costume), and in the 1950s bands based on Amerindian empires – Incas, Aztecs, and Mayans – became very popular. Black Indians for their part, a few of whom still participate in carnival today, have always been considered "African."

If, as we have argued, the popularity of Amerindians has to do with their heroism and marginality, the conflation of Amerindians with Africa is understandable. "In this case," writes Daniel Crowley, "Indian is synonymous with 'wild man' or 'savage' " (Crowley 1956: 206). Like the Warahoons the Black Indians are a striking example of eclecticism, with their black satin shirts decorated with silver and gold beads, their Spanish pantaloons made of broad yellow and black stripes, their earloops and noserings and feathery headdresses. Less visible in our figure 9.5 are the faces blackened with lamp-black or other substances and high-lit with white at cheekbones or around the eyes. Lunging at you with a spear, or with an artificial snake wrapped around one arm, they are, at least for a startled moment, very frightening. In the 1950s Black Indians carried lances, spears, tomahawks, bows and arrows, and drums, and ate fire (Crowley 1956: 206).

In Trinidad as in New Orleans Indian bands created themselves by means of ritual practices embedded in neighborly and other local ties, no less than by using a certain kind of costume. Warahoons and Black Indians were known for their special languages and elaborated performance routines. The masking forms that became dominant during and after the 1950s relied on a spectacle-oriented aesthetic and the combination of carnival artist-entrepreneurs with large pools of individuals ready to buy rather than to make costumes. As bands grew larger, band leaders and carnival artists took advantage of this more general participation and of the increased availability of new material to present Hollywood-like representations of famous characters and stories, including Amerindian themes – Northwest Coast Indians carrying totem poles, Custer's Last Stand, Hopis, Zunis, Seminoles, Mayans, Aztecs, Toltecs, Incas, and so on.

Warahoons and Black Indians were locally generated characters, reflecting influences (Spanish, African, Amerindian) that had been part of the social and cultural fabric of the island for a long time and that gave form and meaning to the rituals. Plains Indian masking, on the other hand, originated in media-transmitted images and was now widely disseminated by the movies which taught everyone how to play this mas. In the short run this evolution produced a spectacular array of Indian costumes and performance forms, since more ritualized and more spectacle-oriented types coexisted and nourished each other. These years were the heyday of the Fancy Indian costumes and of Plains Indian masking. In 1959 Harold Saldenah electrified the Savannah Grandstand audience with hundreds of Cree Indians shrieking and brandishing lances (Anthony 1989: 276). But over a longer period the emphasis on artistic spectacle "civilized" the wild people. The Indians are – and have been since the 1960s – in danger of diluting their distinctiveness to the point of oblivion. A few fringes here and there and headdresses vaguely Amerindian in aura have become what too often passes for Amerindian masking in present-day carnival bands. Few and far between are the grand constructions of yesterday when inspiration exalted the conventional. The Warahoons have disappeared but for a few aging masqueraders (although in recent years groups of children trained in camps organized by the National Carnival Commission portrayed the character in the traditional carnival character festival held on the Friday before carnival). The Black Indians are reduced to a brilliant but very

Fig. 9.5 *Warriors of the Black Continent* Amerindian mas band on a Port of Spain street, carnival 1996. Photograph by Martin Walsh.

small group. The Plains Indian style has proved more enduring, especially in San Fernando, where, from the days of the Wild Indians, Indian mas has been very much alive. Few costumes, however, are as elaborate, while at the same time being successful in conveying a sense of authentic Plains Indian dress, as those produced by the Black Elk.

During our stay in Trinidad we also heard of no other group that was as deeply rooted in the life of its neighborhood. Lionel and Rosemarie Jagessar, also in San Fernando, have for many years created spectacular costumes (nowadays often portraying Amerindians from South American past empires) lavishly decorated with layers upon layers of colored feathers. The aesthetic of these beautifully crafted productions, however, belongs entirely to the realm of the familiar. Their creators' energies, in the feverish months that precede carnival, are mostly focused on the two to four huge costumes that will participate in the prestigious kings and queens competition in the Queen's Park Savannah in Port of Spain. The goal here is primarily to please the eye, in the context of a more and more spectacle-oriented carnival. Indians do survive as a masking motif today, but, with a few exceptions, less as substance than as style.

In the beginning, say the Black Elk, they were led by Wilfred Henry Ramdin, a man who they say "lives like an Indian," dressing simply and eating natural foods, in a small, unpainted dirt-floor place near the foot of San Fernando Hill. In the late 1980s Ramdin ceased to parade with the Black Elk. He now goes to Port of Spain with his own group, although we were told that the two bands sometimes appear together in celebrations before carnival Tuesday.

Ramdin's costume designs and face-painting are exercises in sensuous simplicity. He seems to aim at expressive intensity rather than at accumulating effects, using bright primary colors rather than many mixes and contrasts in flattened costume panels. He employs few feathers, which leave bodily contours and areas of skin intact rather than covered by massy, undulating designs. The etched vividness of his style strikes the spectator in a manner different from the Black Elks' feathery flows (figure 9.6). Black Elk costuming, since the departure of their former leader, has become more exuberant at the risk of losing some intensity. But the band continues to pursue an ideal of historical accuracy, which is akin to Ramdin's vision and sharply different from the Black Indians' and Red Indians' (i.e. Warahoons') eclectic style.

Simplicity versus accumulation of effects, historical authenticity versus rich, bewildering eclecticism: such contrasting tendencies have for decades produced superb inventions deservedly recognized with carnival prizes. But the question here is less this public recognition than the inspiration behind it. If the wild is always, perhaps even only, found by means of contrast with what is tame "here," rather than discovered by immersing the self in the otherness of wilderness "out there," then carnival masking, insofar as it is successful in communicating the wild, brings to the surface qualities that are latent in our everyday existence, qualities that are constantly present but scarcely acknowledged. That too is a function of carnival: like inversion, like satire and parody, like the enlargement of our sense of what is possible, carnival wildness may enlarge our sense of the actual.

Can the Black Elk, with its attendant neighborly practices, maintain the balance it has struck between authenticity and coloristic effects, collective energy and openness? Will the rich eclecticism of the Black Indians and the luminous intensity apparent in Ramdin's costumes be extended? These Amerindian modalities offer attractive alternatives to the commonplace way of responding to ever larger, more vaguely oriented crowds with correspondingly ever larger, more vaguely articulated spectacles which address no challenges to consciousness. For the moment at least, they represent the wild amid the tame.

Fig. 9.6 Ramdin-Jackman group, carnival Tuesday, Port of Spain, 1996.
Photograph by Gordon Means.

NOTE

An earlier version of this chapter is printed in Milla Cozart Riggio (ed.), *The Drama Review*, 42 (3): 147–69 (1998), Cambridge, MA: MIT Press.

1   Black Elk was a revered Lakota Indian medicine man who survived the Wounded Knee massacre and became an eloquent spokesman for Plains Indian spiritual profundity. We thank the Black Elk band for their help and also others interviewed at San Fernando in 1996 (names are listed in the fuller *Drama Review* version of this chapter).

10

THE BLUE DEVILS OF PARAMIN
Tradition and improvisation in a village carnival band

Martin W. Walsh

Some of the most dynamic players in the venues of Trinidad Carnival featuring traditional masquerade are the Blue Devils. A relentless beating on biscuit tins, punctuated by unearthly yelps, marks their passage through the downtown streets of Port of Spain, as a palpable ripple of excitement runs through the spectators, many of whom will be plundered of their snacks or TT dollars by these comic/ horrific images of the demon world. Blue Devils are found throughout Trinidad in such towns as Arima and Point Fortin, but are especially popular in the mountain district of Paramin above the suburb of Maraval to the north of the capital. Blue Devils may be classified as a local variant of the historical character-type of the Jab Molassi (Molasses Devil).[1] It must be borne in mind, however, that many Blue Devil players, past and present, consider the Jab Molassi "somethin' different." With the perversity of true folk practitioners, they often label themselves Jab Jab (a term which they shorten informally to "jab," a practice that will be followed in this chapter). The Jab Jab is, however, a totally different character-type according to the literature.[2]

The present report is based on observations of the Paramin Blue Devils, in action and behind the scenes, during the carnival seasons of 1997, 1998, and 2000, during which I conducted some ten hours of interviews, formal and informal. I focused particularly on the troupe from the mountain trackway of Fatima Trace headed by Andrew Sanoir, better known as "Kootoo."[3] Kootoo's startling "stage presence" and improvisational skills indeed prompted this initial attempt at a performance analysis of the Paramin devil mas'.

EARLIER BLUE DEVILS

Obtaining a "history" of the Blue Devils is by no means easy, the performance tradition being completely oral in transmission and limited exclusively to the brief carnival season. Until very recently the people of Paramin have not given the subject much thought, proud though they are of their tradition. With no records to speak of, one must fall back on anecdotal information and individual impressions.

Many current and retired performers have a general notion that the jab performance has something to do with the end of "slavery days," but none could answer, for example, the practical historical question of when bluing itself began. Andrew's father, Patrick Joseph, at the time in his late seventies (now deceased), had played Blue Devil in the early 1930s. It was a well-established tradition at that time, and so we may with some confidence push the Paramin Blue Devils back to before World War I. However, since there are no patois terms clinging to the performance (other than the word "jab" itself), it is risky to assume that this particular performance, in its current manifestation, goes all the way back to "slavery days."

In Mr Joseph's time the jab dance was performed to tamboo-bamboo (bamboo sections thumped on the road and struck with other sticks), a different sonic effect from the current rhythm section based on the beating of biscuit tins. Though very popular, with "plenty, plenty" jabs, these early bands were small, usually only two percussionists with one jab holding a chain or rope attached to the principal dancer, who was called "King Devil" or sometimes the "Abyssinian Jab."[4]

The players would sequester themselves to blue-up on carnival Monday morning, then surprise the village with their sudden appearance. They would proceed from house to house, extorting from the "terrified" residents a piece of bread or bacon, or a "big penny wit' the King head on it." The rope-man carried a receptacle for the proffered swag that the King Devil usually snapped up in his mouth. Jabs might brandish farm implements such as a pitchfork or cutlass (machete). Young children were known to hide under their beds when they appeared. The group played without masks, their bodies, faces and hair completely covered in bluing. Their appearance was more or less uniform. They wore only a pair of cutoffs furnished with a springy tail. Mr Joseph mentioned fashioning himself a headpiece as King Devil, and I have a separate account of a "cowhead," a skull section painted blue and used for this purpose. But the accoutrements of today's performance – bat wings, forks (tridents), either store-bought or homemade monster masks – were lacking. "Bat wing come after," Mr Joseph recalls. Various cross-fertilizations with Port of Spain Carnival no doubt took place over the years.[5] Even in Mr Joseph's time, the Paramin Blue Devils sometimes ventured downtown to play.

Older players indicated that tensions existed between the jabs and early motorists on the steep and winding trackways of Paramin. Mr Joseph related how a car's fender had once snagged his rope and dragged him some distance down a slope. He did not indicate, however, that this was anything other than an accident, though holding up vehicles for "ransom" – still a common practice of the Blue Devils – might well have been a factor earlier on.

James Sanoir is another son of Patrick Joseph and Andrew's elder brother by some dozen years. He played Blue Devil from the early 1960s to the early 1970s and succeeded his father as Fatima King Devil. In James's time a certain amount of innovation was occurring in the jab performance. He himself played with a macajuel (boa constrictor) that he had procured in the high hinterland and tamed. He would not use the snake directly to terrorize the audience, but would dance with it draped around him. Nowadays it is against the law to employ such partners, but more recent performers occasionally dance with rubber imitations. (Editor's note: In 2003 and 2004 one Blue Devil did carry a six-foot boa constrictor around his neck, using it to threaten the spectators. The mouth of the snake had been taped shut.) Blue Devil fire blowing, on the other hand, is a relatively recent innovation that James disapproves of, finding it "too risky." The general consensus among players of his generation is that present-day youth are going to greater extremes, taking far more risks, and that even the tempo of the pan is more frenetic.

TRAINING (OR THE LACK THEREOF)

For generations, the ranks of the Blue Devils have been replenished from a pool of young adolescents without any direct training of the young by the old, or so my informants maintain. Imitation of the jab dance and vocalizations, as well as practice beating the ubiquitous biscuit tins, however, begins at a fairly early age. The better dancers get noticed by older players and are eventually taken into a band by a kind of "natural selection." James Sanoir was not directly coached by his father but simply "followed along," eventually taking his place as King Devil. James's younger brother Andrew, in turn, took over from him. Little boys seem to spend a good deal of the carnival season in this mimetic process. They often create parallel junior bands complete with homemade props. Some even experiment with bluing. Older boys might help out by beating pan for them. They are likely to turn out for an impromptu performance wherever an audience might gather, for example, after the Patois Mass on the morning of Dimanche Gras. Early in the afternoon of carnival Monday 1998 I followed Andrew around while he beat pan for his two small sons and their friends as they performed a full perambulation of the Fatima area. Andrew lets the boys "create der own t'ing," but is free with advice on road safety, which houses to hit, how to keep up the beat, etc. His involvement as pan man is perhaps not so unusual. The training of the younger generation must be going on all over Paramin in many such informal ways.[6] Andrew's boys fearlessly halted jeeps on the steep traces and lunged at elders hanging around outside the bar. Andrew was proud of them for nabbing 84 TT dollars in their afternoon's work.

As there is no formal training in devil play, so too is there no group rehearsal or designated rehearsal time. While pan beaters need to get back their control over the complicated rhythms every year, the jabs seem to require no such preparation. Joe Felix, known as Pocket, claims to have "never rehearsed, never practiced" when he was playing jab some fifteen to twenty years ago. Many others echo him – jab dancing either comes "natural" or one does not engage in it.

There is, however, an implied code of behavior expected of the Blue Devils. Despite their furious appearance, they are rather circumspect with regard to their audiences, "ain't touchin' nobody," as Mr Joseph phrases it. His son James expresses identical sentiments and Andrew echoes them: "You don't block no one." If a spectator clearly turns away from an approaching jab, he or she is not to be pursued. Even soiling others with blue should be confined to one's friends and neighbors. If a yelping jab demands something, such as a beer or ice cream, and is refused, he simply moves on. Local killjoys might be punished with some minor looting – James once stole a bake out of the oven of a stingy neighbor, juggled with it, and shared it with his rope man – but generally property was respected. Unlike the Wild Indian or Jab Jab bands, Blue Devil groups never had a tradition of challenging each other.

THE PAN, THE BLUE, THE DANCIN'

Although Mr Joseph played jab to tamboo-bamboo back in the 1930s, the tradition for the past fifty years has been driven by pan – biscuit tins slung around the neck and beaten with crude sticks, usually with some other iron percussion (brake drums, cow bells, etc.) and whistles.[7] As in the large steelbands, this rhythm section goes by the name of the "engine room." It keeps up an unrelenting beat. Some tins, given a higher pitch by firing them beforehand, take over during the crescendos of the performance. Beating on the short ends of the tins also produces a different sound from the usual beating on the long sides and is used for various signals to the group. Incompetent and inconsistent drumming can ruin a Jab performance and so the engine room (as the percussive section is called) is considered a vital part of the performance. "Timin'," the "tempo on de pan," is of the essence, everyone agrees. One usually "comes up" as a pan beater and graduates to dancing, but there is no fixed rule. Some pan men never dance, some dancers never beat pan, but a large percentage do both. Everyone knows that carnival is near when the distinctive driving rhythms are heard being practiced up and down the slopes of Paramin.

As far back as anyone can remember Paramin has had Blue Devils, the characteristic color coming from ordinary laundry bluing. Tablets of the bleaching agent are ground up on the performance site and mixed with water, usually by junior members of the team.[8] The dancers begin with a coating of petroleum jelly to fix the color, which otherwise would be sweated off, on the skin. (Earlier performers had used lard, which must have created another, olfactory dimension to the masquerade.) The thick, bright blue liquid is smeared on by hand over every inch of exposed skin and often a paintbrush is used to get a smooth and even finish. A junior member of the band carries along a bucket of this bluing to "freshen up" the dancers. Members of the engine room usually smear a bit on themselves in a gesture of solidarity. Other Blue Devil groups sometimes wear blue boiler-suits for protection in their antics, but Andrew's troupe pride themselves on playing in the old manner, "naked," that is, in briefs and sneakers only, the bluest of the blue.

Blue Devil dancing is recognizably Trinidadian in style, a spread-kneed, angular strut with pelvic grinding, arms extended outward. The most common actions are leaping in the air, lunging at victims, or "rollin' on de groun' an' winin' wit ya partner." Devil winin' indeed can create the impression of undifferentiated, insatiable sexual mania – humping anything at any time. Late in the evening of carnival Monday 1996 I witnessed a devil winin' the front of a maxi-taxi as it attempted to leave Fatima Junction, as well as heaps of jabs winin' on each other as they tumbled down a hillside. Winin' with members of the audience is not common, nor really expected by the dancers. It is strictly up to the initiative of the individual spectator since it would involve considerable soiling.

Current performers deny any particular scenario in what they enact, and yet there is the basic role differentiation of King Devil roped in by an assistant. The "reading" must be that the King Devil is the most possessed, the most dangerous of the jabs, and would tear into the crowd with dire consequences were he not so restrained. Depending on the size of the band (Andrew's can have as many as nine or ten players) there might be two or more jabs also roped in. The larger the troupe the more individual "lines of business" flourish. The King Devil usually is the most active in procuring dollar bills from the spectators by a relentless, "in-your-face" yelping, but the other members of the band also prey upon them. Snow-cones, drinks, fruit and other snacks might be plundered in this way, both for actual refreshment and to create disgusting effects of slobbering, foaming and spitting out. Whole styrofoam cups might be masticated and spewed out again. Often the jabs bite on hidden capsules of red or green food coloring to create quite startling effects of cannibalistic gore. Fire blowing also became quite popular in the 1990s. Ordinary kerosene is taken into the mouth and sprayed out over an open flame creating huge bursts of fire. Players coat their mouths with milk or cream before-hand, but this is the only precaution taken. Andrew has specialized in "eatin' fire," which he claims no other devils want to try at the moment. Since there are many other fire blowers at work in Paramin, it is probably only a matter of time before fire swallowing also enters the general repertory.

PSEUDO-TRANCE AND THEATRICAL TRANSFORMATION

All devil players queried, whether current or retired, agree that a certain trans-formation takes place when one blues-up and begins to hear the beating of the pan, and that both the bluing and the rhythm are required for this particular energizing. James Sanoir describes it thus in an interview:

> You see, when you put de blue on you and you hear de pan, you get a vibes, you get a vibes bring you . . . *jumpy* . . . get you jumpy . . . you feel you could do anyt'ing, yeh, not violence t'ings, but you feel a kinda Happiness in you, Joy.

Another older performer remarked, "You a changed man when you put de blue on you, you change." A current dancer chaffs at the small, demarcated judging areas in Paramin's carnival Monday competition because "when that Jab *in ya head*, in ya head, you can' really perform in a box!"

When Kootoo's group prepares (what they call dressin'), whether behind the grandstand in Port of Spain or on the slope below their homes on carnival Monday, the atmosphere is essentially that of a locker-room during a winning team's suiting up – lots of laughter, joking, one-upmanship, helping each other get ready. Rum or beer might be passed around, but are only casually indulged in. Alcohol does not really fuel the performance. When the pan beaters start warming up, however, dancers in the final stages of their bluing begin to gyrate and let out the character-istic yelps (what Andrew calls bawlin') much like an orchestra tuning up. One might even get a call-and-response effect with the jabs yelping on different tones. This process may start and stop several times before the group is completely welded into a performance unit, at which point they are ready to move on down the road. A jab group unwinds in a similar fashion – intense moments are relived, injuries compared, rum or beer contributed by supporters is passed around and, most importantly, the crumpled TT dollars, stashed in one of the tins of the pan men, are flattened out, counted, and shared among the band members.

Although James Sanoir might talk of a happiness and joy in getting into the Blue Devil role (and all performers characterize their activity in typical Trini fashion as "enjoyin' ya'self wit' ya friends"), the image presented to the carnival spectators is one of elemental rage, insatiable hunger and bestial energy, a blast from hell itself. This does not register as a paradox to the performers, who are, as a rule, friendly, easy-going individuals. The demonic impersonation is not viewed as dangerous in any psychological or spiritual sense, either to the players themselves, or to others. The majority of the Paramin villagers are at least nominally Catholic, but no older people indicated that there was ever a religious objection to the portrayal, even from the local priest.[9] It goes without saying, however, that the jabs completely disappear by Ash Wednesday and are not to be heard of until the next carnival season. Disapproval did exist but it was more a matter of personal discomfort or taste, especially with older women. It was related that Andrew's grandmother wanted nothing to do with the jabs one carnival Monday and consequently had closed up all her windows. She neglected the one over the steep slope behind her house and the devils managed to build a human pyramid and spook her anyway. A contemporary older woman like the late Morilla Montano could still convey an ambiguous relationship to the jabs. Admittedly uncomfortable in their presence, in speaking of them before her death in 2001 she could not refrain from squirming with delight at their "greasy" behavior.

The Blue Devil performance thus does not require any prophylactic activity beforehand, and no player had ever heard of any jab having problems coming out of his role. If the pan keeps beating, the jabs might continue to dance well beyond the boundaries of a particular performance event, but this is strictly for their own pleasure. In earlier decades spectators might have held up a crucifix or saint's medal to turn away an aggressive jab, but this was always in jest. In the Paramin Blue Devils, then, we are not dealing with a spirit-possession performance, as in certain African masked dances or the "riding" of worshippers by the loa in Haitian Vodou, but rather with the skillful simulation thereof. What the Blue Devils do is acting, clearly. They are "only *playin'* de devil." Yet a dancer must truly *seem* possessed. A good jab player never breaks character, and especially not for the purposes of incidental humor. The aural stimulation of the pan and the visual and tactile stimulation of the body-painting evidently create a particularly intense, empathetic brand of impersonation that has elements in common with, one might be tempted to speculate, African modes of religious experience. Not a trace of cultic influence has been noticed by this observer, however.[10]

Many performers, however, credit the jab role with something like special powers. Andrew, for example, claims that he would never consider himself capable of his spontaneous feats of climbing, fire-handling, or uprooting vegetation if he was not so completely in character. "Pan have some kind a meanin'," he claims, imparting extra strength to the dancer. Blue Devils are susceptible to injuries but, like high-performance athletes, they transcend the pain in the adrenalin rush of the game. At the same time, however, the jabs require a certain performative "distance" for their improvisational interactions with the audience and the environment, something like the controlled anarchy of ritual clowns such as the Hopi Koshare. As mentioned earlier, there is an implied code of conduct operating in the performance. In the 1997 Traditional Characters Parade, one of the younger King Devils, riding the wave of his energetic performance, had successfully swept away the crowd from the entrance to one of the upscale shopping malls on Frederick Street, and seemed on the verge of plunging in. Kootoo gave him a quite clear signal to pull back. Jab mayhem was not to be played with wristwatches, calculators and CDs as possible props. Boundaries had been reached: the proper theatre of the Blue Devils remained the street.

IMPROVISATION AND INNOVATION

The Paramin Blue Devil tradition appears to be in a very healthy state of preservation. Unlike many of the traditional masquerades in Trinidad, there has not been a break or a serious decline in the practice. It has deep, local roots and, largely because of its continuous appeal to youth, has never needed to be revived or coaxed back to health by initiatives from the National Carnival Commission. The present Paramin jabs are intensely proud of their tradition and feel that Blue Devil bands from other districts are but pale imitations of their genuine article. Playing jab is "instinct," it is "in de genes."

Dramatic changes have been taking place in recent years, however, largely owing to this very success. For one thing, the Blue Devils' exposure to urban carnival spectators and participants has increased dramatically from the days of Patrick Joseph or even James Sanoir. Numerous, often remunerative venues have opened up from Viey le Cou at Queen's Hall a week before carnival, to NCC events at Carapichaima or San Juan, to the Friday Traditional Characters Parade in downtown Port of Spain, which has grown conspicuously in size and popularity in the last few years. In the 1997 season, Andrew's troupe seemed to be on the road every other day in the two weeks prior to carnival. They were called upon to open the glitzy Dimanche Gras show on the big Savannah stage. (They had also organized a downtown jouvay band that year called *Blue Devils and White Angels*.) In 1998 Andrew was hired by the large mas' band Barbarossa to play jab around their magnificent Blue Devil King costume construction during the Kings and Queens semifinals. The Paramin Blue Devils are indeed achieving something like celebrity status in Trinidad Carnival. Andrew has even appeared, anonymously, on the cover of Earl Lovelace's novel *The Dragon Can't Dance*.

Another development is the annual Jab Jab Competition sponsored by the Paramin Carnival Commission, first held in 1997. The more or less impromptu appearance of Blue Devil bands from dawn to dusk on carnival Monday has now, to some extent, been organized along urban carnival lines to include adjudication and prize-winning. It is hard to imagine how "judging" goes on in such a sweeping, spontaneous display of comic chaos. The brief time slots and small playing areas marked out at Fatima Junction and in front of the Arietas Bar seem ludicrously inadequate. Still, judging proceeds and the idea of a competition with prizes has definitely caught on, especially among the younger players. What the event has also created is an incredible concentration of jab playing, with easily two hundred participants streaming into the village from late afternoon to early evening. Feeding off each other's energy, the various bands collide with each other, hooting in rivalry, as they pour down the various traces toward the judging areas, the living definition of Pandemonium. Carnival Monday night in Paramin, on the other hand, is dominated by the sound-truck and soca music like any other Trinidad fete, although older jabs in their thirties and forties may continue to work the edges of the youthful dance crowd.

There are other developments as well. Colors other than the traditional blue and red have been experimented with, White Devils having appeared recently. Teenage girls are beginning to play (Andrew's sister for example), but so far are not seen in the front ranks of the "shock troops." Elements of the larger carnival world are also creeping in – references to current soca hits, flagmen such as one sees with the

When the parade burst out into the wide open spaces of Independence Square, much of this collective energy dissipated. One noticed immediately how fatigued the Paramin band had become. Uncharacteristically, Andrew turned to me in the crowd pleading for a Carib. Securing an armful of beer bottles I hurried back to the band. Andrew meanwhile was dancing with a concrete block poised on his head. After sloshing a beer, he was up another lamppost, but it was clear he was beginning to wind down from this extraordinary performance.

What might all of this jab playing *mean?* Certainly for the performers themselves it means a good time and a way of making a few dollars as it has always meant.[11] In recent years it has also opened up an arena for achievement that basketball or hip-hop might afford in a North American context. But carnival comes but once a year, and there is no promise (or danger) of "going professional." The new competitive edge to jab playing may have created some new problems and tensions, and one detects a hint of jealousy in some oldtimers regarding the big stage and media opportunities the younger jabs now enjoy; nevertheless, there is little danger that devil mas' will lose its mountain roots or its local appeal. The Paramin Blue Devils are among the most vital traditional characters of Trinidad Carnival, and there are probably more of them than in any previous decade. If the Midnight Robbers and Pierrot Grenades are delicate hothouse plants needing the constant care and nurture of the NCC, the Paramin Blue Devils are hardy, roadside perennials.[12] For the larger context of Trinidad Carnival they may well be supplying that element of "wildness" that Sam Kinser sees as a necessary component of any vital carnival tradition (1999). Celebrating their own blue-smeared, enraged and incontinent bodies, they are the anarchic counterweight to the glitz and glamor of the Savannah stage.

NOTES

1 Under Jab Molassi in his article "The Traditional Masques of Carnival," Daniel Crowley observes, "there are also bands of red, green, or blue devils dressed like the Imps of the Dragon Band with short kandal, tails and pitchforks, but with their bodies covered in ruku or green or blue powder" (1956: 74; see also Harris (1998)). Trinidadian terms used in this chapter can be found in Allsopp (1996). See also the Glossary in this volume.

2 See Crowley (1956: 74–5). Paramin people occasionally use the term *Bad Jab* for their devil type.

3 Andrew likes to call his group "Number One Paramin Blue Devils," but he also works easily with many other devil bands in the district. All jab bands are very loosely organized and often share personnel. Thanks go to the twins Edwin and Edward Joseph who serve as informal "managers" of the troupe. They helped me interpret the village scene and link up with earlier devil players. They also recorded some interviews in 1997 and 1998.

4 The pun is on "abyss." In one of Mr Joseph's old Pierrot Grenade routines he spells out "Mussolini," which might place the Abyssinian Jab at the time of the conquest of Ethiopia.

5 A connection to the props of the elaborate but now defunct Dragon Band is probable. See Crowley above. The horn headdress popular among present-day Blue Devils is perhaps traceable to the urban "Cow Bands" originally organized by abattoir workers.

6 For the Carapichaima venue in 1997 the Fatima Blue Devils brought three "sides." Andrew played King Devil in the first side, and then directed from the sidelines as the apprentice jabs of the second side came on. He would wave and hoot them on to make more of such opportunities

155

as a burning puddle of kerosene. The third side was made up of very young performers for whom Andrew gleefully beat pan.

7   One older player mentioned that heavier cooking oil drums preceded biscuit tins in Blue Devil pan (not to be confused with the motor oil drums which give rise to the steelband).

8   The brand name is "Family Train" with an antique-looking palm tree trademark. A box of several hundred square tablets costs about $30 TT (approx $5US). Earlier the bluing was begged for.

9   The current parish priest, an elderly Tipperaryman, is only amused by the young people's jab playing. He finds they have little historical sense of the masquerade as a response to the trauma of slavery. Unfortunately, I did not have the opportunity to get more of his "bookish" opinions of Paramin Carnival.

10 Damien Joseph compared playing jab to the experience of Shango, but no direct connection to Afro-Caribbean religious practice or cult activity is evident in the masquerade. My son Tilman, who in 2000 became the first white person to play Blue Devil in Paramin, can testify to the ecstatic nature of the experience, something comparable to a really intense "mosh pit."

11 Andrew's group takes in an average of $200 TT per outing, about $35 US, not counting travel expenses and other stipends for performing in sponsored "traditional" events.

12 Few of the traditional character bands come from an unbroken tradition, or have the "critical mass" necessary for a convincing performance. Some exceptions I have noticed are: Rodney Alfred's East Indian Jab Jabs from Couva, now in its third generation, and the Bad Behaviour Sailors from Saparia who, like the Blue Devils, rely on improvised mayhem – kicking each other in the pants, piling up in great heaps on the ground, wining in a chain-dance, etc.

1 True to their adopted demonic code, Blue Devils recoil from water because it is associated with the Christian sacrament of baptism. Trident in hand, Andrew Sanoir, Paramin's top Blue Devil practitioner, enacts this aspect of the mas' during a presentation organized for visitors at the Chagaramas marina, west of Port of Spain. Photograph 1997.

11

PARAMIN BLUE DEVILS
Photographs by Jeffrey Chock

2 Like all fine actors, Sanoir holds his poses so that the details of his performance are manifest. Paramin, carnival Monday, 2002.

3 Apprenticeship begins at a young age. Paramin, carnival Monday, 2002.

4 Disdain and stoicism: another aspect of the Blue Devil's performance. Paramin, carnival Monday, 1999.

5 A rubber-masked devil dares his audience to follow him down the road to perdition. Paramin, carnival Monday, 1997.

6 Paramin's Blue Devil mas' is not the exclusive preserve of men. Carnival Monday, 1999.

7 The tin pan made of a discarded biscuit tin is the driving force of the mas'. Paramin, carnival Monday, 2002.

12

THE JOUVAY POPULAR THEATRE PROCESS
From the street to the stage

Tony Hall

> . . . in that self-defining dawn . . .
>
> Derek Walcott, *The Antilles: Fragments of Epic Memory*
> (Nobel Lecture, December 7, 1992)

Trinidad Carnival has long been associated with theatre – with scripted drama, short sketches and songs, which featured strong "internal dramatic action," and what is often called "theatre of the streets" – featuring acting, song, dance, mime, speech traditions, and elaborate costumes.

One of the first post-emancipation manifestations of theatre connected to the carnival season was the Carnival Tent or Backyard Theatre (Hill 1972: 32). In this setting there were elaborate drum dances such as the belair. There were coronation ceremonies by Borokit bands characterized by Hindu-derived as well as African-derived entertainment, some subtle speechifying as well as elaborate spectacle and dance. There were also Red Indian and Wild Indian playlets, with textured mime and the most remarkable invention in language. There was the satire of Dame Lorraine performances and, by the early twentieth century, the creation of the calypso tent with its calypso war, duet and calypso drama.

The Dame Lorraine show began at midnight on Dimanche Gras, carnival Sunday night. It was a continuation of the mockery of the slave master by the enslaved, which had begun on the estates prior to the period of apprenticeship, 1834–8. This performance in two acts was a burlesque satire of the manners of the eighteenth-century French plantocracy. This Dame Lorraine performance (in Hill's words) "formalized this practice into public theatre for a paying audience" (Hill 1972: 40). These performances lasted till dawn when the heavily costumed performers and their audience would filter onto the street to begin the masquerade on Monday morning: an early version of jouvay.

In 1943, Edric Connor, actor, singer and pioneer folk researcher, in a now famous lecture on West Indian folk music in Port of Spain, demonstrated "the new creation in musical sound" of the steelband and that it could be presented on the concert stage (Hill 1972: 49; Hall 1990: *Late Night Lime* TV interview with Lennox Pierre).

This lecture had a profound effect on a number of pioneer theatre researchers, including Errol Hill and Beryl McBurnie.

In his 1963 and 1964 Dimanche Gras shows, Errol Hill transferred to the big yard of the Queen's Park Savannah stage many of the raw beginnings of the theatre of the yard and the street in the form of the sophisticated political satire of the day. Before that, in 1955 in Trinidad, he had produced *The Ping Pong*, his play about the steelband, which explored both "the strong rhythmic foundation" of the music and the social conditions under which these pioneers of the instrument were forced to live.

Man Better Man, Hill's full-length musical play, written in calypso verse, appeared in 1957 and is still one of the only plays of its kind, which utilizes the calypso idiom so completely for its structure and narrative thrust. In *The Trinidad Carnival: A Mandate for a National Theatre*, Hill attempts to outline a version of a national theatre, grounded in the rhythms of carnival and all the varied elements of theatre found there, using the skills of costume making, the widespread talent for designing and building costumes and properties, the audience participation, choreography and performance, etc.

Others have worked to develop dramatic pieces and other forms of performance out of the carnival and related folk forms. Derek Walcott produced his *Drums and Colours: An Epic Drama* in 1958 as part of the inauguration of the now long-defunct West Indies federation. In this play Walcott attempted to chronicle the history of the islands, from a Caribbean perspective, drawing heavily on carnival pageantry and poetry. Beryl McBurnie with her Little Carib Theatre and Molly Ahye were among the first, in the 1950s, to produce dance dramas based on their research into folk traditions and the struggles for freedom of the Amerindian, African, and East Indian peoples of the islands. Later in the 1970s Astor Johnson took over the mantle with his Repertory Dance Theatre, and in the 1980s Helen Camps successfully produced spectacular plays in the Trinidad Tent Theatre, using the performance traditions of the carnival. In the 1990s, we have the work of playwright Rawle Gibbons, whose *Calypso Trilogy* has been influential, and of musician/composer Geraldine Connor, whose spectacular *Carnival Messiah* produced in England in 2001 and again in 2002 (with productions in Trinidad in 2003 and 2004) has taken carnival theatre to a new level.

As Hill points out, the theatre to be created is taken not just from the perform-ances of the streets but from the basic essence of all the elements of the carnival – from the essence of the mas itself on the road, as Peter Minshall has demonstrated; from the swirling vortex of steel orchestras in the pan yards (as in the offerings of Boogsie Sharpe and Clive Bradley); or from the essence of the extempore, celebratory call and response and social commentary of calypso, soca and chutney, as the late André Tanker and David Rudder have projected.

Working with Peter Minshall, I was able to observe him adapt and transform traditional mas characters through his own meticulous designs – the basic Bat, the Midnight Robber, the Borokit, Moko Jumbie. I witnessed how he incorporated history (particularly the social and design history of the mas) into the present reality of performance without the hampering clogs of nostalgia. From this I learned that traditions are most meaningful when they transform and evolve with the culture that produces them. Therefore, the value of traditional, culture-bearing, mas characters, who embody the history of emancipation and the struggle both for independence and self-definition: characters like the Midnight Robber with his rapid-fire grandiloquent speeches of revenge and imposing hat and gait; the Baby Doll with her instant social action theatre which insists, right there on the street of carnival day, in shaming renegade fathers into child support; the Badly Behaved Sailors satirizing the gay abandon of the Yankee sailor in drunken choreography along the street; all these and more I am now driven to look at more closely.

Throughout Trinidad, at the present time, John Cupid and the National Carnival Commission have established schools in which children learn to embody such culture-bearing characters – so much so that the Traditional Carnival Character festival that takes place on Friday of carnival week has in the last few years virtually become an alternative children's carnival, in which masses of children outnumber the oldtimers performing traditional masquerades. Such an effort of education empowers these children. It gives them a sense of purpose, teaches them valuable lessons from their own history, and helps to preserve and transmit vital cultural traditions, even at the risk of encasing these renegade traditions within the marble vaults of pure mimesis – traditions memorized but not always experienced.

Here emancipation can be seen as the organizing principle around which we can chart and triangulate all our daily efforts. Therefore, when any of these creative impulses, embedded in emancipation cultural traditions, are invoked, a new realization of self emerges, a new understanding of independence "in that self-defining dawn" manifests a jouvay of the collective spirit. These manifestations I call *jouvay process*. This is what we are involved in, a jouvay process. It is ongoing. In this context the theatre wants to probe and bear "witness to the early morning of a culture that is defining itself" (Walcott 1992).

But, as a dramatist, for this to have any concrete meaning, I need a "performance model" based on this formulation. What I call the *jouvay popular theatre process* (JPTP) is such a "performance model." This model assumes the existence of the traditional masquerade characters, not as specific historical figures but as archetypes of human behavior defined within the evolving context of the survival systems of the emancipation tradition in Trinidad. These systems involve processes of creolization, of hybridity, of betweenity, and of assimilation. Moreover, the history of resistance in itself affirms a contrary, paradoxical sensibility sustained throughout the colonial and postcolonial search for personhood and identity.

A JPTP workshop begins by assuming that the daily life of each participant reflects the essential drives and energies of any one or any combination of the hundreds of traditional mas characters, seen as archetypes rather than historical figures. Thus, workshop participants begin their search for the right character or characters, for which they may have an affinity, through an introduction to the history and sociology of the original characters and mas makers of these characters. Second, we go through a range of theatre exercises and games, based on the street performances of the characters, to assist the participants (theatre artists, students or community persons) in their discovery.

In the third stage of the workshop, JPTP participants are asked to create short, improvised dramatic presentations using elements of the street performances of their chosen characters. In these presentations they must play themselves, as the characters, in their own normal everyday life situations. This can be related to the process of spirit possession, which is an important part of the traditional religions of many of the peoples who settled in the West Indies. The traditional mas characters, therefore, manifest in contemporary situations through the JPTP workshop participants.

So you end up with, for instance, the bank manager as Midnight Robber. Only it is not satire: the person playing the Midnight Robber is a real bank manager. It is a way for actors and drama students to understand drama and create theatre, and for community people to better understand themselves and their cultural history. The JPTP, therefore, is a direct way to meditate on jouvay process through a "performance model."

In 1956 the Mighty Sparrow won the Calypso Monarch title in Trinidad when he sang:

> Jean and Dinah
> Rosita and Clementina
> Round the corner posing
> Bet your life is something they selling
> And if you catch them broken
> You can get it all for nothing
> Don't make a row
> Since the Yankees gone, Sparrow take over now.

This heralded a new voice in the calypso arena as well as the new nationalist movement of Premier Dr Eric Williams that was to point the way for an independent Trinidad and Tobago. By 1962 Trinidad and Tobago gained independence from Britain after a West Indian federation of nations, mired in political ambivalence, had failed. Yet, after forty years, Sparrow's voice remained the only one on this issue of the women who were left behind by the Yankees who had occupied the island on the Chaguaramas Naval Base during World War II. The presence of the soldiers on the island with their "yankee dollars" and the resultant power had thrown the local men into dire insecurity. But by 1956, the year of the calypso, most of the soldiers had left for their home, leaving the women behind to fend for themselves among their wounded menfolk. Sparrow's song speaks of the masculine revenge.

My play *Jean and Dinah . . . Who Have Been Locked Away in a World Famous Calypso, Since 1956, Speak Their Minds Publicly* is about those women from whom we have not heard officially. Sparrow's keen observations of the gender politics sparked our attention, and to my mind the women had to reply. To this end, through the JPTP, I created a two-woman play which Earl Lovelace reviewed in the *Trinidad Sunday Express* after attending the play's premiere performance on November 29, 1994 in Port of Spain:

> The two old friends tear at each other, stripping the other of the last little veil of pretence until they stand naked and exposed before each other, evoking the rambunctious poetry of a theatre that is self-confident, passionate and fearlessly their own. We see the soft, delicate shift and shuffle of the fancy sailor dance, and the absurd caricature of baby doll and behind it all the hard life of pimp and prostitute, hard violent men and tough battered women of a pathetic and glamorous heroism, all needing to be rescued for life.
>
> (December 11, 1994)

To build this play I called Susan Sandiford and Rhoma Spencer, two actresses who had always called themselves modern-day jamettes, the defiant warrior-like people of the street who found themselves below the line of respectability in the post-emancipation era.[1] This group comprised drummers, matadors, calinda dancers, batoniers/stickfighters, shantwells/calypsonians, masqueraders/street revelers, prostitutes, etc. Both Rhoma and Susan had already discovered, as students of mine at the University of the West Indies, their full jamette consciousness that allied them with the older women of the street.

By the time we started they were close friends with many of the women from Sparrow's calypso through research they had done on earlier projects. Some of these women had migrated to the United States; others had died. However, Rhoma and Susan were able to improvise monologues and scenes from interviews they had with Jean Clarke (the famous Jean in Town) and other informants. I videotaped the improvisations, which I then had to turn into a play.

The women – "carnival people" through and through – played sailor mas (in all its forms), and they inhabited the pan yards of the "battered lovers" of the "macho bad john" pan men. Yet these women were the stolid keepers of the truth of these men's and their own lives, from the nightclubs to the pan yards. Their drama emerged from the jamette/calinda/warrior essence of the traditional Bad Behaviour Sailor. From that base emerged a Baby Doll monologue by Jean and a mythical Midnight Robber from the dead, Ruby Rab, by Dinah. Each of these forms of mas speaks to a social consciousness: the sailor satirizes American imperialism, and the Baby Doll evokes gender politics, whereas the Midnight Robber seeks to avenge injustices done to his ancestors. The emergence of the Midnight Robber in our workshops was strange, since this is traditionally a male character.

The idea of the play had begun with an interest in the women of the calypso and with no real thoughts of carnival or mas. The women themselves through their spirit had infused the drama with the energy of traditional carnival characters, which emerged from an organic process rather than appearing as arbitrary carnival devices inserted into something called "a carnival play." In fact, even though at times it utilizes the risqué, bawdy humor and viciousness of the jamettes, the relentless, raw and raucous rhythm of carnival, the confrontation and participation peculiar to the carnival of the street, the play consistently uses such elements to draw the audience in. To help viewers appreciate the tumbledown lives of Jean and Dinah, the jamettes who survive partly by infusing their own lives with the spirit of mas, we incorporated their story into a theatre totally derived from the carnival streets that in their essence belonged to Jean and Dinah.

Make a ritual of the sunrise, jouvay!

NOTE

1   By the time the playmaking process ended, Susan Sandiford had been replaced by Rhoma's cousin Penelope Spencer. Rhoma and Penny have performed this drama together in the West Indies, the United States, and Canada frequently, as Lordstreet Theatre Company, since 1994.

1

13

CARNIVAL PEOPLE

Photographs by Pablo Delano

2

3

4

5

6

7

8

9

10

11

12

13

14

15

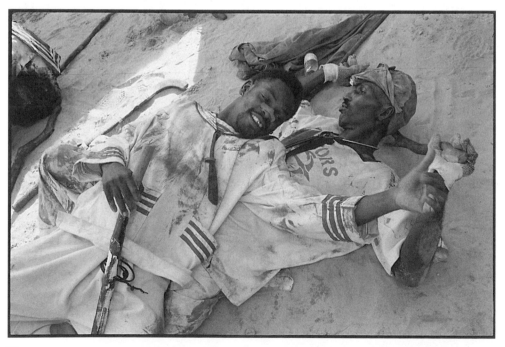

16

17

1 Individual carnival masquerade costume, Carapichaima, carnival Monday, 1997.
2 Nydia Byron, then reigning limbo champion, and Derek Cassanova with others from the Malick Folk Performers, Barataria, 1997.
3 Alyson Brown, *This is Hell*, designed by Peter Minshall, Callaloo Company, Queen's Park Savannah, carnival Tuesday, Port of Spain, 2001.
4 Individual fish costume, Parade of Bands, Queen's Park Savannah, carnival Tuesday, Port of Spain, 2002.
5 Egyptian costumes, Carapichaima, carnival Monday, 1997.
6 Albert Bailey, master wirebender, at home, Woodbrook, 2002.
7 Dragon costume, Carapichaima, carnival Monday, 2001.
8 Soumarie costumes, Port of Spain, Traditional Carnival Character Festival, 2000.
9 Individual costume, Carapichaima, carnival Monday, 2002.
10 Beating iron, Mud Mas, Carapichaima, carnival Monday, 2000.
11 Mud Mas, Carapichaima, carnival Monday, 2000.
12 Winin', Mud Mas, Carapichaima, carnival Monday, 2000.
13 Amerindian costume, Victoria Square, Port of Spain, 2002.
14 Paramin Blue Devil, Victoria Square, Port of Spain, 2002.
15 *Sailors Astray*, Bad Behavior Sailor mas, Carapichaima, carnival Monday, 2002.
16 *Sailors Astray*, Bad Behavior Sailor mas, Carapichaima, carnival Monday, 2002.
17 *Sailors Astray*, Bad Behavior Sailor mas, Carapichaima, carnival Monday, 2002.
18 Blue Devils, Queen's Park Savannah, Port of Spain, carnival Tuesday, 2002.

18

Part III

PAN AND CALYPSO – CARNIVAL BEATS

14

WE JAMMING IT
Introduction to Part III

Milla Cozart Riggio

> From the bongo drum to the roll of the tassa
> Ever since Europe come and she make bassa, bassa,
> We jamming it.
> Calypso, calypso, oh calypso music, yeah! Yeah!
>
> David Rudder

The music of carnival is no less assimilative than carnival masquerades. Whatever their origins and whatever influences they encompass, calinda, kaiso, calypso, soca, rapso, and steel pan are all musical forms (or in the case of pan, instruments), whose structures – like their names – reflect a variety of real and imagined influences that have merged into a new set of Caribbean musics. However – unlike mas – pan and calypso are recognized aspects of the larger African presence throughout the Americas. Often percussive, with a tendency to rely on drums, and yet with melodic, sometimes ballad-like lyrics influenced by the European cultures they partly assimilated, Trinidad Carnival musics are varied and eclectic, their history embedded in what Gordon Rohlehr has called the "whole process of cultural erosion, adaptation, change, and innovation, as well as the concern today with national identity" (1990: 1).

Unlike Part II of this book, the chapters in Part III systematically track, as well as comment on, the evolving history of Trinidad's Carnival musics from the point at which this story is known and can be documented – i.e. from the arrival of the Europeans, the Africans, and ultimately the Asians. There are, of course, hundreds and perhaps thousands of years of history – of music, dance, and the rhythms of life of varying peoples who had passed through and claimed these lands, of voices belonging to the island whose echoes haunt and intensify the assimilative patterns, but which are remarkable mainly for their absence from the recorded histories. Our story begins with the early nineteenth century, with the interaction of the colonizers and the colonized.

Part III, however, begins and ends with the present, acknowledging the role of today's youth in the perennial search for national identity. In an initial lyrical statement that at once mourns the passing of traditions and celebrates "the terror and the truth" of "the jouvay youth massed on Frederick Street, dancing to reggae," award-winning novelist Earl Lovelace affirms that in the Caribbean "the aesthetic is the political," even as he points to the potentially destructive paradox implicit in enshrining music bred of resistance and emancipation in the symbolic citadel of nationhood. Dr Jocelyne Guilbault ends the part by analyzing the music of contemporary, massed youth, the often maligned soca-based "party music" of today, as a defining agent for a new sense of nation that – true to the ethos of the time – confirms and transcends national boundaries, assimilating influences from across the Americas.

In the middle chapters, Dr Dawn Batson, Assistant Professor and Chairman of the Board of the Trinidad and Tobago National Steel Orchestra, tracks the evolution of what she calls the "drum trilogy" from the skin drum to the steel drum – beginning with a tradition that in the early nineteenth century linked fiddle playing and calinda dancing to African drumming, through the incorporation of tamboo bamboo and varieties of other metal instruments (biscuit tins, wheel hubs), noting the cross-fertilization of the (East) Indian tassa ensembles and steel pan. Dr Kim Johnson, who has recently completed his PhD with a carefully researched dissertation that personalizes the history of steel orchestras in the narratives of steelband pioneers, muses on the link between pan and the sense of the fleeting moment, the ephemerality of a music that for him captures the ontology of the modern condition.

In an essay written and massively abridged for this volume, Professor Gordon Rohlehr tracks the "jarring, jamming, carnivalesque collision and clashing counterpoint of rhythms" that constitute the emergence of contemporary soca from "the calypso [that] is a living example of Afro-Caribbean oral tradition adapting itself to a process of continuous change." Pointing to the residual presence of Spanish rhythms so strong that for a time calypso was regarded by some in the 1930s "as an extension of Latin music in the Caribbean," Rohlehr ends his essay by describing the nearly disastrous consequences of assuming that Machel Montano's "'Real Unity' concert of Sunday 26 November 2000" could be transformed into "the bourgeois notion of a 'concert' at which $600 patrons would sit politely in their all-inclusive/exclusive compound."

As part of the story he does not have time to tell, Rohlehr points to forms of music analogous to but different from carnival music, as for instance the pichakaaree competition begun by Ravi Ji as a way for Indo-Trinidadian youths to give voice to their own cultural traditions during the Hindu spring festival of Phagwa. Among the many assimilative influences – including that of English ballads as well as Latin rhythms – that are bound up in the evolution of Trinidad Carnival music, none is stronger or more continuous than the persistent cross-referencing of Afro- and Indo-traditions. True to the character of the island and its peoples, that which is identifiably (East) Indian – instruments such as the tassa drums, rhythms, themes, and lyrics – persistently intermingles with the hybrid, indigenous Afro-based percussive rhythms, even as each set of peoples with their own religions and carefully preserved cultural traditions stalwartly maintains its own independent identity. Visible everywhere, this combination of interaction and separation was driven home to me during carnival season 2002 when Nestor Sullivan of the community-based Pamberi Steel Orchestra in San Juan, Trinidad (also the Director of the Trinidad and Tobago National Steel Orchestra), sat on the steps of the Hindu Temple in the Sea beside a musician who had been playing for Hindu prayers, fingering what was for Nestor a new instrument, hoping to figure out how to incorporate both the rhythms and the tone into his own pan calypso music for the following year.

One of the most striking features of all the musics associated with Trinidad Carnival is the spirit of affirmation that rings through sometimes heart-wrenching lamentations (such as Singing Sandra's 2000 prize-winning calypso monarch entry "Voices from the Ghetto" or Gypsy's earlier controversial "Little Black Boy") and that sustains otherwise banal adaptations such as Sanelle Dempster's 2001 winning Road March "River," which incorporated both melody and adapted lyrics from "When the Saints Go Marching in" in a song that used double entendres to celebrate copulating sexuality. For all the attention given to the role of calypso as political and social satire and to pan as the music evolving from the toughest street environments, there is at the core of Trinidad Carnival music an indomitable spirituality. The musicians of this tradition are, in essence, the high priests of a culture that is – in despite of (rather than because of) the politicians and marketing experts who would commodify their aesthetic traditions – affirmed through its arts. In the lyrical language of David Rudder:

> Cause we're moving with a power and a glory, see how we step in style
> One nation heading to salvation, the Ganges has met the Nile.

Locating the essence of life's interactions in communal celebration rather than the political arena and finding the healing pulse in the rhythms of the dance rather than the posturing for positions of power that often constitutes the basis for international relations removes the cynicism from much of the satire in Trinidad music. Take, for instance, André Tanker's 2002 brilliantly satirical soca composition "Ben Lion," performed with Wendell Manwarren and Three Canal. What is remarkable about this song, Tanker's response to the tragedy of 9/11, is that it contains an astute sense of the political realities of international power and conflict without itself being in any sense political or self-righteous in its call for "one world, a free world" and its welcome of all that world – the Americas and Afghanistan – to one big human party. This song as well as Tanker's equally potent 2003 "Food Fight," points to the healing power of "de fete" as a counterweight to the potentially killing power of international political warfare. There is a basic joy, a sense of celebration, a common bond of humanity that links Tanker's dance-inspiring satire or Rudder's more obviously priestly "High Mas" with Ravi Ji's Mantras of the Year or Pat Bishop's Lydian Singers' resounding "Hallelujah Chorus," sung to the accompaniment of both steel and tassa drums.

The Power and the Glory: In times of fiscal crisis in the United States, when funding for the arts – considered one of the luxuries – is inevitably threatened, the paradoxes of power are highlighted. While the US expansion into the Caribbean has always been capital-driven – attempts to gain power economically through markets – the power of an island such as Trinidad finally comes from the arts. Alas, in their race to capitalize on their oil and natural gas reserves, to replace their street vendors with air-conditioned malls, and to turn their most precious treasures – as, for instance, their music and their carnival arts – into marketable commodities, the politicians and capital developers of Trinidad ironically threaten to silence the music and eradicate the unique richness of their culture. If history can be our guide, these efforts will finally fail. What Lovelace calls the "emancipation jouvay tradition" will hopefully find a new medium of resistance and subversion. So long as the "jamming" goes on, the songs will be sung, the mantras will rejoice, the children of the culture will find and fight their way to some new, subversive, and probably outrageous triumph.

15

THE EMANCIPATION JOUVAY TRADITION AND THE ALMOST LOSS OF PAN

Earl Lovelace

Looking back now to our obligatory carnival Sunday-night fetes that led into jouvay, at whole families linked together, at the lime with friends, the strands of green bush held aloft, old, young, everybody out to Jouvay, it all seems very clear. Yet, for years, hardly any among us realized that, in celebrating jouvay, we were commemorating the celebration of emancipation.

We knew that from 1838, 1 August was the official day of the emancipation celebration. What we did not know was that sometime in the mid-1840s the colonial administration had moved the celebration from that day and tacked it onto carnival. From midnight carnival Sunday the emancipation celebrations began. In effect, jouvay became emancipation. Somewhere along the way the name *emancipation* was withdrawn; but the celebration continued with, poetically, a more appropriate name, one confirming not only the dawn of carnival Monday morning, but asserting the dawning of a new day for those previously enslaved in the island. Jour ouvert, J'ouvert, Jouvay!

By the time we get to the 1950s there is no official celebration of emancipation. August 1 has been given over to Discovery Day or, as some called it, Columbus Day, commemorated in a carnival-style celebration, its central point Columbus Square just off Nelson Street. The picture I have of it before it ceased is of ribbons and maypole dancing and Juju Warriors, and Guarrahoons (Wild Indians) with faces rouged with roocou and freshly cut staves peeled of their skin, chanting in Guarrahoon language and doing their Guarrahoon dance. Here we were carrying on two celebrations, both to do with the celebration of emancipation, and emancipation not even mentioned.

So, instead of blotting the idea of emancipation from the calendar of the country's consciousness, the colonial administration, by tacking emancipation onto carnival, provided emancipation the opportunity to penetrate the official carnival and transform it into a stage for the affirmation of freedom and the expression of the triumphing human spirit in a street theatre of song, dance, speech, sound, and movement. We may reason as well that the colonial government of the 1840s chose carnival as the celebration on which to append emancipation, not simply out of malice but out of their acknowledgment that jouvay, carnival of the street, was itself created and supported by the lower classes of Africans.

It is in emancipation then that we find the genesis of the jouvay carnival characters. Along with parody, ridicule, and the mocking derision of pappyshow, what characterizes these presentations is a sense of threat and violence, ritualized in masquerades: the Devil, Jabmalassie, Midnight Robber, Dragon. All of these masquerades present themselves not only in costume but through their own peculiar song, dance, and/or speech. Along with these we may add the violent art of the stickfighters and their ceremonial kalinda dance and chants. It is into this tradition that the steelband settled when it entered jouvay after World War II.

Steelband belonged here not only because of the spirit of resistance and rebellion it expressed – it had itself grown out of tamboo bamboo and skin drums, was inspired by Orisha chants and Shouters' hymns, and fell easily into the emancipation-jouvay mas playing tradition of Juju Warriors, themselves contributing Flourbag Sailor and Dirty Sailor, Bad Behavior Sailor, Fancy Sailor, and a wave of military-inspired mas.

Steelband was the emancipation jouvay movement's new force. It had arrived at the beginning of a new epoch. The colonialist movement was on its last legs. Self-government and independence were around the corner. The jouvay characters that had maintained their expressions of rebellion and resistance for 120 years were now largely taken for granted, the social conditions out of which they had grown, ignored. The steelband provided a new focus and challenge, not only because of its music but also because of the violence that accompanied it.

Where the violence of the jouvay characters had become formalized into ritual, the steelband presented a violence that was naked, that could not be ignored, that recalled the first fierce jouvay revelers coming onto the streets just after emancipation. And this naked violence was not limited to carnival. It was linked to everyday living. In some ways the steelbands' violence was greater outside of carnival than within it. Bands kept up between themselves ongoing feuds.

But steelband had already become the rallying point especially for the dispossessed jouvay youth, its charisma established even before it hit the streets, the sounds reproduced everywhere in classrooms, schoolboys beating the desks and getting the rhythm, fellars coming back victorious from a football match playing mouth band, imitating the different instruments of the steelband and reproducing pan or drum sounds; fellars all about walking in steelband rhythm and shadowing the wrist movements of a man beating pan. We had something. We, its supporters, its followers, were not awed by the genius that had created it; we shared in its creation. New people were developing new pans, sinking new notes in the steel. Ordinary people were tuning steeldrums, ordinary men and women were becoming arrangers of music. In a sense we had produced the rallying icon for our generation that, if we were mindful, showed us self-confidently embarked upon the mastery of technology, which we would need to compete in the modern world.

At that time steelband was not yet pan. There was no insinuation of its being a single musical instrument; it was a band, with players and men beating iron and men waving flags and various levels of supporters, the principal of which were the bad johns. It was a whole movement that came out at carnival, a gathering of jouvay people complete with flag-man and bad john and jamette woman and man beating iron. There was pride and there was danger. Anything could touch off a fight. And we jumped up in the band with a kind of wariness, feeling ourselves at that time in the heart of a time bomb, listening for the explosion in any discordant sound, alert to run. It was this danger that made the band our own. This was the danger that had to be crossed to lay claim to the bands.

The bad johns were the carriers of that danger, heroes, at least to schoolboys who intuitively knew that they were warriors, heirs to stickfighters now meta-morphosed here in the urban ghettos of Laventille, and John John and Gonzales into fist fighters and head butters. Heroes, Warriors: these terms even in their most limited application traditionally suggest a political consciousness. It is doubtful that the bad johns exhibited any of that; but they were all we had to express the breadth of violence that the poorest had been emancipated into. Just as steelband was showing us the inventiveness, dedication, and genius by which we were to be liberated, the bad johns were displaying the violence we needed to confront if we were to lay claim to that liberation. If the music was to be claimed, you had either to find a way past the bad johns and the violence or open your own band. To claim the aesthetic you had to deal with the political.

Around Port of Spain in the 1950s many "decent" bands began sprouting. Decent people ran to them. But the violence remained until there came the political promise of Dr Eric Williams and his political party, the People's National Move-ment (PNM). Few have failed to observe that the much vaunted cultural creativity expressed in Trinidad and Tobago has come principally from the ordinary African-descended people at the bottom of the economic ladder. This is not surprising. European colonialism was not motivated to create anything since its very rule and mystique rested upon the enlightenment it was introducing to these islands. Its laws, parliament, literature, music, even its brutality: all of it was brought in from the centers of its civilization. Its civilizing mission established a minority that for the purposes of its own advancement and privilege doomed itself to imitation. The remainder, unexposed to the formal colonizing education, were forced to draw upon their own resources of memory, myth, genius, and the consciousness of their circumstances to construct, from the fragments of their broken culture, a new culture by which to live. The very fact that these fragments, whether religious or secular, were continuously under threat forced upon them the need to seek creative means to keep them alive. And this they did in the face of banning, jail, fines, and ostracism. Shango, Shouters, calypso, steelband, carnival – all have come through the fire of colonial disapprobation. The aesthetic would also become the political.

When we woke up to the realization that we were independent and that inde-pendence meant having a culture that we could call our own, we discovered that all we had that might be termed indigenous or native was what had been created or reassembled and maintained here by those at the bottom of the economic ladder.

But we had not all been engaged in the struggle to protect what would eventually become basic to our patrimony. Colonialism with its education, its system of rewards, had produced a diversity that went far beyond what we might call race. And while there were those that transcended these classifications, others benefited from collusion with the colonizers, sharing their contempt for what was being fought for; some were bystanders engaged in what they saw as their own battles. Independence was to face us with the questions: How were the people of this diverse society to access these native elements of what was now being seen as

fueling a culture which all of us were to share? How was this society to authentic-
ally access cultural institutions that grew out of the struggles in particular circumstances by ordinary Black people for their self-affirmation and liberation without
the society embracing the philosophies that inform these institutions? How was it
possible to access the aesthetic without embracing the political?

The simplest solution was to define carnival away from anything political. This
had already begun by linking it to the Greek and the Roman celebration of the two
days of abandon before the Lenten retreat began.

This myth, since its purveyors were in power and since they too had need to
affirm themselves, was given carnival Tuesday in which to express itself; it was given
the Carnival Queen and the Savannah Carnival competitions and the columns of
the *Trinidad Guardian* newspaper which from 1919 to the 1950s ran the Savannah
Carnival, the myth supported by the pronouncements of Eurocentric anthro-
pologists who needed only to speak to be believed. And it was further supported by
a middle class that insisted on being led by colonial definitions that, despite what
was before its own eyes, could find neither the curiosity nor the courage nor the
self-confidence either to follow or to seriously build on the emancipation jouvay
tradition out of which carnival as we know it today was born.

It is against this background that Dr Williams and the PNM were welcomed
into the emancipation jouvay tradition, Williams elevated to the rank of jouvay
character. It was hard to imagine anyone more suited for caricature. He had a
distinctive height, look. He was masked with dark shades. Nobody in public saw his
real face. He was equipped with a hearing aid. In the early days he had a cigarette
dangling from his lips. His speaking voice was unique, his vocabulary and rhythms
a kind of baroque Trinidadian, his cadences echoing the Midnight Robber, his
repartee as swift and sharp as an extempore calypsonian's, his attitude that of the
bad john. In addition he was griot, historian, obeah man, the third brightest man in
the world. This was The Man. The emancipation jouvay tradition claimed him as
its own. Dr Eric Williams for a long time became a fixture in old mas and jouvay-
morning bands, a number of his impersonators vying with each other for the Best
Individual prize.

What became of the political promise anticipated by the emancipation jouvay
movement is a matter that requires much reflection. Was the emancipation jouvay
movement sacrificed for the grander idea of making, of all our people, one nation?
What we know is that Williams stressed the large themes of the independence
epoch. He pointed us to the central concern of knitting together a quite disparate
population. He steered us to a concern for political education. Jouvay people were
invited out from their holes and gutters and shanty towns to the University of
Woodford Square to be lectured on international relations. We were lectured on
constitution reform in Trinidad and Tobago while Black people were not admitted
to work in banks and were finding it impossible to get loans from banks. People
were lectured on the end of colonialism – *Massa Day Done* – while no sensible
program of land reform was ventured into. Perhaps steelband was as much a bless-
ing as an embarrassment. If this venture of nationhood and independence required
that the country be good scholars, how to admit and champion the genius of
ordinary people as expressed by their origination of the steelband? How to elevate
and affirm the steelband movement if doing so would mean pinning oneself to a
certain social program? If it would mean giving stature to another institution that

Fig. 15.1 Dr Eric Williams, first Prime Minister of the Republic of Trinidad and Tobago, 1962–81. Photograph courtesy of the Ministry of Public Administration and Information, Port of Spain.

would not only compete with Williams himself but would elevate the indigenous movement over the educated, elevate the creative over the imitative? Williams couldn't do that. The steelband as symbol and movement remained largely unexplored with little to demonstrate its potential.

And so the opportunity of binding the steelband to indigenous effort, of fulfilling the emancipation jouvay dream of liberating a society to self-confidence and creativity was never undertaken. By the time Williams ended his political career, he had left his emancipation jouvay constituency thoroughly mystified and as distressed as when he had met them. The violence of the steelbands had been removed; and, if over those years we permitted a single bad john, his name was Eric Williams.

In that time, steelband had moved to the Savannah, followed briefly by the emancipation jouvay movement. There it would be subjected to the sanitized rules and regulations of a colonial middle class that continues to address battles that had been long fought and won. Its musical offering remains frozen in the mode of the European classics, the melodic line emphasized at the expense of the rhythmic, the whole wide world of musical possibilities ignored. And is no one even a little bit alarmed that calypso music now played at Panorama by steelbands is less capable of moving people to dance than the deejayed rendition of the same calypso sung by the calypsonian?

Is Panorama to become the final nail in the coffin of pan and the emancipation jouvay movement? Will jouvay survive the loss of pan? Will pan make its way back at the center of the emancipation jouvay movement?

In the first years of Panorama, the supporters of steelband followed the steelbands – no, carried them into the Savannah, along the bull track and onto the Savannah stage; and for a while it looked as if jouvay was going to take over the Savannah; but the Savannah was too small for jouvay. The Savannah could accommodate the music; it could not accommodate the Movement. The organizers of Panorama began to construct more and more fences, to put up barricades, and to employ security. Today, the presence in their numbers of diehard supporters of big bands such as Desperadoes and Renegades helps to maintain the illusion that the emancipation jouvay is in the Savannah. The fact is that, under the insistent weight of security, the numbers of jouvay people in the Savannah have dwindled. Unaccommodated and unwelcomed, they have drifted away. In any event, they didn't want to sit down to a concert, they wanted to get on. They wanted to play.

In the Grandstand now, the Black middle class sit and listen to pan, their baskets with food and drink at their sides. They look at programs and work out which band is playing next and discuss who is likely to win the competition. Here nobody gets up to dance. This is serious business. On the other side, over in the North Stands, there is a mixed gathering of people, on their feet, most of them, the majority in their own contained and rambunctious party. For them, the activities on the stage are the background to their own celebrations, which they carry on most wonderfully during the intervals when the bands are setting up onstage, beating *dudups* and iron and wailing down the place.

Out on the Drag where steelbands assemble and make musical practice runs before they go onstage, longtime supporters, jouvay people from twenty, thirty years back, crowd around the pans, listening for the old sounds, for the emancipation jouvay music. And the youth? Steelband used to be an organizing force for youth. How does the music played now speak to them? Or for them? What irony: now that it has become a national symbol, pan has all but left the emancipation jouvay movement.

Now, after the intense practicing for their single annual offering for the Savannah stage, steelbands bring less and less to the streets. As a result of this fewer people come out to push the pans. Steelbands got their own transportation; steelbands which used to be pushed through Port of Spain now ride on trucks – some, like floats, high up above the emancipation jouvay jam in which they used to be central.

Our failure to consolidate and build on the emancipation jouvay tradition has left it in limbo. This has restored new attempts to define this tradition on the periphery of carnival. This has spawned a debate on the origins of carnival. This is not properly a debate about carnival at all. It is about how people who live here are to lay claim to what valuable has been produced by others in the land. About what price, if any, they are prepared to pay. It is also about the horror of the vision of a carnival torn from its political and social roots, gutted of its power and presented as a neutral aesthetic creation.

Today, the mas is ripe for the picking. It can go anywhere. We face again the same question: How to access the aesthetic without addressing the political?

For a long time the tensions generated by this question have been expressed creatively in carnival: in calypso, both Road March and social commentary; in steelband, classic and calypso; in the mas itself, pretty mas and ole mas. Today, jam and wine have overtaken commentary; classic has stamped itself on the steelbands' presentation of calypso; and old mas has had to be rescued from extinction by having a space on the Friday before carnival. Today the tensions in carnival are expressed between the formal and the extempore; between the chant and the ballad; between the rhythmic and the melodic lines in steelband. What is of particular interest is that, where the spontaneous, the zest, and the spirit belonged to the old emancipation jouvay people, it is now used in the service of a newer jouvay tribe.

The hordes of Bad Behaved Black Devils, Blue Devils, and mud mas in jouvay are now largely of a middle class whose race is Trinidadian. The steelband whose music was the solemn joyful rhythm of a people marching to selfhood is now in the Savannah as the backdrop to the rambunctious revelry in the North Stands. The masquerade figures that affirmed the emancipation jouvay presence in carnival, rescued in part from oblivion by Minshall, have been all but gutted of their force and terror in the translation.

Is there anything to reclaim here? Or are we right on target in producing a totally inclusive and genuinely Trinbagonian celebration?

Carnival is still a monument to the endurance and triumph of the human spirit. It remains the Trinbagonians' existential challenge to that ironic "emancipation" that sought to mock the idea of liberation by "emancipating" people to nothing. Steelband cannot remain indifferent to its role in keeping the spirit of this movement alive. It cannot allow itself to be sidelined to a single tune a year – a hundred men and women in a band playing one tune a year while the youth disappear into the Socarama arena to find a music to sing them and speak for them.

With the emancipation jouvay figures emptied of their force and threat, and steelband tamed and almost put to bed, it is time for us to look elsewhere for the challenge that has always been integral to the emancipation jouvay tradition.

In recent years on carnival days, the jouvay youth massed on Frederick Street, dancing to reggae. In 1998, they found in Machel Montano's "Toro Toro" their own music to place them more properly in carnival. The irony is that music is not deepened by steel: it comes blaring in brass; and we shall need, as we always have needed, to discover once again the courage and goodwill to face the terror and truth of that charge.

RETAKING THE STREETS

Four years later the questions remain: Is Panorama to become the final nail in the coffin of pan and the emancipation jouvay movement? Will jouvay survive the loss of pan? Will pan make its way back to the center of the emancipation jouvay movement?

Today, the dismantling of Panorama is well under way. At its height, it had been one of the grandest festivals on the planet, and, up to 2001, it still brought together all the bands from nearly the whole island for two days. The preliminaries (as they now refer to what we knew as Panorama) are now being held in pan yards. Thirty bands were selected in 2002 for a semifinal show. Even this number the president of Pan Trinbago thinks is too high, so we can expect maybe twenty-five bands next year and fewer the next, until the organizers arrive at an optimum number for their idea of a steelband show. On the other hand, pan is returning to the streets for carnival, more relaxed, more contained, not with quite the fervor as of old, not its main show, more as its exhibition performance. Pan's big show is still the Savannah, still Panorama. At least one organization has had a steelband play at a big carnival fete, as pan used to in what now seems so long ago. This welcome initiative will most likely grow; some of the bigger steelbands have come together to organize regular concerts, and, of course, there is the World Steelband Festival that brings together bands from around the world. Today, pan stands looking in three directions, the streets, the Savannah and the pan yard. The world has changed, it seems as if pan no longer needs to choose which avenue it will take to carry onward the emancipation jouvay tradition.

An earlier version of this chapter is printed in Milla Cozart Riggio (ed.), *The Drama Review,* 42 (3): 54–60 (1998), Cambridge, MA: MIT Press.

16

VOICES OF STEEL
A historical perspective

Dawn K. Batson

ACROSS THE LAND, ACROSS THE SEA, THERE LIES AN ISLE CALLED LA TRINITY . . .[1]

To understand Trinidad's gift to the world, the steelband, one must understand the island and its people. Trinidad, the Trinity, is the home of a rhythmic force that drives the people and the culture: a pitting of three against two, heard in the music, seen in the life, found in the history. The concept of the Trinity confronts the duality of a twin island republic, Trinidad and Tobago.

MOVED BY ANGER, MOVED BY GREED, MOVED BY LOVE AND MOVED BY NEED, A PEOPLE, A PEOPLE INDEED . . .

The mix of cultures and ethnicities that congregated on these small islands played an important role in the development of Trinidadian society. The cultural conflicts, resolutions, and the resulting cultural meld added dynamic force to the creation and evolution of the steelband. Steelbandsmen were mainly of African descent but persons of other races were also deeply involved, the wider society influencing the steelbandsmen.

Music, song, and dance were always important in Trinidad. The people needed some form of release to stave off frustration especially in slave times; but these gatherings also were an opportunity for the people to plan and incite riots. Thus, the ruling class, whether French planters, British colonialists, or "respectable" persons of African or French Creole descent, imposed laws in vain attempts to "tone down" the music, song, and dance of the people. The drum trinity was the first voice heard. Three in one: the bull or bass, the foulé filling in the middle parts, and the cutter, the smallest and most insistent. They gave voice to the confusion, pain, and strength of a people brought against their will from Africa to the New World. The drums witnessed the French planters in their celebration of Mardi Gras. The drums were there as the planters in masked balls combined finery with their imitations of the *nègre-jardins*, as the field slaves were called. The drums laughed as the *nègre-jardins* imitated in return the dances and dress of the planters and sighed as they heard the blowing of the slave driver's horns and the cracking of their whips as the slaves were driven to the cane fields. The drums slapped as the planters imitated scenes of *cannes brûlées* (the burning of the cane) in their Mardi Gras balls and the drums rejoiced as, after emancipation, the Africans mimicked not only the planters but themselves as well in the canboulay (making the word their own) processions. When August 1, 1838, brought full emancipation, we may imagine the canboulay procession celebrating the day as, linked arm in arm, those emancipated paraded through the streets, stickfighters with sticks and flambeau torches, led by their chosen King, Queen, and Prince, women and children bringing up the rear. In the heart of the procession, as always, the drum trinity driving and unifying the people.

In the 1840s the emancipation celebrations and canboulay parades were moved into carnival. Just after midnight on Dimanche Gras the processions began. Led by the chantuelles singing songs of defiance and satire, musicians blowing conch shells, cow horns, and beating drums, stickmen carrying flambeaux and bois (wood for stickfighting), the voices of resistance proclaimed: "When Ah dead bury mih clothes, mama doh cry for me." Folk characters such as the Lagahoo, Soucouyant, and La Diablesse haunted the streets calling out, "Jour Ouvert, jour p'oncore ouvert" (the day is breaking: the day is not yet broken) (Carr 1965). In this way, the jouvert celebrations were born. The music was traditional African call and response with the chantuelle or lead singer singing the verse or lead lines, answered by the crowd singing the chorus.

THEY PLAYED THE DRUM, THEY LAUGHED, THEY CRIED, THEY DANCED, THEY SANG, THEY LIVED, THEY DIED . . . THEY FORMED A SONG AND SAW IT PROVED THEM STRONG . . .

In the late 1800s, the canboulay procession and stickfighting were the mainstays of the carnival. Stick bands divided the city, with each major band having its boundaries which members of other bands were forbidden to cross. Increased urbanization and unemployment created conflict that was enacted in stickfights driven by the drums. Between 1881 and 1883 there were a number of riots connected with the canboulay celebration. The colonial government, apprehensive about the power of the drums, tried to silence them. In 1883, a Music Ordinance was passed effectively banning the beating of any drum, the blowing of any horn, or the use of any other noisy instrument. Banned were any dance, procession assemblage, or collection of persons armed with sticks or weapons of offense numbering ten or more (Rohlehr 1990: 29–30). This Ordinance incited rebellion. In many parts of the country policemen trying to enforce the Ordinance were routed with sticks, stones, and bottles. In 1884 an order fixing the commencement of carnival at 6 a.m. Monday suppressed the canboulay processions and the calindas (Hill 1972: 23–31). These measures, however, did not achieve the desired effect as the people devised different methods of expression, which with each setback grew more and more elaborate.

Banishing the drum from the streets meant that the drum now needed a home. The drum trinity without pause swept into the bamboo that grew all over the island. Tamboo-bamboo bands grew up in "yards" in towns and villages around the country. These yards, as opposed to the huge domains of the stick bands, were based in communities and were more part of neighborhoods than whole regions. "Tamboo" came from the French for drum, *tambour*. Three in one transferred to the lengths of bamboo. The bull became the boom; 5 feet long and 5 inches wide, it was stamped on the ground and became the bass. The foulé, middle mother, kept its name and character, now broken into two pieces of bamboo each 12 inches long, 2 to 3 inches thick and struck together end to end. The cutter still improvised, now made of thin pieces of bamboo of different lengths, held on the shoulder and struck with a stick (Gonzalez 1978). The bands also used the chandler, which was slightly longer than the cutter, split bamboo hit together, bottles filled with varying amounts of water and struck with spoons, chac-chacs (gourds of calabash or wood filled with stones or beans), and scratchers (metal or wood graters scraped with a piece of metal).

Bands from all over the country, some of them over two hundred strong, paraded through the streets. How exhilarating to belong and how frightening to be excluded. The authorities made efforts to clamp down on the bands but they were never banned outright. In the 1920s, the bamboo voice reigned. The (East) Indian tassa ensembles which performed for the Hosay festivals may have affected the rhythms of the later steelbands and vice versa. The tassa ensemble used one cutter which did the soloing, two foulés, a large bass drum, and gynes, small finger cymbals that were used to keep time. Many African-Trinidadians also played in the tassa ensembles.

The 1930s were tumultuous. The voice of Uriah "Buzz" Butler, a trade unionist, inspired labor riots that influenced the mood of the country. The voice of the proletariat became louder and more strident. The bamboo voice, while strong, was found to be easily stilled as the bamboo would burst after repeated pounding. In the search for a louder and longer-lasting sound, young men added metal to the bands. They found that pitches could be made and changed by constant beating. All manner of sound makers were sought: brake drums from cars, dustbin tops stolen from housewives, paint cans, cement drums, cow bells, chac-chacs, and mouth bands (where all the sounds of a brass band were recreated using only the mouth – sometimes real brass buglers played at the front of the bands). Against all this the chantuelles and crowd sang.

In this way, a louder, more durable and more tuneful sound was created. The bamboo was discarded. The rhythms of the drum ensemble were incorporated into these steelbands vieing with each other throughout the island. Simultaneously, persons found that notes could be created on these metal cans and old biscuit tins. One-, two-, and three-note instruments were created. In 1939 and 1940 Alexander's Ragtime Band was the most popular of the new metal bands. Next, the voice of the drums was forged into steel.

These early steelbands were mainly rhythm bands accompanying the crowds. Gradually as the "steelband boys" experimented, more and more instruments were added. The people had a voice that could be developed and improved upon. This new voice of steel mirrored the heart and soul of the drum trinity. The bass, now represented by the cuff boom or slap bass, was made of a biscuit drum "cuffed" or struck with the hand or a ball. The bass was overlaid by the dudup or bass kittle, a caustic-soda drum with two notes and hit with a stick. The lead was taken by the kettle, also known as the tenor kittle or side kettle. Made out of a zinc or paint can, the kettle had three notes and was hit with a stick. Accompanying these were the iron, usually the brake drum of a car, bottle and spoon, chac-chacs, scrapers, and other noise makers.

The people now had creative power and, like birds defending their territory with sound, the voices of the bands became louder, stronger and more melodic. Encounters with the police did not cease, as seen in one incident that occurred in San Fernando, according to the *Evening News* of February 1, 1940:

> Lance-Corporal Sladen told the Court that over 200 pre-carnival revelers were marching along Broadway and other streets beating bottles, spoons and bamboo pipes, and when stopped by a Constable and himself threw bottles and sticks at them and they were forced to seek refuge. They were only able to arrest John Cyrus – one of the smallest men in the crowd.

In the early 1940s, bands continued to experiment with metal. Hamilton "Big Head" Thomas of the Hell Yard band found that burning zinc cans to remove the remaining zinc changed their pitch when struck and started to fashion notes on the cans. At the same time in John John, Winston "Spree" Simon lent a pan to Wilson "Thick Lip" Bartholemew who was noted for his strength. When returned, the pan was badly dented. Restoring its original shape "Spree" found different pitches and began tuning caustic-soda pans. The instrument at this time was in a convex form. Ellie Mannette is credited with sinking the pan, thus allowing the creation of more notes.

Mannette, the holder of an honorary doctorate from the University of the West Indies and a National Endowment of the Arts award in the United States for his contribution to the development of the steelband, remembers:

> During the course of time between 1937 and 1939 there was a gentleman by the name of Spree Simon who invented a four note . . . with the small can . . . created four notes on top of it . . . convex and, I heard about it I did not see . . . sometime later I saw another guy from St James I know, Sonny Roach, with another four note drum playing a little melody on four notes. I was kinda taken back that I could only get two rhythm notes on my drum and cannot get four and said why can't I make four? So I said OK I'm gonna change this whole concept and in 1941 I took the barrels down and made it concave . . . The steelband was born from a very primitive form . . . rhythm, rhythm, rhythm.
>
> (Mannette 2002)

Neville Jules, one of the founders of Trinidad All Stars and a pioneer in the steelband movement, remembers:

> Pan was coming from the river, a place call Hell Yard . . . I listened and then went away. I was ten years old . . . Years later I was in the river playing with "Fisheye" [Rudolph "Fisheye" Ollivierre, a steelbandsman celebrated for his playing skills] . . . the older guys had stopped playing cause they couldn't go on the street [during World War II]. I used to watch Big Head Hamil, he tuned ping-pong, no song, rhythm. Later I started tuning convex pans with dents – ping pong, dudup, biscuit drum, bass drum . . . Big Head was said to be first to play a tune.
>
> (Jules, Interview, 2002)

Norman Darway had this to say: "Victor 'Totee' Wilson was the first to put notes on pan . . . ping pong, ping pong . . . like the QRC clock" (Darway 2002).

From 1942 to 1946 during World War II carnival was banned. Stella Abbott, a Trinidadian music teacher for over sixty years (interviewed at 84 years old), remembers: "at the beginning of the war carnival was still allowed but one year the

Governor banned carnival. I remember the chantuelle singing, 'the Governor say no mas' and the crowd would answer, 'The Governor mother ass,' I don't know if it was related but there was no carnival for the rest of the war[!]" (Abbott, interview, 2002). In spite of the ban on carnival, there were still a number of steelband competitions around the island. The ping-pong was developed and replaced the kittle as the lead pan. On VE Day and VJ Day, the people and the steelbands took to the streets in celebration. The *Evening News* of May 8, 1945, reported, "Dawn – Up earlier than usual, joyous thousands dressed themselves appropriately and paraded in bands, dancing in the street to the crazy rhythm of improvised instruments." The *Trinidad Guardian* on May 9, 1945, reported, "Carnival costumes, packed away since 1940, were shaken out and men donned housecoats and dresses to join in the fun. Scrap metal heaps were searched for brake drums which were mercilessly pounded all day long under flags of all description." The celebrations for VJ Day were even more intense. A *Trinidad Guardian* report of August 1, 1945, stated:

> Standing to lose by these preparations [victory celebrations] are residents of various districts, who are already complaining of being fleeced of their dust bins as the steelband boys get on with the job of assembling instruments which they intend to accompany proceedings. These dust bins which will be used as drums forming part of improvised orchestras can already be heard and were sounded during the weekend as members of the bands which will be seen on the streets prepare for the revelry.

The *Trinidad Guardian* of Saturday, August 18, 1945, reported in a piece headlined "Trinidad Gives Peace A Noisy Welcome": "On both days the steelband boys kept up a deafening din with their improvised instruments which all but crushed recognized orchestras off the streets as revelers showed preference for music thumped out of old iron."

The bands came out on the road with the larger instruments strung around their necks or held in their hands. Stella Abbott (interview, 2002) says, "Coming from Sunday school we were talking about the steel bands and one of the boys said they play melodies now. 'Really,' I said. 'Yes,' he said, 'they play *Mary Had a Little Lamb.*'"

OUT OF OIL THERE CAME THE DRUM . . .

In 1945 the voice, still muted, was in the small pans. Neville Jules:

> Ellie and I were in a competition in Tunapuna, everybody had small pans . . . one guy had a big pan with twelve or thirteen notes . . . the crowd laughed at [him] 'cause everybody else would stand and hold the small pan in one hand and play with the other hand . . . he had to sit and play with the pan on his knee . . . everybody laughed but next competition everybody had big pans . . . I think his name was Cyril "Snatcher" Guy from Tunapuna.
>
> (Jules, interview, 2002)

Ellie Mannette (2002) remembers that "in 1945 we parade in the streets . . . my drum the barracuda was stolen . . . in 1946 I came up with the first 55 gallon drum into a musical instrument."

Some of the bands of the time were Grow More Food, later renamed Tripoli, Hell's Kitchen, Harlem Nightingales and Oval Boys. The advent of the oil drums strengthened the voice of the steelbands and resulted in an improved tonal quality. The steelbands grew up in the communities in meeting places now known as pan yards and great rivalries were engendered between communities with the steelbands being seen as the symbol of the community. As was done in the old canboulay days, the bands paraded with players, women, children and bad johns (the fighters of the communities). The bands took on the aspect of gangs each with their own turf. Many names were taken from films of the time. Carib Tokyo, founded in the 1940s, took its name from the film *Destination Tokyo*, Boys Town, founded in 1951, took its name from the film *Men of Boys Town*, and names such as Red Army, Desperadoes, Renegades and Invaders were calculated to strike fear into the hearts of other bands.

Bands became territorial again, with fights breaking out between the supporters and members of different bands if they felt their territory and property (women, instruments, or music) were threatened. Steelbandsmen were looked down upon by polite society. Parents refused to let their children participate in steelbands. Stella Abbott noted, "parents would beat their boys for playing in the steelbands, they would go get their licks and go back . . . it charmed them" (Abbott, interview, 2002). Needless to say, the authorities were not happy. Famous clashes between steelbands were memorialized by the voices of the calypsonians such as 1954's "Steelband Clash" by the Lord Blakie:

> It was a bacchanal Nineteen fifty Carnival,
> Fight fuh so with Invaders and Tokyo,
> Mih friend run and left he hat
> When dey hit him with ah baseball bat
> Never me again to jump up in a steelband in Port-of-Spain.
> Invaders beating sweet
> Coming up Park Street
> Tokyo coming down beating very slow
> As soon as the two bands clash
> Mamayo if you see cutlass
> Never me again to jump up in a steelband in Port-of-Spain.

The Mighty Sparrow in his calypso "Outcast" also of 1954:

> If your sister talk to a steelbandman
> Your family want to break she hand
> Put she out, lick out every teeth in she mouth
> Pass!
> You outcast!

A MONUMENT TO SOUND AND LIFE, A TRIBUTE TO CREATIVE STRIFE A PEOPLE'S SONG, A PEOPLE'S PRANCE A PEOPLE'S GIFT, A PEOPLE'S CHANCE . . .

Innovations continued into the late 1940s and early 1950s. Tuners added notes as needed for different songs. The ping-pong was first held with one hand and played with one stick. Later on, two sticks were introduced and Ellie Mannette was said to have been one of the first to introduce the wrapping of ping-pong sticks with rubber. As time went on, new pans such as the tune boom and a three-note bass were introduced by Neville Jules. Jules, inspired by the cuatro of the Spanish parang bands, also added the quatro. This instrument was later tuned by Philmore "Boots" Davidson and called the guitar. The balay, chu-fat, grumbler and grundig in the middle section were also added to the steelband.

Many of these instruments have since been discarded. Today the main instruments of the steel orchestra are the tenor which replaced the ping-pong with a range of slightly over three octaves and usually plays the melody, the double tenor used for counter-melodies and harmonies and introduced by Bertie Marshall, also known for his pioneering work on amplification of the instruments, the double second introduced in 1954 by Anthony Williams and used for harmonies, strumming of chords and at times the melody, the double and triple guitars, the cello, the quadraphonic, covering the middle parts, and finally the tenor bass and the six, seven, nine and twelve basses providing the foundation. The frontline or higher pans, rather than being placed around the neck, are today placed on stands, an idea introduced by Anthony Williams. The rhythm section or "engine room" is also of extreme importance and includes the brake drums, the trap set, the chac-chacs, the scratcher, the cow-bell and the congas.

The basic methods of tuning that for the most part are still used today were developed in the 1940s and 1950s. The skirt of the drum was cut to size and the drum sunk with a hammer, the notes grooved in their various sizes with a punch, the steel tempered by heating it on an open fire and then pouring cold water over it, and the notes tuned by hammering the sections. Tuning was often done by ear or with the use of a melodica but today a strobe is used to make the tuning more exact. Many instruments are chromed for longer wear and then re-tuned. In recent times an American company, HydroSteel, has patented a hydroforming process to mass-produce tenor pans. At the moment one hundred and fourteen tenor pans can be produced at a time. The skirts must then be attached and the pans tuned. The pans are made from stainless steel, thus eliminating the need for chroming. Trinidad and Tobago Instruments Limited (TTIL), owned and directed by Michael Cooper, uses a spin-forming process to create mini-pans but uses the traditional method for full-size pans.

TO PLAN TO BUILD TO WORK TOGETHER. TO DREAM TO MAKE OUR WORLD A BETTER PLACE, FOR EVERY CREED AND RACE ...

Not all the voices of polite society were against the steelband movement. Leaders of the Trinidad and Tobago Youth Council defended the pan men. Solicitor Lennox Pierre, Albert Gomes, then a member of the Legislative Council, and Canon Max Farquhar helped to educate the general public about the economic plight of the steelbandsmen. Between 1949 and 1950, a Steelband Association was formed that later came under the leadership of George Goddard, a stalwart champion of the steelband cause. In 1951 the Youth Council sponsored a national steelband of eleven members selected from the best pan men in the country to perform at the Festival of Britain. Rehearsals were held for the first time under a qualified musician, Sergeant Joseph Griffith, who was director of music in St Lucia and a former member of the Trinidad Police Band. Working with tuners, the instruments were chromaticized, simple orchestral scores arranged, and the panmen taught to read a score with the note names identified by Arabic numerals. The band, the Trinidad All Steel Percussion Orchestra (TASPO), debuted at an open-air performance on the South Bank Exhibition Ground on July 26, 1951. Reports from London indicated that, while the initial reaction was one of indulgence when the instruments were first seen, the response soon turned to amazement once the first notes were heard.

The success of TASPO improved the image of the steelband movement in Trinidad. Among the members of the original TASPO was Ellie Mannette, who in his zeal to return to Trinidad to continue work on the instruments turned down the offer of a music scholarship in England. Mannette now teaches and works on the research and development of the instrument at the University of West Virginia in the United States. Sterling Betancourt stayed in England and in 2002 received an MBE for his sterling work in the development of the instrument. (An MBE is a British honour – Member of the Order of the British Empire.) Anthony Williams invented the spider web pan which is today used as the basis of the fourths and fifths tenor. Other members were Dudley Smith, Patsy Haynes, and Granville Sealey, who still plays pan at the Deliverance Temple in Port of Spain.

The official voice of the steelbands was the Steelband Association, which, though formed at an earlier date, was officially registered in January of 1958. The aims of the Association were to develop the steelband in all its aspects; to obtain employment for steelbandsmen; to organize and hold music festivals for steelbands; to encourage, aid, and promote the scientific development of instruments; to provide facilities for training in the art of playing and tuning steelband instruments; and to do all things, matters, and acts for the welfare of steelbands and their members. The Steelband Association was later renamed the National Association of Trinidad and Tobago Steelbandsmen and finally in 1971 renamed Pan Trinbago, today under the leadership of Tobagonian Patrick Arnold.

Many years were to pass before a majority of steelbands consented to join the Association. From its inception, the Association – dealing with fights and rivalries between bands often fueled by poor judging at poorly run competitions – set about to oversee competitions and put competent judges in place. The Association acted as a mediator in many disputes between steelbandsmen. In 1952 the Association successfully lobbied for inclusion in the biennial Trinidad and Tobago Music Festival. This festival, usually adjudicated by British musicians, had as its focus the development of classical music in the country. The involvement of the steelbands was of a high standard and resulted in improvements in the tuning, orchestration, and technical approaches to the instrument. In 1952, Dr Sidney Northcote, the adjudicator, remarked to the audience, "We have witnessed man's ingenuity in trying to get beauty out of something that is absolutely a waste product. That, I do deeply respect" (Maxime 1990).

In 1964 the Association decided to hold its own Steelband Music Festival. Today there is a World Steelband Festival which includes bands from Europe, North America, the Caribbean, and, of course, Trinidad and Tobago. Music written for the instrument has been promoted, and the repertoire of music written specifically for the instrument has grown.

In 1963, the Association, with the help of the then Carnival Development Committee, organized the Panorama competition which became the major competition for steelbands. The Panorama steelbands usually ranged in size from fifty to one hundred members or, at the height, one hundred and twenty. Panorama arrangers with a proven track record became viable commodities, with many bands paying large sums to obtain the services of arrangers such as Ray Holman, one of the first to write and arrange his own music, Len "Boogsie" Sharpe, a phenomenal player, arranger, and composer, Jit Samaroo, whose work with his family band Samaroo Jets and the Renegades Steel Orchestra has won him international kudos, and Clive Bradley, gifted teacher and brilliant arranger. Tuners such as Bertram Kelman, Bertie Marshall, Tony Slater, the late Leo Coker, Roland Harrigan, Michael Kernahan, and others have been and are in demand as bands struggle to achieve a good sound.

MUSIC'S NOT THE ONLY VOICE THAT STRIVES TO GIVE OUR CHILDREN CHOICE. ART AND SCIENCE HAND IN HAND TAKE ON A JOURNEY TO A LAND OF POSSIBLE HOPE AND POSSIBLE PLAN...

The government of Trinidad and Tobago has over the years acted ambivalently towards the steelband movement. The independence struggle leader, Dr Eric Williams, leader of the PNM (People's National Movement) political party, promoted the steelband as a source of national pride using steelbands for many official functions. Dr Williams also pushed for corporate sponsorship of the bands. Later governments promoted the steelband in various ways – the steelband is the official national instrument of Trinidad and Tobago – but there has been no major push toward economic independence for the steelbandsmen. The Trinidad and Tobago National Steel Orchestra was formed in August 1998 and the Board of Directors put in place in November of 2000. Members of this orchestra are now pursuing an Associate of Arts degree in Music Performance under the College of Science, Technology, and Applied Arts of Trinidad and Tobago (COSTAATT). Despite this, much more needs to be done for the instrument and its proponents in terms of research and exposure.

What about the women of the steelbands? Women have always played an important role in the steelband movement. The first all-girl steelband led by Hazel Henley, Girl Pat, was formed in the 1950s, and Cynthia Davis of Tripoli was one of the first women to play pan on the road. Women have been involved as arrangers, conductors, judges, and performers. Women have also been the cause of many steelband clashes. In addition, the work of pioneers such as Frederick "Mando" Wilson and his cousin Victor "Totee" Wilson, Oscar Pile, Austin Simmonds, George Beckles, Allan Gervais, Zigilee, "Patch Eye," Rudy Wells, Rudolph Charles, Denzil Hernandez, and many others deserves greater recognition. The steelband's future is now in the hands not only of Trinidadians, but in the hands of many across the world. A new story has begun.

NOTE

1   All section headers are taken from Dawn K. Batson, "The Essence," © 1996.

17

NOTES ON PAN

Kim Johnson

Pan, which are called steel drums in the US, can be found throughout the world. There are hundreds of collegiate steelbands in the US today, including at least one in Alaska, as well as numerous community bands and many individual professional pannists. *Pan News*, a Swiss steelband newsletter, lists over 125 full-time bands. The Nigerian army has a steelband, as do the Dutch police service and as did, until 1999, the US Navy. There are bands all over Europe, in Japan, Venezuela, Kuwait. And of course they are common in the Caribbean. To most people outside of Trinidad a steelband is a small group of kids, or perhaps a five- or six-man ensemble on a cruise ship or at a beachfront hotel, which plays pop tunes or "Yellow Bird" on pans. That, to a Trinidadian, is as anemic as the worst muzak. The real thing can be heard live only from the gigantic, pulsing orchestras known as conventional steelbands. What these are, how they evolved, their relationship to the society, are the subject of the following notes.

In his memoirs, John Slater (1995), founder of an early steelband, recalls that one of his childhood pastimes in the 1930s at Easter Boys Government School was drumming: "Roderick 'Tench' Waldron and I loved to beat our fingers on the desk as if we were drumming, while at the same time singing calypsos (in our teacher's absence of course)," recalls Slater. "But whenever we got caught, we used to suffer the consequences." Over three decades later, I too, as a secondary schoolboy in the late 1960s and early 1970s, drummed. It was nothing unusual, we all did it in my class. I am not sure when we started but by third form a teacher could not leave the class unsupervised for a moment without our striking up a racket, pounding away on our desks. We sometimes drummed to annoy a teacher but mainly we drummed for its own sake. The trancelike pleasure we got from the drumming was akin to the sensuous pleasure we discovered later in dancing.

Sometimes our drumming was accompanied by oral imitation of instruments – this boy the bass, that one the saxophone. One boy, a rather dull, otherwise untalented youth, would at the slightest instigation launch into a marvelous electric guitar whine. "Guitar Mouth," he was nicknamed. Many years later, in researching the history of the steelband movement, I discovered that "mouth bands" had been commonplace among working-class black youth as a means of transportation: if a gang had to walk somewhere – say, they were returning from a party – they would start up a mouth band which would "play" all the way home. Indeed, mouth bands even became a didactic tool: when the members of Casablanca Steel Orchestra wanted to learn a piece of music, they would listen outside a party to how the regular dance bands played it. Each youth would take the part of a particular instrument, and they would then tramp back to their pan yard, each one singing the lines of their chosen instrument, until they could transfer what they had learnt onto their pans.

"Twelve o'clock, one o'clock sometimes we outside [a party] and them don't know, we outside because we didn't like to dance, we like the music, so I always outside listening," Raymond "One Man" Mark, an early steelband captain, told me in an interview (1995):

> Sometimes I have a little side with me and we outside and we singing different parts we go play on the pan and when the thing done we gone back up the road, we eh stopping because if you stop you go forget. We sing until we go in the pan yard. Any hour and we gone in and we get it and remember it.

It was through this method that the band learned "Ruby," a calypso played by Sel Duncan's dance band on Henry Street, and surprised other pan men: "When we come out on the road with that all them fellas want to know where we get that tune" (Mark, interview, 1995).

I have asked many Trinidadians if they drummed on desks in school. Without exception they replied as if the answer was so obvious that the question was silly: "Of course." Thus did it strike me how the compelling urge to drum and the inchoate pleasure it gave were deeply rooted in Trinidadian hearts.

George Yeates, a captain of Desperadoes Steel Orchestra in the 1950s, recalled:

> The young people [in the ghetto] had to travel some distance to fetch water from a public stand-pipe. They used pitch-oil [kerosene] tins and zinc buckets, and on their way down to the stand-pipes, they would keep a rhythm so that the distance was not felt; and there we believe the thought of Steel Bands was originated.

> (in Goddard 1991: 23)

Discussing this with Ernest Brown, an African-American researcher who has studied black music in Africa and in the US, I asked the same question. He thought for a while. "No," he said. "We were more into sports" (interview, 1997).

Yet you do not hear it in calypso, which has not the overwhelming percussive foundation one would have expected, and which you can hear, for instance, in Cuban or Dominican music, even though the Hispanic countries have a far smaller proportion of Africans. So how was this powerful compulsion to drum manifest in Trinidad? Where was the energy channeled?

When I asked Jeffrey Beddoe – a priest in the Yoruba religion of Orisha, a drummer, and the brother of the late Trinidadian master-drummer Andrew Beddoe – where did our impulse to drum find an outlet, he replied, "It all went into pan" (interview, n.d.).

The steelband that won the 1997 Panorama competition, Renegades Steel Orchestra, did so for the third consecutive time. This victory not only gave

Renegades the first Panorama hat-trick ever, it also gave the steelband their then unprecedented ninth victory. It all has been accomplished on the basis of an unusual partnership between the band and its arranger and musical director, Jit Samaroo. The East Port of Spain band was of no musical significance throughout the 1950s and 1960s but was notorious for its belligerence. Even today many people still refer to Renegades by the name a small faction of the band called itself in the 1960s: Lawbreakers. And yet the arranger that this gang of black, urban youth teamed up with in 1971, Jit Samaroo, was a shy, quiet Hindu teenager from a small rural village in the Lipinot Valley, where the main musical tradition is Venezuelan-derived "parang" music of string bands (for more information, see Bellour, Johnson, and Riggio 2002). The Renegades–Samaroo combination seems unlikely, but from a wider perspective it really is not. The steelband movement, despite its Afro-Trinidadian origins and its fierce rivalries, has always been inclusive. Every one of the top bands is wheeled onto the Panorama stage by throngs of partisans who are quite clearly not slum dwellers.

"I wonder how many of them are from Laventille," remarked a colleague when Desperadoes took the stage with its enormous crowd of supporters. There were many more than a handful of white people who were obviously foreign amongst the crowd of men and women from Laventille, the ghetto home of the band. I knew why they were there. I too can recall pushing pans as a child when steelbands paraded on the streets for carnival. It was a mark of belonging, an honor even, to be a part of one of the huge caravans that filled the streets with rivers of music. I too must have stood out starkly as a middle-class child amongst the more plebeian steelband supporters, but I never met the slightest hint of rejection.

If the original percussive impulse was African, it became highly creolized – that is, is combined with other musical influences, including that of Europe and other New World countries. So the early development of pan is largely a story of the young men of Trinidad in the 1940s striving to create a melodic instrument out of a drum, moving it away from being a purely percussive instrument of rhythm, and laboring to acquire virtuosity of performance and composition with it. They began with rhymes and progressed to nursery rhymes, choruses for simple songs, then entire songs. By 1952 they were attempting European art music for the Music Festival.

Technically, this progression represented a growing complexity of the instrument and of the ensembles. Pans acquired more notes, which were in turn tuned more accurately. Steelbands acquired more pans, which gave them a wider and ultimately symphonic range. As important as this was the burgeoning social complexity of the steelband movement as musical inclusiveness mirrored social inclusiveness. The first barriers to be broken were those of age and sex. Daisy James, for instance, unknown to her mother, played for Casablanca Steel Orchestra during the mid-1940s when she was just a child. The men in the band, some of whom were the most feared hooligans in Port of Spain, had to hold the pan that she played because it was too heavy for a little girl. True, there was something of the mascot about her presence there, but the more important reason she was allowed into what would have otherwise been an exclusive club was her ability to play the instrument. Like-wise, by 1950, when it was clear that pan was a melodic instrument, you got the involvement of middle-class white and Chinese youths in the steelband movement with bands such as Dixieland, Silver Stars, Stromboli, and Starlight. There was even in Tunapuna at the time an East Indian band, Saraswatee, which played Indian music. So when Jit Samaroo teamed up with Renegades, it was nothing unusual.

"It brings people together, both playing and listening, in a way that no other kind of music seems to," Lady Berkley, the wife of the twentieth Baron Berkley, remarked enthusiastically on December 7, 1994, in the London *Times*. She played piano, clarinet, accordion, and guitar. "But," she explained, "the thing about those instruments is that you play them by yourself, and I didn't feel comfortable with the idea of a proper orchestra." So she joined the London Melodians, an English branch of a Trinidadian steelband, Melodians. The London Melodians comprise about twenty members, but the full extent to which pan brings people together is manifest in the large "conventional" steelbands for which there is at present an upper limit of 120 players in the Panorama competition. That is larger than a fully constituted symphony orchestra. The gravitational force that attracts and musically synchronizes so many players is rhythm. The dominating rhythm comes from the continuous, bright, metronomic clanging of the brake-hub percussion that is the most primitive instrument in the ensemble. It has undergone almost no change since metal was introduced into the bamboo stamping tubes in the 1930s. And it is still to many Trinidadians the heart of the steelband. That is why that section of the band is popularly known as the "engine room."

When a group of Trinidadians needs a single instrument to make noise on during an outing, ultimately it is the iron they will carry. You can hear it on bus excursions to the beach and at trade-union demonstrations, the sharp clanging that compels Trinidadian hips to sway and their feet slowly to shuffle with a kind of sensuous irresistibility. As David Rudder sang with brilliant double entendre in "The Engine Room": "If you iron good you is king" (1987).

That is nothing new. Drums have been used for centuries to coordinate people. Soldiers marched steadfastly to their death to the beat of a drum corps. A rhythm can be almost hypnotic, transcending individuality, merging the collective, reducing fear. The early steelbands – aggressively masculine in their origins – were martial organizations too, down to the bugles. They fought one another, and they fought the police. The test was to continue playing throughout the melée, no matter what.

All instruments in a steel orchestra are percussive, and every player fits into a song's unifying rhythm. That is what makes feasible the coordination of so many players with neither scores nor conductor. But what makes it attractive for both players and their audience is that pans are as much melodic instruments as they are rhythmic. (Who would listen to 120 drummers banging away simultaneously on timpani or congas?) The urge to drum was leavened by a desire to play melodies. Were it not for this simultaneously melodic impulse, pan would never have evolved beyond the initial five or six notes of a West African *zana mbira*, or thumb piano.

Ever so often the lament is heard that pan men cannot read music. It is an opinion that is most often shaped by a formal training in classical music and by the desire to provide a greater musical flexibility to the steel ensemble in a variety of performance venues. But the point is not far-fetched. Indeed, at least one band insists its players learn to read music. After all, steelband music, including the Panorama arrangement that every steelband essays annually, is highly orchestrated, and the method of rote learning requires weeks of practice. Then, even when a tune has been mastered, that lasts only as long as the players' recall. A year later it is gone. So what could be more practical than having the players able to read a score? And yet nothing could be more irrelevant. Most pan men are amateurs with hardly a continuous use for the skill. No steelband arrangers score music for their bands, and indeed those who could do so number but one or two. If they did, who would read the scores? That is not how steelband music is arranged or composed – by an isolated musician creating in the solitude of his study. Instead, the pannist is there in the pan yard with the band, and the tune grows as it is practiced, with players making contributions, the arranger tailoring the piece to suit the skill of the band and the taste of the players. From the preliminary to the semifinal to the final stages of all steelband competitions, the tune changes according to the judges' comments and the way it feels when it is performed before the crowd.

Besides, who wants to hear last year's Panorama tune? Until the late 1970s steelbands played at parties. And they played on the road for carnival, on public holidays, or whenever the mood took them, even when it was illegal. But for every steelband the moment of glory, the apotheosis they hunger for, has always been found in a competition. It is what they are remembered by. Mention, for instance, the defunct Sun Valley steelband to any aficionado, and he will recall how the band won the first island-wide competition in 1946. Nowadays the main competition is Panorama, but in the first two decades of the steelband movement many competitions were organized by private impresarios. Indeed, on the road, steelbands even competed informally against one another.

Before the bands grew too large and were pushed off the streets by louder, cheaper DJs, whenever two of them met on the road at carnival, if they did not fight, they competed musically. Some emphasized their orchestration; others were good in improvisation. "Revving" it was called, improvisation bringing to mind the urgency of cars readying for a race. Bands sought one another to hold these impromptu competitions on the road. None of this is surprising to a Trinidadian, for rivalry, both martial and aesthetic, has for the past century been the motor in our culture. Calypsonians compete, masqueraders compete. Robbers competed in grandiloquent rhetoric, Jab Jabs competed with whips, Fancy Indians competed with invented languages, Pierrot Grenades competed with nonsense rhyme – so it was inevitable that steelbands would compete with music.

The great band of the 1940s and 1950s was Invaders. When in 1996 I interviewed Neville Jules, the former captain of Trinidad All Stars, he recalled those days for me:

> When Invaders coming up from Woodbrook they coming up with a crowd and we now, we now, we in Charlotte Street, we couldn't even have half the crowd that Invaders had so we just figured we want to get a name like Invaders. So any time we hear Invaders in town we looking for them. It come like a guy is the world's champion in boxing, but you would be glad to get a chance to box with that man cause even if you eh beat him, if you show good you build up yourself. So we used to look for Invaders. And then it become a regular thing. So we started now to surprise them by practising so that nobody would know what we doing and I think the first year we really started that was with "Skokian".

That was when orchestration, which was more suited to Jules's temperament, began to replace improvisation. Then in 1957 Trinidad All Stars met Crossfire from

St James. Crossfire switched into their best tune, "Another Night Like This." Trinidad All Stars geared up to follow them and do battle, but a police officer, thinking the road already too congested with steelbands, shunted All Stars in another direction.
Jules (interview 1996) continues:

> Crossfire was still playing "Another Night Like This" and, well of course that was sounding better than what we were playing because they playing their best tune. We were playing maybe our second or third best tune so everybody start to jump. "O Gawd, Crossfire blah blah blah! Crossfire!" When we was coming up Henry Street the following year somebody say, "Crossfire." That was the only year we was never really looking for Invaders cause we wanted to get Crossfire. And we swing into Duke Street, and we wait for them right there, and as they come we hit them Beethoven's Minuet in G. That was the end of them.

Out of such competition was born the "bomb" steelband competition in which, until the 1970s, bands played secretly rehearsed classical or pop tunes to calypso tempo with an aim to surprise the listeners. That is, on jouvert morning they dropped their "bombs."

The music was the moment. I have heard Lennon and McCartney's "Penny Lane" countless times; it is a song I have loved. But it cannot be severed from that early morning in the 1970s when, just as daylight was seeping into the carnival Monday atmosphere, I heard Starlift steelband play it. The shock of recognition and pleasure can never be repeated.

The moment was all, and despite their orchestration, bomb tunes were exercises in immediacy. Consequently, to understand them we must explore the aesthetics and the ontology of ephemera in relationship to modernity. There is a sense in which all music only exists at the moment it sounds. Beethoven's symphonies only really exist, that is, are only realized, while they are being performed. In this sense music cannot be written; scratchings on paper are not music, they are only instructions on how to make a particular piece of music – a score is no more music than a recipe is food. Nevertheless, the gulf separating "written" from "ephemeral" music can be in some ways greater than the similarity between them. This has to do with the ways in which music engages with time, and here is where the ephemeral diverges from the written. The transcription of music constitutes an attempt to deny time, or at best to transcend it, whereas the ephemeralization of music seeks to outwit time. What does this mean?

Musical notation is usually thought to have been an outcome of the growing complexity of European music: "As the separate voices gained greater freedom, more accurate means had to be found to indicate the way these voices were expected to blend," argue Yehudi Menuhin and Curtis Davis in *The Music of Man*. "Notation came partly from the need of many people to work together, and music naturally reflected this social fact" (1980: 73). Maybe, maybe not. Notation certainly allowed the creation of long, structurally complex works, which could thereafter be performed far and wide. Its architectural permanence protected the works from the attrition of human memory. But it also paved the way for the domination of composers over performers. The latter became mere "interpreters" of a composition. This is how the writing of music facilitated a suppression of living composers by dead ones.

Facilitated, not caused. The root cause lay deeper, in the ontological value accorded in Europe to permanence. "The dominant ideal of Western literate culture calls for the creation of poetic and plastic forms that shall outlast bronze and break the tooth of time," declares George Steiner, who also notes in passing that "there is in non-Western culture a long history of the production of complex, highly inventive artifacts in materials intended for almost immediate consumption or destruction" (1972: 175) – that is, the production of aesthetic transience.

The quintessential African art form, music – which is often inseparable from dance and, the most transient of art forms, masquerade – does not seek to break the tooth of time. Its radically different ontology seeks rather to outwit it. This is what Thelonious Monk meant when he said, "Writing about music is like dancing about architecture" (in Gabbard 1995: 3). Ephemeral music derives its value from its temporality; it is a celebration of the transient uniqueness of the present. This moment is unique, and its music will never be repeated, it says. The musician taps his foot as the metronome in his head says: now, now, now, now.

How does such ephemerality seek to outwit time? The answer is found in the relationship between musician and audience. Whereas written music is realized through the relationship between the composer and the musician who later interprets the score, the moment of improvised music is created through the relationship between musician and audience. The first case is a form of power; the second is a kind of communion that transcends the solitude of the individual.

The momentary communion of musician and audience is intrinsic to the aesthetic Africans brought to the New World, and not only through improvisation. A call–response structure involves both parties in the creation of the music, removing the barriers between them. So too does the dancing and hand-clapping associated with the music. The emphasis on rhythm and repetition, and the centrality of drums, also has the same effect. African-derived music in different countries found different ways to manifest the aesthetic of transient immediacy. Emphatic improvisation is the path jazz took, but there are other ways.

Although steelbands in Trinidad are often heard at shows and concerts, their contemporary *raison d'être* has always been to compete regularly in the performance of intricate music. From the 1970s on the music became highly orchestrated, and improvisation was out of the question. And yet, the aesthetic of immediacy is so deeply ingrained in the Trinidadian sensibility that these hugely popular events are as completely ephemeralized as any improvisation. New tunes are arranged for each band for each competition – you rarely hear last year's tune. And the competitions are conducted with all the fervor and partisanship and excitement and here-and-now uniqueness of a sporting event.

Combining aesthetics and sport is not unusual for a Trinidadian. C.L.R. James did so most profoundly in his magnum opus, *Beyond a Boundary* (1963), relating them to the wider sociopolitical formation. He emphasized that the Greek origins of democracy emerged from their annual competitions in both theatrical works and athletics. On the cricket pitches of Eton and Harrow, James demonstrated, the nineteenth-century ruling class of Britain learned their code of honor. In a similar vein, I feel that the communal steelband of Trinidad, and the Afro-American music of the New World in general, can be most fruitfully understood in the context of the general existential condition of modernity.

Fig. 17.1 San Fernando SeaBees on the road, carnival 1956. These masqueraders play steel "pan 'round de neck," an early form of steel pan before the instruments were mounted on stands and carried in racks. Pan around the neck still appears in Trinidad Carnival as a traditional form of pan competition. Photograph courtesy of Nestor Sullivan of Pamberi Steel Orchestra and the National Steel Orchestra of Trinidad and Tobago.

What constitutes modernity? Usually its constituents are found in the Renaissance rise of humanism and individualism, or in the Reformation spread of secularism, or in the growth of science and technology, or bureaucratic organization (although, as James often pointed out, the earliest systems of industrialized mass productions were the mines and plantations of the New World). For me, modernity is first and foremost the condition of rootlessness or, to borrow a phrase from Georg Lukács, "transcendental homelessness" (1971: 61). According to John Berger in *And Our Faces, My Heart, Brief as Photos* (1984), home in traditional society was the center of the real, of everything which made sense; all the rest was chaos. Home was the center of the world where the vertical line between the underworld below and the heavens above crossed the horizontal line of geography.

Emigration breaks that crossing of lines. "To emigrate is always to dismantle the center of the world, and so to move into a lost, disoriented one of fragments," says Berger, describing a condition that has come to be normal for most of mankind, which has lost continuity with the dead and the gods alike (1984: 57). To Berger, the irreversible loss of home has spawned, since the massive migrations of the nineteenth century, the modern centrality of romantic sexual love, the longing for the fusion of two displaced, rootless individuals.

But the vast and largely forced migrations of the nineteenth and twentieth centuries were prefigured by the slave trading of Africans. Millions were uprooted from one continent to another, from a traditional to an industrial environment. Families were dispersed, nations dissolved, languages dissipated. For the African slaves, the middle passage that uprooted them irrevocably shattered the crossing of the vertical and horizontal lines that constituted home. Their background was different from that of other people confronting the attrition of modernity, however, and so too was their response. Descartes established a disembodied mind within the solitary modern Europe, and Rousseau defined his freedom and solitude in terms of an autonomous individual who formed a social contract with others. Whereas New World Africans experienced modernity, both its racial oppression and its eradication of tribal horizons, as an urge for collective liberation of the mind and body. These diasporic Africans salvaged the shards of tradition and culture and collected anything else they could find in that holocaust, and out of the debris they created a culture that embraces all to collectively celebrate the unique beauty of the present. That is the music of the Americans and, indeed, of the modern world.

An earlier version of this chapter is printed in Milla Cozart Riggio (ed.), *The Drama Review*, 42 (3) (1998): 61–73, Cambridge, MA: MIT Press.

18

CALYPSO REINVENTS ITSELF[1]

Gordon Rohlehr

The calypso is a living example of Afro-Caribbean oral tradition adapting itself to a process of continuous change. Its history reflects the immigration of Europeans, Africans, Asians and Caribbean people into an island that had known 299 years (1498–1797) of Spanish rule, and was, through ongoing contact with Venezuela, to retain strong Hispanic cultural ties. The Trinidad experience involved a process of continuous indigenization, enacted on ground stolen from reduced though not erased Amerindian communities to create out of this teeming welter of ethnicities a restless and, according to V.S. Naipaul, "half-formed" society, sufficiently flexible to accommodate the paradox of homogeneity and difference: a jarring, jamming, carnivalesque collision and clashing counterpoint of rhythms.

The Trinidad Carnival and the calypso are both theatres in and metaphors through which the drama of Trinidad's social history is encoded and enacted, historically a celebratory mass/mas theatre of contested social space: the domain of the stickfighter, the Wild Indian, the Pierrot Grenade, the Midnight Robber, the chantwel and his descendant, the calypsonian, and the pan man of the emerging steelband movement into the 1960s. The contestation of these carnivalesque figures with rhetoric or blows – often rhetoric *and* blows – mirrored the confrontation taking place within the social process itself.

The calypso had its roots in a complex of songs and dances which, in spite of prohibitive legislation both during and after slavery, were kept alive at the regular weekend "dance assemblies" of the African "nations" who had been brought into the Archipelago. Prominent in this process was the transgression of sacred and secular forms and the assimilation of different dances into each other. The minuet was Africanized into the belair, which Errol Hill (1972) regards as the true ancestor of the narrative calypso, drums replacing string bass and altering the entire rhythmic foundation of the song. The stanzaic structure of the belair and the litanic call-and-response structure of the calinda merged in the calypsos of the first four decades of the twentieth century, which normally had an eight- or sixteen-bar narrative stanza followed by a litanic refrain.

Because it has been so open to change, Trinidad society has always generated questions about the nature of tradition and periodic alarm at the erosion of traditional forms. As early as 1883 the French Creole editor of *Fair Play*, Henry Schuller Billouin, deplored the songs and drum dances of the black community of Port of Spain, claiming that they had degenerated from African and French Creole songs and dances of earlier decades. He called for the banning of "drum dances" and the stickfighting and picong songs that were sung on those occasions (March 1, 1883). Other commentators from that period blamed migrants from the southern Caribbean, while the editor of the *Trinidad Review*, Jacob Thomas, explained that the scurrilous songs and lascivious dances were the bequest of belly-dancing prostitutes from Curaçao (*The Trinidad Review*, August 9, 1883). One hundred years later, in the 1980s, Jamaican "dub" and "dancehall" music, particularly the sexually aggressive performance style of the "dancehall queens," was being blamed for the "degeneration" of Trinidad's calypso and soca music into ultra-simplistic lyrics and sexualized "wine-and-jam" performance. "Traditional" music was again being defended against the evils inherent in "invasions" from rival Caribbean musics.

Yet, between the 1880s and the 1980s Trinidad's music had constantly been reinventing itself. During the first decade of the twentieth century, old-time singers of "single-tone" or four-line calypsos in Creole French resisted the efforts of George "Jamesie" Adilla, the Duke of Marlborough and Phillip Garcia, the Lord Executor, to improve the calypso by singing eight-line "double-tone" calypsos in highly rhetorical English. The initial result of this confrontation between tradition and innovation was that newcomers were forced to flee Port of Spain because they could not endure the fierceness of the old-time picong in Creole French (Pitts 1962).

By the second decade of the twentieth century, it was clear that the reinvention of what since 1901 had begun to be called "calypso" did not mean the death of traditional structures but their incorporation into new ones. Thus, calinda litanies coexisted beside rhymed couplets, quatrains and octaves; in time, combinations of these would constitute the fundamental forms of most "ballad" or narrative calypsos from the 1930s to the 1950s. The Sans Humanité or Oratorical mode, which had been a contested innovation during the first decade of the twentieth century, became a revered traditional structure during the next two decades. Though it was superseded by narrative/ballad calypsos in the 1920s and 1930s, it retained its place in what one might term "a calypso memory-bank," and still informs minor-key compositions.

Calypso melody, too, was under constant pressure from the variety of rival musics that coexisted in Trinidad in the early twentieth century. The Roaring Lion's "Caroline" was a makeover of the English folk-song "Oh Where Have You Been, Billy Boy." Several folk-melodies from other Caribbean islands – for example, "Sly Mongoose" from Jamaica, "Brown Skin Girl" from the Grenadines, "Stone Cold Dead" from Barbados, "L'Année Pasée" from Martinique – were assimilated into the emerging Trinidad calypso. Latin American song forms, promoted by the prolific bandleader Lionel Belasco, were so popular in the Trinidad of the 1920s and 1930s that Ralph Perez, the Decca agent who recorded most of the calypsos between 1937 and 1939, viewed calypso as an extension of Latin music in the Caribbean and a variation on the songs he had already included in Decca's Latin American collection.

Performances of calypsos in the tents of the 1920s were rivaled by vaudeville shows featuring variety acts, comedy, music of other Caribbean territories and of North America. Between 1920 and 1927, the calypsonian Lord Beginner (Egbert Moore) was a comedian in a vaudeville show even as he did his apprenticeship "hiding in the back," as he termed it, of a minor calypso tent in Belmont. What he and other men, such as Bill Rogers (Augustus Hinds), popularizer of British Guiana's Bhagee/Bargee music, began in the 1930s would be replicated two decades later in the 1950s by Barbadian composer and singer Irving Burgie (Lord Burgess) and the American/Jamaican folk singer Harry Belafonte (Rohlehr 1990).

Recordings of calypso music from the 1930s (Harlequin HQ CD 1992) reflect the influence of boogie-woogie piano, the rigidity of jazz-type bass lines, and New-Orleans-style instrumentation. A jazz straitjacket was forcibly imposed on the fluid prosody of calypso which, with its history of Latin-style syncopation and its roots in calinda, belair and bamboula, had only recently sorted out the transition from French Creole to English prosody. Yet the encounters of calypso with other musics were never entirely one-sided. The presence in New Orleans music since the 1920s of compositions such as "Panama" or Jelly Roll Morton's "Winin' Boy Blues" (White, sound recordings, 1991) suggests that some dialogue had been taking place between the musics of the islands and those of the Mississippi delta. In *Their Eyes Were Watching God*, Zora Neale Hurston describes the seepage of Caribbean work-songs and folk-songs into America via immigrants working in what poet Kamau Braithwaite later calls the "painfields" of Panama and Florida (1973).

In Trinidad, constant self-invention has resulted in the society's preoccupation with the contradictory forces of tradition and change, and in the generation of hybrid forms. Single-tone calinda, calypso callendar, and creole carnival song reflected the persistence of early African Creole litanic forms in transition between their function as "folk" music and their reinvented status as the pulse of an emerging popular, commercial music. The American presence, induced through jazz music, radio, and cinema, was reflected in the many "calypso swing" songs and the occasional calypso foxtrot. A "Calypso Shouter" suggests the early impact of the Shouters (Spiritual Baptists) on the Trinidad public. For even as the Shouters were mockingly identified by several calypsonians, their hymns were being recorded and popularized by the same singers (Spottswood 1985). The same was true of the prohibited Orisha religions, fragments of whose sacred chants entered into the calypsos of Lion, Tiger, Caresser, Cobra and Beginner and resurfaced three decades later in Sparrow and Duke, then twenty years after that as stylized rhythmic figures in the compositions of André Tanker and David Rudder, and as sacred chants in the music of Ella Andall (sound recordings, 2000).

Such evidence illustrates the contradictory pull of change and tradition in the formation of the Trinidad calypso. Tradition was fiercely defended, particularly when change seemed to threaten the erosion of old, established forms. Lord Executor, who began his career between 1899 and 1901 and was a major voice in the introduction of the eight-verse, oratorical calypso in English, rejected the advent on the calypso scene of jazz-styled big bands. Executor's "sad" lament in "Calypso" that "outside fashions are idolized" has been repeated by calypsonian after calypsonian throughout the five decades since he delivered it (Pitts 1962).

The 1950s were significant in the "reinvention" of calypso. Simultaneously, there was the emergence in Trinidad of the "Little," then the "Mighty" Sparrow (Slinger

Francisco) and of Harry Belafonte in America. Sparrow, who began as a roving night club singer in 1954, won both the Calypso King and the Road March titles in 1956 with "Jean and Dinah." Belafonte released his calypso album (1988) in late 1956, and by 1957 Belafonte's style was successfully challenging rock 'n' roll in the international popular music market. Sparrow was the greater phenomenon, though the world would never quite recognize this. A calypsonian's lot was far from easy. The Calypso King in 1956 received $25 and a silver cup. So the calypsonian had to do more than compose and perform. He needed to create and access his market and sell and promote his product at home and abroad, while retaining sufficient creative energy to produce ten new songs every year. In the more than 120 he recorded between 1956 and 1963, Sparrow logically collaborated with skilled song writers, for which he was criticized as breaching the tradition that requires a true calypsonian to compose his – or more recently her – own songs.

In contrast, Belafonte's success – based on a relatively small output of Caribbean folk-songs that included the occasional calypso, and of songs composed in the folk-song mode – led to an acceleration of the process that since the 1930s had propelled the calypso outwards from its parochial roots in Trinidad into the US, UK, Jamaica, the Bahamas, Surinam, Panama, Guyana, Venezuela, Ghana and Sierra Leone (among other places), where singers regularly began to call themselves "calypsonians."

Various factors determined this interface of diasporan Afro-Caribbean musics. First, they were part of what diasporan Africans had refashioned out of the debris of forced migrations, violent disrupture, plantation slavery and its grim aftermath, which the Mighty Sparrow in "The Slave" (1963) describes as hunger, destitution, illiteracy, loss of motivation and direction, and erasure of identity. Such musics were, therefore, tough, flexible, stridently self-assertive and capable of fulfilling some of the traditional functions of ancestral African musics: the call to work or battle, celebration or lamentation, praise or censure, complaint or satire. Such musics wore the emblem of Anansi, trickster, shape-shifter and survivor. They adapted themselves to local circumstances, while pursuing the objectives of freedom and space. Chief among the challenges were recurrent legislative attempts to regulate or censor both songs and singers. From the Music Ordinance of 1883 in Trinidad, to the Theatres and Dance Halls Ordinance of 1934 on to the more recent "Clause Seven" of the Equality of Opportunities Act of the late 1990s (Rohlehr 2002), grassroots Afro-Creole music in Trinidad has had to circumvent legislation designed to control or even abolish social commentary critical of elites in positions of power. Mask, disguise, verbal coding, and shape-shifting were strategies of both self-defense and attack.

If musical forms such as mento, goombay, or beguine temporarily yielded space in the late 1950s to "calypso," it was because something called calypso had, through Belafonte's international success, become the vehicle that diasporan Africans, all the children of Anansi, had perceived would take them into the freedom of "vacant interstellar space" (Milton, "Samson Agonistes"; Coltrane, sound recordings, 1974). For a subaltern music to access the market at all, it needed to operate via a US intermediary. In the 1950s and 1960s, Belafonte – clean, brown, smooth, tall, handsome, and half-Jamaican – was the ideal player for that role; but there were others: Robert Mitchum (who recorded Sparrow's "Jean and Dinah" as early as 1957), Dorothy Dandridge, the Andrews Sisters, Maya Angelou, Sarah Vaughan, and Sonny Rollins. Crossing-over, then (and now), required the metropolitan intermediary and a consequent loss of control by the original creators of the music, over its style and content. After Belafonte, distinctly different folk singers from throughout the Caribbean would, for as long as it was profitable, call themselves "calypsonians" or "calypso singers."

The commercial contact between market-seeking calypsonian and controlling, withholding metropole inevitably necessitated a change in the form and content of the calypso away from its sociopolitical relevance within its own community towards its simplification and commodification for the market, as illustrated in the contrast between Lord Invader's bitterly protesting lament about prostitution and social distress, "Rum and Coca Cola" (1946), and the Andrews Sisters' successful Shangri-La version of the same song. There was, however, almost as much resentment as there was complaisance behind these calypso masks which, significantly, were being worn at the same time as ten of the cricket-playing islands came briefly together to form the West Indian Federation (1958–61). The new nationalism of independence, which followed the break-up of the Federation, led to a hasty quest for iconic national cultural forms – calypso, steelband, carnival in Trinidad; mento, ska, pantomime, jonkunnu in Jamaica; goombay and jonkunnu in the Bahamas. Island nationalisms, then, virtually put paid to that period when "calypso" became the vehicle that had propelled the musics of the African Caribbean diaspora into world prominence. Trinidad itself became more defensive and jealous of its claim to being the homeland of calypso.

The first two decades of the Sparrow era (1956–76) were marked by contestations, with first Melody (1958–63) – who had composed songs for Belafonte in a relationship for which Melody later felt he had not received sufficient recognition – and then Kitchener (1963–70). While such contestations revitalized the tradition of man-to-man confrontation characteristic of carnival culture, many innovatory calypsos grew out of them. The Sparrow/Melody exchange resulted in over a score of songs in which these two antagonists threw jibes at each other that varied from good-natured to abrasive, from harshly coarse to smoothly sophisticated (Sparrow/Melody 1957–62). Melody interrogated Sparrow's kingship and the machismo on which it was constructed. Sparrow mocked Melody's supposed ugliness, personal hygiene and inability to attract women. The tradition of picong was both maintained and reinvented, not as an exchange of spontaneous extemporized insults but in carefully crafted full-length calypsos. Throughout this period the two men remained the best of friends and were frequently on tour together.

A remarkably creative era, these five pre-independence years saw Sparrow's investiture as monarch of a new age. If Kitchener, Spoiler, and Melody defined the spirit of the post-World-War-II decade (1945–55), Sparrow's calypsos sparkled with the self-confidence and machismo of a decade (1956–66) marked by a new nationalism that was initially regional (i.e. the West Indian Federation) then parochial (i.e. the separate achievement of independence by Jamaica and Trinidad (1962), then Barbados and Guyana (1966)). Sparrow's calypsos (1959, 1963) were a channel for the bravado, self-assertiveness, and strident, yet paradoxically fragile, masculine self-confidence that seemed inseparable from the politics of this new nationalism. Indeed, Sparrow compared his own battles against his many critics with those that the country's premier, Dr Eric Williams, was fighting against his rivals in politics and the press. Williams, the political hero, and Sparrow, the culture hero, were equal warriors in the same national cause, accepted and rejected by Trinidad's capricious publics, fragmented by class, ethnicity, gender, and generationally determined tastes.

If "society in Trinidad" was constantly passing judgment on Sparrow, Sparrow was equally forthright in his condemnation of society as hypocritical and guilty of "false pride" ("Popularity Contest," 1963). When Lord Kitchener returned to Trinidad in January 1963, after fifteen years in the UK, the contradictions were further emphasized. Kitchener was, quite inaccurately, remembered as a rooted traditionalist, in spite of his having led the newly arrived group of calypsonians who called themselves the Young Brigade in rebellion against the Old Guard (sometimes known as the Old Brigade) in 1946. Sparrow, in contrast, was seen as an innovator who had not only changed the structure of calypso but had also committed the unforgivable sin of singing other people's compositions. A kind of nostalgic mythology had begun to be invented around the figure of Kitchener.

For all its awkwardness and sourness, the Sparrow–Kitchener rivalry revitalized calypso, leading to innovation by both bards and awakening in other calypsonians the desire to defeat both champions. Since steelbands were an important component in determining the Road March winner, Kitchener undertook the task of composing calypsos that could highlight the percussive strengths of pan in both Road March and Panorama competitions – finding the medium between long melody lines that would afford the pan men room for variation and short rhythmic lines that would inspire the revelers to dance. With others joining in, a substantial and still growing body of "pan calypsos" has been the result: the late 1990s saw a competition for pan calypsos; over the last five years more than twenty of these calypsos have been composed annually, some years over forty!

By the mid-1980s, Kitchener had arrived at a series of templates for structuring different types of calypso. While accepting the sixteen-bar stanza and eight-bar chorus as a basic calypso structure, Kitchener held that a calypso composed for the steelband needed to carry either twenty-four or thirty-two bars in both stanza and chorus. A "message" calypso, that is, a slow didactic ballad of the Chalkdust, Stalin, or Pretender type, needed an expanded structure of thirty-two bars in both stanza and chorus. Such expansiveness gave the singer "time to relate what you want to relate." A party calypso, on the other hand, required no more than eight bars each for stanza and chorus. Verbally, such a calypso had much less to say (Kitchener 1986).

In none of these categories – pan, message, or party calypso – was the calypso stagnant. In the case of the Road March, the Kitchener/Sparrow monopoly drove younger singers either to despair or to greater efforts to break the stranglehold. Notions of how to do this varied from Maestro's call for more tempo ("Tempo," 1975, and "Fiery," 1976) to Shadow's demon-driven quest in "Bass Man" (1974) and "Constant Jamming" (1976) for a deeper, more resonant and hypnotically monotonal bass line. Maestro's call for more tempo, echoed in Calypso Rose's "Gimme More Tempo," the 1977 Road March, would, apart from Squibby in the mid-1970s, fall on deaf ears until Christopher "Tambu" Herbert burst on the scene in the late 1980s. Shadow's threat to defeat both Kitchener and Sparrow, made in 1971 in his own name, but containing the desire of a younger generation, since Composer's "Cacadah" (1964), for a place on the calypso stage, would take a mere three years to be fulfilled.

By the mid-1970s, whatever generation gap had originally existed between Sparrow and Kitchener had virtually closed. Another "generation" of singers had moved to center stage. Sparrow and Kitchener were a settled issue: homage, public recognition, honor needed to be paid to both in equal measure. The two singers had become a sort of dyad in the public mind, voices of a generation whose cycle had closed.

A new debate had opened up within Trinidad's calypso universe. This time the issue was not one of tradition (Kitchener) versus change (Sparrow) but one of serious calypsos (i.e. moral, didactic or political calypsos) versus party or celebration songs with their emphasis on melodic sweetness and rhythm. Chalkdust's "Kaiso versus Soca" (1978) defined the terms of this debate in which singers such as Valentino, Chalkdust, and Stalin found themselves in one camp and singers such as Kitchener and Shorty in the other. Matters had come to a head in 1977 when the Carnival Development Committee proposed a special prize for the best political calypso, and Kitchener was loud in his disapproval of serious, solemn, and heavy songs at Dimanche Gras when most people were seeking joyful release from the burden of their everyday lives. However, Calypso Rose, a woman, had twice beaten Kitchener at his own game of mindless celebration; his own masquerade was now dominating the calypso stage and yet he could no longer find a place on it.

Rose's prolonged wailing mode of delivery, a possible inheritance from her Spiritual Baptist/Shouter roots, has now become the signature style of a significant number of current female soca singers. Denyse Plummer, Sanelle Dempster, and Allison Hinds have all imitated it, while the United Sisters in their chanterelle mode (for example in "Whoa Donkey" (1994) and "Four Women to One Man" (1995)) have also benefited from Rose's signature style. Maestro's call for "more tempo," echoed by Rose in 1977, had relocated raw energy at the center of carnival music, which was augmented when Penguin (Sedley Joseph), a secondary school teacher, revitalized the Jab Jab rhythm in 1980's "The Devil."

Among the many reasons why calypso has constantly reinvented itself is the fact that calypsonians reinvent themselves by stepping out of their time and generation forward into each new age and trend. Thus, Kitchener, who had many times before expressed dissatisfaction with the emerging soca of the 1970s, contributed substantially to this emergence with his immensely popular "Sugar Bum" (1978). Since "Sugar Bum" sounded rather like an uptempo reggae, it made quite an impact – so says Byron Lee – on Jamaicans. It also brought to a head the issue of defining what was a true calypso; for here was Kitchener, who had always been touted as a preserver of tradition, sanctioning the intermarriage of calypso and reggae.

The issue, a hardy perennial, had arisen in 1960 with Sparrow's "Rose" and would recur three decades later with Shadow's "Poverty Is Hell" (1993/4). In 1978, Kitchener insisted in one of his many interviews: "soca is nothing else but a variation, an offshoot of calypso" (*The Sun*, 1978). He considered his colleagues as being "very stupid . . . to think that anything can remain stagnant" (Harper 1978), and pointed to the changes that had occurred in calypso since Lion's time:

> The Calypso was once sung in patois; Lion was in those times. The Mighty Growler then added a swing in Calypso . . . Growler's styling continued until Sparrow took over with a ballad type of Calypso in 1956 and the people loved it. Now Lord Shorty,

who has been experimenting for years, has come up with the soca beat . . . God bless Lord Shorty . . . I am warning those calypsonians who feel the "soca" is not Calypso to watch the waves. Those who cannot ride on the crest of the waves will have to fall by the wayside. For years they have been clamouring for a change in Calypso and now it is here they have failed to recognize it.

The "soca" beat is the only beat to fight against The American "soul" and Jamaican Reggae. We should be proud of the "soca" instead of trying to cry it down. I Kitchener say "soca" is Calypso and I should know because throughout my life I have identified myself as a calypsonian and nothing else. No one can tell me what is Calypso or not.

(Harper 1978)

Here was a peculiar state of affairs: soca music was being rejected by traditionalists because it seemed to have incorporated elements from reggae and American soul; yet the same soca music was being promoted by Kitchener as Trinidad's only weapon against the total incursion of foreign musics.

Sparrow, a notable innovator over the first fifteen years of his calypso life, had in "Robbery with V" (1961) identified originality, stage personality, and melodic variety as the criteria by which he measured excellence. In a 1969 interview (Jacobs 1969), he placed emphasis on entertainment value, sweetness of melody, and heightened rhythm. He noted that the age favored celebratory calypso at the expense of humor and satire, a shift in emphasis that paralleled the movement in carnival away from historical or realistic portrayals towards imagination and fantasy. Sixteen years later, in 1985, Sparrow reminisced that many of his inno-vations – which had been misunderstood in their time – had become standard features of what was now being called "soca." Indeed, twenty-five years before, explaining to Chubby Checker why a young Trinidadian girl from Boissiere village had been able to out-twist him at his Astor Theatre show in Trinidad, Sparrow asserted that the musically all-inclusive calypso already contained the means of absorbing and transcending the twist or any other new thing on the stage. The folk heritage of limbo, Shango, and bongo had inculcated skill, flexibility and panache that were equal to any challenge or test, regardless of its source (Boyke 1985).

One of the explanations usually offered for the emergence of soca music in the 1970s is that in the 1960s both singers and musicians believed that calypso had become a dying art-form, badly in need of vitalization. The fact that such a senti-ment is even more pervasive in the first decade of the twenty-first century after "soca" music has itself gone through several permutations suggests that the notion of a dying calypso signifies something larger and deeper: the intuition of new and insecure identities constructed not on the solid achievements of the past but on the ruins of ancestral lifestyles. However, a close examination of the music of the 1960s and 1970s does not support in any way the myth of a dying art-form, of a calypso that was melodically or rhythmically deficient. There was no lack of either rhythm or rhyme in the 1960s, an era, as we have seen, in which the combined talents of Kitchener, Terror, Sparrow, and Melody were in the process of engendering calypsos with expanded structures designed specifically for pan on the road.

There were, clearly, several tributaries of rhythm and sound that contributed to that torrent of song that in the 1970s came to be called "soca." Several persons are considered to have contributed to its genesis and development: Ras Shorty I, Maestro, Arrow, Merchant, Kitchener, Superblue, Sparrow, Calypso Rose, and Eddy Grant in the 1970s and 1980s, and Preacher, Ronnie McIntosh, Machel Montano, Allison Hinds and Square One, Krosfyah, Sound Revolution, Sanelle Dempster, Bunji Garlin, and a host of other voices and bands in the 1990s. Two voices that have claimed authorship of the soca genre stand out: Eddy Grant and Lord Shorty (or Ras Shorty I as he came to be called in the late 1970s).

Guyana-born and domiciled in England for twenty-three years, Grant relocated to Barbados in the 1980s after achieving phenomenal success as a composer, performer, and producer of his own wide repertoire of songs. Grant brought back to the Caribbean his notion of a global market and his sense of the necessity for Caribbean musicians to conceive of themselves as making music for the world. Grant "conceived" of something he called "kaisoul": "an amalgam of pop music, soul music and calypso music which was 'Black-skinned Blue-eyed Boys' [1970], which, I believe, was the first Soca recording" (interview, 1994). Grant's experiments with crossover rhythms were part of the phenomenon of countering a sense of decay with new forms that in themselves feed the illusion of loss that is as ancient as the calypso itself.

Ras Shorty I (Garfield Blackman) was born in 1941 in Lengua, a village of cane and peasant farming whose population is so overwhelmingly Indo-Trinidadian that even the small percentage of Afro-Trinidadians who live in that community resemble their Indian neighbors in carriage, in gesture, and in understanding of Bhojpuri that is still spoken there. Nurtured on both calypso and Indian folk and popular musics, Shorty learned to play the *dholak* and the *dhantal* and was experimenting with integrating these musics, it is said, since his first calypso composition, "Mango Long" (1958). After that adventure, his songs became a mixture of comic narrative and here he demonstrated not only a familiarity with several of the popular Indian songs but considerable skill in rendering them in illustration of his initial assertion that Indian singers had been improving ("going for higher") over the years. The narrative sections of "Indian Singers" were undoubtedly calypso, while its choruses were quotations from current Indian songs.

It would take Shorty a few more "years of toil, burning the midnight oil" ("Wh(om) God Bless," 1979) before he would with "Indrani" (1973), "Kalo Gee Bull" (1974) and the massively popular "Endless Vibrations" (1975) effect the perfect blend of calypso and East Indian rhythms while, paradoxically, calling for a change in "the accent of Carnival/To a groovy, groovy bacchanal." Shorty, at this critical period in the mid-1970s – the period of Shadow's "Bass Man," Maestro's "Tempo," Squibby's "Iron Man," and Kitchener's "Rainorama" – seemed to half-believe the myth that calypso was dying and in need of renewal in order to compete with both reggae and soul, the musics preferred by a growing cohort of the nation's youth. Standing at a crossroads of infinite possibility, he began to point in two directions at the same time. On the one hand, he was calling for change in the direction of American "soul" culture – ("groovy, groovy," "ride on, ride on/right on, right on," "rock your boat") – and on the other hand he was pontificating about Trinidadians' need for cultural anchorage in the country's indigenous sounds.

Shorty's advice as "pointer-man," man-at-the-crossroads-of-possibility, was that the nation should be free to appreciate whatever it pleased, but should never forget its roots. In envisaging a new sound, Shorty dreamed of a rhythm that would incorporate the different, yet subtly interconnected universes of Afro-Creole, Indo-Creole and African-American popular musics and thus reach out simultaneously to several of the accessible publics in Trinidad and Tobago.

The paradox of Shorty, however, did not end with this Janus-faced focus on local and foreign traditional and new. "I Make Music" (1976) and "Soul Calypso Music" (1975) both suggest that Shorty was moving into a musical space that contained neither the traditional Trinidad mélange nor the new foreign sound. This was totally new space and sound. Similarly, "Om Shanti" (1979), composed by Shorty and Steve Rabathally, was a radically new achievement: the marriage of calypso and Hindu mantra. Another experiment in fusion was conducted from his home in the Piparo forest where he had retreated after the collapse of his life as calypso superstar, phallic hero, and macho man. Shorty began composing devotional music that he called "Jamoo." Given the many dimensions of Shorty's secular and sacred existences and the many directions towards which his creative spirit simul-taneously moved, one would imagine that he would understand and accept the many radical changes that the music that he in 1977 named "SOKAH: the Soul of Calypso" underwent throughout the 1990s. Shorty, however, considered most of these changes to be for the worse, and with "That Ain't Good Enough" (1993) and "Latrine Singers" (1996) he magisterially condemned all his "disciples" in soca for singing "tata" (feces), before his death in 2000.

Soca was and has continued to be the fruit of a series of contradictions, con-testations, crossings-over, comfortable and uncomfortable compromises. Like the calypso of which it was in the 1970s a still indistinguishable offshoot, soca was diverse, multilayered and many-ancestored. The 1980s, age of Blue Boy at one end and David Rudder, Chris Tambu Herbert and Charlie's Roots at the other, with Arrow and Shadow deeply entrenched in the middle, simply added to calypso's and soca's diversity. Social and political calypsos, only peripherally treated in this chapter, went through as many stages, phases and dimensions of change as did soca or "party" music. David Rudder rather sardonically suggests in "Panama" (1988) that one of those changes has been the extension of the narrative stanza to accom-modate the incremental growth of political corruption.

Another change is the growth in metaphorical density in a significant number of political calypsos. This development, however, contrasts with the even more sig-nificant trend of plain, harsh, unadorned invective that has characterized many of the political calypsos of the 1990s. These two trends require special and detailed analysis and can be only mentioned here (see Rohlehr 1985, 1992: and also Hall, K. and Benn, D. 2000). Special study, too, needs to be made of the extraordinary manipulation of political calypsos in Trinidad's trilogy of general elections, 2000, 2001, and 2002. Political calypsos are neither dead nor dormant. As with other categories of calypso, there are more political songs available and wider coverage of issues each year. There is, unfortunately, no corresponding increase in the coverage that is given to political calypsos in the electronic media.

Middle-of-the-road genteel soca achieved its apex in the early 1990s with the band Taxi and the "action song" "Dollar Wine," along with the mischievous and smoothly subtle "Frenchman," whose rhythm was mildly reggae- and dancehall-flavored. This was well-bred, bourgeois soca, doing what the bourgeoisie did best: malingering on the edges of real energy while defending the ambience of the gated community of privilege. Quite different from genteel soca but intersecting it at its edges is what one may term "ritual" soca. This may have started with the Tobago-nian duo of Shadow and Calypso Rose, though one fully recognizes calypso's age-old linkages with Orisha worship and the Baptist faith (Sparrow 1984).

In this vein, Superblue shot into prominence with "Soca Baptist" (1980), whose irreverent intermarrying of the sacred and the secular prompted the Spiritual Baptist community to call for its prohibition. Later in the 1980s in a calypso entitled "Zingay," Blue's preacher, clad in blue robes like Superblue himself, is a prophet armed against demonic forces: unemployment, recession, retrenchment, unhappiness, hunger. Clearly, Superblue viewed his music as an agency of national and personal healing and as a protection against the terrible tribulations facing almost everyone in the trammels of "pressure," "fire," "obeah" and "thunder."

David Rudder has often assumed the role of "high priest" in what he calls "the holy temple of soca" and has been consciously engaged in enhancing the ritual elements of Trinidad's carnival music. His efforts have won him deeply devoted fans from every stratum of society, but particularly from among the genteel bourgeoisie in quest of a soca that still combines rhythmic vitality with lyrical intelligence, as had always been the case with the best of traditional calypso. It is this bourgeoisie too that has been largely responsible for the reinvention of jouvay into a more elaborate ritual of rebirth. Such ritual has demanded its own music, and over the last decade there have been several songs composed about jouvay. These songs carry a slow beat that is meant to resuscitate the old-time "chip" and shuffle of the traditional steelbands. The best example of ritual jouvay music is the Laventille Rhythm Section's 1998 mud mas chant, "Jouvay," a joyous parody of the church's rituals of anointment and baptism in which dwellers of the late twentieth century reach backwards and downwards towards their origin: earth.

There has also been "dancehall soca" and its earthier relative, "ragga soca." Here the story turns to Byron Lee, the opportunistic popularizer of Jamaica's ska in the early 1960s, who has also been a vital link between the musics of Trinidad and Jamaica (Lee 1992). Grasping the fact that Trinidad's Carnival had historically provided the most vital context for the flowering of that island's music, Lee – who made his first contact with Trinidad music when he visited in 1963 and was intrigued by the percussion (the iron, brake drum, and jamming syncopation) – promoted, first, street dancing in the Halfway Tree area of Kingston and then carnival and a calypso tent.

The 1980s, too, was the time when Jamaican dancehall music spread throughout the southern Caribbean with one of the main agencies of its dissemination being the minibus or maxi-taxi, as it is called in Trinidad and Tobago. The themes of sex and violence that had evoked harsh and continuous condemnation when they surfaced in the calypsos of Sparrow and others in the 1950s and 1960s resurfaced in maxi-taxi dancehall, without mask or metaphor. Public outcry resulted in a ban being placed on the loud playing of music on public transport. Sound systems of above a certain size were forbidden. This did not, of course, diminish the popularity of the Jamaican sound; and the current generation of Trinidadian and Tobagonian singers in their late teens or early twenties, both male and female, are as much products of dancehall as they are of soca. It is normal now at carnival shows for the season's soca fare to be presented in the form of a drama of compet-ing male and female sexualities, reminiscent of the much more intense gender contestation that has for some time dominated Jamaican dancehall.

Related to ragga soca is rapso, a hybrid with its own history of constant metamorphosis. Rapso, like rap, hip-hop and dancehall, involves talking or at best chanting to a beat. Lancelot Layne is usually credited with having invented this form of "talk-song" (my name for it) in the late 1960s, time too of the emergence of Eddy Grant's "Kaisoul." Rapso has served both political and entertainment agendas and has, like soca, attracted both bourgeois and proletarian practitioners.

Finally, there is chutney soca, the latter-day fusion of Indo-Trinidadian music and calypso. The interface of these two bodies of music has seen various phases from the 1920s and 1930s of "Bhagi Pholourie," "Gi Sita Ram Gi," and "Dookani" where, seen through the eye of the Creole – Afro, Hispanic, or Portuguese – the entire Indian presence was represented as a curious, at times laughable, at times exotic Other (Rohlehr 1990). This mode of representation did not readily change; it was simply augmented by other images of the Indo-Trinidadian as rival, threat, an antagonist more dangerous than exotic. These new images were, in their turn, qualified by highly flattering ones that commended the diligence, intelligence and acumen of the race (e.g. Chalkdust's "Ram the Magician," 1984) and recommended Hinduism as a source of spiritual strength, wisdom and solace (e.g. Ras Shorty I's "Om Shanti Om," 1979).

Sparrow's "Maharajin" (1982), "Maharajin Sister" (1983) and "Maharajin's Cousin" (1984) were updates of Atilla's and Executor's "Dookani" or King Fighter's "Sookie" (1964) in that the women in these calypsos were rustic, exotic, sexually alluring and unattainable. Such calypsos presented favorable stereotypes of ethnic Indian communities, probably in the hope that this would make possible the penetration by calypso of the growing but as yet untapped Indo-Trinidadian market. Musically, these calypsos required cooperation between calypso arrangers and Indian musicians. The incorporation of Bhojpuri sentences in their choruses also required interethnic collaboration. The reverse became true soon after, as Indian singers sought the help of calypsonians and Black song-writers as they crossed over into the domain of calypso.

The transition in 1987 of Drupatee Ramgoonai from singer of Hindu devotional songs to calypso was a major leap forward for the hybrid soca chutney form. Drupatee's emergence, however, was greeted with consternation by ethnic Hindu purists who deplored the intermixing of races and cultural forms. These ethnic purists were little different from the aesthetic purists who had deplored even the slightest deviation from what they considered the true, pure form of calypso.

The story of chutney's (chatnee according to some experts) journey towards calypso/soca has been one of the commercialization of a folk music. It has also been a story of male expropriation of a female mode; the original chutney music was exclusively female, involving mainly the performance of mature women at Hindu weddings, behind closed doors where neither males nor children were allowed. Over the years, chutney had made the journey from the matikor's closed space to the public stage where it was promoted, some complained, by non-Hindu producers with only commercial profit in mind. Indrani Rampersad felt that the issue now involved "the fight for the mighty dollar versus that for morality" (1990). Between the 1980s and the 1990s, debate raged within the Hindu community over what should be done about the now public performance of Hindu sexuality. Chutney, some said, was even worse than carnival in that its "lewd and vulgar dancing" was being performed nearly every weekend, while carnival was only once a year. Some commentators even called for police censorship of chutney shows.

Ravi Ji, a Hindu thinker and activist of Central Trinidad, noted that "chatnee," starting from humble beginnings in folk-songs sung at excursions, had now grown "to register a dynamic presence in the cultural landscape of Trinidad and Tobago" (1990). The song form had also moved beyond Trinidad and was now popular in the Caribbean, Fiji, the United States, Canada and India, making a similar journey to the one calypso had made since the 1950s. The movement from the matikor to the open public stage then involved the transgression of women into an arena already controlled by men. Female performance in this arena of rhythm, alcoholic intoxication and license was directly related to Indian women's desire for visibility within their own and the wider national community.

Virtually all of this controversy sounded like cyclic repetition of debates that had been taking place since the French Creole and British elites became confronted in the mid nineteenth century with the phenomenon of "jamette carnival." The desire to control the behavior of an underclass and especially to monitor women's public performance; the call for censorship by means of police intervention; the moral self-righteousness of an emergent bourgeoisie – all these things had happened before.

Chutney, then, was an arena of contestation within its ethnic community, long before the question arose of its encountering calypso and soca in their own arena of tooth and fang. Political and cultural activists of the Hindu community such as Ravi Ji and Kamal Persad sensed the potential of chutney as a politically adversarial music to become the Indo-Trinidadian alternative to the predominantly Afro-Creole form of the political calypso or to carnival. Another alternative to political calypsos would be provided in the spring Hindu festival of Phagwa by an innovative song form called pichakaaree, the name taken from the gun that shoots the colored liquid called abeer during Phagwa.

Trinidad had always been a country of multiple cultural identities in covert or open competition with each other for iconic representation and visibility. The Afro-Creole versus Indo-Trinidadian (or Trinidad-Indian as some ethnic nationalists prefer) phase of such contestation has been the most recent and crucial manifestation of this phenomenon. Chutney, calypso, soca, pichakaaree, carnival, Divali, emancipation, Indian Arrival Day have, in this context of competing ethnicities, all assumed iconic status, serving as metaphors of the larger contestation perpetually alive beneath the face of the ongoing masquerade.

The uniting of cultures would insulate the society against the fissures that had again become painfully evident when the Creole-Indian coalition party, the NAR, split into its constituent fragments in 1988. Foreshadowing David Rudder's magnificent dream "The Ganges and the Nile" (2000) by more than a decade, Delamo proclaimed:

> Now who come out to divide and rule
> Eh go use we as no tool
> Anytime they coming racial
> I dougla, I staying neutral.

(Constance 1991: 43)

When for the carnival season of 1996 two businessmen, George Singh and Colin Talma, promoted the first National Chutney Soca competition, it was immediately recognized by many to be the musical inscription of the new UNC regime that had first come to power in 1995 with its slogan of "national unity." Speaking on the night of the finals to a Skinner Park crowd of 18,000, Basdeo Panday, the new Prime Minister, commended the cross-cultural nature of the competition as "a step in the direction of national unity" (Danny 1996: 3).

Chutney soca, a newcomer to the carnival's broad "national" and multiethnic stage, was clearly only one part of what was happening in carnival in 1996. Calypsonians Cro Cro, Sugar Aloes, Chalkdust, Watchman, and David Rudder, among others, were interrogating Panday's "national unity." By far the greatest attempt to illustrate Trinidad's national unity via iconic performance was Machel Montano's potentially healing "Real Unity" concert of Sunday, November 26, 2000. "Real Unity" had arisen from the heart of soca, chutney and dancehall, out of the symbolic meeting of Rudder's "Ganges and Nile" (the UNC used this as a political campaign song and as Panday's signature tune in the trilogy of elections, 2000, 2001, and 2002). But just as Rudder's song had been appropriated by the very "mind-benders" it had sought to dismiss and leave behind, Machel's "Real Unity" was silently and swiftly embraced as the perfect apotheosis of the chutney soca concept: equal visibility on the national cultural stage. It was breathtaking in scope, this occasion that was meant to unite the calypso superstars of the 1950s and 1960s with their soca, ragga, dancehall and chutney counterparts of the 1980s and 1990s. Machel was touted as "one of the major assets this country has produced in culture in the last two decades" (Blood 2000: 8). The song "Real Unity," after which the concert had been named, celebrated the myth of racial harmony and interracial love, in terms not substantially different from Sparrow's "Maharajin" (1982) and Iwer George's controversial "Bottom in the Road" (1998). "Real Unity" declared that one was free to "jam" on any member of any race that one pleased in Trinidad's "united nation." The idea attracted all sorts and conditions of people, from the hedonistic, apolitical youth to the vote-seeking politicians for whom every occasion, fete or funeral, had become susceptible to manipulation.

Everything was perfect except the ill-assembled scaffolding upon which the ramps containing the VIP seats had been erected. These ramps could not bear the collective weight of so many big shots, among whom "stormers" soon mingled in classless unity. As soon as Machel took the stage and said "jump," patrons started to jump. The ramps began to sway, then to wine, then to dingolay, then to buckle and finally to collapse into a wilderness of twisted steel, broken plywood and scattered chairs, and a soca chorus of screams and groans (account reconstructed from television replays of the catastrophe, as well as eyewitness accounts in the press of late November 2000). The bourgeois notion of a "concert" at which $600 patrons would sit politely in their all-inclusive/exclusive compound was instantly superseded by the reality of a typical Machel "bram," at which patrons had for a decade been invited to "get on bad," "free up," "misbehave," and "mash up the place." After the $600 patrons departed and the injured were taken to hospital, some by the very pirogues on which a few of the stormers had come, Machel and company resumed the concert at 11:30 p.m. and performed until 3:00 a.m., giving the $80 and $70 patrons, who stood on solid unshakable ground, what they had come for.

From all that has been said above, it should be clear that calypso reinvents itself, not only in hope of finding formulae to penetrate external markets but also and primarily in response to complex pressures within Trinidad's parochial and infinitely complicated society. Hybrid song forms reflect alliances, transgressions and contestations that are constantly taking place in a society that is restless, hyperactive, driven, as David Rudder suggested in 1997 or 1998, by an excess of adrenaline, and imperfectly contained and defined by a multitude of shifting and intersecting boundaries. The reinvention of calypso is a function of the society's constant self-renewal; but self-renewal suggests either the constant death or waning of identities, and the discontinuity that ensues as younger and younger generations try to supplant the entrenched hierarchies of the old and fossilized.

NOTE

1   This chapter has been condensed from Professor Rohlehr's much longer, forthcoming study of the evolution of calypso by Milla Cozart Riggio, who takes the responsibility for disjunctures created in the editorial process.

19

ON REDEFINING THE NATION THROUGH PARTY MUSIC

Jocelyne Guilbault

This chapter examines identity politics by focusing on a popular music usually found in the bins of record stores under the label "international music" or "world music." While this project falls into an important new trend in academic studies, popular musics that are deemed profit-oriented, known not for their focus on text but rather for their focus on pleasure, dance, and sexualized bodies, have rarely been studied in relation to the notion of nation. My hope is to fill part of this gap by exploring soca from Trinidad, a popular music also often called "party music," that emerged in the mid-1970s and has been a dominating force in the carnival music industry since the late 1980s.

My aim is in part to challenge the commonly held view that soca is merely the product of commercial interests, the result of the homogenizing effect of globalization, and the embodiment of the threat to local culture's integrity. As Line Grenier writes about global pop, "in keeping with the high/low cultural hierarchy that it reproduces, [such a view] involves, albeit implicitly, the uncritical privileging of some musical genres deemed autonomous, 'authentic,' and empowering, over pop and other mainstream genres deemed strictly profit-driven, alienating, and 'false' " (in press: 3). Positing party songs as trivial and interchangeable commodities not only ignores the artistic investment of its makers but also neglects the aesthetic discrimination and value-judgments of its consumers. It also overlooks the ways in which soca's success – its ability to communicate, to sell, and to endure as a genre – is based not simply on reproducing familiarity but also on cultivating difference.

Party music, like any other music, can be understood only by grasping the conjuncture that has permitted it to arise. Thus, it is important to position soca in relation to calypso, of which it is a musical offshoot and with which it shares the same space, namely, carnival. Since 1993, soca has used the conceptual framework and infrastructure of competitions that informs the calypso music industry to gain legitimacy and recognition. Because carnival and its competitions have historically served, in Gayle Wald's expression, as the "authenticating" spaces of national culture in Trinidad, soca, I contend, has helped to change definitions of the national (2002). This study examines how soca functions to critique prescriptive ideologies of national identity.

I focus on three discursive spaces through which soca has been articulated: first, soca's sounds, which perform their own version of nation in carnival by functioning as sites of encounters between styles, genres, musical strategies, and technologies, and as sites of ethnic, racial, and gendered social relations; second, soca's producers or consumers linked to the nationalist discourses in which, or against which, soca is figured; and third, the diasporic circuits in which soca travels. My goal in looking at these spaces is to offer different takes on soca's articulations of nation.

TAKE 1: SOCA'S ARTICULATIONS OF NATION THROUGH SOUNDS

I begin by focusing on soca's sounds, not only because they constitute a privileged point of entry for me as a musician, but also because soca's sounds first spurred controversy. Here, I draw on Josh Kun's notion of "audiotopia" (inspired by Michel Foucault's concept of "heterotopia") to explore soca's unique configuration of spaces through sounds or, to use Kun's words:

> music's ability to act effectively as an agent of intense utopian longing and its uncanny ability to bring together several sites normally deemed incompatible, not only in the space of a particular piece of music itself, but in the production of social space and mapping of geographical space that music makes possible.

(Kun 1997: 289)

Soca arose in the early 1970s out of an attempt to bring together the two largest communities of the island of Trinidad. According to one of soca's most respected founders, the late Garfield Blackman, known as Ras Shorty I (formerly as Lord Shorty), soca music aimed "to unite the East Indian and African peoples" and "to fight 'racialism' among them." From its beginning, soca illustrates how global movements can give force to local desires. Drawing on the civil rights movement in the United States and its major impact in many other countries (Zuberi 2001; Dunn 2001), Ras Shorty I seized this particular moment to fight the colonial legacy of ethnic or racial divisions in the newly independent nation-state of Trinidad and Tobago through music. He fused calypso – the unofficial emblem of the nation-state, which until then had featured Afro-Creole performers almost exclusively – with Indian musical elements to bond and represent musically the two historically divided Trinidadian communities.

Initially, arrangements of soca songs that featured Indian instruments[1] had to be revised – retaining the Indian rhythms but playing them on instruments typically heard in the calypso rhythm section because, in the words of Ras Shorty I, "many Afro-Trinidadians felt that these new additions were spoiling their music." Eventually, however, soca's new sounds succeeded in gaining acceptance and became the dominant music during carnival by the late 1980s. Although Indian sounds have nearly disappeared in soca today, it would be hasty to conclude that the initial efforts made through soca to bring together the Indian and Afro-Trinidadian communities were in vain. Soca, in fact, provided the possibility for the Indian community to gain visibility in the local carnival scene. By the mid-1980s, soca (then predominantly heard as an Afro-Trinidadian music) was (re)appropriated by the Indian community to produce chutney soca, a fusion that unmistakably merges the sounds of the two musical traditions.[2] In 1993 with the creation of Indian-owned radio stations, and in 1995 with the additional support of an elected government headed for the first time by an Indian Prime Minister, chutney soca became more audible. With the launching of yearly competitions during carnival in 1996, chutney soca acquired legitimacy. Through this process, the new sounds of both soca and chutney soca have arguably redrawn the map of carnival space, bringing to the fore the question of who and what, in ethnic terms, constitutes the national.

In line with its initial mission, soca has continued to draw the voices of new subjects into the carnival scene. In contrast with traditionally male-dominated calypso, soca has featured a significant number of solo female artists or frontliners since the 1990s. In recognition of women's contributions to the carnival scene, Rituals, one of the most important Trinidadian record labels, issued a ground-breaking compilation entitled *Soca Divas* in the year 2000. Just as Ras Shorty I's motivation for bringing the Indian and Afro-Creole communities together was partly related to social movements that transcended Trinidad's sociopolitical boundaries, so too the significant role women have come to play in soca is related to issues on a far larger scale than the local (see Grenier in press: 10), influenced, for example, by the growing prominence of women in other Caribbean popular musics, such as dancehall and zouk, and transnational practices such as rap. Along with these relatively new musics and their new gender politics, soca has provided a space for Trinidadian female artists not only to join regional and international move-ments but also to participate as song or mass leaders in the prominent public sphere where the national is articulated.

In addition to featuring the voices of new subjects, soca has articulated other types of relationships through its sounds. In songs such as "Jab Molassie" by Superblue, "Jab Jab" by Machel Montano, and "Vampire" by Maximus Dan, new relationships with tradition have been forged. As Kun describes it in reference to other musics from the southern hemisphere, "the sounds of tradition . . . meet the sounds of the post-industrial, the sounds of the machine, and the sounds of (post)modern technology" (Kun 1997: 304). Old musical techniques (such as repetition, call-and-response, and rhythmic patterns typical of traditional carnival characters such as Jab Molassie or Jab Jab) and old calypso songs have not been abandoned but have been reconfigured – for example, Maximus Dan's 2002 song "Vampire" featured excerpts of Black Stalin's song "Vampire Year" recorded in 1982. The rearticulation of traditional material with contemporary sounds from multiple cultural and national locations is not a new strategy in Caribbean Creole cultures, where mixes and remixes have always been common. But in the post-colonial context, in which modalities of cultural hybridity – such as forced assimi-lation, internalized self-rejection, or commercial cooption – have caused much resentment, soca's open celebration of the creolization process makes any claim that the national can be defined exclusively in terms of a fixed tradition harder to sustain.

Importing new music technologies into soca has been part of what Nestor Garcia Canclini has termed "cultural reconversion" – a process that reflects Leopold Senghor's motto "not to be assimilated, but to assimilate" – by using whatever is available to reinforce the local cultural capital (cited in Kun 1997: 304–5, and in conversation). Such cultural reconversion takes place, for example, when the drum machine is used to make soca sounds palatable to contemporary audiences. It also takes place when Machel Montano appropriates a Jamaican dancehall rhythm to create a break in his 1997 fast-paced soca song "Big Truck" to provide a breathing space before returning to his fast soca section with a renewed intensity. Similarly, when soca artists rely on "riddims" (derived from a well-known Jamaican practice, fixed, pre-recorded instrumental rhythm section tracks created by producers or arrangers that are used by different artists) to create their own soca songs, the local cultural capital is not lost.[3] Rather, following Canclini's argument, it is re-articulated through a multiplicity of subjectivities and senses of belonging that inextricably interrelate the local and the global, the national and the transnational (Canclini cited in Kun 1997: 305). Because soca bands and singers perform mainly in the authenticating space of carnival where Trinidadianness is publicly enunciated, soca sounds become an effective site for witnessing how the bonds and boundaries of national culture are negotiated.

The question is, how do these forms of connections enacted through soca sounds come to matter, for whom, and why? In an attempt to explore these questions further, I turn next to soca's "culture of production" and "production of culture," as articulated by soca artists in creative tension with the traditional discourses of nationhood (for elaboration of the symbiotic relationship between "culture of production" and "production of culture," see Negus 1999).

TAKE 2: SOCA'S PRODUCERS AND CONSUMERS IN RELATIONSHIP TO NATIONALIST DISCOURSES

It is well known that music has often entered nationalist discourses. But how has a music deemed profit-driven, associated with parties – but not with political parties of any sort – been relevant to nationalist projects? In our case, what conventions does soca reinforce or challenge in the nationalist discourses? Before attempting to answer these questions, I want first to clarify how music – and which music – has been historically connected to nationalist discourses in Trinidad.

Drawing on the work of Thomas Turino, I use "nationalist discourse" to refer explicitly to "a political movement or ideology that bases the idea of legitimate sovereignty on a coterminous relationship between a 'nation' and a state" and the expression "musical nationalism" to refer specifically "to musical styles, activities, and discourses that are explicitly part of nationalist political movements and pro-grams" (Turino 2000: 13–14). On the basis of these definitions, the music, space, and format most associated with the nationalist project in Trinidad have been calypso, carnival, and competitions. State-sponsored organization of calypso competitions has linked this music to nation-building, independence and post-independence themes (see Rohlehr 1990; Liverpool 1993, 2001; Trotman 1993; Regis 1999).

To summarize briefly: in the 1960s and 1970s the nationalist construction of calypso in Trinidad developed under the leadership of the first Prime Minister, Oxford-trained black scholar Dr Eric Williams, and then was renewed during the Black Power movement. Seen as central in the promotion of national culture, calypso was thought of as bringing the kind of new consciousness needed to eliminate the false sense of self that people experienced under the colonial regime.

Because of calypso's emphasis on the word, on speaking the reality as it is expressed in everyday language, social activists and intellectuals, including C.L.R. James, saw calypso as synonymous with "being authentic" by providing "a oneness of mind and physical reality" (Trotman 1993: 24–5). Calypso's emphasis on language had the power to bring change. Whereas during the colonial period calypso became the focus of attention because of its perceived role in the struggle for survival, during the 1960s and the 1970s calypso increased its prominence by being associated with the processes of cultural identification and political emancipation.

Thus, any music challenging the prominence of calypso in the carnival space and using competitions similar to those associated with calypso to establish its legitimacy would be confronted by nationalist discourses and set in comparison to calypso. In the 1990s, programs on the state-owned television channel (TT&T), talk shows on local radio stations, columns and open letters in daily newspapers, cultural critiques in monthly reviews, and academic articles expressed concerns about soca's commercialization, reliance on technology, and impact on morality.

Over the past fifteen years, nationalists, cultural activists, and populist artists have regarded with suspicion, if not antagonism, the commercialization of soca which they attribute to Anglo-American influence. Debates about soca have been part of a much larger nationalist discussion that opposes political-cultural values to market values and procedures, Trinidadian nationalism to foreign influence and domination. On the basis of such views, the problems raised by soca center on cultural importation and export quality.

For many observers, when soca songs entered international markets, they began to exhibit the typical symptoms of commodification – resembling many and any other popular musics. According to Rohlehr, "Soca has in two decades moved from being a trade name for a variety of calypso-crossover rhythms to a fairly rigid song form with standard chord structure, melodic lines, and lyrics" (1998: 91). Its songs have become simplified and homogenized. They all resort to similar gimmicks involving both self-promotion and the adoption of the basic methodology of all advertising: repetition (Rohlehr 1998; Alleyne 1995). On the whole, the commercialization of soca is thus equated with loss: a narrative quality diminished through the loss of humor and rhetorical or storytelling skills; and a musical sensibility diminished through a reliance on repetition instead of creativity.

At issue is how local artists, in their attempts to penetrate the international market, have allegedly fallen prey to the "rules" of the global market: turning original musical compositions (here meaning traditional calypso) into cultural commodities and adopting foreign aesthetics at the expense of local musical values. Interestingly, even though calypso – like other musics linked to nationalist projects – is widely acknowledged to have been mediated by foreign music, in nationalist discourses it retains an aura of rootedness and authenticity as a cultural practice associated with the masses, especially the Trinidadian black working class.[4]

Linked to the anguish over foreign influence and its homogenizing impact, the widespread use of sound technologies in soca, particularly drum machines and samplers, has been met with great concern because of the allegedly detrimental effects of technology on both craftsmanship and creativity. In the words of a journalist commenting on soca:

Incorporating digital samples of other songs became easier with desktop audio systems. With the coming of affordable CD recordable systems, anyone who wished to become a soca artist could put something together on the desktop and burn ten or so CDs for the radio stations . . . Faster and faster. Leaving less and less time to think, to reflect, to contemplate this festival we are creating . . . There was a time when the calypsonian thought long and hard about the events of the day and fashioned songs which used irony and parable to tell stories richly flavoured with their opinions.

(Mark Lyndersay, "Bring the Rhythm Down," *Trinidad Express*, February 18, 1998)

As Nabeel Zuberi notes, musical developments such as soca's use of technology are often framed in oppositional terms: "either an older organic and authentic form of musical expression representing a community has been destroyed by the new technologies, or ethnicity melts away in this synthesized global melange" (2001: 132). Indeed, the fact that some of soca's major hits, such as Machel Montano's "Come Dig It" or Edwin Yearwood's "Redemption," have been associated, and even confused at times, with American-style house music and R&B raises questions about whether such crossovers embody a local or even regional Caribbean identity. Either way, technology is conceived as a threat to the survival and expression of difference. As Zuberi notes in relation to musics using digital technologies, soca makes it "more problematic to claim that sounds are readable as arising directly from specific identities and localities" (2001: 132). Soca thus troubles the traditional expression and definition of nation in Trinidad by transgressing not only the normative aesthetics of calypso but also the definitions of identity circumscribed by place.

At another level, soca's focus on pleasure, dance, and sexualized bodies has constituted another main area of contention. Even though lyrically some soca songs include social commentaries (for example, in 2002 André Tanker's critique of Osama bin Laden in "Ben Lion"), most party songs either vigorously invite participants to jam and wine or focus on relations with the opposite sex. As a whole, soca songs are thus seen at best as lacking any political value or as culti-vating an escapist attitude. At worst, their focus on jamming and wining is thought to encourage sexual looseness, and also to undermine consensual standards of decency. Interestingly, the wining dance movements prevalent in soca are found in many of the Afro-Creole traditions in Trinidad and in the Caribbean and are hence not new. But the central importance they have acquired in soca both on stage and among fans has been criticized, not because they foreground a new cultural politics that links identity and culture irrevocably with the expression of sexuality, but rather because this new politics challenges the norms of who can express sexuality and to what extent.

As Simon Frith (1996) has argued in his work on popular discrimination, such critiques are more than musical judgments. They imply not only ethical but also moral evaluations and assessments. Just as Jamaica's DJs have been said to "steer the dancehall side of roots culture away from political and historical themes and towards 'slackness' " – which Paul Gilroy translates as "crude and often insulting wordplay pronouncing on sexuality and sexual antagonism" (Gilroy quoted by Cooper 1993: 141) – soca artists have been seen as steering carnival music away from its language of sociopolitical resistance and critiques of a regressive form of identity politics: the lyrics are deemed shallow, and their yearnings are judged to be limited to the immediate needs of the body. It is noteworthy that expressions of emancipation or resistance to hegemonic tendencies – like those articulated by some female performances – have not been read in nationalist discourses as such, it could be surmised, less because these expressions are politically irrelevant than because they may undermine some of the tenets of the nationalist project, as it has traditionally been defined.

A contrasting perspective on soca emerges, however, when considered in relation to the new nation-building discourse of soca producers or consumers. Over the past eight years in Trinidad, Barbados, and Antigua, most soca singers and arrangers I interviewed who have been active since the late 1980s explained their approaches to soca as reactions to implicit rules and traditions in calypso. In musical terms, calypso not only sounded old (as it did for Ras Shorty I in the 1970s or more recently for Edwin Yearwood and Nicholas Brancker, the leader and main arranger of Krosfyah, a famous Barbadian soca band) but its structure – three verses alternating with a refrain – also seemed too confining, with the focus nearly exclusively on the lyrics at the expense of the melodies: "the lyrical content of 90 percent of the songs don't cater for the younger people and only talk about politics, guns ... and everything negative in society" (Yearwood, interview, Barbados, August 6, 1997).

Yearwood and Brancker illustrate the generation gap, difference in musical tastes, and relationship to the process of nation-building that separate most soca artists from traditional calypsonians. Most new-wave soca artists were born after their countries gained independence and thus take as a given their countries' nationhood. As Robin Balliger indicates, soca artists "enact a form of politics exemplary of the 'post-national' period: instead of an enfranchised public partici-pating in a critical, modernist, national dialogue, alienation shifts power away from state authority, political promises and 'representation,' to what is immediately known and experienced" (Balliger 2000: 118). In this sense, the work of soca artists has less to do with dismissing the idea of nation than with attempting to renew its formulation in contemporary terms – in line with the new cultural politics of neoliberalism and globalization. Concretely, they aim to redraw the carnival space where the national culture is authenticated in at least two ways: by turning their attention to youth and by reimagining soca sounds in ways that extend the carnival music industry beyond the local scene, connecting it with today's regional and international markets.

> What does bring we together
> If yuh come from near or far
> Jump and wave and get on bad
> Soca make yuh catch ah glad
> ("Soca" by Machel Montano and Xtatic, 2000)

As stated in "Soca," a song by the reputed Trinidadian soca artist Machel Montano and his band Xtatic,[5] soca is designed to encourage the formation of what anthropologist Arjun Appadurai has called "a community of sentiment," that is, a community of people who begin to imagine and feel things together (1996: 8). To achieve a sing-along feel and sense of togetherness, the soca artists I interviewed were clear about the strategies they use: they give greater importance to the back-ground vocalists than used to be true of calypso. To boost the energy level and to "vent frustration or express emotions that may not be possible to channel in any other way," they speed up the rhythm from the typical 100 beats per minute in calypso to 120 and up to 140 beats per minute, and place the rhythm section forefront in the final mix (quotation from Nicholas Brancker, interview, Barbados, March 12, 1997). They also infuse the song texts with a series of hook lines based on call-and-response exchanges.

To a much greater extent than calypso, soca performances are designed, in the words of Krosfyah's leader, "to cater equally for the feel, the audio, and the visual" (Yearwood, interview, Barbados, August 6, 1997). In this spirit, most soca artists have devoted a great deal of attention to lighting and theatrics, to producing catchy tunes that involve constant interaction with the crowd, and to performing choreographed or freestyle moves to make the whole stage come alive. For the soca audience, this calls for dancing. In fact, leading people not only to sing but also to dance has become the criterion in the Caribbean for evaluating soca songs and artists. The repeated calls in soca songs to "jump and wave," "move to the right, move to the left," "get yourself a partner," "follow me," "start to wine," and "go down low" make physical participation and acting together central to creating a sense of community. As Balliger reported in her study on soca audiences, soca music is not so much about a politics of representation, as about a politics of presence: a face-to-face encounter and solidarity among peers. It is also about a politics of pleasure, of emotional joy and release in the temporary community of the "fete" through dancing – "not in the deferral of satisfaction through hard work" (Balliger 2000: 118–19).

TAKE 3: SOCA'S ARTICULATION THROUGH DIASPORA

Numerous publications have richly documented the importance of overseas carnivals for Trinidadians and other Caribbean population groups in diaspora and the crucial role that popular culture, most particularly music, has played in such contexts. But few, if any, have addressed the particular role that soca has played in diasporic spaces. What kinds of identities does it perform and for whom? In soca's transnational circuits, is the notion of nation reinforced or abandoned?

By entering the long tradition of overseas carnivals (the first overseas Caribbean carnival began in the late 1920s in Harlem: Nurse 2000: 96; Hintzen 2001: 42), soca has taken on the overseas carnivals' original mandates: namely, to assert a pan-West-Indian cultural identity and to provide a means of resistance in an otherwise alienating environment (Nurse 2000: 103; Ho 2001; also see Nurse, Connor and Farrar, and Kasinitz in this volume). Yet soca performers reach Caribbean diasporic population groups markedly different from those of the early twentieth century. The frequency with which migrants can now travel back and forth between their new homes and their mother countries and the ease with which they can exchange daily news with their friends and relatives still living in the Caribbean have given a new twist to the meaning of migration. With today's access to mass communication and modern technology, the traditional meaning of "home" defined by referring to a specific place or locality has become ever more blurred and indeterminate.

Paradoxically, despite these changes, immigrant population groups' need to maintain ideas of cultural and ethnic distinction has become more salient than

(Gupta and Ferguson 1992: 10). In the face of adversities such as racial dis-
.nination and ethnic ghettoization, visible diasporic minorities have felt pressed
,einforce their collective identities so that they can fight for political spaces. For
Caribbean population groups abroad, and for Trinidadians especially, the means of
reinforcing this sense of collective identity has been through carnival, through
calypso and, over the past fifteen years, through soca.

Interestingly, as Percy Hintzen (2001: 43) has noted in relation to New York's
West Indian diaspora,

> country-specific identities do not disappear on Labor Day [time when West Indian
> Carnival is celebrated in New York] but are reflected in patterns of participation at
> the carnival festivities that publicize national rather than regional identity. On the day
> of the parade, a profusion of flags represents the various countries, and designated
> sections of the parade route have become country-specific gathering places.

Since these remarks apply equally well to most other West Indian diasporic communities, the question then is how soca has catered simultaneously for both a pan-
West-Indian and a Trinidadian identity: by being hybrid in form and influence –
like overseas carnivals themselves – and simultaneously embodying a culture of
resistance and one of cooptation – thereby defying the simplistic generalization
that the two cultures are by definition opposed to each other (see Nurse 2000: 103).
Its trademark of sounding multiple cultural and national locations and embodying
various musical sensibilities undoubtedly stems from appreciating, to use Stuart
Hall's words, "the dialogic strategies . . . essential to the diaspora aesthetic"
(quoted by Nurse 2000: 105).

As Gayatri Gopinath suggested in relation to bhangra, reading soca as embodying West Indian diasporic aesthetics "allows for a far more complicated understanding of diaspora, in that *it demands a radical reworking of the hierarchical
relation between diaspora and the nation*" (Gopinath 1995: 204; italics in the
original). On the one hand, soca's incorporation of diasporic sensibilities from
different Caribbean cultures and communities creates a network of alliances that
"displaces the 'home' country from its privileged position as originary site"
(ibid.). On the other hand, the performance of soca's diasporic aesthetics in the
nation reconfigures the very terms by which the nation is constituted – making the
diaspora part of its economy, both culturally and financially. Reading soca as
embodying diasporic aesthetics also highlights the ways in which soca constructs
its audience: formed by both national and diasporic subjects whose identities
are "not singular or monolithic and are instead multiple, shifting, and often self-
contradictory . . . made up of heterogeneous and heteronomous representations of
gender, race, and class" (Marcia Tucker quoted by Nurse 2000: 105).

The problem is that, even though soca may aim to reach an audience that is
"heterogeneous," in reality soca's constituency in the carnival sphere is mostly
black.[6] This raises the question whether the carnival that soca helps to articulate
should be simply portrayed as a "black" or Afro-Caribbean thing instead of a
"Caribbean" festival (Nurse 2000: 103). In other words, the issue of racial and
ethnic representation in the diasporic celebration of the nation and the region
continues to be raised particularly by the Indo-Caribbean community in relation to
what music and whom the overseas carnivals continue to privilege.

Just as soca (re)produces in diaspora some of the tensions from "home" when performing the nation, soca also experiences in diaspora the same marginal positioning that "home" – and the nation it represents – has historically held vis-à-vis First World societies. It faces the legacies of postcolonial conditions: lack of access to political and economic leverage and insufficient organizational capability to control its circulation and to maximize its commercial returns (for instance, those made possible by legal copyright protections). Soca is racially marked, and thus heavily confined to predefined markets and possibilities. In the same ways Keith Nurse has remarked about overseas carnivals, the limitations faced by soca "are systemic in nature in that they relate to large-scale, long-term processes such as colonialist discourse (Bhabha 1994) . . . and imperialism (Ado 1986)" (quoted by Nurse 2000: 109). And yet, along with the expansion of overseas carnivals beyond the confines of the immigration populations they represent, soca has reinforced some old alliances and created new ones – racially, ethnically, culturally, economically, and politically. In "this act of transnational, transcultural, and transgressive politics," to borrow Nurse's wording (2000: 107), soca could be said to have strengthened both national and pan-West-Indian identities at home and abroad.

SOCA AS A NEW CULTURAL FORMATION

Soca has radically altered the carnival music scene since the late 1980s. In conclusion, inspired by Herman Gray's use of the term, I want to suggest that soca's deployment might point to a new "cultural formation," one that has not only remapped collective identities but also reformulated in fundamental ways what is taken to be authentic in national culture. Through soca, a constellation of new social relations, shifts in sensibility and desire, strategic use of new technologies, and involvement of dominant institutions and infrastructures have come together in revolutionary ways.

As we have seen, some of the social, political, and cultural moves that this new formation has encouraged stand in contrast with traditional dominant ideologies locally, and have been met with resistance. In addition to rethinking the bounds and boundaries of the nation – whom it includes and excludes and what geographical spaces partake in its embodiment – this new cultural formation enacted through soca has embraced a diasporic aesthetics and identity politics that have posed vexing questions about the ethics and politics of representation, not just for Trinidadians. Indeed, I am struck by the ways in which the worries about the images and representations circulated through soca echo those concerning other black diasporic musics such as dancehall and rap and are profoundly related to broader issues raised by and through the African diaspora. Scholars such as Gordon Rohlehr from Trinidad and Paul Gilroy from Britain use strikingly similar terms when addressing their preoccupations about the ethical, cultural, and political future of the national and black self-representation through popular musics that in their views lack political vision. They see these musics as underwritten by cultural and market values steeped in hedonism, short-term pleasure, and social irresponsibility, and as withdrawing dangerously from collective black struggle. But, as Gray remarks, "These images are made under very specific discursive conditions and social relations. Such circumstances set the limits of possibility for imagining, producing, and circulating different kinds of representations." He adds, "What may be a cause for worry are not so much the images alone as the cultural frameworks and social conditions out of which they are generated and the cultural desires to which they respond" (Gray 2001: 88).

Following Gray's recommendation, the work of cultural critics should not be simply about documenting the rise of a new cultural formation, but also "critically interrogating the conditions of cultural production and evaluating the politics that it proposes and enacts" (ibid.). In that sense, tracing how soca has worked effectively to change the notion of nation in Trinidad and Tobago as I have tried to do here marks only the first step of a large critical enterprise.

NOTES

1   Ras Shorty I's musical arrangement of "Indrani" recorded in 1973, for example, featured, in addition to the mandolin, two Indian musical instruments: the *dholak* (double-head barrel drum played with bare hands) and the *dantal* (also spelled *dandtal*, a metal rod struck by a U-shaped clapper).

2   Chutney soca combines two already hybrid forms: the Indo-Trinidadian music called "chutney" developed from Bhojpuri folk-songs and Hindu wedding music, and soca, as described above, derived from calypso and Indian rhythmic patterns.

3   For example, in carnival 2002, a soca riddim called "Best Riddim" (riddims are often named) created by producer Sheldon "Shel Shok" Benjamin was used by Trinidadian artists Bunji Garlin ("We Doh Watch Face"), by Denise Belfon ("De Jammet"), and by Benjai ("Over & Over"). I thank Christopher Edmonds for this information.

4   This comment is inspired by Christopher Dunn's own assessment of a similar situation in Brazil (2002: 72).

5   In contrast with the calypso tradition where artists are expected to be the authors of their own songs – even though this, in practice, is not always the case – many soca songs are often written in collaboration with other people. Over the years, Machel Montano has regularly credited various members of his group as co-writers of his songs, as is the case for "Soca," which was co-written with Daryl Henry and Vincent Rivers, and performed by Daryl Henry a.k.a. Farmer Nappy.

6   In festivals throughout Europe where soca is also performed, large crowds of white people attend.

Part IV

CARNIVAL DIASPORA

20

THE FESTIVAL HEARD ROUND THE WORLD
Introduction to Part IV

Milla Cozart Riggio

Of the three largest and most inclusive carnivals in the Americas – in Rio de Janeiro, New Orleans, and Trinidad – Trinidad Carnival alone has established its own diaspora. Indeed, despite its having been imitated in more than sixty North American and European cities as well as other Caribbean islands, and its having influenced celebrations in other places such as Japan and Australia, Trinidad Carnival remains one of the most copied but least known major festivals. Still not listed in the *Encyclopedia Britannica* under carnival, the festival that is arguably the only truly national carnival in the world[1] has created a centrifugal pattern of dispersion that radiates outwardly and inwardly. Many thousands of West Indians – often from islands other than Trinidad – not only come "home" to Port of Spain for carnival each year, they also take carnival home with them. Those who live in the United States and Canada often follow diasporic carnivals from Toronto to Brooklyn to Miami and places between and beyond throughout the summer, traveling with their families and friends, usually in cars or buses, from city to city in a series of weekend carnival pilgrimages.

One of the keys to understanding the phenomenon of the Trinidad Carnival diaspora lies in the conscious decision of the scholars and statesmen leading the path to independence from Britain in the 1950s and early 1960s to use carnival as the identifying signifier of the newly independent nation. The Trinidad economy has a strong multinational element to it, established primarily by its history of oil and natural gas production. Moreover, the leaders of Trinidad, as in other newly emerging West Indian nations, were more than politicians; men such as Eric Williams, J.D. Elder, C.L.R. James, and Lloyd Best were statesmen and often trained scholars (some with PhDs from English or American universities), authors of significant books as well as shapers of political independence.

However, neither the economy nor the educational system of Trinidad was truly autonomous. Both were derived from and interlocked with the nations from which the emerging democracy wished to separate itself. What were truly indigenous were the varied folk art forms – music, dance, masquerade – that had emerged over a century and a half of resistance and assimilation, resulting finally in the extraordinary panoply of carnival. Faced with the dilemma of how to preserve culture while also developing nationhood, the shapers of the new nation elected to turn to the festival that since World War II had come to symbolize Trinidadian identity. Taking the pannists off the streets and into the national performance venues, giving calypsonians the privilege not only of critiquing the government but also of helping to authenticate it, establishing a costumed queen of masquerade bands to counter the ballgown Carnival Queen competition that had remained the bastion primarily of Whiteness on the island, Prime Minister Williams and his fellows converted folk aesthetics into national symbols. The romance between the Prime Minister and the culture that had to a large extent developed in and from the streets would not last. But by the time the Black Power movement of 1970 crystallized the rupture, carnival had already been enthroned as the festival of the nation.

Meanwhile, the establishment of the new nation coincided with a large-scale emigration of West Indians from their home islands in the 1960s, to fill the labor forces of Canada, Britain, and the United States. As carnival became the signifier of national identity, so too it became a gauge of nostalgic identification for those émigrés, who would remember not only the masquerades and music but also the food (peas and rice, for instance) and the varied senses of community of their homeland. The process was simple.

What is not so easy to understand is why Trinidad Carnival should have provided the blueprint for the nostalgic performances of identity for West Indian communities, such as those of Notting Hill or Toronto, in which Trinidadians were themselves in the minority of West Indian immigrants. In the chapters to follow, Keith Nurse attempts to explain that phenomenon in terms (among others) of the kinetic power of the Trinidad masquerade costumes, even as he defines ways in which the Trinidad Carnival in its many new locations has become a more assimilative, pan-Caribbean festival, incorporating Jamaican reggae, jerk pork, and other culinary and aesthetic influences from other islands. It is true that the form of masquerade known as "fancy mas" or "pretty mas," with its sense of playing royal and its spectacular individual king and queen costumes, along with decorated bikini costumes for women, often dominates the diasporic carnivals, along with steelbands and calypso or soca music. It is also true that carnival in Britain has from its beginnings in the 1960s incorporated elements of satire and traditional characters, as well as grotesquely comic, often cross-dressing costumes. Moreover, stilt walkers of the Moko Jumbie variety are increasingly common in many diasporic carnivals. Nevertheless, the satirical and/or threatening traditional culture-bearing characters, such as the Midnight Robber, the Pierrot Grenade, or the Moko Jumbie – traditions that have been revived within the last decade in Trinidad – have followed into the diaspora very slowly, usually as a result of a self-conscious effort at education by cultural researchers such as John Cupid of the National Carnival Commission.[2]

One of the features that characterizes diasporic carnivals is that of reiterative recall. Sometimes the designs for mas bands, and even some larger individual costumes themselves, will be taken from Trinidad to Toronto, Brooklyn, Notting Hill, or other places, where the designs may be given new thematic names and larger costumes – once automatically discarded at the end of carnival – recycled. Thus, the diasporic carnivals (some of which, because they are held in densely populated areas, at times draw more massive crowds than in Trinidad) become literal reminders not only of the homeland or the festival in general but of the carnival of any given year.

One interesting phenomenon of this kind is provided by the annual Road March competition. Many non-West-Indian visitors to Trinidad complain about the end-less repetition of music in the annual carnival: not only is the music sometimes intolerably loud but the same songs are played over and over, until at last one is played enough times to win the road title. In the years I have been attending carnival (annually since 1995), it is customary each year to complain about that year's Road March offerings: the songs are said to be terrible, degenerating, worse than one could remember. Then the festival ends; those who have come "home" for the festival return to their varied cities, armed with tapes or CDs of this year's music purchased at the airport. Suddenly, the Road March compositions that seemed banal during the festival are in themselves vital mnemonic devices. Play the song, and you are back in the festival. The very repetition that drove one crazy becomes the mechanism of cultural memory, propelling backwards in time and place.

Obviously, carnival in Trinidad – where the majority of citizens are either African or (East) Indian in ethnic origin – is a different kind of festival (celebrating the nation) than the event in which a minority population nostalgically celebrates its homeland elsewhere. In this sense, the diasporic Trinidad carnivals have something in common with the Shi'ite festival of Hosay in Trinidad, which throughout the late nineteenth century was celebrated by Indian indentured workers throughout the south of the island, by Hindus as well as (probably more than) by Muslims. A spectacular religious procession that was contested in the actual homeland became for a time a cultural unifier for the laborers known perjoratively as "coolies" (a word roughly equivalent to "nigger" for Africans), perhaps in part because of the spectacle that may have linked this professional commemoration with carnival, or perhaps because those celebrating Hosay claimed always to be worshipping at a shrine that contained a small clod of Indian earth, brought over in the ships of 1845.

The difference between being a majority and a minority population is significant, even to a people that does not make its own laws or feel that it has full control of its own economy or its own future. Always to see some variety of one's own face – rather than faces of other races or cultures – mirrored in those around you provides a kind of implicit confidence that does not exist when one is in a minority. Correspondingly, carnival in Trinidad – which celebrates an entire nation – is very different from the contained and regulated parades in the diaspora. The latent violence in Trinidad emerges from the mythos of resistance, the danger implicit in the clashing of territorial bands, or the basic dialectic of carnival itself. In other places, such as Notting Hill, violence erupts mainly between those celebrating the festival and the enforcement officers or threatened local citizens in the culture or city that hosts it. The festival exists not only as a nostalgic reminder of home but also as a way of taking and claiming space in the new society. As a result, diasporic carnivals are often as much food festivals as they are parades or masquerades. All those things that both remind of home and allow one to stake out aesthetic and communal space in a new society become important.

In the three chapters that follow in this section, Keith Nurse first analyzes the diasporic spread of carnival within the economic and cultural parameters of globalization itself. The final two essays examine two (or really three) of the major diasporic carnivals: Geraldine Connor and Max Farrar compare Notting Hill in London to the festival in Leeds. Philip Kasinitz focuses on Labor Day in Brooklyn. Other festivals might as well have been chosen – Toronto, Miami, Boston, Atlanta, Chicago, Montreal – with equal interest. Moreover, we have not considered the spread of Trinidad-style carnival throughout the Caribbean itself – notably in Jamaica where it was introduced only a few decades ago, partly by Chinese-Jamaican musician Byron Lee, who plays regularly in Trinidad at carnival season, or in Martinique or other islands. Typically, these other Caribbean festivals occur at times other than carnival Monday and Tuesday, so as not to compete with carnival in Trinidad. In the chapters that follow, we do not intend to privilege the carnivals in any specific location. But we do hope that, by analyzing the dynamics of relocating the festival in particular places, we will be able to get at some of the major recurrent issues involved in the diasporic spread of carnival.

NOTES

1   Carnival in other places may exist throughout the nation, as, for instance, in Brazil or Italy. However, in those countries carnival – for the most part an urban festive form – tends to remain local and separate, so that one thinks of carnival in Rio as separate and different from carnival in Bahla, or Venetian carnival as different from that of Rome. Though there are regional carnivals in Trinidad, however, those participating in the festival tend to cross the island, often moving from town to town, with many flocking to Port of Spain, known as the Mecca of carnival. Since the 1920s (and more especially the 1940s), Tobagonians have also developed carnival, sometimes celebrating in Trinidad and sometimes staying home, but for the most part following the carnival forms developed historically in Trinidad.

2   Under the leadership of Cecil Alfred, mentored by Trinidadian cultural researcher John Cupid, carnival in Montreal – scheduled the weekend before Caribana in Toronto – has self-consciously incorporated the traditional carnival characters in its development. This is an exceptional case, at least in North America.

21

GLOBALIZATION IN REVERSE
Diaspora and the export of Trinidad Carnival

Keith Nurse

> People carnivalling and playing marse in Brooklyn; they playing marse in Montreal,
> in Toronto and Miami, they playing marse in Calgary, and in Antigua, in St. Lucia,
> and Jamaica; they playing marse in New York and Notting Hill, moving and moving
> and in the moving they throwing out the seeds that defy the holding in the ships
> crawling across the Atlantic . . .
>
> (Phillip 1998)

Trinidad Carnival has come under greater scrutiny from local and international
scholars in recent years (Burton 1997; Cowley 1996; Hill 1993; Riggio 1998b;
Rohlehr 1990). However, most of the research takes a historical, ethnographic,
anthropological and/or sociological perspective. In addition, by and large, the
unit of analysis has been that of the nation-state of Trinidad and Tobago. Consequently, few analysts have looked at Trinidad Carnival within the framework of
the globalization of culture. This is symptomatic of a lacuna in the field of popular
culture, as Manning observes: "While Third World countries are well known as
importers of metropolitan popular culture, the reverse process – the export of
cultural products and performances from the Third World – has evoked less discussion" (1990: 20). This chapter attempts to redress this lacuna in the literature.
The approach used here is built on two planks. The first argument is that the case
study of the export of Trinidad Carnival illustrates the intersection of globalization
and diasporization. The Caribbean enjoys a peculiar circumstance in that it is both
a recipient and a sender of diasporas (Cohen 1997). The Caribbean has been a
destination for several migrations (forced and voluntary) that relate to the region's
history of incorporation into the modern capitalist world-system over the last five
hundred years (James 1980; Mintz 1974). The Caribbean has also exported a large
share of its population to countries in the North Atlantic, especially since the
1960s. The contemporary diasporization of Caribbean people fits into Stuart Hall's
notion of double or "twice diasporised" (1989).

The second argument critiques the literature on globalization (Kofman and
Youngs 1996; Waters 1995) and global culture (Featherstone 1994; King 1991),

which tends to focus on the recent acceleration in the flow of technology, goods, and resources and sees the flows principally as a north-to-south or center-to-periphery direction. Much of the literature on globalization does not capture the long history of global capitalism or the impact of contemporary diasporas on the north. However, "culturally, the periphery is greatly influenced by the society of the center, but the reverse is also the case" (Patterson 1994: 109). Therefore, the aim of the chapter is to examine the counter flow, the periphery-to-center cultural flows, or what Patterson calls the "extraordinary process of periphery-induced creolization in the cosmopolis" (1994: 109). In this respect the chapter is a case study of "globalization in reverse," a take on what Jamaican poet Louise Bennett calls "colonization in reverse."[1]

THE DIASPORIC CARIBBEAN CARNIVALS

Trinidad's carnival, which has long been a source of inspiration for carnivals in the Caribbean region, has been exported outside the region and is now considered truly global. The globalization of Trinidad Carnival is directly related to the spread and expansion of a Caribbean diaspora in the North Atlantic, especially after World War II, in response to the demand for cheap immigrant labor. Almost every major city in North America and England has a Caribbean-style carnival that is, in large part, modeled after the one found in Trinidad. In each respective site it is the largest festival or event in terms of attendance and the generation of economic activity. For instance, Notting Hill Carnival in London, the largest festival of popular culture in Europe, attracts over two million people over two days of activities and generates estimated economic impact of £93 million. Labor Day in New York and Caribana in Toronto are similarly the largest events in the USA and Canada (see Table 21.1 below for further details). As such, the diasporic Caribbean carnivals are arguably "the world's most popular transnational celebration" (Manning 1990: 36).

It is estimated that there are over sixty diasporic Caribbean carnivals in North America and Europe (see Table 21.2 below). No other carnival can claim to have spawned so many offspring. These festivals are modeled on the Trinidad Carnival or borrow heavily from it in that they incorporate the three main art forms (pan, mas, and calypso) and the Afro-Creole celebratory traditions (street parade or theater). Organized by the diasporic Caribbean communities, the diasporic carnivals have come to symbolize the quest for "psychic, if not physical return" to an imagined ancestral past (Nettleford 1988: 197) and the search for a "pan-Caribbean

Table 21.1 The economic impact of diasporic Caribbean carnivals

Diasporic carnivals	Attendance	Estimated expenditures
Caribana, Toronto	1 million	Cnd $200 million
Labor Day, New York	3.5 million	US $30 million
Notting Hill, London	2 million	Stg. £93 million

Source: Nurse 1997; LDA 2003.

Table 21.2 Diasporic Caribbean carnivals: regions and cities (audience figures are given where known)

In the UK (30):	In Europe (4):
Barrow-in-Furness	Nice – France
Bedford (20,000)	Nyon – Switzerland
Birmingham (600,000)	Rotterdam – Netherlands
Bradford	Stockholm – Sweden
Bristol (40,000)	
Coventry	**In Canada (7):**
Derby	Calgary
Dover	Edmonton
Hereford	Montreal
High Wycombe (30,000)	Ottawa
Huddersfield	Toronto (1 million)
Leeds (300,000)	Vancouver
Leicester (100,000)	Winnipeg
Liverpool	
Luton (100,000)	**In the USA (20):**
Manchester (30,000)	Atlanta
Norwich	Baltimore
Nottingham	Boston
Notting Hill – London (2 million)	Cambridge – Massachusetts
Oxford (20,000)	Chicago
Plymouth	Dallas
Preston	Detroit
Reading	Hartford
Sheffield	Houston
Southampton	Jacksonville
Stafford	Miami
Swindon	New York (2 million)
Waltham Forest – London	Oakland
Woking	Orlando
Wolverhampton	Philadelphia
	Rochester
	San Francisco
	Tallahassee
	Washington DC
	Westchester

Source: Nurse 1999.

unity, a demonstration of the fragile but persistent belief that "All o' we is one" (Manning 1990: 22). In the UK alone, there are as many as thirty carnivals that fall into this category. They are held during the summer months rather than in the pre-Lenten or Shrovetide period associated with the Christian calendar. The main parade routes are generally through the city center or within the confines of the immigrant community – the former is predominant, especially with the larger carnivals.

Like their parent, the diasporic carnivals are hybrid in form and influence. The Jonkonnu masks of Jamaica and the Bahamas, which are not reflected in the Trinidad Carnival, are clearly evident in many of these carnivals, thereby making them pan-Caribbean in scope. The carnivals have over time incorporated carnivalesque traditions from other immigrant communities: South Americans (e.g. Brazilians and Colombians), Africans and Asians. For instance, it is not uncharacteristic to see Brazilian samba drummers and dancers parading through the streets of London, Toronto or New York during Notting Hill, Caribana or Labor Day. The white populations have also become participants, largely as spectators, but increasingly as festival managers, masqueraders, and pan players.

Another development is that the art forms and the celebratory traditions of the diasporic Caribbean carnivals have been borrowed, appropriated or integrated into European carnivals. Indeed, in some instances, the European carnivals have been totally transformed or "colonized." Examples of this are the Barrow-in-Furness and Luton carnivals where there is a long tradition of British carnival. One also finds a similar trend taking place in carnivals in France, Germany, the Netherlands, Switzerland, and Sweden, as they draw inspiration from the success of the Notting Hill Carnival. It is observed that many European carnivals, especially in the UK, have become less rebellious and more commercial with the rise of modern industrial culture. In fact, Shohat and Stam argue that "European real-life carnivals have generally degenerated into the ossified repetition of perennial rituals" (1994: 302).

The first diasporic Caribbean carnival began in the 1920s in Harlem, New York. This festival was later to become the Labor Day celebrations in 1947, the name that it goes by today (Nunley and Bettelheim 1988: 166). The major diasporic Caribbean carnivals, for example, Notting Hill and Caribana, became institutionalized during the mid- to late 1960s at the peak of Caribbean migration. Nunley and Bettelheim (1988) relate the growth of the carnivals to the rise in nationalism in the Caribbean with the independence movement of the 1960s. The emergence of the carnivals can also be related to the rise of "Black Power" consciousness. The growth in the number and size of the diasporic Caribbean carnivals came in two waves. The first wave involved the consolidation of the early carnivals during the 1960s until the mid-1970s. From the mid-1970s two parallel developments took place: the early carnivals expanded in size by broadening the appeal of the festival, for example through the introduction of sound systems playing reggae or house music; and a number of smaller carnivals emerged as satellites to the larger, older ones.

CARNIVAL AND DIASPORIC IDENTITY

The diasporic Caribbean carnivals have developed into a means to affirm cultural identity and promote sociopolitical integration within the Caribbean diasporic community as well as with the host society. The diversity in participation suggests that the diasporic Caribbean carnivals have become multicultural or polyethnic festivals (Cohen 1982; 1993). For instance, Manning (1990: 35) argues that the diasporic Caribbean carnivals provide a kind of social therapy that overcomes the separation and isolation imposed by the diaspora and restores to West Indian immigrants both a sense of community with each other and sense of connection to the culture that they claim as a birthright. Politically, however, there is more to these carnivals than cultural nostalgia. They are also a means through which West Indians seek and symbolize integration into the metropolitan society, by coming to terms with the opportunities, as well as the constraints, that surround them.

Manning's explanation of the significance of carnivals to the Caribbean diaspora is supported by the observations of Dabydeen (1988: 40):

> For those of us resident in Britain, the Notting Hill Carnival is our living link with this ancestral history, our chief means of keeping in touch with the ghosts of "back home." In a society which constantly threatens or diminishes black efforts, carnival has become an occasion for self-assertion, for striking back – not with bricks and bottles but by beating pan, by conjuring music from steel, itself a symbol of the way we can convert steely oppression into celebration. We take over the drab streets and infuse them with our colours. The memory of the hardship of the cold winter gone, and that to come, is eclipsed in the heat of music. We regroup our scattered black communities from Birmingham, Manchester, Glasgow and all over the kingdom to one spot in London: a coming together of proud celebration.

Dabydeen (1988: 40) goes on to to illustrate that the carnivals are an integrative force in an otherwise segregated social milieu:

> We also pull in crowds of native whites, Europeans, Japanese, Arabs, to witness and participate in our entertainment, bringing alien peoples together in a swamp or community of festivity. Carnival breaks down barriers of colour, race, nationality, age, gender. And the police who would normally arrest us for doing those things (making noise, exhibitionism, drinking, or simply being black) are made to smile and be ever so courteous, giving direction, telling you the time, crossing old people over to the other side, undertaking all manner of unusual tasks. They fear that bricks and bottles would fly if they behaved as normal. Thus the sight of smiling policemen is absorbed into the general masquerade.

From another perspective, it is argued that the diasporic carnivals reflect rather than contest institutionalized social hierarchies. In each of the major diasporic carnivals the festival has been represented in a way that fits into the colonialist discourse of race, gender, nation, and empire (Bhabha 1994). The festival has suffered from racial and sexual stigmas and stereotypes in the media, which are based on constructions of "otherness" and "blackness." This situation became heightened as the carnivals became larger and therefore more threatening to the prevailing order. In the early phase, from the mid-1960s to the mid-1970s, the carnivals were viewed as exotic, received little if any press, and were essentially tolerated by the state authorities. From the mid-1970s, as attendance at the festivals grew, the carnivals became more menacing, and policing escalated, resulting in a backlash from the immigrant Caribbean community. Violent clashes between the British police and the Notting Hill Carnival came to the fore in the mid- to late 1970s (Gutzmore 1993). Similar confrontations occurred in the other major diasporic carnivals in New York and Toronto (Buff 1997; Manning 1983, 1990).

Through a gendered lens "black" male participants in the festivals have been portrayed as "dangerous" and "criminal." Female participants, on the other hand, are viewed as "erotic" and "promiscuous" (Hernandez-Ramdwar 1996).

These modes of representation have come in tandem with heightened surveillance mechanisms from the state and the police. In the case of London, the annual expenditure by the state on the policing of the festival in the late 1990s was in excess of £3 million, ten times more than public investment for the staging of the festival. It can thus be argued that the politics of cultural representation has negatively affected the viability of the diasporic carnivals. The adverse publicity and racialized stigmas of violence, crime, and disorder have allowed for the blockage of investments from the public and private sectors in spite of the fact that the carnivals have proven to be violence-free relative to other large public events or festivals. In the case of the UK, for instance, official figures show that Notting Hill, which attracts two million people, has fewer reported incidents of crime than the Glastonbury rock festival which attracts 60,000 people.[2] Yet the general perception is that Notting Hill is more violence-prone.

Under increased surveillance the carnivals became more contained and controlled during the 1980s. The perspective of governments, business leaders, and the media began changing when it was recognized that the carnivals were major tourist attractions and generated significant earnings in visitor expenditures. For example, the publication of a 1990 visitor survey of Caribana, which showed that the festival generated Cnd $96 million from 500,000 attendees (Decima 1991), eventually resulted in the Provincial Minister of Tourism and Recreation visiting Trinidad in 1995 to see how the parent festival operated. Provincial funding for the festival increased, accordingly. In 1995, for the first time, London's Notting Hill Carnival was sponsored by a large multinational corporation. The Coca-Cola company, under its product Lilt, a "tropical" beverage, paid the organizers £150,000 for the festival to be called the "Lilt Notting Hill Carnival" and for exclusive rights to advertise along the masquerade route and to sell its soft drinks. That same year the BBC produced and televised a program on the thirty-year history of Notting Hill Carnival. By the mid-1990s, as one Canadian analyst puts it, the carnivals were reduced to a few journalistic essentials: "the policing and control of the crowd, the potential for violence, the weather, island images, the size of the crowd, the city economy and, most recently, the great potential benefit for the provincial tourist industry" (Gallaugher 1995). These developments created concern among some analysts. For example, Awam Amkpa (1993: 6) argues that

> strategies for incorporating and neutralizing the political efficacies of carnivals by black communities are already at work. Transnational corporations are beginning to sponsor some of the festivals and are contributing to creating a mass commercialized audience under the guise of bogus multiculturalisms.

Another analyst saw the increasing role of the state in these terms:

> The funding bodies appear to treat it as a social policy as part of the race relations syndrome: a neutralised form of exotica to entertain the tourists, providing images of Black women dancing with policemen, or failing this, footage for the media to construct distortions and mis(sed)representations. Moreover, this view also sees that,

if not for the problems it causes the police, courts, local authorities, and auditors, Carnival could be another enterprising venture.

(McMillan 1990: 13–14)

In this respect one can argue that the sociopolitical and cultural conflicts, based on race, class, gender, ethnicity, nation, and empire, that are evident in the Trinidad Carnival were transplanted to the metropolitan context. In many ways the diasporic Caribbean carnivals, like the Trinidad parent, have become trapped between the negative imagery of stigmas and stereotypes, the cooptive strategies of capitalist and state organizations and the desires of the carnivalists for official funding and validation.

For the host societies, in North America and Europe, the diasporic Caribbean carnivals also allowed for an open and public display of the socioeconomic and politicocultural tensions that exist between the organs of oppression (i.e. the state, police, media, church, school) and the Caribbean population. The carnivalesque aesthetic and politics confronted the hegemonic discourse and modes of representation as they relate to stereotypes of race, sexual behavior, and criminal activity. At one level it has forced a multiculturalism onto the agenda. In other ways, it illustrates how little things have changed in terms of the hegemonic colonialist discourse and imperialist structures.

CARNIVAL AND THE CULTURAL POLITICAL ECONOMY

There is some debate as to whether the diasporic carnivals have lost their revolutionary potential, whether they have been coopted and incorporated into the capitalist production system. The issue, however, is that the host societies have not remained untouched by the carnivals. They have forced a Caribbean consciousness on their host societies. The Caribbean carnivals have not only grown in size, they have also "colonized" other carnivals, especially in Europe. This has occurred largely because the Trinidad-inspired carnivals have a competitive advantage in the kinetic movement of the costumes and the vibrancy of the music and dancing. Thus, "once the liberating forces of mas are felt by citizens of these cities, they may learn to play mas as well" (Nunley and Bettelheim 1988: 181). They have reintroduced magic, fantasy, and wonderment into the long-ossified carnivals of Europe and its diaspora (North America). From this perspective one can argue that the diasporic Caribbean carnivals are a powerful transcultural force which has expanded the geo-economic and geo-political space for Caribbean people, at home and abroad. Amkpa (1993: 6), in commenting on the Caribbean carnivals in the UK, for instance, notes that:

> As victims of enforced hybridity due to displacements and marginalizations experienced in the histories of the islands, the carnival performances recall the African and the Asian origins of communities, and these do not only hybridize the identities of people they share spaces with, but also the dominant culture to whose centre they have migrated.

It is also that the Caribbean carnivals, because they are forged from the struggles against slavery, abhor closure and are inherently democratic and participatory. One of the negative consequences of this is that the carnivals have the characteristics of free or collective goods and thus allow for free riding. At most of the carnivals the people who make money contribute little if any financial resource in terms of grants or business sponsorship (e.g. the hotels, restaurants, bars, airlines, ground transportation, state authorities) while the organizers of the festival generally run on meagre financial resources. As a result, the Caribbean carnivals exhibit something of a contradiction: the carnivals generate large earnings (e.g. visitor and audience expenditures) but the organizing units retain very little of the profits.

The diasporic Caribbean carnivals are faced with the challenge of producing what can be defined as a public good – a street festival which is subject to high levels of free riding from key stakeholders such as hoteliers, travel and transport agencies, restaurateurs, broadcasters, and unlicensed concessionaires. In this sense the carnivals are not easily comparable to closed festivals which have greater control over the appropriation of economic value by non-contributing entities.

Moreover, the growth of the festival has outpaced the management capabilities of the early developers, and updating managerial skills has been slower than required. For this reason most of the carnivals find themselves in a position of resource-dependency upon state and city authorities or corporate entities. The contributions are then generally viewed as subsidies rather than investments in the public art process or festival tourism. When the carnivals are funded, the amounts granted generally are small relative to the mainstream arts and to the economic impact that the festival makes.

The carnivals have suffered from negative press and publicity in terms of crime, racial tension, and mismanagement, which have devalued the corporate leverage and media value of the festival and blocked investment from the public and private sectors. In part this scenario can be explained by the tendency of the diasporic Caribbean carnivals to draw on carnivalesque, popular culture, and anti-establishment themes that are resistant to and critical of official and hegemonic culture. However, because of the parallels with the large carnivals in the Americas (e.g. Rio Carnival, Trinidad Carnival, and New Orleans Mardi Gras) it can be argued that the challenge of attracting resources is linked to the larger multicultural question of race, ethnicity, and class.

The diasporic Caribbean carnivals are at a historical turning point. In the last decade they have grown in size and popularity beyond anyone's wildest dreams. The diasporic Caribbean carnivals have grown from being the bane of their respective cities to becoming an indispensable feature of popular culture, multiculturalism, and cultural tourism. They have also outgrown the managerial and entrepreneurial capabilities of the festival organizers as exemplified by the problems of indebtedness in Caribana and the charges of mismanagement that have affected carnivals such as Notting Hill. These problems are further compounded by the factionalism and fragmentation found in many of the carnivals, the most notable example being Miami Carnival. Faced with a less than co-operative governmental and corporate sector, the carnival organizers have thrived by leveraging political capital, largely under the banner of multiculturalism. However, the increased recognition of the importance of the economic benefits of the carnivals is bringing new political concerns. The carnivals are now considered too vital to the respective cities to be left up to the vagaries of diasporic politics. This is evident in the recently commissioned economic impact study of the Notting Hill Carnival by the London Development Agency.

This scenario establishes an interesting context for the future of the diasporic carnivals. In the current recession-plagued period where most developed country state agencies find themselves under severe financial constraints there is a strong temptation to cut funds to the Arts, especially so-called multicultural or ethnic art. The shift in the political spectrum to the right-of-center has also made for a less supportive environment. These trends signal that the stakeholders involved in putting on the carnivals must begin to develop a strategy to enhance their income-earning prospects independent of philanthropic public support; in the form of corporate investments based on crass commercialism. Failure in this regard is likely to result in the carnivals being disbanded or taken over by state agencies or corporate entities.

These concerns raise the issue of political consciousness and praxis within the Caribbean community. In terms of the transnational cultural politics of carnival, the Caribbean diaspora is not a homogeneous group. There are a number of schisms that impact the politics of the diasporic carnivals. Jamaicans outnumber other islanders (e.g. Trinidadians) by a significant ratio, notably in the UK, and consequently there has been a strong contest between both groups over what should be in the carnival: reggae versus calypso; static sound systems versus mobile sound-trucks. In part, the position of Jamaicans can be explained by the strength of their popular culture in the metropolitan context. Another major conflict has been between Afro-Caribbean and Indo-Caribbean groups, especially in Toronto, where there is a sizable Indian population from Guyana and Trinidad. Much heated debate has emerged as to whether the festival should be portrayed as a "Caribbean" festival rather than a "black" or "Afro-Caribbean" thing. The former, being viewed as more inclusive, was favored by the Indo-Caribbean community. This contrasts with the situation in the UK where the carnival has shifted from a "Caribbean thing" to being a "black British" and even a national festival. The success of the carnivals has encouraged the jockeying for positions of power and ownership within the festival. In many respects these contestations mirror the inherent fragmentation of a multiethnic community and the process of continuous negotiation of identity that follows.

CONCLUSION

For the Caribbean diaspora, carnival has emerged as a basis for asserting a pan-Caribbean cultural identity and as a mode of resistance in an otherwise alienating environment. The carnivals have also allowed for integration as well as contestation with the dominant white population in addition to the other immigrant communities within the host societies. In tandem, the carnivals have had to confront colonialist and imperialist discourses and practices reminiscent of the threats that the parent carnival faced in the nineteenth century. Financial challenges along with schisms based on race, ethnicity, gender, and nationality have factored in the Caribbean community's ability to capitalize on the geopolitical, economic, and cultural space that the festival has created. These conclusions reinforce the view that carnivals, like other popular culture forms, involve the aestheticization of politics and are keenly contested by different interest groups and social forces (Cohen 1993) and thus defy simplistic generalizations which view transgression and cooptation in oppositional terms.

The chapter argues that the diasporic Caribbean carnivals are products of and responses to the processes of globalization as well as transcultural social formations. This illustrates that carnival as a cultural activity is not just about merriment, colorful pageantry, revelry and street theatre, although there is a lot of that taking place. Carnival is born out of the struggle of marginalized peoples to shape a cultural identity through resistance, liberation, and catharsis. These values have facilitated its replication wherever the Caribbean diaspora is found. The diasporic carnivals have acted as a bond between the diasporic community and those at home, promoting much travel and contributing to the growth of a cultural industry in Trinidad and Tobago with strong export capabilities (Nurse 1997). It is also observed that the sheer size and economic impact of the diasporic Caribbean carnivals have made them an important basis for transnational diasporic politics.

NOTES

1　Louise Bennett's poem entitled "Colonisation in Reverse" chronicles the wave of Jamaican and Caribbean migration and its sociocultural impact on England in the 1960s (see Markham 1989: 62–3).

2　In 1992 the Glastonbury rock festival had 636 reported crimes compared to the 80 reported for Notting Hill (*So Yu Going to Carnival*, 9 (January, 1995): 88–9).

22

CARNIVAL IN LEEDS AND LONDON
Making new black British subjectivities

Geraldine Connor and Max Farrar

Participating in carnival undermines the possibility of writing an objective account. This extraordinary experience, at once creative, transgressive, and intensely pleasurable, melts the cool detachment of the traditional academic. Both the authors of this chapter, one formed at the center, as the British defined it, of an empire, the other at its margin, made their way to carnival from quite different positions, but we find ourselves united in our love of the whirlwind of art, passion, and struggle that carnival unleashes every year. We recognize that there are almost as many ways of analyzing carnival as there are cities that host this marvelous spectacle, but in this chapter we articulate a common perspective, which, though infused with our own subjectivity, nevertheless makes a serious effort to interpret the two largest Caribbean carnivals in the UK.[1]

The carnivals in Leeds and London, celebrated over the Bank Holiday weekends at the end of August every year since 1967, symbolize the creative, surreptitiously political, energies of men and women formed in the English-speaking Caribbean in the 1930s, 1940s, and 1950s. Seeking a new life either in London, the cosmopolitan capital city of a recently abandoned empire, or in Leeds, a northern city at the end of its life as an industrial machine for that empire, these men and women were inspired by their recent memories of the massive Trinidad Carnival, or the smaller, but equally vibrant carnival in St Kitts-Nevis. For many, carnival had a special place as an embodied, artistic representation of the pleasures, pains, and protests of their lives in their islands of origin. As they found their place in the frequently unloving Mother Country, reuniting with their children or making new families in Britain, many of their children grew up within households in which the politics and art of carnival were central. Others, perhaps not deeply involved in the preparations, learned that the carnival summer Bank Holiday was a specially joyous, and specifically Caribbean, highlight of their year. These younger people today join with their parents and grandparents in the making of carnival.

But the analysis of carnival cannot be limited to mere description of its pleasures. This chapter offers an understanding of the carnivals in Leeds and London structured by the following themes: first, the long history of the Trinidad Carnival being used as a vehicle for protest against the injustices of colonial subjugation has been transported into the UK carnival tradition; the latter must be understood in the context of opposition to white British racism; second, the occupation by carnival revelers of specific neighborhoods of the major cities, and the struggle, particularly in London, to maintain that public, mobile presence on the streets, is an essential component of the British carnival tradition; the demand to occupy the streets takes particular force because carnival is an essentially embodied, performative art form; third, because of these two phenomena, carnival has been one of the anvils on which new black British identifications have been forged. Over nearly forty years in the UK, new concepts of black British identity, in which the creative and expressive arts are a central feature, have emerged. New subjects, formerly colonized, sometimes anticolonial, and now postcolonial, have formed themselves throughout the postwar period of black settlement in the UK, and carnival has been an important instrument in this transformation.

THE UK CARNIVAL: THE CONTEXT OF RACISM

Trinidadian/British poet, publisher, and political activist John La Rose has pointed out that Caribbean migrants had already formed their artistic, political, and social lives before they arrived in the UK: "We did not come alive in Britain" (Harris 1996: 240). One aspect of that history is the anticolonial struggles for independence in the islands of the English-speaking Caribbean (James 1985; Parry and Sherlock 1971; Richards 1989). Another is the experience of carnival. The earliest recollection of carnival for one of the authors of this chapter was as a child growing up in Trinidad, sitting on the bleachers of the Queen's Park Savannah (Port of Spain) in scorching hot sun and seeing her fantasy come alive: the steel orchestra Silver Stars' portrayal of *Gulliver's Travels*. It was 1963. Right in front of her were all the children of Lilliput in glorious costumed splendor, exactly as she had imagined it from reading the book, surrounding the amazing, tied up and nailed down, giant-sized Gulliver. The band was designed by Pat Chu Foon. To add to the delight, this was her first encounter with steelband in all its glory. The band that impressed her the most was Guinness Cavaliers. Lord Kitchener's kaiso of that year was "De road make to walk on carnival day," but the Mighty Sparrow was also a serious contender with "Dan is de man in de van." The sailor bands, all in white, with masqueraders numbering in the thousands – you had to duck the talcum powder! (Hill (1972: 106–10) provides a detailed description of the stage show at Trinidad's first independence carnival of 1963.) Not only did this leave a lifelong impression on her, it shaped her work as a creative artist in both Britain and the UK. In the mid-1970s she played a tee shirt mas of which her memories are just as vivid. She jumped up all over Notting Hill behind Miguel Barabas and his percussion crew, playing on the back of a pick-up truck.

Peter Minshall was designing for Notting Hill Carnival in those days, his famous "Hummingbird" costume taking shape at that time. On the road Ebony steelband played a Peters and Lee hit, "Don't Make Me Wait Too Long." Ebony's mas band that year was called *Colour My Soul* and depicted all the national colors of the different Caribbean islands: Grenada, Trinidad, Jamaica. London Carnival would not have been the same if we did not all dance the night away in one of the now late Charles Applewhite's legendary carnival fetes. The latest calypso import from Trinidad that year was Shadow's "Bassman" – bom bom pudi bom bom!

In a similar vein, the founders of the Leeds Carnival drew their inspiration from the childhood memories. Ian Charles joined his first mas camp – a Sailor band – when he left his home in Arima to go to college in Port of Spain. Arthur France was "always fascinated by carnival" in his home island of St Kitts, despite the fact that his parents would not let him attend, because of the sometimes physical rivalry between the steelbands. "When I was a child I remember seeing Levi Jeffers and other men who are now in Leeds in a play called *David and Goliath* which they put on the road," he recalls. Ian Charles always wanted to be in a troupe of robbers: "They would catch you on the corner and pull out their guns – you couldn't get away until you paid them something!" (LWICC 1988)

This chapter's other author first encountered carnival in Leeds in the early 1970s. With none of the rich history of the Trinidad Carnival to inform him, shaped instead in England by a commitment to anti-racist politics, attending a Carnival Queen show at the Mecca Ballroom came as a cultural shock. These were early examples of carnival art in Leeds, produced by people from the small islands of St Kitts-Nevis, with help from West Indian students studying at Leeds University, but the costumes and the performance were so clearly superior to anything he had seen at an English fete that he immediately recognized them as magnificent examples of popular art. The program for that year lists seven Queen contestants, music of a type he had never dreamed he would hear (the Wilberforce steelband), and songs by Lord Silkie, who had heard calypso in St Kitts, and was determined to continue the tradition in the somewhat colder climate of Leeds (Farrar 2001).

His abiding memory of that night is symptomatic of the troubled relationship between black and white in the UK: his rising desire to join the joyous, expressive spectacle of black culture, and his deep embarrassment as he and the other white people demonstrated how far they needed to travel to catch the spirit. A few days later, as the carnival procession gathered in the park opposite his house, he photo-graphed the event for *Chapeltown News*, the local community newspaper. These are long shots – having few connections with the revelers, fearing rejection as an unwelcome, possibly racist, outsider, he pointed his camera and hoped for the best.

His caution was well-founded. Racism by whites against black citizens, and the increasingly militant response, was the context in which black–white relationships were inevitably placed. By the 1970s, most of Britain's black population had ten to twenty years' experience of that hostility. Although social scientists disagreed on exact proportions of the white population who revealed "extremely prejudiced" attitudes in surveys in the 1950s, Anthony Richmond concluded that it was around one-third of the population (Richmond 1961: 247). Searching for a place to rent, black British citizens found notices in the window reading "No coloureds" (see photo in Hiro 1992). It could get much worse. Wallace Collins described, on his first night in London in 1954, meeting "a big fellow with side-burns" lunging at him with a knife and shouting "You blacks, you niggers, why don't you go back to the jungle" (Collins (1961) cited in Fryer 1984: 375). These big fellows, so-called Teddy Boys, aided and abetted by fascists, set off violent riots against black residents in Notting Hill in 1958 (Pilkington 1988; Fryer 1984: 378–80; Hiro 1992: 39–40). It is important to note that Sir Oswald Mosley, standing as the British Union of Fascists' candidate for the Notting Hill area in the 1959 general election, was not able to stir up any further disorder, and received a derisory number of votes (Benewick 1972: 16).

Nevertheless, carnival was created in Britain as one of the responses by black settlers to the disenfranchisement, blatant racism, and victimization they experienced in the 1950s and 1960s. It should be understood as a very specific response – one which asserted the positive contribution that black people would make to the cultural life of Britain. Shortly after the Notting Hill "race" riots, Claudia Jones initiated the carnival tradition in the UK. Scholars differ in their accounts of the first carnival event,[2] but the authoritative account is Marika Sherwood's. Reproducing the souvenir brochure for the night, Sherwood explains that it took place at St Pancras Town Hall in central London on January 30, 1959, with a cabaret program directed by Edric Connor, choreography by Stanley Jack, with stage decor by Rhoda Mills and Charles Grant. Artists included Cleo Laine, The Southlanders, Boscoe Holder Troupe, Mike McKenzie Trio, the Mighty Terror, Pearl Prescod, Sepia Serendares, Fitroy Coleman, Corinne Skinner-Carter, Trinidad All Stars and Hi-Fi steelbands, West Indian Students Dance Band, and Rupert Nurse and his Orchestra (Sherwood 1999: 54–6). Jones, whose family had emigrated to the US from Trinidad when she was 9, had been arrested and served with a deportation order in 1951 because of her Communist Party activity. Trinidad was extremely reluctant to admit her, and she arrived in London in 1955 (Sherwood 1999: 22–6). Jones founded the *West Indian Gazette*, which included contributions from leading Caribbean novelists such as George Lamming and Andrew Salkey, as well as British and international news. Jones "had a distinct socialist and anti-imperialist perspective" (Alleyne 2002: 28), but she also had a particular perspective on the arts. In the 1959 brochure she wrote of the "event of Notting Hill and Nottingham" (both areas had experienced "race" riots in 1958) as the context for "our Caribbean Carnival," arguing that if carnival had

> evoked the wholehearted response from the peoples from the Islands of the Caribbean in the new West Indies Federation, this is itself testament to the role of the arts in bringing people together for common aims, and to its fusing of the cultural, spiritual, as well as political and economic interests of West Indians in the UK and at home.
>
> (Jones, cited in Sherwood 1999: 157)

By 1962, the event at the Seymour Hall had attracted the Mighty Sparrow, one of the most politically acute of the Trinidadian calypsonians, and the *West Indian Gazette* organized another performance at the Manchester Free Trade Hall in the north of England (Sherwood 1999: 161). Jones died in 1964, but the tradition she had established was directly utilized in the first Notting Hill street fair which included a distinctive West Indian Carnival presence in 1966. Darcus Howe, writer, broadcaster, and former editor of the radical monthly *Race Today*,[3] remembers "five hundred revelers and a makeshift steelband in a swift turnaround along Great Western Road, Westbourne Park and thence onto Powis Square" (Howe, interview with Geraldine Connor).

The initiative for this event came from Rhaune Laslett, a woman of Native American and Russian descent who was president of the London Free School. She organized cultural events and a street procession with the aim of familiarizing white and black people with each other's customs, improving the image of Notting Hill, and generating warmth and happiness (Cohen 1993: 10–11).

By 1969, Laslett's fair had included an Afro-Cuban band, the London Irish Girl Pipers, Russ Henderson's West Indian three-man band, the Asian Music Circle, the Gordon Bulgarians, a Turkish Cypriot band, the British Tzchekoslovak Friendship band, a New Orleans marching band, the Concord Multi-racial Group, and the Trinidad Folk Singers. But all had appeared "within an unmistakenly British – if not English – cultural framework" (Cohen 1993: 19).

It took some time for the Notting Hill Carnival to take on a completely Caribbean form, organized by British black people. From 1971 onwards, the conventions of the Trinidad Carnival, particularly the steel pan orchestra, were introduced, and leadership came from West Indians.[4] One of the main movers of this turn was Lesley Palmer, a teacher and musician, born in Trinidad but raised in London, who went back to Trinidad to study its carnival, returning in 1973 to work on mobilizing steel and mas bands (Cohen 1993: 26; Palmer 1986).

The context in which carnival was created in London and Leeds is political in the sense that making culture cannot be divorced from the social and political system in which that culture is located. Carnival is one of the various modes of action by which black settlers and their children changed the cultural life of Britain. Arthur France explains the political context very clearly: carnival was established in Leeds in 1967 as a means of taking the heat out of the racial strife of the day. France, one of the originators of the Leeds West Indian Carnival, was a leading member, with Calvin Beech and Gertrude Paul, of the United Caribbean Association (formed in 1964) in Leeds, which had already initiated a series of lobbies and demonstrations against racial discrimination in the city. Remembering carnival in his native St Kitts, France recognized the need to produce an event which would celebrate West Indian culture, as well as provide time off from the conflictual business of demanding equal rights in a resistant white society.[5]

The origin of the Leeds Carnival lies in a fete organized in 1966 at Kitson College (now Leeds College of Technology) by two students, Frankie Davis (from Trinidad) and Tony Lewis (from Jamaica). The British Soul band Jimmy James and the Vagabonds played, Marlene Samlal Singh organized a troupe of people dressed as Red Indians, and Frankie Davis wore his costume on the bus from Roundhay Road to the town center. The party ended at the British Council's International House, off North Street.

Arthur France, who still chairs the Leeds Carnival Committee, had first suggested starting a carnival in 1966. He approached the United Caribbean Association for backing, but it initially rejected the idea, and then set up a committee which did not deliver. To push his idea forward, France then selected another committee, which included Willie Robinson, Wally Thompson, Irwin and Rounica, Samlal Singh, Rose McAlister, Ken Thomas, Anson Shepherd, Calvin Beech, and Vanta Paul. By 1967, the carnival preparations were under way. Ma Buck was centrally involved in the organizing, and Ian Charles's home in Manor Drive, Leeds 6, was turned into a mas camp in which three costumes were produced. A similar fate befell Samlal Singh's home in Lunan Place, Leeds 8. The first Queen Show was held in the Jubilee Hall, on Savile Place, off Chapeltown Road, Leeds 7. The Sun Goddess – worn by Vicky Cielto, designed by Veronica Samlalsingh, Tyrone Irwin, George Baboolal, and Clive Watkins – took first prize. Betty Bertie designed and made a costume called The Snow Queen, and Wally Thompson made one called The Gondola.

Willie Robinson made Cleopatra, a costume worn by Gloria Viechwech, while the fifth costume was called The Hawaiian Queen.

The Gay Carnival Steel Band, which later became the Boscoe Steel Band, including Roy Buchanan, Rex Watley, Curtland, Dabbo, Tuddy, Vince, Clark, Desmond, and others, played steel pan music in the procession that year, joined by the Invaders, also from Leeds (led by Prentice), the St Christopher Steel Band from Birmingham, and another band from Manchester. Troupes on the road included the Cheyenne Indians (with Ian Charles as the Chief), the Fantasia Britannia troupe (led by Vanta Paul), and the Sailors (organized by Willie Robinson), and Veronica Samlalsingh and Anson Shepherd produced a children's band. The procession wound its way from Potternewton Park to the Leeds Town Hall, where a crowd of about a thousand people were entertained by a steelband competition judged by Junior Telford from London, who had brought the first Trinidadian steelband to Europe. That night, the Last Lap dance was held at the Leeds Town Hall. Telford took the news back to London, and the Leeds troupes were invited to attend the Notting Hill street fair.[6] Leeds rests its claim to be the first West Indian carnival in the UK on the fact that it was the first to be exclusively Caribbean in form, and the first to be run by a black British organization.

Refusing the racial assumptions of imperial British culture, carnival has appropriated and reformulated European aesthetics, combining them with African traditions, and created a new cultural space as a tool for liberation. As Brian Alleyne (2002: 67) points out, despite differences in detail, the existing studies of the British Carnival all

> see the development of carnival in Britain in terms of a struggle by West Indians to make a public expression of a collective identity in the face of a structurally racist and hostile social reality in Britain. They have treated the carnival as one instance of the ongoing struggle of Black people to forge social and political space in Britain.

THE EMBODIED SPATIAL PRACTICES OF CARNIVAL

The established order in hierarchically organized societies always perceives the gathering of crowds of the "lower orders" as a potential threat. The history of the Trinidad Carnival, from the time when the former slaves began to participate en masse in festivities that had probably been reserved primarily for the master class, is a history of prohibitions and bans (Pearse 1956a). From the first procession, Leeds Carnival organizers have always been careful in negotiating the route and the stewarding with the West Yorkshire Police Force, and Inspector Roy Exley's helpful response to the Leeds committee's approach is warmly commemorated in its 25th Anniversary brochure (LWICC 1992). Nevertheless, as Willie Robinson, a participant in the first Leeds Carnival, recollects: "As a measure of the insecurity of the West Indian [sic] community in Leeds, some still believed that those taking part would be arrested on the day" (LWICC 1987: 8).

Early support from the local council for the Notting Hill Carnival evaporated in 1966, seemingly because the Free School was believed by councilors to be a subversive organization – the Free School was at the heart of organizing local black and white tenants against slum landlords (Cohen 1993: 13–14, citing *Kensington News* press reports from July 1966 onwards).

Notting Hill's carnival subsequently obtained significant support from a variety of sources, but in 1976 it was the scene of major violent protest – described in the mass media as rioting – by young black men against the Metropolitan Police. Fifteen hundred policemen were deployed that year, and used what some observers described as "highhanded and severe" methods in their dealings with the youth (Cohen 1993: 34); 325 policemen were hospitalized, and sixty people were arrested (*Race Today*, September, 1976: 170). This was the starting point for a concerted and long-running effort to remove the carnival from the streets of Notting Hill. The police and the council were faced with determined resistance from the Carnival Development Committee (CDC), chaired by Darcus Howe, whose arguments in various issues of *Race Today* were summarized in his 1978 pamphlet *The Road Make to Walk on Carnival Day*. The use of a title borrowed from Lord Kitchener's calypso was one of several markers of the CDC's solidarity with the working-class pan and mas men and women who saw the history of carnival as one aspect of the emancipation struggle. Abner Cohen states that the intense argument between this tendency, and the rival Carnival and Arts Committee (CAC), with its moderate, middle-class black leadership, was finally resolved in favor of the CAC in 1981, when the Arts Council intervened to change the funding arrangements for the carnival (Cohen 1993: 45–51).

In a critical review of Cohen's book, David Roussel-Milner, friend of Claudia Jones, a founder of the Martin Luther King Foundation, carnivalist and Arts Council worker until 1985 (Sherwood 1999: 14, and passim), argues that the CAC was formed in order to divide the Notting Hill Carnival movement, and that the Arts Council used the existence of two committees as an excuse to withdraw support. He strongly implies that there was a conspiracy between the police, the Arts Council, and the local authorities "to take control of carnival" (Roussel-Milner 1996: 9).

When the CAC collapsed in 1988, the Carnival Enterprise Committee took over, chaired by barrister Claire Holder, and major changes were introduced to the organization of carnival in Notting Hill. A new framework was imposed by the police, which included strict enforcement of an early end to the event; a 75 percent reduction in the numbers of sound systems allowed; prevention of dancing behind the mas bands; intensive video surveillance and interception of black youths; strict adherence by the procession to the agreed route. Perhaps most significant of all, the black youths who had formerly coalesced around sound systems were now completely separated from the mobile carnival procession (Cohen 1993: 65–70). Since then, Notting Hill Carnival has become a commercialized, highly respectable event. Having been subjected to "an overwhelming onslaught from different directions intended to force it out or confine in within a strait-jacket" (Cohen 1993: 9), it may appear now to be fully contained within the parameters laid down by the establishment.

To draw this conclusion would be to overlook the spatial politics of carnival, and the embodied performances that it enacts. Henri Lefebvre (1976: 31) argued that "Space is permeated with social relations . . . shaped and moulded from historical and natural elements." As we have seen, Notting Hill is just such a space. According to Darcus Howe: "We have captured the streets of Notting Hill and transformed it into an arena of cultural rebellion" (Cohen 1993: 111). The "we" here is significantly ambiguous; Howe probably refers primarily to black (Caribbean) people, but might well include all those white and other non-white residents who have supported carnival and other local struggles. Michael Keith refers to this area as a "symbolic location" and argues that Notting Hill, in the period 1975 to 1988, was "the spatial realization of a deeply rooted historical struggle" (Keith 1993: 123–9). In this perspective, the ascendancy of a group of black Britons described by their opponents as "yuppie capitalists," "coconuts," and "lackeys" (Cohen 1993: 68) might be regarded as one moment in the dialectic. That process took another turn in 2002 when Claire Holder, who at least grew up in Trinidad in dialogue with carnival, was deposed as Chief Executive of the Notting Hill Carnival Trust and replaced by Professor Chris Mullard. According to Darcus Howe, this was the result of a coup organized by Lee Jasper, the black British adviser to the Lord Mayor of London (2002). The Mayor's interest in carnival is well known (Jasper 2001), but Mullard strongly denied this allegation, arguing that there was no pressure from the Lord Mayor's office. His position as Chair of the Trust was short-term, with the objective of restoring democratic involvement of all parties engaged in the Notting Hill Carnival (Mullard 2002).

If a fully democratic process was to emerge, the radical tendency within the London Carnival movement, exemplified by the Association for a People's Carnival and the People's War sound system (Alleyne 2002: 66–74), might well take control and restore "the working class tradition" in the London Carnival. The formation of the Notting Hill International Carnival Committee, with its democratic constitution and membership composed of mas bands, steelbands, sound systems, calypsonians, participating music bands, and Notting Hill tenants and residents' association, indicated that such a process was in motion (La Rose 1990).

Support for this proposition comes from the Leeds Carnival. Under the leadership of people dedicated to the earlier forms of carnival, who learned from the conflict in London, and who maintained firm opposition to hyper-commercialization, Leeds Carnival has not only maintained a trouble-free procession throughout its long history but has also nurtured designers, steelbands, soca sounds, and mas bands with deep roots in the black communities of northern England. Stripping itself of political rhetoric, negotiating carefully with the police, securing the support of all the mas camps, with professional public relations provided by Susan Pitter, Leeds Carnival has finessed the politics of space. It has successfully varied its route, initially processing through Chapeltown and the city center, then basing itself only in Chapeltown, and (in 2002) agreeing to the city council's request for it to enter the city center again, holding the Carnival Queen contest on a specially constructed catwalk in the new Millennium Square outside the Civic Hall. It is likely that in future years the Bank Holiday Monday procession will enter the city center and hold a show in the Square. This development is a further indication of the British-Caribbean peoples in Leeds moving from the margin to the center (Julien and Mercer 1996).[7]

Another pointer to the complexity of the cultural politics of carnival lies in the special form of embodied performativity that it represents. Mikhail Bakhtin provided an analysis of Rabelais's representation of the sixteenth-century carnival in France which is relevant to an understanding of the London and Leeds West Indian Carnivals today. "[C]arnival is one of Bakhtin's great obsessions, because in his understanding of it, carnival, like the novel, is a *means of displaying otherness*:

Fig. 22.1 Sharon Clements in *The Lost Ship* mas band, designed by Hughbon Condor, Queen of the Leeds Carnival 2002. Photograph by Max Farrar.

carnival makes familiar relations strange" (Holquist 1990: 89). One form of this display of "otherness" is the use of extraordinary costume and often bizarre cosmetics to transform the body's appearance radically. This is a new type of body, one which is often transgressive of conventional norms. Bakhtin produced a vision of what he called "the grotesque body":

> A body in the act of becoming. It is never finished, never completed: it is continually built, created, and builds and creates another body . . . Eating, drinking, defecation . . . copulation, pregnancy, dismemberment, swallowing up by another body . . . In all these events, the beginning of life and end of life are closely linked and interwoven.
>
> (Bakhtin, *Rabelais and his World* (1984), cited in Holquist 1990: 89)

Fig. 22.2 Transgressive bodies: Michael Paul and Hebrew Rawlins cross-dressing at the Leeds West Indian Carnival, 2002. Photograph by Max Farrar.

Bakhtin's concept of dialogism – that thoughts, words, and existences take place *only* as dialogue with the other (Roberts 1994: 247) – applies to carnival because this is one of the sites in which the grotesque body is displayed. In carnival, all bodies are in dialogue. It would be surprising if all the excesses which Bakhtin described in the Rabelaisian, fictional carnivalesque world of the mid sixteenth century had survived intact in the twenty-first-century carnival in the UK (indeed, we would argue that this reduction of excess should be addressed by carnival in the UK today); but Bakhtin's general point about "grotesque bodies" remains highly relevant. In the Leeds Carnival of 2001 people played mas dressed in rags and smeared in cosmetics to represent mud, and Captain Wenham's Masqueraders troupe (which was a major feature of the Leeds Carnival until very recently) were dressed in tatters and wore grotesque masks. Benji's troupe once appeared as pall-bearers, carrying a body in a gorilla mask, playing dead. In 2001 Ruth Bundey appeared in an elephant's mask (referencing the Hindu god Gamesh). The regular appearance in the Leeds Carnival of men who delight in dressing as women (Hebrew Rawlins and Michael Paul being the best examples) is another aspect of this playful transgressiveness (see figure 22.2).[8]

In contemporary carnival in the UK, the "grotesque" is in dialogue with its opposite, "beauty," and, perhaps in keeping with the postmodern obsession with the perfection of form according to increasingly globalized notions of what constitutes beauty, this beauty form now predominates. It is important to note, however, that, in both the Leeds and the London carnivals, costumes are worn by people of all shapes and sizes, and aesthetic standards are mainly judged according to the artistry of the costume, rather than the beauty of the wearer. Holquist writes that these bodies, for Bakhtin, and we would argue for today's carnival, "militate against monadism, the illusion of closed-off bodies or isolated psyches in bourgeois individualism, and the concept of a pristine, closed-off, static identity and truth wherever it may be found." The Caribbean carnival is thus one source of resistance to the "egotism of the West" that Bakhtin denounced (Holquist 1990: 90).

NEW BLACK SUBJECTIVITIES

Around the middle of the twentieth century, when British citizens from the West Indies were beginning to settle in the UK, George Lamming wrote:

> It is the brevity of the West Indian's history and the fragmentary nature of the different cultures which have fused into something new; it is the absolute dependence on the values in that language of his coloniser which has given him a special relation to the word, colonialism. It is not merely a political definition; it is not merely the result of certain economic arrangements. It started as these, and grew somewhat deeper. Colonialism is at the very base and structure of the West Indian cultural awareness. His reluctance in asking for complete, political freedom . . . is due to the fear that he has never had to stand. A foreign or absent Mother has always cradled his judgement.
>
> (Lamming [1960] 1995: 15)

This was the ideological context in which the carnival movement in the UK was created. It is one which we would argue has almost, but not entirely, disappeared. Stuart Hall has analyzed the change that became observable in the 1980s. He argued that, in an earlier period of cultural politics, when black people were "placed, positioned at the margins . . . blacks have typically been the objects, but rarely the subjects, of the practices of representation."

Now, as a political struggle over representation itself emerged, there was

> the recognition of the extraordinary diversity of subjective positions, social experiences and cultural identities which compose the category "black"; that is, the recognition that "black" is essentially a politically and culturally *constructed* category, which cannot be grounded in a set of fixed trans-cultural or transcendental racial categories and which therefore has no guarantees in nature.

Thus it is no longer possible to hypothesize an "essential black subject." Instead, we are "plunged headlong into the maelstrom of a continuously contingent, unguaranteed, political argument and debate, a critical politics, a politics of criticism" (Hall [1989] 1996: 442–4).

The debate that raged around carnival in London was a critical moment in the representation of the conflicting subjective and political positions which are evident in black British culture today. The actual practice of carnival then reproduces a variety of subjectivities on the streets of UK cities. Thus in Leeds we see the truck hired over the past five years or so by the Pan African Cultural Group, wearing African clothes and playing African instruments, representing themselves quite clearly as Africans and Africanists, but not Afro-centrics: they use Kwame Nkrumah's socialist concept of Pan-Africanism, and some of the members are white. The Godfather's truck carries a precarious pile of speaker boxes, along with a crew of older men who may well be in suspenders and brassieres, blasting out soca hits recently imported, usually from Trinidad. These men are emphatically Caribbeans, but their Bacchanalian followers, some of whom are their children, are equally emphatically black British, identifying with soca as one of a variety of musical interests, which will include soul, R&B, UK garage, hip-hop, and reggae.

While this wide variety of styles and identifications will be evident throughout the Notting Hill Carnival, in Leeds, with the Committee's insistence on fore-grounding the steel pan and soca traditions, sound systems will be confined to the periphery of the carnival. The willingness of the young Leeds Carnival revelers to accept this limitation during the carnival period is one indication of the fluidity of the identifications that they make.

Thus, many of these new black subjects have moved beyond the essentialism of an earlier individualistic, tunnel-visioned consciousness toward a state of multi-consciousness or interculturalism. Consciously or subconsciously, they have moved toward the notion that cultural identities are actively constructed through particular communication processes, social practices, and articulations within specific circumstances. In doing so, they have constructed a new cultural space and place. This new position insists upon cultural negotiation which involves a process of linking together several elements that may not necessarily have had any previous relation to each other. This articulation represents a movement between alternative conceptions of truth, a movement toward a many-stranded consciousness that moves beyond the limited definition of hybridization as a mixing of only two strands.

Carnival plays a crucial part in blending the wide variety of identifications that are available in postmodern, or late-modern, Britain. Inherent within the aesthetic of carnival is the seamless fusion of arts practice and community engagement. In particular, carnival is now seen and often used as an effective creative tool for bringing disparate communities together in common celebration. It has repeatedly demonstrated the potential it offers for communication and unification across social, cultural and political boundaries, and more recently carnival has been seen as a model for artistic and social co-operation, integration and cohesion, ultimately offering a creative opportunity for social and political change. Despite the commonalities that can be drawn between the carnival activities of various British Caribbean communities, the nature and form of artistic expression is also characterized by a diversity that is reflective of the differences and complexities evidenced within particular areas of the Caribbean diaspora. This cross-fertilization of celebratory archetypes reflects influences from a variety of communities including Trinidadian, Barbadian, Dominican, and Jamaican. In fact the Liverpool Carnival is a blend of cultural tradition from six Caribbean islands.

But the carnival tradition in the UK is more than simply a means of unifying people whose origins lie in the various islands of the Caribbean sea. Thus the Bradford Carnival has embraced contributions from Dominica and Barbados in the Caribbean, but also includes Asian and white English cultural forms. The Unity Day Carnival in Wolverhampton reflects Barbadian, white English and Asian influences. At Notting Hill, the reggae of Jamaica is heard alongside the soca and steelband of Trinidad, the samba of Brazil, and the jungle, drum'n'bass and garage of Britain.

In fact British carnival practice has acquired its particular uniqueness and flavor precisely because it has embraced alternative immigrant communities – African, Asian, South American – all of whom have their own specific celebratory promenade traditions from which they can draw.

This diversity is also reflected in the increasingly common practice for the formal aspects and ideologies integral to Caribbean-style carnival to be borrowed, appropriated and integrated, to enhance, and transform British carnival and British celebratory traditions. Having been witnessed first in the early Notting Hill street fairs, this transformation can be seen to great effect at the Barrow-in-Furness and Luton carnivals as well as the Fish Quay Festival in North Shields, Newcastle, where there is a long and established tradition of carnival to build upon. A more understated approach has been taken at events such as the High Wycombe, Reading and Dover carnivals.

Tom Fleming (1998) has produced the most sustained analysis of carnival in the UK (in Leeds and in Bristol) which draws upon sociologies of space and identity, but our final example of the potential for carnival to formulate and express new identities and new cultural practices comes from Geraldine Connor's work *Carnival Messiah*. This massive production, staged in 1999 and 2002 by the West Yorkshire Playhouse in Leeds and in 2003 and 2004 in Port of Spain, represents a unique fusion of the Caribbean Carnival with European opera. Geraldine Connor describes herself as a "New European" – "a living exponent of the meeting of Europe, Africa and Asia four centuries ago . . . I carry all that cultural baggage with me." She writes:

> *Carnival Messiah* drags Handel's best-known work kicking and screaming into the new millennium . . . By superimposing traditional Western European musical and theatrical devices on the traditional Trinidad Carnival practice, an holistic, organic metamorphosis occurs . . . [it] creates a natural bridge of cross-fertilisation . . . *Carnival Messiah* subverts the ideology of homogenisation; instead, it celebrates difference and otherness . . . [which does not] equate to cultural separatism or imply a kind of cultural assimilation. It should instead explore issues of divergence and "otherness" in terms of cultural parallels and divergences, cultural uniqueness and similarities.
>
> (Connor 2002)

This model of identities forged in cultural and political practice takes us beyond the entrenched positions imposed by racism. "New European" might be a self-identity

Fig. 22.3 *Carnival Messiah* was first performed at the West Yorkshire Playhouse in Leeds and fused carnival traditions and music with Handel's *Messiah*. Written and directed by Geraldine Connor, it used professional actors and a cast of over one hundred people drawn from the local community. Photograph by Tim Smith, 1999. For comparative carnival costumes see figures 7.6, 8.1–8.3.

to be adopted by those of us in Europe who read the history of that continent as one of migration and cultural interchange, who recognize the implausibility of describing as "white European" those whose skin colors vary from pink to olive, and who through cultural and political practice work toward the abolition of the category known as white (Roediger 1994; Ware and Back 2002).

CONCLUSION

This chapter has provided the bones of a history of carnival in London and in Leeds, and it has offered an interpretation of carnival practice. Accepting that carnival is an intensely subjective experience performed by people who cannot escape their cultural and political histories, and thus that there are many "truths" to be constructed around carnival, it has nevertheless argued that the tradition in the UK is best understood as a subtle, cultural/political response to white racism. Its subtlety lies in its production of an invisible politics, a politics which is normally non-confrontational. Carnival in the UK understands that the anti-human negativity of racism is effectively challenged by the embodied, human performance of art – an art which has been created "by the people, for the people," which occupies and transforms public space. This is an art led by dark-skinned people, which demonstrates their centrality to the UK cities in which they have settled, and which includes all people of good will, whatever their pigmentation. As Geraldine Connor (2002) puts it: "This new cultural space then becomes a tool of liberation for all."

NOTES

1   This chapter arises from a paper presented by Geraldine Connor titled "Carnival as an instrument of postcolonial liberation – In search of a liberative potential for the post-modern West Indian subject" at the World Conference on Carnival, Showcasing the Caribbean held at Trinity College, Hartford, CT, in 1998. The overall argument in this chapter is similar to the one made at the conference, and whole paragraphs have been lifted from that speech. But, whereas the speech contained the lyric of carnival, this chapter has the drone of academe, providing another textual indicator of the problems and possibilities of hybridizing cultures.

2   Anne Walmsley's meticulously researched book on the Caribbean Arts Movement says that Jones "coordinated the first West Indian Carnival in Britain, at Porchester Hall, Bayswater" (Walmsley 1992: 21).

3   Howe is related to the late C.L.R. James, and *Race Today*, published under Howe's editorship in London from 1974 until 1982, is the most significant British exemplar of that eminent Trinidadian Marxist's cultural politics (see Buhle 1988; Farred 1996).

4   Close readers may be puzzled by the shifting signifiers in this chapter. "West Indian" is used to reflect the language of the 1960s and early 1970s. In fact the Leeds Carnival insists to this day on calling itself the Leeds *West Indian* Carnival. In the 1980s, the term "African-Caribbean" began to replace "West Indian." The authors of this chapter use the term "Caribbean" to reflect the importance of the other national heritages, apart from African, among people of Caribbean descent. Alternatively, we use "black British." Unlike some writers we use the lower case for "black," because we do not want to fetishize the color of human skin. Because of the persistence of racism, these are intensely political categories and we recognize that there are several other terms which other authors prefer.

5   Arthur France made this point in a speech given to the conference of Black and Asian Studies Association (BASA) held in Leeds on October 19, 1996. The point has been followed in Max Farrar's conversations with Arthur France, in which he confirms that this was his approach to the formation of Carnival in Leeds. BASA (formerly ASACHIB, Secretary: Marika Sherwood) has a Newsletter obtainable from the Institute of Commonwealth Studies, 28 Russell Square, London WC1B 5DS.

6   This account of the origins of Leeds Carnival is almost identical to the one in Farrar (2001). Arthur France recalls taking one of his early troupes to the Notting Hill Carnival on a very wet August Bank Holiday Monday. Both Palmer (1986) and Cohen (1993: 18) give 1968 as the year of the torrential rain. Palmer (1986) recalls " 'man' from the north [Leeds] joining 'man' from Trinidad, and 'man' from the Grove . . . pulling the pan . . . the rain so steady."

7   This account holds true in general, but the Leeds Carnival has not always been harmonious. Three people died at the Leeds Carnival in 1990. Two were deliberate murders. One was accidental – a ricochet from gunshot. None of the alleged perpetrators, or victims, was from Leeds (Farrar 2001). The Committee moved swiftly to change the arrangements made by sound systems, with full co-operation from the sound crews. The dissension that has occasionally taken place about the organization of the Leeds Carnival has always been amicably resolved.

8   To get closer to the Leeds Carnival visit the website "Celebrating 35 years of the Leeds West Indian Carnival," developed by Pavilion in Leeds, at www.newmasmedia.co.uk.

23

"NEW YORK EQUALIZE YOU?" CHANGE AND CONTINUITY IN BROOKLYN'S LABOR DAY CARNIVAL[1]

Philip Kasinitz

It has become something of a cliché to declare that New York, and specifically Brooklyn, is both the largest city and the cultural capital of the anglophone Caribbean. Like most clichés, this is in some ways true and in some ways misleading. West Indians and their US-born children now number over one million in the New York metropolitan area (Vickerman and Kasinitz 1999). If West Indians from the various new nations that constituted the British West Indies before 1962 are considered together, they are the largest immigrant group in New York – comprising roughly 24 percent of New York's immigrant and second-generation population and almost half of the Black population (Waters 1999).[2] Much of the soca, calypso, and reggae consumed in the Caribbean is now produced in New York, often by artists based there at least part time. Many of the region's intellectual and cultural leaders now live and work in New York, as do a surprising number of its politicians, at least when out of power. Many Caribbean products can now be obtained more cheaply and more easily in New York than in many parts of the Caribbean. Indeed, Milton Vickerman has recently argued that actual travel to the Caribbean is increasingly unnecessary for West Indians seeking to maintain a strong ethnic affiliation. Today, the middle-class black sections of Brooklyn and Queens have come to constitute a prosperous West Indian world which many immigrants and their children now find preferable to the impoverished original (Vickerman 2001).

And yet, for all of this, New York is not a Caribbean city. West Indians in New York face a social context utterly different than the one they knew in the Caribbean, and nowhere is this more apparent than in matters of class and race. Whether they choose to identify with, or distance themselves from, native African Americans, West Indian New Yorkers find their lives shaped by race in a thousand large and small ways different from the way race operated "back home" (Foner 2001; Waters 1999; Vickerman 1998). In this new context, Caribbean cultural activity can never really be a simple effort to retain traditions from "back home." Cultural forms inevitably take on new and different meanings (see Buff 2001).

Nowhere is this more obviously true than in Brooklyn's West Indian–American carnival, the annual event that culminates in the huge street celebration which draws one to two million participants and spectators each year to Eastern Parkway on the US Labor Day (the first Monday of September), with an increasing number of competitions and performances taking place the previous weekend. Given the nature of carnival it could hardly be otherwise. The carnival tradition is one in which social meanings are always in flux. It is an arena in which ordinary people can critique and challenge the conditions that shape their lives. As the late Frank Manning wrote,

> Celebration does not resolve or remove ambiguity and conflict, but rather it embellishes them. It locates these social facts . . . in a performance context in which they can be thought about, acted upon and aesthetically appreciated. The celebrants' hope . . . is that the rhythm of performance will find an echo in life, if only for the moment.
>
> (Manning 1984)

As an event in which the participants' social identities are both crystallized and transformed, the Labor Day Carnival struggles uneasily between two different models of ethnic assertion: the Caribbean, and specifically Trinidadian Carnival, on the one hand, New York's own tradition of "ethnic" parade – such as the St Patrick's Day Parade and the Puerto Rican Day Parade – on the other. Yet now larger than the events it is modeled on, carnival is increasingly struggling to create something new, something that is rooted in the Caribbean, but in many ways is also very much a product of New York.

ETHNICITY DANCES IN THE STREET: "OLE MAS" COMES TO BROOKLYN

Brooklyn's Labor Day Carnival is an event that from its beginnings mixed extravagant fantasy and gritty reality, escapist fun and serious purpose. Next to the stilt walkers and the fantastic dragon, signs with commentary about United States and Caribbean politics sometimes appear. A band of masqueraders in elaborate "African" garb is accompanied by slogans about black pride and African unity. And the year the Duvaliers were overthrown, the old blue and red flag of pre-Papa-Doc Haiti waved above some of the most uninhibited of the dancers. New York politicians, always drawn to a crowd, started to come to carnival in the early 1980s. As the decade went on, national political figures began to add Brooklyn to their Labor Day itineraries. Then, in 1991, the eyes of the nation were focused on Crown Heights as carnival followed closely on the heels of serious racial disturbances. Since that time the event has become the annual occasion for the New York press to assess the state of the West Indian community, now the largest immigrant group in this city of immigrants. Today the Labor Day procession is a defining moment in the political and cultural life of Caribbean New York. Both its location and its schedule are now considered inviolable.

Held annually since 1969 in Brooklyn's Crown Heights, carnival brings together people from throughout New York and other North American cities. The crowd includes young toughs and United Nations Ambassadors, dreadlocked rastas and churchgoing grandmothers – a virtual cross-section of Caribbean America. In recent years, many of the community's more respectable members have complained about the raucousness of the carnival. Still, they continue to come, and to bring their American-born children. As a festival in which people play with the idea of identity, it is fitting that carnival has become the most visible public symbol of New York's West Indian community. Like the West Indian community itself, Brooklyn's Carnival is now too massive to ignore, and thus serves to make visible a group of people who, caught between their status as Blacks in a racially divided city and as immigrants distinct from the larger African-American community, have long felt invisible (see Bryce-Laporte 1972). A festival full of uncertainties and contradictions, carnival also presents an appropriately ambiguous public face for a people whose role in the city's civic life remains in flux. Like its diasporic cousin, the London Carnival studied by Abner Cohen (1980a, 1982), it is a "contested terrain," a unique social space in which social and political realities are subject to redefinition. Thus, carnival is a sphere in which the potential for both conformist and oppositional politics is always present simultaneously. It is not merely a reflection of politics, – it *is* politics – a realm where new ideas about power relations may be articulated in the context of a public drama.

The Trinidad Carnival served as a model for the Brooklyn celebration, with its masquerades, ritualized violence, penchant for satirical calypso music, confrontational politics, and status as a nation-building festival. A new, status-conscious elite paradoxically took its cultural cues from the poor, converting symbols and slogans of equality – "All O' We Is One" – into expressions of national unity (Hill 1972). Trinidad is traditionally a source of employment for persons from smaller islands. Thus, over the years, Trinidad's carnival forms and traditions were spread by returning migrants to parts of the Caribbean that had their own pre-Lenten carnival traditions, as well as to Protestant territories in which the fete was unknown. Migrants from Trinidad and neighboring islands began to hold pre-Lenten dances in New York during the 1920s. Then, in 1947 Jesse Wardle, a Trinidadian immigrant, obtained a parade permit for a carnival procession from 110th Street to 142nd Street in Harlem. Held on Labor Day, a time of year more suitable than February for outdoor celebrations in New York, this event was sponsored by Congressman Adam Clayton Powell (interestingly, one of the few prominent New York black politicians of the period who was not of Caribbean descent). As Lord Invader (1955) described the event:

> Labor Day I felt happy,
> Because I played Carnival in New York City.
> Seventh Avenue was jumpin',
> Everybody was shakin'.
> From 110th to 142nd,
> We had bands of every description.
> This is the first time New York ever had,
> Carnival on the streets like Trinidad.

Although dominated by Trinidadian organizers, this street carnival was from its inception self-consciously pan-West-Indian. Caribbean unity, albeit on Trinidadian terms, was a central theme. The sheer numbers of people involved in such a highly visible event helped to promote a sense of group identity. Scheduling the event on Labor Day helped to break the always tenuous connection to Catholicism of the pre-Lenten carnival and facilitated the participation of West Indians of all religions.

In 1964, following a bottle-throwing incident between African-Americans and Caribbean revelers (coming on the heels of a more serious outbreak of violence in 1961), the parade permit for carnival in Harlem was revoked by city officials nervous about racial unrest. The next year, Rufus Gorin, a Trinidad-born band-leader and longtime participant in the Harlem Carnival, attempted to organize a new Labor Day Carnival in Brooklyn, where large numbers of West Indian immigrants had by then settled. The small ad hoc committee he headed initially met resistance from the city, which was hesitant to sponsor a large street gathering of Blacks during that riot-torn period. Gorin was once even arrested in full carnival regalia. However, in 1971, the group, now headed by Carlos Lezama, a Trinidadian immigrant[3] and machinist for the New York City Transit Authority, obtained permission to hold carnival on Eastern Parkway, Frederick Law Olmstead's stately boulevard which runs through the heart of central Brooklyn's black neigh-borhoods. This broad Parkway is uniquely suited to the huge event – although one can hardly imagine a use more distant from Olmstead's genteel vision.

The number of West Indians in New York had already begun to swell following the 1965 immigration reforms. Over the next three decades, the community and the event grew together. The area immediately south of Eastern Parkway – which some in the community are now campaigning to have renamed "Caribbean Parkway" – soon became the cultural and demographic center of West Indian settlement in New York. The ad hoc committee is now a permanent organization known as the West Indian American Day Carnival Association (WIADCA) and is headed by Lezama and his daughter.

Despite its massive growth, the format of Brooklyn's carnival has changed little over the years. During the week prior to Labor Day Monday a series of concerts, steelband contests, and children's pageants are held on the grounds of the Brooklyn Museum. The events climax with a huge carnival procession on Eastern Parkway on Labor Day itself. These "official" carnival activities are accompanied by dozens of affiliated dances, concerts, and parties in West Indian neighborhoods around the city. In contrast to most of New York's numerous "ethnic" festivals, the carnival lacks a centralized structure. The WIADCA obtains the needed permits and deals with city officials. As the event has grown, it has also worked inter-mittently with the city tourism and economic development officials in an attempt to make the event more "tourist friendly." Yet its members are more coordinators than organizers, and they have had a frustratingly difficult time in getting carnival participants to agree to even minor changes in the way things are done.

The dozens of dances, shows, and parties throughout the city that complement the parade are run by individual promoters who operate independently of the WIADCA. The various steelbands rehearse throughout the summer in "pan yards" scattered throughout Brooklyn and Queens. While some participate in a WIADCA-sponsored steelband contest and show at the Brooklyn Museum a few days before Labor Day, others do not, and in recent years band leaders have organized rival steelband shows in other locations. Indeed at times in the late 1990s relations between the band leaders and the organization reached such a head that a "strike" by the band leaders was often threatened, although never completely carried out. Yet, while other groups may offer rival shows and supplementary events, the WIADCA's culminating procession on Labor Day itself is now clearly sacrosanct. It is the one event everyone attends, and no one has seriously proposed a rival or replacement since an attempt to create a more "respectable" Labor Day event in Manhattan failed miserably in the early 1980s.

The "mas" (masquerade) bands are also privately organized, and their leaders are also frequently at odds with the Association. Each mas band is composed of several dozen to several hundred elaborately costumed revelers who dance to live or recorded music in the carnival procession. They are loosely organized around themes that emphasize fantasy (*Galactic Splendor*, *Splendors of the Far East*, *Party in Space*), ethnicity (*Caribbean Unite*), or current events (*Cry for Freedom*, *Tribute to Bob Marley*). Historical themes, with costumes influenced by Hollywood epics (*Extracts from Rome*), are particularly popular, as are those which use popular culture references in bizarre juxtapositions: one band recently used the theme *Ponderosa in Hell*: its masqueraders, clad in black and red, wore cowboy hats, toy six-guns, tin stars, devil masks and wings. In general, costumes are loosely co-ordinated but by no means uniform. In some bands all members are in costume, although in most only a few members wear elaborate outfits while the majority simply wear matching tee shirts. All bands, however, feature at least one or two (and often a dozen) extremely complex and fantastic outfits that are not so much costumes as small, one-person floats. The leaders of these bands invest a tremendous amount of time and energy in carnival preparations. Sponsoring a band is expensive, and, while most of the leaders can be described as "middle class," none is wealthy. Yet they frequently report investing thousands of dollars out of pocket for band expenses. Although some of this money is recouped through the sale of costumes, at best the bands break even, and many lose money. While the leaders may be involved in preparations throughout the year, the costume makers usually start to work in the early summer, with work coming to a feverish pitch in the month preceding the carnival. Typically this work – men constructing the mechanical parts of costumes, women sewing – takes place in rented storefronts, basements, social clubs and private homes.

This investment of money and preparation time, as well as the bonding effect of the common effort, serves to differentiate the thousands of core participants from the hundreds of thousands of more casual revelers who march along in matching tee shirts on Labor Day. Thus, in 2002, when pouring rains kept the Labor Day crowds down, these core participants came out nonetheless. As one woman in a gold-spangled bikini over a gold, semi-see-through body suit and a two-foot-high gold and silver head piece explained, "Of course I am here! Where else am I going to wear this?"

In the actual Labor Day procession each masquerade band half marches and half dances (or in Trinidadian terms "chips") around a flatbed truck that may carry a calypso group or a steelband, but in recent years has been more likely to sport a huge sound system playing recorded calypso or soca music. The trucks display banners announcing the name of the band's leader, its theme and its sponsors: usually local businesses or politicians, occasionally social service organizations or labor unions. Sometimes the vehicle itself becomes part of the display: a local shipping company decorates its delivery van as an outrageous version of a cargo ship, complete with real shipping barrels on the roof.

The lack of central organizational authority is evident in the form of the carnival parade itself. The procession starts around noon with a group of dignitaries, grand marshals (usually local business leaders, celebrities, and politicians), and city officials who march, or rather saunter, down the Parkway. But they do not draw much attention, for the main body of the carnival may be a mile or more behind them. Next come several carloads of West Indian–American beauty contest winners who are likewise largely ignored. The crowds that line the Parkway, eating, drinking, and talking to friends, show little interest in these "parade" elements that are grafted rather uneasily onto the carnival form. The real carnival begins when more than a dozen large masquerade bands, surrounding flatbed trucks carrying musicians or sound systems, start down Eastern Parkway, theoretically in order. This structure breaks down almost immediately, bands stop, change direction, or simply get bogged down in a dancing mass of humanity. The distinction between participant and spectator quickly disappears, despite the concerted efforts of the police to maintain it. Some bands do not even finish the three-mile route in the allotted six hours. As a dramatic event, carnival is strikingly leaderless. There are themes and a certain ebb and flow, but no particular center or head.

Community leaders and politicians seeking local recognition and support are naturally attracted to huge gatherings such as carnival. Yet the event itself subverts notions of leadership and presents a throng of autonomous individuals. This presents politicians and the WIADCA officials with a dilemma: how does one "lead" an event without a head or even a very clear direction? In recent years politicians and the WIADCA have tried to tighten control over the procession. This became a critical issue in 1995, when two hours of the event were covered on live television. On the whole, however, efforts to remake carnival more in the mold of a traditional ethnic parade have met with only modest success.

CARNIVAL AND ETHNIC IDENTITY

Brooklyn's carnival is an "ethnic" event in a city where ethnicity is enormously politically salient. Yet while carnival clearly asserts a massive presence in New York, it does not offer the opportunity to make a strategic statement: it is too anarchic to be manipulated or to support a structure. The WIADCA leadership strives to project an image of ethnic distinctiveness and solidarity, self-consciously invoking New York's tradition of ethnic politics. As Lezama writes: "To West Indians, as one of the many ethnic minorities in New York, the need for social collaboration, the introduction of a feeling of community and brotherhood are variables critical to us in maintaining our existence within the wider sphere of other ethnic groups" (WIADCA souvenir brochure, 1983). A former Association officer puts it more directly: "We expect the powers that be to recognize carnival as part of our culture, as the culture of any other group is recognized." This notion, that West Indians are an ethnic group like other ethnic groups, implies the presence of clearly recognized political leaders to whom the "powers that be" can pay deference and who may serve as brokers between the state and the ethnic population. The WIADCA presents itself as such a group, yet its claims to leadership over the event are problematic.

Yet, if carnival does not create group leaders, it does assert group boundaries. More than any other event it visibly embodies the emerging pan-West-Indian identity now evident in New York. As early as 1976, the calypsonian Mighty Sparrow sang:

> You can be from St. Cleo, or from John John
> In New York, all that done.
> They haven't to know who is who,
> New York equalize you!
> Bajan, Grenadian, Jamaican, "toute monde,"
> Drinking they rum, beating they bottle and spoon.
> Nobody could watch me and honestly say,
>   they don't like to be in Brooklyn on Labor Day!

It is worth noting that the pan-ethnic identity Sparrow sings about is very much a creation of the New York context. Indeed, he invokes a classic New York image: at a time when cultural critics in the academy are seeing "resistance" everywhere in postmodern culture, Sparrow's New York is that stubbornly modernist city in which the newcomers can remake themselves. New York's carnival, for him, is not about clinging to Caribbean tradition, but rather the opportunity to create something which, while rooted in the Caribbean, is essentially new. This assertion of a New-York-based pan-West-Indian identity is one of the reasons why carnival has become so important in New York, despite the fact that the majority of Afro-Caribbean New Yorkers come from nations with no carnival tradition. The importance of carnival lies in the fact that, while it is unquestionably "ethnic," its tradition of satire, inversion, creativity, and innovation leaves the content of West Indian identity unfixed. It thus creates a space in which a reformulation of identity and a realignment of social relations are possible.

Of course, to the extent that Trinidadian symbols have been central to the carnival, the defining of this new West Indian identity takes place on unequal terms. While people throughout the anglophone Caribbean and Haiti attend carnival along with growing numbers of Latinos and African-Americans, the WIADCA, the steelbands and the masquerade bands are still dominated by Trinidadians. Carnival is highly developed in Trinidad, and naturally Trinidadians bring with them the skills to mount the festival. Yet this Trinidadian tradition is put forward as an expression of West Indian identity. Thus, in New York, carnival continually vacillates between its Trinidadian roots and its pan-Caribbean agenda.

Music has played a central role in the negotiation of cultural politics that occurs during carnival. In its early years the concerts presented on the Brooklyn Museum grounds featured overwhelmingly Trinidadian entertainers. The 1974 carnival program lists a steelband competition, an ole mas competition, a costume competition, and a "calypso tent" – all distinctly Trinidadian cultural forms. By 1976, however, the WIADCA – which, as Hill (1994) notes, was still almost entirely Trinidadian – added a "Night in the Caribbean" on the Saturday before carnival. This concert featured Jamaican reggae, Haitian dance troupes, and even a group from Costa Rica. In 1983, in an attempt to include more Jamaicans and more young people in general, the organizers added "Reggae Night" to the festivities on the Thursday night preceding Labor Day. The reggae concert was both part of the carnival and distinctly separate from the weekend's other events. "The Jamaicans," Lezama noted to the *Jamaican Weekly Gleaner*, August 15, 1983, "wanted their own night." In 1987, a "Haitian Night" was added as well.

These divisions can also be seen on Eastern Parkway itself. In the late 1970s Hill and Abrahamson (1980) observed that young reggae fans tended to group around sound systems at one end of Eastern Parkway and on side streets, listening to recorded Jamaican music, while Trinidad-style street "jump up" predominated in the middle of the carnival throng. Of course not all young reggae fans are Jamaican. However, many young New York West Indians choose to express themselves in the Jamaican mode, just as their elders tend to articulate their ethnicity in terms of Trinidadian origin. By the 1980s a few reggae bands mounted on trucks joined in the procession, and both reggae and soca could be heard throughout the Parkway. In the 1990s soca dominated the mas bands, but it was contemporary reggae, Jamaican dancehall music and African-American hip-hop that poured out of the windows and the sound systems set up along the side streets.

While the WIADCA has sought to encourage the participation of all West Indians, it continues to define the "real" carnival traditions in Trinidadian terms. The Association and other Trinidadian groups have sought funding to train young United-States-born West Indians in such skills as costume making and steelband music, thus promoting their own particular definition of West Indian culture. They have also sponsored an annual "Kiddie Carnival," held during the afternoons preceding the Saturday and Sunday night carnival shows. In an event modeled on the much more massive children's carnivals of Trinidad, children compete for prizes for the best costumes and chip and wine to calypso on the big stage as proud parents fawn and flashbulbs click. The WIADCA sees these events as ways to pass on "ethnic traditions" to the young. Indeed, for many middle-aged parents, Kiddie Carnival is a far more acceptable version of West Indian culture than the rasta-influenced, Jamaican-based hybrid of the late 1970s or the gangsta-rap-influenced versions of dancehall music favored by the youth of the 1990s.

In the late 1980s, leaders of the steelbands and several of the larger mas bands took their own step toward restoring the "authentic" Trinidadian roots of carnival – albeit one which favored the more raucous and less respectable side of the Trinidadian tradition than that put forward by the WIADCA. Tired of being literally drowned out by the recorded music from the sound-trucks that now dominate Eastern Parkway on Labor Day, they created their own central Brooklyn procession. Known as j'ouvert ("break of day"), sometimes spelled "jou-vay," this parade starts at 3:00 a.m. on Labor Day morning, a time when nothing is likely to drown out the steelbands. Even at that hour the jouvay celebration draws tens of thousands of revelers, most of whom later make their way to the more pan-Caribbean Eastern Parkway procession (Allen and Slater 1998). Jouvay is a loud, hard-partying event, with dancers with blackened bodies, spontaneous drumming as well as plenty of steel pan. On the one hand, it is far more consistent with older Trinidadian traditions, some of which are now being eclipsed in Trinidad as well (see Brown 1990). On the other hand, it is also something of a protest against the WIADCA's increasing respectability as well as against the behavior of the police, who during the Guiliani administration became far more aggressive in closing down pan yards for excessive noise and other "quality of life" violations. In this sense jouvay is both more traditional than the Eastern Parkway fete and, at the same time, more consistent with the confrontational racial politics favored by many younger West Indians and West Indian–Americans. For these young people, the WIADCA's "ethnic" model fits imperfectly on the reality of a group that, despite their ethnic distinctiveness, find their life chances far more shaped by their racial identity as black people in America.[4]

CARNIVAL, RACE, AND POLITICS

The underlying ambiguity of the West Indian community's relationship with the rest of black New York comes to the surface in the carnival. Despite frequent talk of black unity and allusions to Pan-Africanism, carnival, by its nature, differentiates West Indians from other Blacks. The early organizers believed that these differences should remain within a narrowly defined "cultural" realm. Carnival provided an arena where they might be expressed far more directly than they could be in the realm of government and politics. In recent years, however, politics has come more openly into the carnival. In 1984, New York's leading black radio station, WLIB, arranged a carnival appearance by the Reverend Jesse Jackson. The following year a number of politicians (only a few West Indian) seized upon carnival as an opportunity to get their message across and had undertaken partial sponsorship of mas bands so that their names would appear on the band trucks. Thus, signs saluting "City Councilwoman Rhoda Jacobs" and the "Greater Flatbush Independent Democratic Club" and urging "Andrew Stein for City Council President," "Roy Innis for Congress" (in 1986), and even "Free South Africa" hung alongside those naming Caribbean bakeries, shipping companies, and restaurants. Yet the question of whether carnival should be explicitly political soon became a source of controversy in the community. As Colin Moore, an activist associated with the left wing of New York's Caribbean leadership, wrote in the *Caribbean News* in 1985,

> the organizers of the carnival have not outgrown their parochial roots. The gentlemen from Laventille, Sangre Grande and Arima still view carnival as an opportunity to "play mas." They could not perceive its broader cultural implications or political significance. As a result of this shortsightedness, this gerontocracy of aging "mas men" has been unable to impose the discipline, organization and creativity necessary to transform the carnival from a Laventille affair into a Caribbean event, from a Brooklyn Road March into a citywide media event, from a backyard bacchanal into a significant political event.

A few years later, tragic events would, indeed, turn carnival into a political event, whether the "aging mas men" wanted it so or not.

Since its early days the Brooklyn Carnival had survived several attempts by Hasidic Jews of the Lubavitcher sect, whose World Headquarters is on the Eastern Parkway along the carnival route, to have it banned or moved. Over the years, as the rest of the Jewish population of Crown Heights moved out (and West Indians moved in), members of this tight-knit Hasidic sect had chosen to stay and to continue to build institutions in the area. Indeed during the 1970s and 1980s their numbers had grown steadily and they continued to buy large amounts of property in the neighborhood. Yet, despite widespread feeling among West Indians that the small Hasidic community wielded power far out of proportion to its numbers in Crown Heights, the Jewish group had been notably unsuccessful in their efforts to stop the carnival. Indeed resistance to the festival may have actually helped the WIADCA forge close relationships with local politicians, many of them Jewish. During the 1980s, as the numbers of both Caribbean and Hasidic residents grew in Crown Heights, tensions over real estate, crime, and the actions of Hasidic security patrols often strained relations between the groups. Yet by and large they lived together peacefully, if not amicably.

Then on August 19, 1991, a car driven by a Hasidic Jew – part of the Lubavitch Grand Rebbe Menachem Schneerson's motorcade – jumped a curb in Crown Heights, killing a seven-year-old Guyanese boy named Gavin Cato. Rumors, eventually disproved, quickly spread throughout the neighborhood that a Hasidic ambulance service had ignored the child while rushing the uninjured driver from the scene. Several hours later a group of about twenty black youths fatally stabbed a Hasidic student named Yankel Rosenbaum. Three nights of rioting followed in which groups of Blacks and Hasidim clashed in the streets, Jewish families were attacked in their homes, and stores belonging to black, white, and Asian merchants were looted. Black youths marched to the World Headquarters of the Lubavitcher Hasidic sect on Eastern Parkway, where some hurled rocks and bottles and shouted anti-Semitic slogans. Mayor David Dinkins, the city's first African-American mayor, repeatedly called for calm and was himself briefly trapped by rock-throwing black youths during a condolence call on the Cato family.

By week's end a massive police presence had quelled the violence, yet the anger remained on both sides, At a loss to explain the outburst in the generally stable Caribbean community, some observers attributed the violence to young people "from the projects" spurred on by "outside agitators" – in other words, to a native African-American "underclass." This analysis was half true at best. While most of the Caribbean community was horrified by the violence, many youths in the streets were immigrants and their grievances went far beyond the accident. "This is like a trench town," a Jamaican teenager told a reporter from *New York Newsday*, "The wicked and the rich have had their day. Now we can stand up and be heard." In fact, one of the most shocking things about Crown Heights was that resentment of the Hasidim seemed just as common among home-owning, middle-class Caribbean immigrants as among poor Blacks, whether native or foreign-born.

Caribbean community leaders, while denouncing the violence and condemning anti-Semitism, gave voice to their own longstanding grievances against the Hasidim. The easy equivalence they drew between the accident and the murder revealed the depth of their sense of historical injustice. For their part, the Hasidic leadership saw the killing as only the latest chapter in their own narrative of victimization. They were quick to describe the Crown Heights events as a "pogrom" and even to draw comparisons to Kristallnacht. Both "sides" – if one can talk about "sides" in a riot – perceived themselves as victims. Empathy was in critically short supply.

The African-American activists who dominated media coverage of the Crown Heights events proved more effective as lightning rods for popular discontent than the Caribbean leadership. But, as tempers cooled, many in the Caribbean community came to see these activists as exploiting a tragic situation. One of the most visible, Sonny Carson, hurt his own cause with clumsy attempts at ethnic politics, such as unfurling a Guyanese flag at Gavin Cato's funeral.[5]

The Crown Heights riot occurred less than two weeks before Labor Day. Understandably, city officials viewed the prospect of hundreds of thousands of carnival revelers on Eastern Parkway with considerable trepidation. Hasidic leaders called once more for the event to be canceled, and several African-American politicians suggested that it might be moved to a less charged location. Yet the WIADCA insisted that carnival should go forward on Eastern Parkway, as always. "Nothing is going to happen!" Lezama insisted on the Thursday before Labor Day. "I am going to walk down the Parkway and if the head Rabbi wants to come with me, he is welcome! This is what the city needs now!"

Going ahead with carnival was an enormous risk. Violence would gravely threaten its future and any overture to the Hasidim would certainly be attacked by some in the black community as a sell out: "a shame before God" is how Sonny Carson described it. Yet Lezama, who has made carnival his life's work, understood the community. He first made it clear that the event would not be moved and that he would not consider bowing to Hasidic pressure. Once that was established, however, he surprised many by putting aside years of bad feelings and inviting representatives of the Hasidic community to join the event. To the surprise of many more, they accepted. On Labor Day the crowd was a bit more subdued than usual, but it greeted the Rabbis politely, and the day came off without incident: "Peace on the Parkway" was the year's slogan. The deep wounds that drive New York's racial politics were not healed, or even forgotten. Yet, for most of the people on the Parkway, two weeks of tension had been enough. For one day, at least, peace on the Parkway seemed like a good idea.

The ambivalence with which the Caribbean community viewed the riot was, not surprisingly, best captured in a calypso. In 1992 the Mighty Sparrow's "Crown Heights Justice" was among the most memorable songs of that year's Trinidad Carnival, and the following Labor Day it could be heard throughout central Brooklyn. On the one hand it was a call for peace:

> Why do we have this confrontation?
> Violence will not solve our situation.
> We must learn to live in peace, live in Peace!
> Preacherman, Rabbi, Priest, live in Peace!

Sparrow goes on to invoke harmony between West Indians and Jews:

> History will show from slavery to holocaust,
> The whole world know, so we have to live in peace,
> No reason to fight like beasts; live in peace!
> Pain and suffering we have borne,
> Blacks and Jews should live as one,
> And celebrate; here life is great!
> No Swastika. No slave master!
> Instead we fight the endless fight,
> Right here, where we live, here in Crown Heights . . .

This call for harmony is followed by a reiteration of longstanding grievances:

> My reason for being upset is plain to see,
> The special treatment you get from Albany . . .
> No cops on my block to complain to,
> But police around the clock to protect you – from who?

The song's refrain put the emphasis on justice, along with a quote from Marcus Garvey:

> All we want is Justice!
> Don't deny the Justice!
> All the excuses, all the lies,

Can't stifle the children's cries.
For the little boy who died,
And the little girl who cried, Ethiopia will rise-again! . . .
The system is pregnant with fault, but it mustn't fail.
Guilty drivers go to jail!
That's what we call justice!

Conspicuous by its absence was any mention of "justice" for the Hasidic scholar who died not by accident but at the hands of an angry mob.

In 1994 controversy with the Hasidic community arose again, with the convergence of Labor Day and Rosh Hashanah. Again Lezama rebuffed attempts by city officials to have the event rescheduled. He and other West Indian community leaders argued that carnival might not be as old as Rosh Hashanah, but it was no less important and should be treated with the same respect. Yet once the City assured the continuation of the event on the Parkway, Lezama went out of his way to reassure the Hasidic leadership that the event would end on time, and to coordinate the activities of the two communities in a less confrontational manner. Some members of the Hasidic community could not be placated, while some Caribbeans and African-Americans criticized Lezama for being overly solicitous of Hasidic support. Yet the majorities in both communities seemed satisfied, if not completely happy, with the division of scarce public spaces at these sacred times of the year. And make no mistake about it: carnival has now sanctified both the Eastern Parkway site and the Labor Day date, for New York's West Indian community.

The controversy in 1994 also resulted in an increase in media attention. Carnival has given the New York media the opportunity to review the state of the Caribbean community and to question the identity of a people who are both black and immigrant in a city usually divided between Blacks and the children of immigrants. And the peaceful end of the 1994 controversy appealed to the media's comfort with ethnic celebration over racial confrontation. Thus in 1995, two hours of carnival were televised live for the first time, and Lezama's "aging mas men" occupied center stage. Their particular version of pan-Caribbean ethnic identity enjoyed a uniquely prominent position in the community's efforts to define itself, at least for the moment.

Since that time, with Lezama and his contemporaries beginning to fade from the scene, the WIADCA has begun to face an inevitable succession crisis. This largely voluntary association started out running a small block party and thirty years later found themselves running the largest regularly scheduled public event in North America. They generally did so with remarkable skill, grace, and energy. Yet they also resisted new blood, were reluctant to formalize their procedures, and were often suspicious of those outside their circle. Today, US-born and raised West Indian New Yorkers, many of non-Trinidadian origin, are coming to play a leadership role in the event. As these second-generation Caribbean New Yorkers take over carnival, it remains to be seen whether they will make it into something more in keeping with the typical "ethnic parade," along the lines of St Patrick's Day or the Puerto Rican Day parades. On the other hand, many of those who now "play mas" on the Parkway are, in fact, new immigrants, who came from a very different Caribbean than the one Lezama and his colleagues left more than half a century ago. Will these newcomers seek to "keep it real" in a traditional Port of Spain mode, as the growth of jouvay seems to suggest? It is, of course, too early to say. For now, carnival remains the place for presenting and dramatizing the idea of a Caribbean community in New York. So long as carnival remains in flux, it will continue to provide the social and temporal space in which notions of group identity can be played with and contested if never completely resolved. It will thus continue to interest anyone trying to make sense of the changing ethnic landscape of this increasingly global city.

NOTES

1　Portions of this chapter have been previously published in Philip Kasinitz, *Caribbean New York: Black Immigrants and the Politics of Race* (Ithaca: Cornell University Press, 1992) and are reprinted with permission.

2　Terminology becomes difficult when differentiating between Afro-Caribbean immigrants and other Black Americans. Both can and do use the term "African-American." For purposes of clarity, I use "West Indian" and "Afro-Caribbean" to refer to the immigrants and their children, "native African-American" to refer to blacks whose forebears have been in the US more than two generations, and "Blacks" to refer to both groups.

3　Lezama was actually born in Venezuela, to Trinidadian parents. Like many English-speaking West Indian immigrants born in Spanish-speaking nations, he considers himself West Indian, not Latino.

4　It is worth noting that the Black victims in the most celebrated cases of police brutality and mob violence over the last decade and a half have almost all been black immigrants, not native African-Americans: Michael Stewart, killed in Howard Beach, and Yusef Hawkins, killed in Bensonhurst, were from Trinidad; Patrick Dorismond, killed by the police, and Abner Louima, police torture victim, were both Haitian; Amadou Diallo, mistakenly shot forty-one times by the police, was from West Africa.

5　For more on Carson and his ambivalent relations with the Caribbean community see Kim (2000).

TRINIDAD CARNIVAL GLOSSARY

Carol Martin

Trinidadian carnival terms, like carnival, resist definitive definitions, making this glossary almost antithetical to carnival. Yet Trinidadian carnival terms indicate important distinctions between African, East Indian, and European influences while foregrounding Trinidadians' conception of carnival as a dynamic social and political event. So wherever possible this glossary includes multiple spellings, resulting from transcriptions of terms from a vibrant oral culture, competing definitions, and multiple histories. The aim of assembling this glossary is to indicate, from sometimes competing and contradictory explanations, an understanding of what carnival – a defining event of Trinidad and Tobago culture – has been and what it is becoming.

[Editor's note: For this volume some features, such as capitalization and spelling, have been normalized for the sake of consistency, though in Trinidadian usage, they are not so standardized. We have, however, left the multiple spellings that reflect the richness of an oral culture in the glossary, which now contains variants the reader may not find in the text. However, some textual variants remain, as for instance the variation between mas' and mas, or the capitalization of Jouvay or Grandstand and North Stand, when such terms are used with particular emphasis.]

Terms in *italics* have their own entries in the glossary.

authentic Indian   See *Black Indian* and *Fancy Indian*.

Baby Doll   A traditional carnival character in which girls demand financial support from accused "fathers" in the crowd. This mas now exists primarily as a revival of a mas that was popular in the 1930s and 1940s. See *traditional mas*.

bacchanal   Rowdy behavior, a party; any situation in which there is excessive confusion.

Bad Behaviour Sailors   Traditional carnival characters in sailor suits, often wearing slogans such as "Sailors Astray," who roll on the ground and in the gutter to simulate drunkenness. Some bad behaviour sailor costumes include a red and white cotton jersey fabric sack worn over the head with eyeholes and a dangling red phallic nose (sometimes referred to as "long-nose sailors"). Also known as Dirty Sailors.

bad johns   Street-toughened fighters connected to communities and *steelbands*, who aggressively defend territory, dignity, and honor.

band   This term denotes either a music band, such as a brass band or a calypso band, or a group of performers who masquerade ("play mas") together on carnival Monday or Tuesday or in Children's Carnival. In the latter case, the term may be used to designate one entire group of traditional characters (traditional character bands), of jouvay players who belong to one group (jouvay band), or one group of masqueraders, known as a mas band. A single mas band may have as few as twenty-five people or as many as ten thousand or more masqueraders. Each mas band is designated by a specific name, which often refers to the theme of the costumes in a particular year. The term also implies territorial gangs. See *calypso*, *devil bands*, *jouvay*, *mas bând*, and *traditional mas*.

Bat   A traditional carnival character who mimes bats.

bele, bélé, belle, belair, bel air   A dance, originally from the French *bel air*, known throughout the West Indies. Possibly it comes from the Bele tribe on the Senegal River, West Africa. In the nineteenth century, it was a topical satiric or eulogistic song, and also a drum dance.

Black Indian   A traditional carnival character with a painted black face inspired by African and indigenous peoples. Costumes are predominantly black, often with large, elaborate feathered and beaded headdresses of many kinds. Black Indians say they speak an unidentifiable but "original people's " language.

Black-and-white-face Minstrels   Minstrels in whiteface, who play banjos, guitars, or now most often *cuatros* and sing plantation songs from the southern US, and who developed from Trinidadians imitating American whites in blackface. Other instruments include clappers and chac-chacs.

Blue Devils   Covered in blue mud, spewing red drool to imitate blood, Blue Devils typically act berserk, sexual, and ravenous. To a degree their costumes are open to personal preference and can include pitchforks, various kinds of masks, wings, and horns. In Paramin, the mountain village home to an important Blue Devil band, laundry bluing is mixed with vaseline to make the mud. Blue Devils from Paramin also refer to themselves as *Jab Jabs* although they are more like *Jab Molassis* than Jab Jabs, both of whom are devils. See *Jab Jabs* and *Jab Molassi*.

bois, poui   The wooden stick used in *stickfighting*, from the French word for wood, *bois*. Poui is another name for bois, named for the poui tree whose wood is used to make the sticks. Bois can also be cut from gasparee, balata, or anare wood. Stickfighters give their sticks names such as "teaser" or "pleaser." A "mounted stick" is one that has been treated, often by an *obeah* priest, insuring injury to an opponent.

bongo wakes   All-night wakes for the dead at the home of the deceased in which bongo drums and other instruments are played.

Burrokeet, Burokit, Burroquite, Burokeet   A traditional carnival character in a donkey costume. From the Spanish *burroquito*, little donkey. The structure is made from wire covered with fabric or papier-mâché and a cloth that hangs from the frame to cover the masquerader's legs. Very familiar to European, Middle Eastern, and Indian communities, this masquerade predates medieval times; see *Soumarie*.

caiso, kaiso, cariso, caliso   Early names for calypso. See *calypso*.

calinda   See *kalinda*.

callaloo   A traditional Trinidad dish typically made of a mixture of ingredients including leaves of the dasheen plant, ochro (okra), crab, and salt meat. The term is sometimes popularly used to refer to the cultural mix that is found in Trinidad. Callaloo is also the name of Peter Minshall's mas-making company.

calypso   The music and rhythm native to Trinidad closely associated with *lavway*, the call-and-response of *stickfighting*. Stickfighting chants endowed calypso with rhythm, melodies, and a combative, satirical manner. Although the word is probably from the Hausa *caiso*, a praise/critical singer of West Africa, when it was transcribed into English in the mid twentieth century its reference was changed to Calypso, the Greek muse of music and daughter of the Titan Atlas.

Calypso Monarch, Calypso King   The traditional calypso title of "Calypso King" was changed to "Calypso Monarch" in the 1970s when Calypso Rose was the first woman to win this title.

canboulay, *cannes brulees*, *cannes brûlées*   Derived from the French for "burning cane" (though other definitions as improbable as the patois for "cane rat" have been suggested). Canboulay is a celebration of resistance and emancipation, reenacting the days when enslaved Africans were driven with cracking whips to put out fires set by vandals on sugarcane plantations. Cane was also burnt before harvesting to control reptiles, centipedes, scorpions, and other pests. Thus, canboulay may have been associated both with dangerous and cruel forced labor and with the harvest festivals at the end of a season of heavy labor marked by the final burning of the cane stubs. Canboulay used to be celebrated on August 1, the date of emancipation. Subsequently it was moved to midnight of *Dimanche Gras*. Contemporary *jouvay*, which begins the two days of celebration before Ash Wednesday, was thus originally a celebration of emancipation. See *jouvay* and *Dimanche Gras*.

carnival dances   See *chip, fireman, jump-and-wave*, and *wine*.

carnival Monday   The Monday before Ash Wednesday when people play *jouvay* in the early morning hours. Carnival Monday any *band* (fancy or traditional) or individual may *play mas* with all or part of their costumes, or even in alternative attire. Carapichaima has the largest regional Monday carnival on the island. Monday evening *devil bands* congregate in Paramin mountain village. A variety of Monday night *fetes* and *steelband* competitions occur in various locations. See *jouvay, play mas, fete, devil bands*, and *steelband*.

carnival Tuesday   This is the last day of carnival before Ash Wednesday. It is the day all the *pretty mas*, the pageantry, the big *mas bands* come out into the streets. Revelers come into the streets as early as 8:00 a.m. to *play mas* at the many competition sites and anywhere they feel like it. The day ends with *las lap*.

Cedula of Population, Cédula de Población   The invitation, issued first in 1776 and then extended in 1783, by King Charles III of Spain for foreigners to settle in Trinidad. A memorandum from Grenadian French planter Roume de St Laurent, who visited Trinidad in 1777, initiated the immigration. All foreign settlers had to be Roman Catholic subjects of nations in alliance with Spain, and had to agree to abide by Spanish laws. This migration – fueled by the incentive of free land – created a large French population within the Spanish state. Land was also given to Free Colored and African Creole planters; those who had fought with England in the war of 1812 took up this offer.

chantwell, chantrel, chantuelle, shantwell   The lead singer of *canboulay* and *kalinda* bands, an early version of a calypsonian who calls for the response in a call-and-response song. Also, the lead singer in Shango and Rada worship. From the French *chanterelle*, solo singer.

chip, chipping, chippin, chippin'   Shuffling to the down beat of a carnival song in a manner that has subtle rhythmic reverberations in the rest of the body. Chippin is a ubiquitous, simple carnival dance uniting people – young and old – in a pulsing flow of group movement. Everyone who *plays mas* chips.

chutney   A bawdy folk music from India brought by indentured laborers.

chutney soca, soca chutney   The fusion of African and East Indian music of Trinidad and Tobago. Chutney soca mixes African and East Indian rhythms, uses Hindi words and Indian instruments such as the harmonium and hand drum, and Indian dances. Chutney soca includes contributions of East Indians such as Sandar Popo and Drupartee Ramgoonai.

Creole   In Trinidad, Creole designates identification with both foreign ancestry and native birth. In the nineteenth century, there were two Creole traditions: French and African. More recently this idea of Creole has been contested by some Indo-Trinidadians who have begun to identify themselves as Indo-Creole. The term is also used to indicate the hybrid Caribbean language also sometimes termed as French patois.

cuatro   A four-string guitar believed to have been introduced to Trinidad by Venezuelans, used in Christmas *parang* music as well as in minstrel and other bands. See *parang music*.

Dame Lorraine   A traditional carnival character who originally mocked French plantation wives. In carnival, cross-dressing men as well as women played the character, but it is now primarily a female masquerade. The all-over floral print dress of this *mas* is augmented with a padded posterior and breasts, and sometimes a pregnant belly. Formerly this masquerade took the form of Dame Lorraine plays.

devil bands   Bands that play *jouvay* by wearing horns and tails and carrying pitchforks. See *jouvay*.

Dimanche Gras   French for "fat Sunday," the Sunday before Ash Wednesday. Dimanche Gras activities of various kinds take place throughout the island, including the Dimanche Gras show at *Queen's Park Savannah*.

Dragon   A traditional carnival character traced back to 1908 when Patrick Jones, inspired by Dante's *The Inferno*, created a dragon-type depiction of Lucifer.

East Indian   A term used in the West Indies for those whose ancestors immigrated to the Caribbean from (any part of) India, initially used to distinguish them from native populations known as "Indian" or "Amerindian."

engine room   The percussion section of a *steelband* consisting of drums, tambourines, bells, brake drums, scrapers, and rattles. The engine room, like that of a ship, drives the band. Also the percussion section of a *Jab Molassi* band.

English Catholic   Trinidad term for the Church of England. English Catholic is an expansion of the acronym EC (English Church), used primarily in reference to schools.

extempo   A competitive form of *calypso* in which opponents extemporaneously compose and sing clever and humorous repartee; usually in a competitive duel.

Fancy Indian   A traditional carnival character also sometimes colloquially called *authentic Indian*. This character is arguably carnival's most carefully researched. Players' study goes beyond costumes and dance styles to include lifestyle, religious beliefs, and social structures especially of the Seminole, Cherokee, Cree, and Plain tribes. Fancy Indians wear war bonnets with brightly colored feathers, and their costumes have embroidery, beads, chokers, shields, and painted tunics.

Fancy Sailor   See *Fireman*, *King Sailor*, *Sailor*.

fete   A party with music, dance, and food, from the French word *fête* meaning festival.

Fireman   A traditional carnival character, costumed to aggrandize the image of the sailor who stokes the ship's engine. A type of *Fancy Sailor*, firemen wear blue or gray rather than white costumes, don pipes, black beards, goggles, hats that look like crowns, and long stokers with animal decorations such as dragons or fire at the tip. The firemen's dance is a distinctive sliding step that recalls stoking the engine. See *King Sailor*, *Sailor*.

flambeau   A glass bottle filled with a wick and kerosene and lit. Sometimes *Blue Devils* carry flambeaux and spit kerosene through the flames to create clouds of fire in the streets.

fol   The heart-shaped breastplate, usually covered with mirrors, worn by *stickfighters*, *Jab Jabs*, Clowns, *Neg Jardins*, and *Pierrot Grenades*.

free coloureds   Persons of color in the Caribbean, who were not enslaved. This term ordinarily refers to mulatto or mixed-blood brown-skinned persons, rather than darker-skinned Africans. They were part of the overall Creole population, given certain privileges but often restricted, even though they might be both wealthy and educated. In Trinidad, under Governor Chacon, they were forbidden to serve in the Cabildo, or government. Restrictions varied throughout the nineteenth century. When population is figured, the free coloured are often grouped with the Africans (or "blacks") as persons of color.

gayelle   The *stickfighting* arena – a circle created by spectators.

Grandstand, Grand Stand, Grand Stands   The permanent spectator stand on the south side of the *Queen's Park Savannah* in Port of Spain.

Guarahoon, Warahoon, Warraoun, Guarrahoon   A traditional carnival character derived from the Guaro people of the Orinoco River region of Venezuela who, until the 1930s, regularly rowed in their pirogues to Trinidad. There are two opposing descriptions of Guarahoons: painted red with *rookoo* dye and wearing entirely red clothing and zig-zagging through the streets; and, painted black suggesting a reference to *Black Indians* and runaway enslaved Africans who intermarried with native Indian tribes. Guarahoons are also colloquially called *Red Indians* and, less frequently, *Wild Indians*. Until the 1950s, Guarahoons were said to have spoken several authentic Indian languages.

iron band   A predecessor to *steelbands*, iron bands consist of brake drums and oil drums.

Jab Jab   A traditional carnival character that looks like a happy medieval European clown but is nevertheless a whip-carrying devil. A Jab Jab wears a painted mask made of thin wire mesh (probably buckram) covering his entire face. His costume consists of red and yellow, red and black, or yellow and black horizontal striped dagged shirts and pants. Marabou feathers line the seams of his often sequined and appliquéd shirt and pants. His head is hooded, and his costume can also be embellished with a cape and breastplate. The Jab Jabs' fierceness is revealed in their songs and chants. Traditionally, they attack rival groups of Jab Jabs. They crack their whips in the air and challenge one another to exchange lashes. Jab Jab derives from the French *diable*, modulated into the patois *jiable* and from that to Jab Jab, twin devils or double devil. Blue Devils in Paramin call themselves Jab Jabs (or Jabs).

Jab Molassi, Jab Molassie, Jab Molasi, jabmalassie   A traditional carnival devil character. A Jab Molassi's costume consists of covering the entire body, including face and hair, with originally molasses, and now mud, tar, and/or grease, often in different colors – blue, red, white. *Blue Devils* are a form of Jab Molassi.

jam and wine   See *wine*.

jamette, jamet   Jamette or jamet refers to followers of *canboulay* bands in the latter half of the nineteenth-century carnival. Carnival during this period is sometimes called "jamette carnival." Jamette also refers to women who followed *kalinda*. Later its usage designated prostitutes and street-tough women who followed *steelbands*. A word of disputed origins, jamette may be from the French *diametre* meaning boundary, border.

jouvay, j'ouvert, jouvert, jourvert, jour ouvert, jou ouvert   Trinidadian jouvay is derived from the French *jour ouvert*, the opening day of carnival which begins (often officially 2:00 a.m.) the Monday morning before Ash Wednesday. Jouvay is a nocturnal *mas* that breaks up shortly after dawn. Thousands of revelers in old clothes covered with mud, or as *Blue* or *Red Devils*, or drenched in black oil (Oil Men) fill the streets. They *chip* and *wine* as they follow steelbands or sound systems on tractor-trailors, or they create their own music by beating biscuit tins. Contemporary jouvay, the two days of celebration before Ash Wednesday, was originally a celebration of emancipation. Especially among middle-class Trinidadians "j'ouvert" has again regained popular usage. For some, the French pronunciation obscures the Trinidadian transformation of carnival from a celebration of the European plantocracy to the African-inspired carnival of emancipation.

jouvay devil bands   Jouvay devil bands *chip* to big trucks carrying massive and powerful sound systems, to *pan* carried through the streets on street racks, or to rhythms beaten on biscuit tins the Monday morning before Ash Wednesday. The registration fee for a jouvay devil band may include the cost of a costume, drinks on the road, and perhaps a *fete* in a jouvay yard before going on the road.

jump-and-wave   An exuberant dance of simultaneous jumping and waving the arms that, when done in large groups of masqueraders, creates an elating sense of mass movement – the individual in continuous bodily flow with the group.

jump up   To participate in carnival masquerade, especially *pretty mas*. The term also describes those who crash a band or play *las lap* in street clothes. A man might jump up in a band in street clothes to protect his girlfriend or keep her company.

kalinda, kalenda, calinda, calenda, calender, calenda, batille bois The *stickfight*, its dance, and its songs derived from a mock-combat dance of African origin that was a popular form of entertainment on plantations throughout the islands. Perhaps partially derived from quarterstaffs, the hardwood sticks the enslaved carried to beat snakes, officially banned in 1810. The kalinda is the dance referred to by French planters as the origin of *canboulay*. Gatka is a stickfight dance practiced by Trinidadians of East Indian descent. (Forms of East Indian martial arts that may be related to gatka include parikanda, the martial art related to Chhau dances of Orissa and Bihar in north India, and the Punjabi gutka.) See *stickfighting*.

kalinda chants Chants handed down from one generation of *chantwells* to the next, used to embolden *stickfighters*.

King Sailor, Fancy Sailor A traditional character who wears an elaborate costume consisting of multicolored large sequins, feathers, borders of bright tulle and feather boas, epaulets, medals, badges, small mirrors, and sometimes bottle caps affixed onto white shirts and pants and topped with a bandolier. The most famous leader of Fancy Sailor bands is recently retired Jason Griffith of Belmont (Port of Spain), who worked with Jim Harding, an originator of the sailor mas.

las lap Literally the very last time for music, dance, and drink before Ash Wednesday. A well-known las lap takes place in Port of Spain at the St James roundabout (traffic circle) in the cool of the night after the hot carnival Tuesday. With a slow and softer tempo, las lap is an opportunity to wind down. At midnight the final ritual takes place when the police van arrives to end the action, signaling the end of carnival for the year.

lavway The *calypso* call-and-response, also used in *stickfighting*. A good lavway makes use of double entendres in a melodically interlocked call-and-response. A French patois word that comes from *le vrai* (the truth) or perhaps *le voix* (the voice).

liming To spend time talking, laughing, drinking with other people.

mas, mas' Mas is the Trinidadian word for masquerade. Some people prefer "mas" to carnival. Mas is part of the triumvirate: *calypso*, *pan*, and *mas*. See *play mas*.

mas band A group of mas players ranging in size from a few dozen to several thousand often under the direction of one individual who designs the costumes. Mas bands compete for prizes in three major categories: large bands (always eight hundred or more, ranging up to as many as eight thousand in one band), medium bands (ordinarily 251–799), small bands (ordinarily 51–250), and, for the first time in 1998, mini-bands (11–50). These size categories may vary. Large bands have separate sections with different costumes unified by an overall theme, dancing or *jumping up* behind powerful sound systems mounted on big trucks. Costumes, performance, and music all comprise a band. Well-known past band-leaders include George Bailey, Stephen Lee Heung, and Harold Saldenah, among others. At present, some of the foremost bandleaders include Peter Minshall, Stephen Derek, Albert Bailey, Wayne Berkeley, and Richard Afong.

mas camp The location where the costumes of a specific *band* are assembled and distributed and where rehearsals, if any, are held.

masquerade To dress in carnival costume, dance, and parade in the streets. See *mas* and *play mas*.

Midnight Robber   A traditional carnival character who accosts spectators with an audacious barrage of slang and double talk aimed at getting them to give up their cash. Midnight Robber's speech – his robber talk – is dangerous, bombastic, and boastful. He brags about the strength of his villainy, his murders of millions. Often the robber is avenging wrongs done to his family generations ago. The Midnight Robber's costume includes a whistle to announce himself, frilly trousers, an embroidered shirt, a cape, a fake gun or dagger, and a huge brimmed hat usually adorned with items depicting the theme of the robber's speech for that year. A coffin often appears on either the robber's hat or his shoes. The robber can be dressed fully in black, or he may dress as a Fancy Robber wearing an excess of decorations. The Midnight Robber disputably originates in the traditions of Western African griots or storytellers with influence also from American western movies.

military mas   Mas that includes representations of any form of military.

minstrels   See *Black-and-white-face Minstrels*.

Moko Jumbie   When this stilt-walking traditional carnival character is asked where he is from, he responds that he has walked all the way across the Atlantic Ocean from the West Coast of Africa. A Moko Jumbie is the spirit of Moko, the *Orisha* (god) of fate and retribution who emphasizes that even as he endured centuries of brutal treatment he remains "tall, tall, tall." His head touches the sky, as he stands astride the crossroads to waylay unwary late-night travelers. Moko Jumbies are found throughout the West Indies. Traditional Moko Jumbies wear long pants or skirts (covering the stilts) and cover their faces. Now, any stilt walker in carnival might be called a Moko Jumbie.

mounted stick   A *bois* that has been treated or ritually poisoned by an *obeah* healer to insure injury to an opponent.

mud mas   Mud mas is played during *jouvay* following *Dimanche Gras*; also sometimes played on *carnival Monday* and *Tuesday*. Revelers coming from *fetes*, performances, and their homes cover themselves with brown, red, white, green, or blue mud and dance through the street until dawn. Some feel that experiencing sunrise after dancing all night covered with mud is a mystical or transcendental experience essential to carnival.

National Carnival Commission (NCC)   The National Carnival Commission of Trinidad and Tobago succeeded the Carnival Development Committee (CDC), and was formed in 1991 to make carnival a viable national, cultural, and commercial enterprise; to provide a managerial and organizational infrastructure for presentation and marketing of carnival performances and products; and to establish ongoing research and preservation of carnival.

Neg Jardin, Negre Jardins, Negres Jardins, Negue Jardin   An early masquerade, apparently played by liberated Trinidadians in satiric mockery of their former enslavement and by plantation owners as derisive imitation of the enslaved.

North Stands, North Stand   The temporary viewing stand built each year in the *Queen's Park Savannah* across the stage from the *Grand Stands*. In the North Stands groups of observers, known as posses, stake out and claim their viewing territory for carnival competitions. North Stand viewers have a mystique of participation – chanting, waving, dancing – that carries throughout the carnival season but is strongest at the *Panorama* prelims. However, since 2002 the prelims have been held in individual pan yards, changing the rhythm of the season and challenging the mystique of the North Stands on prelim day.

obeah   A West African system of medicine which uses skulls, bones, shells, and feathers and is often a theme in carnival bands.

ole mas, old mas, ol' mas   An old style of satiric and parodical masquerade involving acting out puns. Old clothes, also an important part of *jouvay*, are usually worn. Some now resist the use of this term, preferring *traditional mas* instead.

Orisha, Orixa   In Trinidad, Orisha is the traditional religion of people descended from the Yoruba of West Africa. Candomblé and Cuban Santeria are offshoots of this religion. In Trinidad, as well as elsewhere in the Caribbean and Brazil, the religion is commonly called *Shango* after one of its principal gods. Orisha means "god" in the Yoruba language of West Africa.

pan   A melodic percussion instrument unique to Trinidad, the steeldrum, made initially out of discarded oil drums. Sometimes refers to other metal containers such as biscuit tins, or to the music created by beating pan. See *Panorama, pan rand de neck, pan yard*, and *steel band*.

Panorama   The carnival season *steelband* competition begun in 1963, with the finals currently held on the weekend before Ash Wednesday. Under the control of Pan Trinbago, Panorama has four competition divisions: North, South, East, and West. It is divided into preliminary competitions (prelims), semifinals, and finals. Regional competitions are part of the national competition, though each region has its own champion. Panorama prelims are legendary for the energy of its supporters in the *North Stands* of the Queen's Park Savannah, though since 2002 prelims have been held in the pan yards.

pan round de neck   A *steelband* that carries its pans suspended from a sash tied around the neck. Also called traditional steelband. This is an early form of *pan* that is still played competitively.

pan yard   The practice area and home of a *steelband*. The concept of "yard" merges the Trinidad concept of barracks with the African idea of a central space surrounded by dwellings, and includes a sense of home as well as a gathering place. Pan yards are where pannists and others often *lime* as well as play pan, and may have seats for spectators and vending stands. See *pan*.

parang   Traditional Spanish-Trinidadian Christmas music involving serenading from house to house and, in more recent times, playing private and public performances and competitions during the long parang season lasting from early October to January 6.

patois   See *Creole*.

picong   An acerbic, satirical, or taunting verbal exchange.

Pierrot Grenade   A traditional carnival character, a jester in the guise of a schoolmaster, with pretensions to learning while dressed in rags. The proof of Pierrot Grenade's wisdom is his ability to spell any polysyllabic word, in his own unique way, weaving a story with each syllable. His costume consists of many small strips of brightly colored fabric, sometimes a book, a schoolmaster's whip, and previously – although not necessarily now – a mask or face paint. The name is French patois for a Grenadian clown.

Pissenlit, Pisse en Lit, Pisenlit   Performed at least until the 1950s when it was finally outlawed for vulgarity (having been periodically outlawed earlier, as in 1895), Pissenlit was played by men dressed as women in transparent nightgowns and carrying or wearing only menstrual cloths stained with blood. In French, *pis en lit* means to piss in bed. Occasionally revived today.

play mas, play mas', masquerade, play mask   To put on a costume and participate in a *mas band* or *jump up* in the streets. This is the key action of carnival from which everything else comes. The expression "to play mas" is part of Trinidadian vernacular, connected to the idea "to play yourself" or "do your thing." See *mas*, *band*, and *jump up*.

poui   See *bois* and *kalinda*.

pretty mas, fancy mas   Today's dominant form of masquerade emphasizing beautiful costumes with elaborate decorations. To some extent, pretty mas developed as middle-class participation in carnival increased, although the Afro-Creole carnival also emphasized "dressing up and looking good," from early on in the nineteenth century. Some feel that growth of pretty mas has led to the decline of traditional characters, the eclipse of *ole mas*, and commercialization of carnival. Many pretty mas costumes are now decorated bikini-style garments.

Queen's Park Savannah   The Queen's Park Savannah was sold by the Pechier family to the people of Trinidad and Tobago in 1817. The family reserved a lot of 6,000 square feet to be used as a family burial ground. The Savannah served as cricket and football grounds with no permanent structure for either. However, as early as the 1850s horseracing paddocks, grandstands, and a racecourse were built under the patronage of Governor Lord Harris. After the Victory Carnival of 1919, some carnival competitions were held in the Savannah, which slowly became the central competitive arena for carnival. A permanent grandstand was eventually erected on the south side.

rapso   Rapso combines rap and *calypso*, and was influenced by the *chantwell* and the speech of traditional characters such as the *Midnight Robber* and *Pierrot Grenade*. Brother Resistance, one of rapso's major originators, described rapso as the poetry of *calypso*, the consciousness of *soca*, and the power of the word. See *calypso* and *soca*.

Red Indian   A colloquial name now considered a misnomer for *Guarahoon*. The confusion of Red Indian with Guarahoon probably originates with conflating North American Indians with the *mas* derived from the Guaro of Venezuela in which the skin is covered with red dye.

Road March   A music competition on the streets of Port of Spain on carnival Monday and Tuesday. The *calypso* or *soca* which is played most often as *mas bands* pass through the downtown performance venue or cross the *Queen's Park Savannah* stage on those two days is ruled the Road March winner for the year. Thus, this competition is determined entirely by what song those who control the music trucks providing music for the masqueraders choose to play as the *bands* cross the stage or through the venue. There is no predetermined agreement about this music.

rookoo, roucou   A berry whose juice is used for red color, especially for *Guarahoons*.

Sailor   A traditional carnival character dating to the nineteenth century, influenced by American naval presence during World War II. There are several specific types of sailors, each with its own costumes and dances or movements. See *Bad Behaviour Sailors*, *Fancy Sailors*, *firemen*, and *King Sailor*.

Shango   One of the principal Yoruba gods of West Africa, the Caribbean, and Brazil. The religion itself is often called Shango in Trinidad. See *Orisha*.

soca   Described by Ras Shorty I, one of the main originators, as the soul of *calypso*, soca is a fusion of East Indian rhythms with the African musical structure of calypso inflected with influences from North American soul music. Sometimes identified as "party music," today soca is a generic term used for most of the new music coming out of Trinidad and Tobago.

Soumarie, Sou-marie, Sumari   A traditional carnival character consisting of an Indian horse and rider. An East Indian version of *Burokeet*.

sound system   Mobile amplification systems consisting of many bass boxes, mid-range boxes, high-end boxes, and amps hauled through the streets on a sound-blasting juggernaut eighteen-wheel tractor-trailer. Thousands of masqueraders follow each of these mobile sound systems, a part of carnival since the 1970s.

steelband, steel band, steel orchestra   Musical groups consisting of steeldrums, with a percussive *engine room*, that emerged in Trinidad in the 1940s from the African working class. The music has an African aesthetic: repetitive, syncopated, with a strong beat and dense polyrhythms. Street orchestras also play European classical music and popular tunes.

stickfighter   One who practices the martial art of stickfighting. Stickfighers usually frequent a particular gayelle, which may have a recognized champion. They often challenge each other to stickfights within the *gayelle*. A "gayelle" is literally the circle in which a stickfight takes place, often in front of a pub. But the term also implies a collective sense of stickfighters who belong to one group, identified by the place of the gayelle. Stickfighters from one gayelle will not ordinarily fight others from the same gayelle in an open competition, though the competitions organized by the National Carnival Commission have challenged this practice.

stickfighting, stick fighting, stick play   A martial art probably originating in African stick play, enhanced in Trinidad with the sticks used on plantations for protection against snakes. Stickfighting is accompanied by drumming and by chants or songs called *lavways*, sung by singers known as *chantwells*. Stickfighting has a strong ritual element and involves dancing and clever footwork as well as fighting. There is also an Indian form of stickfighting, referred to in Trinidad as kalariyapayyatt or gatka and other kinds of Indian martial arts. See *kalinda*.

tamboo bamboo, tambour-bamboo, tambour bands   Polyrhythmic percussion made by beating bamboo sticks of varying lengths against the ground (hence "tambour" or drum). Probably derived from Ghana, this rhythmic beating led to beating metal piles by the youths of Laventille, who later invented the steel drum.

tassa drums   East-Indian-derived drums made from goat skins stretched over clay bases. Tassa drums are carried with a shoulder strap and played with sticks. Large bass drums, struck by the hands, or by one hand and one stick, are sometimes called tassa.

traditional mas   Traditional mas includes traditional characters, *vintage calypso*, *pan*, and *ole mas*. Traditional mas bands are local and individual in tone as distinct from the massive *fancy mas* bands. In traditional mas, the interactions of traditional characters are typically

293

on a small scale. Characters interact with spectators in close proximity. *Baby Dolls*, *Moko Jumbies*, *Blue Devils*, and *Midnight Robbers* provoke spectators into giving them money. The stories of *Pierrot Grenades* are meant to be heard, as is the robber talk of the *Midnight Robber* and the lost language of *Black Indians*. Both men and women now perform many traditional characters.

Victory Carnival of 1919   Banned for two years because of World War I, carnival resumed in 1919 with the Victory Carnival, organized by the newly established *Trinidad Guardian* newspaper, despite talk by the British colonial authorities of banning it for good, marking victory in war and for carnival. Carnival gradually became a national expression with extensive media coverage.

vintage calypso   An early narrative form of *calypso* in which calypsonians dressed in felt hats and tailored suits spun actual incidents into pointed social and political commentary.

White-face Minstrels   See *Black-and-White-face Minstrels*.

Wild Indians   Wild Indian is a term no longer acceptable to some people in Trinidad or Tobago as it connotes savagery. But it continues to be used as a reference to various forms of Amerindian masquerade.

wine, win', wining   Dancing emphasizing fluid pelvis rotations, either alone or in full physical contact front or back with another person. The expression comes from winding the hips in a circle. The erotic movement can be traced to various African dances. *Jam* and *wine* have approximately the same meaning.

An extended version of this glossary is printed in Milla Cozart Riggio (ed.), *The Drama Review*, 42(3): 220–35 (1998), Cambridge, MA: MIT Press.

WORKS CITED

UNPUBLISHED INTERVIEWS

Abbott, Stella, interview with Dawn Batson, Barataria, Trinidad (June 6, 2002).

Anonymous San Fernando Amerindian Masquerader, interview with Hélène Bellour and Samuel Kinser (1996).

Barrow, Carlton "Zigilee," interview with Kim Johnson, Port of Spain (February 20, 1993).

Beddoe, Jeffrey, personal communication with Kim Johnson (n.d.).

Brancker, Nicholas, interview with Jocelyne Guilbault, Barbados (March 12, 1997).

Brown, Ernest, personal communication with Kim Johnson (1997).

Christopher, Bolo, personal communication with Carlisle Chang (1997).

Constance, Zeno, interview with Burton Sankeralli (1997).

Edwards, Frances, personal communication with Jacob D. Elder and Lennox Pierre (1954).

Ganase, Pat, interview with Skye Hernandez (1997).

Girdharrie, Solo, interview with Skye Hernandez (1997).

Grant, Eddy, as interviewed on *The Breakfast Club*, TV 6, Port of Spain (January 28, 1994).

Howe, Darcus, interview with Geraldine Connor (n.d.).

Howe, Darcus, interview with Max Farrar (June 8, 2002).

Jules, Neville, interview with Dawn Batson, Port of Spain (June 6, 2002).

Jules, Neville, interview with Kim Johnson (1996).

Kitchener, Lord, interview with Gordon Rohlehr (1986).

Lezama, Carlos, interview with Philip Kasinitz (1991).

Mark, Raymond, "One Man," interview with Kim Johnson (1995).

Mullard, Chris, interview with Max Farrar (September 27, 2002).

Pierre, Lennox, interview with Tony Hall on *Late Night Lime*, produced by Christopher Laird (1990).

Ravi Ji (Ravindranath Maharaj), interview with Burton Sankeralli (1997).

Ravi Ji (Ravindranath Maharaj), interview with Milla Cozart Riggio (2004).

Sanoir, Andrew, interviews with Martin W. Walsh (1997, 1998, 2000).

Sanoir, James, interviews with Martin W. Walsh (1997, 1998, 2000).

Yearwood, Edwin, interview with Jocelyne Guilbault (Barbados, August 6, 1997).

TRINIDAD NEWSPAPERS

Chronicle

Daily News

Evening News

Fair Play

New Era

Palladium

Port-of-Spain Gazette

Recorder

Review

San Fernando Gazette

Sunday Guardian

Trinidad Guardian

SOUND RECORDINGS

—— (1992) *Trinidad: 1912–1941*, Harlequin HQ CD, West Sussex, England: Interstate Music.

Andall, E. (nd, c 2000) *Oriki Ogun: A Suite of Chants to Ogun*, EACD 0006, Sealots, Port of Spain: Coral Studios.

Belafonte, H. (1988) *Harry Belafonte: All Time Greatest Hits*, 6877–2–R, RCA, BMG Music.

Coltrane, J. (1974) *Interstellar Space*, ASD9277, ABC Impulse.

Lord Invader (Rupert Grant) (1946) *Calypso at Midnight*, New York: Rounder.

—— (1955) *Labor Day*, Folkways Records.

Louisana Repertory Jazz Ensemble of New Orleans, *Marching, Ragging and Mourning: Brass Band of New Orleans*, 1900–20.

Mighty Sparrow, The (1963) "The Outcast," in *The Outcast*, NLP 4199, National.

—— (1976) *Mas in Brooklyn*, Recording Artists Productions.

—— (1992) *Crown Heights Justice*, Charlie's Records 004.

Mitchum, R. (1995) *Calypso Is Like so, Scamp*, SCP 9701–2, Capital Records.

Ras Shorty I (1978) *Soca Explosion*, SCR 1004. New York: Charlie's Records.

Soca Divas (2000), Rituals, CO7200.

White, M. (1991) *Dr. Michael White Crescent City Serenade*, Antillies: Island Records.

BOOKS AND ARTICLES

Abimbola, W. (1975) "Iwapele: The Concept of Good Character in Ifa Literary Corpus," in W. Abimbola (ed.) *Yoruba Oral Tradition*, Ife: University of Ife.

Abiodun, R. (1994) "Understanding Yoruba Art and Aesthetics: the Concept of Ashe," *African Arts*, 27 (3): 68–78, 102.

Ado, H. (1986) *Imperialism: The Permanent Stage of Capitalism*, Tokyo: United Nations University.

Aho, W.R. (1987) "Steelband Music in Trinidad and Tobago: the Creation of a People's Music," *Latin American Music Review*, 8 (1): 26–58.

Allen, R. and Slater, L. (1998) "Steel Pan Grows in Brooklyn: Trinidadian Music and Cultural Identity," in R. Allen and L. Wilcken (eds) *Island Sounds in the Global City: Caribbean Popular Music and Identity in New York*, New York: ISAM and the New York Folklore Society.

Alleyne, B. (2002) *Radicals Against Race: Black Activists and Cultural Politics*, Oxford and New York: Berg.

Alleyne, M.R. (1995) "The Transnationalisation of Caribbean Music: Capitalism and Cultural Intertextuality," PhD dissertation, University of the West Indies.

Allsopp, R. (1996) *Dictionary of Caribbean English Usage*, Oxford: Oxford University Press.

Amkpa, A. (1993) "Floating Signification," *Hybrid*, 3, June/July: 5–6.

Anderson, M. and Kreamer, C. (1989) *Wild Spirits, Strong Medicine: African Art and the Wilderness*, New York: The Center for African Art.

Anthony, M. (1989) *Parade of the Carnivals of Trinidad 1839–1989*, Port of Spain: Circle Press.

Appadurai, A. (1996) *Modernity at Large: Cultural Dimensions of Globalization*, Minneapolis: University of Minnesota Press.

Arnoldi, M.J. and Kreamer, C. (eds) (1995) *Crowning Achievements: African Arts of Dressing the Head*, Los Angeles: Fowler Museum of Cultural History.

Aronson, L. (1980) "Patronage and Akwete Weaving," *African Arts*, 13 (3): 62–6, 91.

Aumis, F. *et al.* (1992) *Femmes: livre d'or de la femme créole*, Pointe-a-Pitre: Raphy Diffusion.

Bakhtin, M. ([1968] 1984) *Rabelais and his World*, tr. Helene Iswolsky, Bloomington: Indiana University Press.

Balliger, R. (2000) "Noisy Spaces: Popular Music Consumption, Social Fragmentation, and the Cultural Politics of Globalization in Trinidad," PhD dissertation, Stanford University.

Barnard, M. (1996) *Fashion as Communication*, London: Routledge.

Barnes, R. and Eicher, J. (eds) (1993) *Dress and Gender*, Oxford and Providence: Berg.

Batson, D. (1995) "Pan into the Twenty-first Century: The Steelband as an Economic Force," PhD dissertation, University of Miami.

Bayley, F.W.N. (1833) *Four Years Residence in the West Indies*, London: William Kidd.

Bellour, H., Johnson, K., and Riggio, M. (2002) *Renegades: The History of the Renegades Steel Orchestra of Trinidad and Tobago*, London: Macmillan Caribbean.

Benewick, R. (1972) *The Fascist Movement in Britain*, London: Penguin.

Benitez-Rojo, A. (1995) "The Polyrhythmic Paradigm: the Caribbean and the Post-modern Era," in Lawrence Hyatt and Rex Nettleford (eds) (1995) *Race, Discourse and the Origin of the Americas – A New World View*, Washington DC: Smithsonian Institution Press.

Berger, J. (1972) *Ways of Seeing*, London: Penguin.

—— (1984) *And Our Faces, My Heart, Brief as Photos*, London: Writers and Readers Publishing Cooperative Society.

Berkley, Lady (1994) *The London Times*, December 7: n.p.

Bettelheim, J. (1979) "The Afro-American Jonkonnu Festival: Playing the Forces and Operating the Cloth," PhD dissertation, Yale University.

Bhabha, H. (1994) *The Location of Culture*, London: Routledge.

Billouin, H.S. (1883) *Fair Play*, March 18: n.p.

Birth, K. (1999) *Any Time Is Trinidad Time: Social Meanings and Temporal Consciousness*, Gainesville: University Press of Florida.

Blake, F.I.R. (1995) *The Trinidad and Tobago Steel Pan: History and Evolution*, Port of Spain: Felix I.R. Blake.

Blake, W. ([1794] 1967) "London" in *Songs of Innocence and Experience*, Paris: The Trianon Press.

Blood, P.R. (2000) "And a Child Shall Lead Them," *Trinidad Guardian*, November 25: 8.

Borde, P.G.L. (1876) *The History of Trinidad under the Spanish Government*, vols I and II, reprinted (1982) Port of Spain: Paria Publishing.

Boyke, R., coordinator (1985) Conversation from "Calypso Symposium." Office of Key Publications, Port of Spain, January 7.

Brathwaite, K. (1973) *The Arrivants: A New World Trilogy*, Oxford: Oxford University Press.

Brereton, B. (1979) *Race Relations in Colonial Trinidad*, Cambridge: Cambridge University Press.

—— (1981) *A History of Modern Trinidad, 1783–1962*, Kingston: Heinemann.

Brierly, J.N. (1912) *Trinidad Then and Now*, Port of Spain: J.N. Brierly.

Brown, E. (1990) "Against the Odds: The Impact of Social Forces on Carnival, Calypso and Steelband in Trinidad," *Black Perspectives in Music*, 18: 81–100.

Bryce-Laporte, R.S. (1972) "Black Immigrants: The Experience of Invisibility and Inequality," *Journal of Black Studies*, 3: 29–56.

Buff, R. (1997) " 'Mas' in Brooklyn: Immigration, Race and the Cultural Politics of Carnival," in J. Adjaye and A. Andrews (eds) *Language, Rhythm, and Sound: Black Popular Cultures into the Twenty-first Century*, Pittsburgh: University of Pittsburgh Press, 221–40.

—— (2001) *Immigration and the Political Economy of Home: West Indian Brooklyn and American Indian Minneapolis 1945–1992*, Berkeley: University of California Press.

Buhle, P. (1988) *C.L.R. James: The Artist as Revolutionary*, London and New York: Verso.

Burke, P. ([1978] 1994) *Popular Culture in Early Modern Europe*, Aldershot: Ashgate.

Burton, R. (1997) *Afro-Creole: Power, Opposition, and Play in the Caribbean*, Ithaca: Cornell University Press.

Buscher, G. (1869, rpt 1969) "John Jacob Thomas," in J.J. Thomas, *The Theory and Practice of Creole Grammar*, Port of Spain: The Chronicle Publishing Office, rpt London: New Beacon Books.

Caillois, R. (1950) *L'Homme et le Sacré*, Paris: Gallimard.

Campbell, C. (1992) *Cedulants and Capitulants*, Port of Spain: Paria Publishing.

Carmichael, (Mrs) A.C. (1833) *Domestic Manners and Social Conditions of the White, Coloured, and Negro Population of the West Indies*, 2 vols, reprinted (1961) London: Treacher.

Carnival Program Book (1974, 1976, 1977, 1983) West Indian American Carnival Day Association: Brooklyn, New York.

Carr, A. (1965) "Jour Ouvert: An Aspect of Trinidad Carnival," in Downtown Carnival Competition Programme, n.p.

Catannés, H. (1923) *Les Fastnachtspiele de Hans Sachs*, Strassbourg.

Chalamelle, E.F. (1901) *Some Reflections on the Carnival of Trinidad*, Port of Spain: Fair Play.

Cohen, A. (1980a) "Drama and Politics in the Development of a London Carnival," *Man*, 15: 65–86.

—— (1980b) *The Politics of Elite Culture: Explorations in the Dramaturgy of Power*, Berkeley: University of California Press.

—— (1982) "A Polyethnic London Carnival as a Contested Cultural Performance," *Ethnic and Racial Studies*, 5 (1): 23–41.

—— (1993) *Masquerade Politics: Explorations in the Structure of Urban Cultural Movements*, Berkeley: University of California Press, in conjunction with Oxford: Berg.

Cohen, R. (1997) *Global Diasporas: An Introduction*, London: UCL Press.

Collins, W. (1961) *Jamaican Migrant*, London: Routledge & Kegan Paul.

Connor, G. (2002) *Carnival Messiah*, Leeds: West Yorkshire Playhouse.

Constance, Z. (1991) *Tassa, Chutney and Soca: The East Indian Contribution to the Calypso*, San Fernando, Trinidad: Constance, Z., 43.

Cooper, C. (1993) *Noise in the Blood: Orality, Gender and the "Vulgar" Body of Jamaican Popular Culture*, London: Macmillan.

Cowley, J. (1996) *Carnival, Canboulay and Calypso: Traditions in the Making*, Cambridge: Cambridge University Press.

Crowley, D. (1956) "The Traditional Masques of Carnival," *Caribbean Quarterly*, 3 & 4: 42–90, 194–223, reprinted in G. Benon (ed.) *Trinidad Carnival*, Port of Spain: Paria Publishing, 42–90.

Dabydeen, D. (1988) "Man to Pan," *New Statesman & Society*, August 26: 40–1.

DaMatta, R. (1991) *Carnivals, Rogues, and Heroes: An Interpretation of the Brazilian Dilemma*, tr. John Drury, Notre Dame, Ind.: Notre Dame University Press.

Danny, P. (1996) "Sonny Mann Beats Them All," *Express*, January 29: 3.

Darway, N. (2002) Lecture on St James contribution to the steelband, given at the "We Beat Festival" at the St James Amphitheater, St James, June 3.

Day, C. (1852) *Five Years' Residence in the West Indies*, 2 vols, London: Colburn and Co.

Decima (1991) *A Report to the Caribbean Cultural Committee on Caribana, 1990 Survey*, Toronto: Decima Research.

DeLeon, R. (1988) *Calypso from France to Trinidad: 800 Years of History by the Roaring Lion*, Mount Lambert, Trinidad: Raphael DeLeon.

De Verteuil, A. (1984) *The Years of Revolt, Trinidad 1881–1884*, Port of Spain: Paria Publishing.

—— (1994) *The Germans in Trinidad*, Port of Spain: Litho Press.

De Verteuil, L.A.A. ([1858], 1884) *Trinidad: Its Geography, Natural Resources, Administration, Present Conditions and Prospects*, London: Ward and Hall; 2nd edition 1884: London and New York: Cassell.

Dickens, C. (1854) *Hard Times*, serially published in *Household Words*. London: April–October.

Drewal, H.J. (1977) "The Arts of Egungun among Yoruba Peoples," *African Arts* 11 (3): 18–19.

Drewal, M.T. and Drewal, H.J. (1983) *Gelede: A Study of Art and Feminine Power among the Yoruba*, Bloomington: Indiana University Press.

Dunn, C. (2001) *Brutality Garden: Tropicalia and the Emergence of a Brazilian Counterculture*, Chapel Hill: University of North Carolina Press.

—— (2002) "Tropicalia, Counterculture, and the Diasporic Imagination in Brazil," in C. Perrone and C. Dunn (eds) *Brazilian Popular Music and Globalization*, New York: Routledge, 72–95.

Elder, J.D. (1964) "Color, Music, and Conflict: A Study of Aggression in Trinidad with Reference to the Role of Traditional Music," *Ethnomusicology* 8: 129–36.

—— (1966) "Kalinda: song of the battling troubadors of Trinidad," *Journal of the Folklore Institute*, 3 (2): n.p.

—— (1969) *From Congo Drum to Steelband: A Socio-historical Account of the Emergence and Evolution of the Trinidad Steel Orchestra*, St Augustine, Trinidad: University of the West Indies.

Elie, J.P. (1990) *A Short History of Arima: 1749–1990*, Port of Spain: Jean Elie.

—— (1997) "The Amerindians of Santa Rosa de Arima: The Construction of an Ethnic Identity," M.A. thesis, University of London.

Espinet, C.S. and Pitts, H. (1944) *Land of the Calypso*, Port of Spain: C.S. Espinet and H. Pitts.

Falassi, A. (1987) "Festival: Definition and Morphology," in A. Falassi (ed.) *Time Out of Time*, Albuquerque: University of New Mexico Press.

Fanon, F. (1967) *Dying Colonialism*, New York: Grove Press.

Farrar, M. (2001) *A Short History of the Leeds West Indian Carnival, 1967–2000*, Leeds: West Yorkshire Archive Service. Accessible from the Leeds section of "Moving Here" on the UK's Public Record Office website at http://www.pro.gov.uk.

Farred, G. (ed.) (1996) *Rethinking C.L.R. James*, Oxford and Cambridge, MA: Blackwell.

Featherstone, M. (ed.) (1994) *Global Culture: Nationalism, Globalization and Modernity*, London: Sage.

Fleming, T. (1998) "Re-articulating Tradition, Translating Place: Collective Memories of Carnival in Leeds and Bristol," PhD dissertation, Department of Geography, University of Sheffield, England.

Foner, N. (2001) *Islands in the City*, Berkeley: University of California Press.

Foster, H.B. (1997) *New Raiments of Self: African-American Clothing in the Antebellum South*, Oxford: Berg.

Foucault, M. (1972) *The Archeology of Knowledge*, London: Tavistock Publications.

Franco, P. (2000) "The 'Unruly Woman' in Nineteenth-century Trinidad," *Small Axe 7*, March: 60–76.

Fraser, L.M. (1881) "History of Carnival," *C.O. 295/289*, no. 6460, 131, Colonial Office Correspondence, Trinidad: Public Records Office.

Frazer, Sir J. (1922) *The Golden Bough: A Study in Magic and Religion: Abridged Edition*, New York: Macmillan.

Freidenberg, J. and Kasinitz, P. (1990) "Los Rituales Publicos y la Politizacion de la Etnicidad en Nueva York," *Desarrollo Economico*, 117 (Junio): 109–32.

Friedmann, J. and Weaver, C. (1979) *Territory and Function: The Evolution of Regional Planning*, Berkeley: University of California Press.

Frith, S. (1996) "Genre Rules," in *Performing Rites: On the Value of Popular Music*, Berkeley: University of California Press, 75–95.

Fryer, P. (1984) *Staying Power: The History of Black People in Britain*, London: Pluto Press.

Gabbard, K. (1995) "Introduction: Writing the Other History," in K. Gabbard (ed.), *Representing Jazz*, Durham, NC: Duke University Press.

Gallaugher, A. (1995) "Constructing Caribbean Culture in Toronto: The Representation of Caribana," in A. Ruprecht and C. Taiana (eds) *The Reordering of Culture in the Hood: Latin America, the Caribbean and Canada*, Ottawa: Carleton University Press, 397–407.

Garaud, L. (1895) *Trois Ans à la Martinique*, Paris: Librairie D'Education Nationale.

Gilmore, D. (1998) *Carnival and Culture: Sex, Symbol, and Status in Spain*, New Haven: Yale University Press.

Glissant, E. (1995) "Creolization in the Making of the Americas," in Lawrence Hyatt and Rex Nettleford (eds) (1995) *Race, Discourse and the Origin of the Americas – A New World View*, Washington DC: Smithsonian Institution Press.

Goddard, G. (1991) *Forty Years in the Steelbands, 1939–1979*, London: Karia Press.

Goffman, E. (1965) "Attitudes and Rationalizations Regarding Body Exposure," in M.E. Roach and J. Eicher (eds) *Dress, Adornment and the Social Order*, New York: John Wiley & Sons, Inc.

Gonzalez, S. (1978) *Steelband Saga: A Story of the Steelband – the First 25 Years*, Port of Spain: National Heritage Library.

Gopinath, G. (1995) "Bombay, U.K., Yuba City: Bhangra Music and the Engendering of Diaspora," *Diaspora*, 4 (3): 303–30.

Gray, H. (2001) "Prefiguring a Black Cultural Formation: the new conditions of black cultural production," in D.T. Goldberg, M. Musheno, and L.C. Bower (eds) *Between Law and Culture: Relocating Legal Studies*, Minneapolis: University of Minnesota Press.

Grenier, L. (in press) "Circulation, Valorization and Location in Global Pop Music: the fame of Celine Dion in Quebec," in *Enciclopedia della Musica Einaudi*, Turin: Einaudi.

Grimm, J. and Grimm, W. (eds) (1812) *Kinder- und Hausmärchen*, Berlin: Verlage des Herausgebers.

Gupta, A. and Ferguson, J. (1992) "Beyond 'Culture': Space, Identity, and the Politics of Difference," *Cultural Anthropology*, 7 (1): 6–23.

Gutzmore, C. (1993) "Carnival, the State and the Black Masses in the United Kingdom," in W. James and C. Harris (eds) *Inside Babylon: The Caribbean Diaspora in Britain*, London: Verso.

Hall, H. (1982) "Inside Brooklyn's Carnival," *Everybody's Magazine*, November.

Hall, K. and Bern, D. (2000) *Contending with Destiny: The Caribbean in the 21st Century*, Kingston, Jamaica: Ian Randle Publishers.

Hall, S. (1989; 2nd edn 1996) "New Ethnicities," in D. Morley and K.-H. Chen, *Stuart Hall: Critical Dialogues in Cultural Studies*, London and New York: Routledge.

—— (1991) *Myths of Caribbean Identity*, Coventry: University of Warwick, Centre for Caribbean Studies.

—— (1997, rpt 2001) "The Spectacle of the 'Other,' " in Stuart Hall (ed.) *Representation: Cultural Representations and Signifying Practices*, London: Sage.

Hall, T. (1998a) " 'They Want to See George Band': Tobago mas according to George Leacock," in M. Riggio (ed.) *Trinidad and Tobago Carnival*, special edition of *The Drama Review*, 42 (3): 44–53.

—— (1998b) "Lennox Pierre: an interview by Tony Hall," in M. Riggio (ed.) *Trinidad and Tobago Carnival*, special edition of *The Drama Review*, 42 (3): 41.

Handelman, D. and Shulman, D. (1991) *Myths of Caribbean Identity*, Coventry: University of Warwick, Centre for Caribbean Studies.

—— (1997) *God Inside Out: Sivas' Game of Dice*, New York: Oxford University Press.

Harper, P. (1978) "Kitchener: Soca is Calypso," *Evening News*, January 4.

Harris, M. (1998) "The Impotence of Dragons: Playing Devil in the Trinidad Carnival," in M. Riggio (ed.) *Trinidad and Tobago Carnival*, special edition of *The Drama Review*, 42 (3): 108–23.

—— (2002) *Carnivals and Other Festivals*, Austin: University of Texas Press.

Harris, R. (1996) "Openings, Absences and Omissions: Aspects of the Treatment of 'Race', Culture and Ethnicity in British Cultural Studies," *Cultural Studies*, 10 (2), May.

Harvey, D. (1989). *The Condition of Postmodernity: An Enquiry into the Origins of Cultural Change*, Cambridge, MA: Basil Blackwell.

Hayden, D. (1995) *The Power of Place: Urban Landscapes as Public History*, Cambridge, MA: MIT Press.

Hearn, L. (1890; 2nd edn 1923) *Two Years in the French West Indies*, New York: Harper & Brothers Publishers.

Hernandez, E. (1998) "Carnival and the Commmunity in Tobago," in M. Riggio (ed.) *Trinidad and Tobago Carnival*, special edition of *The Drama Review*, 42 (3): 48–9.

Hernandez-Ramdwar, C. (1996) "De-coding Caribana: The Contradiction of a Canadian Carnival," Caribbean Studies Association, XXI Annual Conference, San Juan, Puerto Rico.

Hill, D.R. (1993) *Calypso Calaloo: Early Carnival Music in Trinidad*, Gainesville: University of Florida Press.

—— (1994) "A History of West Indian Carnival in New York to 1978," *New York Folklore*, 20 (1–2): 47–66.

Hill, D. and Abrahamson, R. (1980) "West Indian Carnival in Brooklyn," *Natural History*, 88: 72–84.

Hill, E. (1972; 2nd edn 1997) *Trinidad Carnival: Mandate for a National Theatre*, Austin: University of Texas Press and London: New Beacon.

Hintzen, P. (2001) *West Indian in the West: Self-representations in an Immigrant Community*, New York: New York University Press.

Hiro, D. (1992) *Black British, White British: A History of Race Relations in Britain*, 2nd edn, London: Paladin.

Ho, C.G.T. (2001) "Globalization and Diaspora-ization of Caribbean People and Popular Culture," *Wadabagei: A Journal of the Caribbean and its Diaspora*, 4 (1): 1–38.

Holquist, M. (1990) *Dialogism: Bakhtin and his World*, London and New York: Routledge.

Hollander, A. (1993 [1975]) *Seeing Through Clothes*, New York: Viking Press.

Honour, H. (ed.) (1977) *L'Amerique vue par l'Europe*, Paris: Editions des Musées Nationaux.

Houk, J.T. (1995) *Spirits, Blood, and Drums: The Orisha Religion in Trinidad*, Philadelphia: Temple University Press.

Howe, D. (1978) *The Road Make to Walk on Carnival Day*, London: Race Today Publications.

Hyatt, V.L. and Nettleford, R. (eds) (1995) *Race, Discourse and the Origin of the Americas – A New World View*, Washington DC: Smithsonian Institution Press.

Inniss, L.O. (1932) *Reminiscences of Old Trinidad*, Port of Spain: L.O. Innis.

Jacobs, C. (1969) "Now Birdie Speaks His Mind," interview with the Mighty Sparrow, *Trinidad Guardian*, March 2.

James, C.L.R. (1963) *Beyond a Boundary*, London: Hutchinson & Co.

—— (1980) *The Black Jacobins*, London: Allison & Busby.

—— (1985) *A History of Negro Revolt*, London: Race Today Publications.

Jasper, L. (2001) "Don't Spoil the Carnival," *Guardian* [London], August 22.

Julien, I. and Mercer, K. (1996) "De Margin and de Center," in D. Morley and K.-H. Chen (eds) *Stuart Hall: Critical Dialogues in Cultural Studies*, London and New York: Routledge.

Kasinitz, P. (1992) *Caribbean New York: Black Immigrants and the Politics of Race*, Ithaca: Cornell University Press.

Kasinitz, P. and Freidenberg, J. (1987) "Caribbean Public Celebrations in New York City: the Puerto Rican Parade and the West Indian Carnival," in C. Sutton and E. Chaney (eds) *Caribbean Life in New York City: Social and Cultural Dimensions*, Staten Island, NY: Center for Migration Studies, 327–49.

Keith, M. (1993) *Race, Riots and Policing*, London: UCL Press.

Kennedy, D. (2003) *Oxford Encyclopedia of Theatre and Performance*, Oxford: Oxford University Press.

Kim, C.J. (2000) *Bitter Fruit*, Princeton: Princeton University Press.

King, A. (ed.) (1991) *Culture, Globalization and the World-System*, London: Macmillan.

Kinser, S. (1990) *Carnival American Style: Mardi Gras at New Orleans and Mobile*, Chicago: University of Chicago Press.

—— (1995) "Violence Ritually Enjoined: the Mardi Gras Indians of New Orleans," *Cahiers de Littérature Orale*, 37: 115–49.

—— (1999) "Why Is Carnival so Wild?" in K. Eisenbichler and W. Huesken (eds) *Carnival and the Carnivalesque: The Fool, the Reformer, the Wildman, and Others in Early Modern Theatre*, Amsterdam and Atlanta: Rodopi.

Knight, F.W. (1978) *The Caribbean: The Genesis of a Fragmented Nationalism*, New York: Oxford University Press.

Kofman, E. and Youngs, G. (eds) (1996) *Globalization: Theory and Practice*, London: Pinter.

Kun, J. (1997) "Against Easy Listening: Audiotopic Readings and Transnational Soundings," in C.F. Delgado and J.E. Muños (eds) *Every-Night Life: Culture and Dance in Latin/o America*, Durham, NC: Duke University Press.

Lamming, G. (1960; 2nd edn 1995) "The Occasion for Speaking," in B. Ashcroft, G. Griffiths, and H. Tiffin (eds) *The Postcolonial Studies Reader*, London and New York: Routledge.

La Rose, M. (1990) *Documents in the Struggle for a Representative and Democratic Carnival, 1989/1990*, London: New Beacon Books.

Lawlor, C. (1993) "The World Turned Upside Down," *Hybrid*, 3, June/July: 2–4.

Lawson, E.T. (1985) *Religions of Africa: Traditions in Transformation*, San Francisco: Harper & Row.

LDA (2003) *The Economic Impact of the Notting Hill Carnival*, London: London Development Authority.

Lee, B. (1992) "The Internationalization of Calypso," Seminar at University of the West Indies, St Augustine, February 13.

Lefebvre, H. (1976) "Reflections on the Politics of Space," *Antipode*, 8 (2).

—— (1991) *The Production of Space*, tr. D. Nicholson-Smith, Oxford: Blackwell.

Lezama, C. (1983a) *West Indian American Day Carnival Association (WIADCA) Souvenir Brochure*, Brooklyn, NY: WIADCA.

—— (1983b) in *Jamaican Weekly Gleaner*, August 15.

Liverpool, H. (1993) "Rituals of Power and Rebellion: The Carnival Tradition in Trinidad and Tobago," Dissertation, University of Michigan.

—— (1998) "Origins of Rituals and Customs in the Trinidad Carnival: African or European?" in M. Riggio (ed.) *Trinidad and Tobago Carnival*, special edition of *The Drama Review*, 42 (3): 24–37.

—— (2001) *Rituals of Power and Rebellion: The Carnival Tradition in Trinidad & Tobago, 1763–1962*, Chicago: Frontline Distribution/Research Associates School Times Publications.

Lovelace, Earl (1979) *The Dragon Can't Dance*, London: Longman.

—— (1994) Review of Tony Hall's "Jean and Dinah", *Trinidad Sunday Express*, December 11.

Lukács, G. (1971) *The Theory of the Novel*, Cambridge, MA: MIT Press.

Lyndersay, M. (1998) "Bring the Rhythm Down," *Express*, February 18: 9.

LWICC (1987) *Leeds Westindian Carnival Official Magazine*, Leeds: Leeds West Indian Centre.

—— (1988) *Leeds Westindian Carnival 21st Anniversary Brochure*, London: Caribbean Times.

—— (1992) "We Didn't Know What We Were Getting Into," in *Hot This Year: The Official Carnival Magazine*, Leeds: Leeds West Indian Centre.

McMillan, M. (1990) *Cultural Grounding: Live Art and Cultural Diversity: Action Research Project*, London: Arts Council of Great Britain.

Mails, Thomas (1972) *Mystic Warrior of the Plains*, Garden City, NY: Doubleday Press.

Mannette, E. (2002) Lecture on his involvement with steelband, given at the European Preliminaries of the World Steelband Festival, Sète, France, May 25.

Manning, F. (1983) "Carnival and the West Indian Diaspora," *The Round Table*, 286: 186–96.

—— (1984) "Symbolic Expression of Politics: Cricket and Carnival," in F. Manning (ed.) *The Celebration of Society: Perspectives on Contemporary Cultural Performance*, Bowling Green, OH: Bowling Green University Popular Press.

—— (1990) "Overseas Caribbean Carnivals: The Arts and Politics of a Transnational Celebration," in J. Lent (ed.) *Caribbean Popular Culture*, Bowling Green, OH: Bowling Green University Popular Press.

Markham, E.A. (1989) *Hinterland: Caribbean Poetry from the West Indies and Britain*, Newcastle upon Tyne: Bloodaxe Books.

Martin, Carol (1998) "Trinidad Carnival Glossary," in M. Riggio (ed.) *Trinidad and Tobago Carnival*, special edition of *The Drama Review*, 42(3): 220–35.

Martinez, C. (2001) "Towards a First Approach to the Experience, Perception and Imagination of Spatial Practices," unpublished paper presented at the Hemispheric Institute of Performance and Politics annual encuentro, Monterrey, Mexico.

Maxime, G. (1990) *Steelband Music Festivals, 1952–1989*, Port of Spain: Maxime.

Menuhin, Y. and Davis, C. (1980) *The Music of Man*, London: MacDonald General Books.

Millett, T.M. (1993) *The Chinese in Trinidad*, Port of Spain: Imprint Publications.

Mintz, S. (1974) *Caribbean Transformations*, Baltimore: Johns Hopkins University Press.

Moore, C. (1985) "Some Reflections on the Labor Day Carnival," *New York Carib News*, September 24: 15.

Morris, P. (ed.) (1994) *The Bakhtin Reader*, London and New York: Arnold.

Mullard, C. (2002) "Time to Party – The Whole of Britain Needs the Notting Hill Carnival's Celebration of Cultural Diversity," *Guardian* [London], August 24.

Naipaul, V.S. (1969) *The Loss of El Dorado: A History*, London: André Deutsch.

Negus, K. (1999) *Music Genres and Corporate Cultures*, New York: Routledge.

Nettleford, R. (1988) "Implications for Caribbean Development," in J. Nunley and J. Bettelheim (eds) *Caribbean Festival Arts*, London: University of Washington Press.

—— (2001) "Texture and Diversity: The Cultural Life of the Caribbean," lecture presented at the presentation of the Premios Principe Claus, December 11, Luis Carcamo-Huechante; published as "Textra y diversidad: La Vida Cultueral del Caribe," in *Prince Claus Find*, special issue on *Carnival*, The Hague, Netherlands, 8–17.

Nunley, J. and Bettelheim, J. (eds) (1988) *Caribbean Festival Arts*, London: University of Washington Press.

Nurse, K. (1997) "The Trinidad and Tobago Entertainment Industry: structure and export capabilities," *Caribbean Dialogue*, 3 (3): 13–38.

—— (1999 rpt 2000) "Globalization and Trinidad Carnival: Diaspora, Hybridity and Identity in Global Culture," *Cultural Studies*, 13 (4): 661–90; reprinted in R.R. Premdas (ed.)

Identity, Ethnicity and Culture in the Caribbean, Trinidad: School of Continuing Studies, University of the West Indies, 80–119.

Ottley, R. (1995) *Calypsonians From Then to Now*, part I, Port of Spain: Ottley.

Palmer, L. (1986) "Memories of Notting Hill Carnival," in *Masquerading – the Art of the Notting Hill Carnival*, London: Arts Council.

Parry, J.H. and Sherlock, P. (1971) *A Short History of the West Indies*, London: Macmillan.

Patterson, O. (1994) "Ecumenical America: Global Culture and the American Cosmos," *World Policy Journal*, 11 (2): 103–17.

Pearse, A. (1956a) "Carnival in Nineteenth Century Trinidad," *Caribbean Quarterly*, 4 (3 & 4): 175–93; reprinted in G. Besson (ed.) (1988) *Trinidad Carnival*, Port of Spain: Paria Publishing.

—— (1956b) "Mitto Sampson on Calypso Legends of the Nineteenth Century," *Caribbean Quarterly*, 4 (3 & 4): 250–62; reprinted in G. Besson (ed.) (1988) *Trinidad Carnival*, Port of Spain: Paria Publishing, 40–63.

Phillip, N.M. (1998) "Race, Space and the Poetics of Moving," in K.M. Balutansky and M.-A. Sourieau (eds) *Caribbean Creolization: Reflections on the Cultural Dynamics of Language, Literature and Identity*, Gainesville: University of Florida Press, 129–53.

Pilkington, E. (1988) *Beyond the Mother Country: West Indians and the Notting Hill White Riots*, London: IB Tauris.

Pitts, H. (1962) "Calypso from Patois to its Present Form," *Guardian Independence Supplement*, August 26: n.p.

Powrie, B.E. (1956) "The Changing Attitudes of the Coloured Middleclass Towards Carnival," *Caribbean Quarterly* 4: 224–32; reprinted in G. Besson (ed.) (1988) *Trinidad Carnival*, Port of Spain: Paria Publishing, 91–107.

Quevedo, R. (1962) "History of Calypso," in *This Country of Ours*, Port of Spain: PNM.

Rampersad, I. (1990) "Chutney's Excesses: Ravana's triumph," *Trinidad Guardian*, December 11: 9.

Ravi Ji (1990) "Chutney Phenomenon," *Sunday Guardian*, November 11: 35.

Regalado, M. and Munoz, A. (2004) "The Entroida in Laza, Spain: A Continuing Tradition," in Barbara Mauldin (ed.) *Carnaval!*, Los Angeles, CA: UCLA Fowler Museum of Cultural History.

Regis, L. (1999) *The Political Calypso: True Opposition in Trinidad and Tobago*, Miami: University Press of Florida.

Remedi, G. (1996) *Murgas: El teatro de los tablados*, Montevideo: Ediciones Trilce.

—— (2003) *Carnival Theater: Uruguay's Popular Performers and National Culture*, translated by Amy Ferlazzo, Minneapolis, Minn.: University of Minnesota Press.

Richards, G.L. (1989) "Masters and Servants: The Growth of the Labour Movement in St Christopher-Nevis, 1896 to 1956," PhD dissertation, University of Cambridge.

Richmond, A.H. (1961) *The Colour Problem: A Study of Racial Relations*, Harmondsworth: Penguin.

Riggio, M. (1998a) "Resistance and Identity: Carnival in Trinidad and Tobago," in M. Riggio (ed.) *Trinidad and Tobago Carnival*, special issue of *The Drama Review*, 42 (3): 7–23.

—— (ed.) (1998b) *Trinidad and Tobago Carnival*, special issue of *The Drama Review*, 42 (3).

—— (1999) "Massing the Universe: Trini Party for the World," unpublished paper delivered at the World Conference on Carnival III, Port of Spain, Trinidad.

—— (2003) "Carnival," in D. Kennedy (ed.) *The Oxford Encyclopedia of Theatre and Performance*, Oxford: Oxford University Press, 226–8.

Roach, J. (1996) *Cities of the Dead: Circum-Atlantic Performance*, New York: Columbia University Press.

Roach, M.E. and Eicher, J. (eds) (1965) *Dress, Adornment and the Social Order*, New York: John Wiley & Sons, Inc.

Roberts, G. (1994) "Glossary," in P. Morris (ed.) *The Bakhtin Reader*, London and New York: Arnold.

Roediger, D. (1994) *Towards the Abolition of Whiteness*, London: Verso.

Rohlehr, G. (1985) "Man Talking to Man: Calypso and Social Confrontation in Trinidad 1970 to the Present," *Caribbean Quarterly*, 31 (2), June: 1–13.

—— (1990) *Calypso and Society in Pre-Independence Trinidad*, Port of Spain: G. Rohlehr.

—— (1992) "Apocalypse and the Soca Fires of 1990," in G. Rohlehr, *The Shape of That Hurt and Other Essays*, Port of Spain: Longman.

—— (1998) "We Getting the Kaiso that We Deserve: Calypso and the World Music Market," in M. Riggio (ed.) *Trinidad and Tobago Carnival*, special edition of *The Drama Review*, 42 (3): 82–95.

—— (2000) "Change and Prophecy in the Trinidad and Tobago Calypso, Towards the Twenty-first Century," in K. Hall and D. Benn (eds) *Contending with Destiny: The Caribbean in the Twenty-first Century*, London: Ian Randle Publishers, 542–74.

—— (2002) "The Calypsonian as Artist: Freedom and Responsibility," *Small Axe 9*, March, London.

Rosemain, J. (1986) *La Musique dans la Société Antillaise, 1635–1902*, Paris: Editions L'Harmattan.

Roussel-Milner, D. (1996) "False History of Notting Hill Carnival: a review of Professor Abner Cohen's *Masquerade Politics*," *Association for a People's Carnival Newsletter*, 7, August, London.

Sankeralli, B. (1986) "The Experiences of Disorder in the Calypso: A Philosophical Study," unpublished Caribbean Studies thesis, University of the West Indies.

—— (1995a) "Indians in a Creole Caribbean," presented at ISER-NCIC Conference, "Challenge and Change: the Indian Diaspora in its Historical and Contemporary Contexts," University of the West Indies, St Augustine.

—— (1995b) "Of Hijab and Hallelujah," *Caribbean Window*, 1 (1): 22.

—— (1996) "Ethnicity and the Problem of Religion in Trinidadian Folk," paper presented at the Workshop on African, Indian, and Indigenous Religions of the Caribbean, University of the West Indies, St Augustine.

Schechner, R. (1988 [1993]) *The Future of Ritual: Writings on Culture and Performance*, London and New York: Routledge.

Scott, J. (1990) *Domination and the Art of Resistance*, New Haven: Yale University Press.

Sherwood, M. (1999) *Claudia Jones: A Life in Exile*, London: Lawrence and Wishart.

Shohat, E. and Stam. R. (1994) *Unthinking Eurocentrism: Multiculturalism and the Media*, London: Routledge.

Singh, J.F. (1997) "Traditional Carnival Characters," in R. Balleram (ed.) *Carapichaima Carnival Committee: Golden Anniversary Celebrations: 1947–1997*, Carapichaima: Carapichaima Carnival Committee.

Singh, K. (1988) *Bloodstained Tombs: The Muharran Massacre 1884*, London: Macmillan.

Slater, J. (1995) *The Advent of the Steelband and my Life and Times with It, 1939–1995*, Port of Spain: John Slater.

Smart, I.I. and Nehusi, K.S.K. (eds) (2000) *Ah Come Back Home: Perspectives on the Trinidad and Tobago Carnival*, Washington DC: Original World Press.

Smith, K. (ed.) (1986) "Lord Kitchener: I came back to fight Sparrow!" in *Sparrow the Legend: Calypso King of the World*, Port of Spain: Inprint Caribbean Ltd.

Smith, M. (1994) *Mardi Gras Indians*, Gretna, LA: Pelican Publishing Co.

So Yu Going to Carnival (1995) Ah Wee Travel Agency, 9 January, pp. 88–9.

Sparrow, The Mighty (1984) *Trinidad Guardian*, March 23.

Spottswood, R. (1985) "Discography of West Indian Records, 1912–45," in D. Hill, *Calypsonians Speak for the Record*, unpublished MS, University of the West Indies Library, Trinidad: St Augustine.

Steiner, G. (1972) "Extraterritorial," in *Papers on Literature and the Language Revolution*, Harmondsworth: Penguin.

Stuempfle, S. (1995) *The Steelband Movement: The Forging of a National Art in Trinidad and Tobago*, Philadelphia: University of Pennsylvania Press.

Tawney, R.H. (1926) *Religion and the Rise of Capitalism*, New York: Harcourt, Brace & World.

Thomas, J.J. (1869; rpt 1969) *The Theory and Practice of Creole Grammar*, Port of Spain: The Chronicle Publishing Office; rpt London: New Beacon Books.

—— (1883) *The Trinidad Review*, August 9: n.p.

Trotman, A.V. (1993) "African-Caribbean Perspectives of Worldview: C.L.R. James Explores the Authentic Voice," PhD dissertation, York University.

Tulloch, C. (1997–8) "Fashioned in Black and White: Women's Dress in Jamaica, 1880–1907," *Things*, 7, winter: 29–53.

Turino, T. (2000) *Nationalists, Cosmopolitans, and Popular Music in Zimbabwe*, Chicago: University of Chicago Press.

Turner, V. (1988) *The Anthropology of Performance*, New York: Performing Arts Journal Publications.

Twycross, M. and Carpenter, S. (2001) *Masks and Masking in Medieval and Early Tudor England*, Aldershot: Ashgate.

Vickerman, M. (1998) *Cross Currents: West Indian Immigrants and Race*, New York: Oxford University Press.

—— (2001) "Tweaking a Monolith: The West Indian Immigrant Encounter with 'Blackness'," in Nancy Foner (ed.) *Islands in the City: West Indian Migration to New York*, Berkeley: University of California Press, 237–56.

Vickerman, M. and Kasinitz, P. (1999) "West Indians, Haitians and Dominicans," in Elliot Barkhan (ed.) *Ethnic Groups in the United States*, Westport, CT: Greenwood Academic Press.

Walcott, D. (1974) "The Muse of History," reprinted in D. Walcott (1998) *What the Twilight Said*, New York: Farrar, Straus & Giroux.

—— (1992) "The Antilles: Fragments of Epic Memory," Nobel Lecture, December.

—— (1998) *What the Twilight Said*, New York: Farrar, Straus & Giroux.

Wald, G. (2002) "I Want it That Way: Teenybopper Music and the Girling of Boy Bands," *Genders*, 35, http://www.genders.org/g35/g35 wald.html.

Wallerstein, I. (1983) *Historical Capitalism*, London: Verso.

Walmsley, A. (1992) *The Caribbean Artists Movement, 1966–1972: A Literary and Cultural History*, London and Port of Spain: New Beacon Books.

Ware, V. and Back, L. (2002) *Out of Whiteness: Color, Politics, and Culture*, Chicago and London: Chicago University Press.

Waters, M. (1995) *Globalization*, London: Routledge.

Waters, M.C. (1999) *Black Identities: West Indian Immigrant Dreams and American Realities*, New York and Cambridge: Harvard University Press and the Russell Sage Foundation.

Weber, M. (1930) *The Protestant Ethic and the Spirit of Capitalism*, tr. Talcot Parsons, New York: Scribner (first English translation of *Die protestantische Ethik, und der Geist des Kapitalismus*).

Weiner, A. and Schneider, J. (eds) (1989) *Cloth and Human Experience*, Washington DC: Smithsonian Institution Press.

White, S. and White, G. (1998) *Stylin: African-American Expressive Culture*, Ithaca and London: Cornell University Press.

Wilbert, J. (1993) *Mystic Endowment: Religious Ethnography of the Warao Indians*, Berkeley: University of California Press.

Zuberi, N. (2001) *Sounds English: Transnational Popular Music*, Chicago: University of Illinois Press.

INDEX

NOTE: Page numbers in italics mean information is in an illustration or caption. Page numbers followed by *n* indicate a note; *glos* means that there is a Glossary entry. References are to Trinidad Carnival unless otherwise indicated.

eBooks – at www.eBookstore.tandf.co.uk

A library at your fingertips!

eBooks are electronic versions of printed books. You can store them on your PC/laptop or browse them online.

They have advantages for anyone needing rapid access to a wide variety of published, copyright information.

eBooks can help your research by enabling you to bookmark chapters, annotate text and use instant searches to find specific words or phrases. Several eBook files would fit on even a small laptop or PDA.

NEW: Save money by eSubscribing: cheap, online access to any eBook for as long as you need it.

Annual subscription packages

We now offer special low-cost bulk subscriptions to packages of eBooks in certain subject areas. These are available to libraries or to individuals.

For more information please contact webmaster.ebooks@tandf.co.uk

We're continually developing the eBook concept, so keep up to date by visiting the website.

www.eBookstore.tandf.co.uk